CONTROVERSIES IN TAX LAW

Tax and tax controversies have captured the attention of Americans throughout history. These topics have not only generated debate and discussion in households, boardrooms, and classrooms across the country and throughout generations—they have led to violent struggles and, in some cases, wartime struggles. In this book, thirteen prominent scholars explore why taxation has played a prominent role in American legal and political debates, highlighting the reality that individual viewpoints are shaped by economic, philosophical, historical perspectives. The essays are informative, timely, and fascinating—a must read for students both inside and outside the classroom.

Nancy Staudt, Dean and Howard & Caroline Cayne Professor of Law,
Washington University in St. Louis School of Law, USA

With essays covering everything from the tax policy contributions of early-twentieth-century home economists to the future of the corporate income tax, and reflecting both traditional and critical analytical approaches, this volume deserves the attention of anyone with an interest in tax policy. You may not agree with all of the arguments in this provocative collection, but you will be challenged and you will not be bored.

Lawrence A. Zelenak, Pamela B. Gann Professor of Law,
Duke University Law School, USA

This edited volume which includes a point-counterpoint approach to tax law, demonstrates the intellectual depth of the field. By creating a space for scholars to engage with contrary viewpoints, Ashgate Publishing is creating a new gold standard for the legal academy.

Dorothy A. Brown, Vice Provost and Professor of Law,
Emory University School of Law, USA

Controversies in American Constitutional Law

Series Editors:

Jon Yorke and Anne Richardson Oakes, Centre for American Legal Studies,
School of Law, Birmingham City University, UK

Controversies in American Constitutional Law presents and engages with the contemporary developments and policies which mould and challenge US constitutional law and practice. It deals with the full spectrum of constitutional issues, publishing work by scholars from a range of disciplines who tackle current legal issues by reference to their underlying legal and political histories and the philosophical perspectives that they represent. Its cross-disciplinary approach encourages analysis of past, present and future challenges to the idea of US constitutionalism and the power structures upon which it rests. The series provides a forum for scholars to challenge the boundaries of US constitutional law and engages with the continual process of constitutional refinement for the protection of individual rights and liberties, within an evolving framework of legitimate government.

CALS promotes research, scholarship, and educative programs in all areas of US law, and is the home of the *British Journal of American Legal Studies*. Faculty members have extensive experience in submitting *amicus curiae* briefs to the United States Supreme Court and lower federal courts, and advising on criminal justice issues in many states. CALS coordinates the largest British law undergraduate internship program to the United States. Through this program, and members' research, CALS has created relationships with over 100 partners in over 25 states. CALS faculty advise public bodies, provide professional training, and speak at conferences across the USA.

Controversies in Tax Law

A Matter of Perspective

Edited by

ANTHONY C. INFANTI
University of Pittsburgh, USA

Routledge
Taylor & Francis Group
LONDON AND NEW YORK

First published 2015 by Ashgate Publishing

Published 2016 by Routledge
2 Park Square, Milton Park, Abingdon, Oxon OX14 4RN
711 Third Avenue, New York, NY 10017, USA

First issued in paperback 2017

Routledge is an imprint of the Taylor & Francis Group, an informa business

British Library Cataloguing in Publication Data
A catalogue record for this book is available from the British Library

Library of Congress Cataloging-in-Publication Data
Infanti, Anthony C., 1968- author.
Controversies in tax law : a matter of perspective / by Anthony C. Infanti.
pages cm. -- (Controversies in American constitutional law)
Includes bibliographical references and index.
ISBN 978-1-4724-1492-2 (hardback)
1. Taxation--Law and legislation--United States. 2. Tax administration and procedure--United States. 3. Corporations--Taxation--Law and legislation--United States. I. Title.
KF6289.I493 2015
343.7304--dc23

2014041038

ISBN 13: 978-1-138-08983-9 (pbk)
ISBN 13: 978-1-4724-1492-2 (hbk)

Contents

Notes on Contributors

Bradley T. Borden is a professor of law at Brooklyn Law School in Brooklyn, New York. His teaching and scholarship focus on partnership and real estate taxation.

Yariv Brauner is the University of Florida Research Foundation Professor and a professor of law with the Levin College of Law at the University of Florida. He joined the Florida faculty in 2006. He has been a visiting professor or a guest speaker in various universities in the United States and abroad. He is an author of articles published in professional journals and law reviews, and a coauthor of *U.S. International Taxation—Cases and Materials* (with Reuven S. Avi-Yonah and Diane M. Ring), now in its third edition.

Adam Chodorow is the Willard H. Pedrick Distinguished Research Scholar at the Sandra Day O'Connor College of Law at Arizona State University, where he teaches tax and business law. His research and writing focus on a variety of contemporary tax issues, including valuing companies for estate tax purposes when buy-sell agreements are disregarded, reforming the flexible spending account rules to allow excess contributions to be donated to charity, and taxing virtual income. He has also written on the links between religious taxation and the federal income tax and the normative justification for a charitable donation in Chinese tax law.

Bridget J. Crawford is a professor at Pace Law School in White Plains, NY. Her primary teaching fields are taxation and wills, trusts, and estates. She is the editor (with Anthony Infanti) of *Critical Tax Theory: An Introduction* (Cambridge University Press 2009). Her scholarly interests include the intersection of gender and tax policy.

Joseph M. Dodge is the Stearns Weaver Miller Weissler Alhadeff & Sitterson Professor, Florida State University College of Law. Before entering teaching, he engaged in private law practice in Tokyo (1967–1969), Honolulu (1969–1971), and Washington, D.C. (1971–1972). He has taught at the University of Detroit School of Law (1973–1978), the University of Texas Law School (1978–2001), and Florida State University College of Law (2001–2014). He also visited at UCLA Law School (1982–1983) and the University of Utah (2000). He taught mainly various courses in taxation and gratuitous transfers. His books include *The Logic of Tax* (1989), coursebooks (many with coauthors) in individual income tax, estates and trusts, and estate and gift taxation, and student study texts in the same areas. He has published over 60 articles in law reviews and tax journals and given assorted professional and academic talks and seminars.

Wendy C. Gerzog is a professor at the University of Baltimore School of Law, teaching classes in tax and estate planning. She is an Academic Fellow of the American College of Trust and Estate Counsel and an elected member of the American Law Institute. She has written extensively on the gift and estate tax issues of valuation, marital deduction, family limited partnerships, and charitable transfers. She coauthored a textbook, *Federal Taxation of Gratuitous Transfers: Law and Planning*, with Joseph Dodge and Bridget Crawford (who are also contributors to this volume). She created and, for many years, wrote the Estate and Gift Rap column for *Tax Notes*.

Stephanie Hunter McMahon is a professor of law at the University of Cincinnati College of Law who teaches courses in both tax law and legal history, and her research often combines her interest in these areas. In particular, her work has explored how women have been, and continue to be, affected by taxation, and how women have used issues of taxation to further their own rights. After graduating from law school, she practiced tax in New York City for a few years before returning to school and graduating with a PhD in history from the University of Virginia. She has a strong interest in examining how different groups of people with different backgrounds and different experiences understand and influence fiscal issues in American history.

Anthony C. Infanti is Senior Associate Dean for Academic Affairs and a professor of law at the University of Pittsburgh School of Law, teaching courses in the tax area. His scholarly work has focused on two ostensibly quite different, but, in reality, quite related areas: (1) the intersection of tax and comparative legal theory; and (2) critical tax theory (i.e., the impact of the tax system on traditionally subordinated groups). He has received both the University of Pittsburgh Chancellor's Distinguished Teaching Award as well as an Excellence-in-Teaching Award from the graduating students of the University of Pittsburgh School of Law. He is an elected member of the American Law Institute and of the American Bar Foundation.

Steve R. Johnson is University Professor of Law at the Florida State University College of Law, where he teaches, among others, courses in federal taxation of individuals, business entities, and international transactions. He also is a member of the faculty of the Graduate Tax Program at the University of Alabama School of Law. He is coauthor of two texts: *Civil Tax Procedure* and *Tax Crimes*. He has written scores of tax articles and book chapters, and he is a frequent speaker at tax law conferences. His work has been cited in numerous academic articles and books and in decisions of the U.S. Supreme Court, several federal district courts and circuit courts, Bankruptcy Court, the Court of Federal Claims, and the U.S. Tax Court.

Carolyn C. Jones is the F. Wendell Miller Professor of Law at the University of Iowa College of Law where she was formerly the dean. Her research interest is in the legal history of taxation, and she has written on taxation in the context of the woman suffrage movement, debates about the role of the National Council of Churches in tax policy, popular tax narratives, and World War II tax propaganda and women's work in that time.

Lily Kahng is a professor of law at Seattle University School of Law. She teaches federal income taxation, corporate taxation, partnership taxation, estate and gift taxation, and tax policy. Her research interests include taxation of women and families, tax administration, comparative tax, and critical tax theory. Before joining the Seattle University faculty in 2001, she was an associate professor at Cornell Law School and served as an attorney advisor in the Office of Tax Legislative Counsel in the U.S. Department of the Treasury. From 1991 to 1993, she was acting assistant professor at New York University Law School. She began her legal career as an associate at the New York law firm of Simpson Thacher & Bartlett, and then was a vice president of mergers and acquisitions at the investment bank of Salomon Brothers, New York.

Andrea Monroe is an associate professor of law at Temple University's Beasley School of Law, where she teaches courses in taxation, partnership taxation, tax policy, and torts. Her current research examines the intersection of partnership taxation, tax abuse, and tax administration. Before joining the Temple faculty, she taught at the Northwestern University School of Law as a visiting assistant professor.

Henry Ordower is Professor of Law and past Co-Director of the Center for International and Comparative Law and Director of the Berlin Summer Program at Saint Louis University School of Law. He teaches U.S. income taxation courses—individual, partnership, corporate, and international—as well as corporation finance. His research and writing focuses on U.S. and comparative taxation and the operation and regulation of private investment companies. His recent research addresses issues of tax distribution and its role in the growing disparity between high- and low-income individuals. He maintains an active consulting practice advising in tax planning, hedge and private equity funds, and business structure, and providing expert testimony on taxation and business organizations in complex litigation matters. He has been elected to membership in the American College of Tax Counsel, the European Association of Tax Law Professors, and the International Academy of Comparative Law.

For Hien and Rose Mai.

List of Abbreviations

2010 Act	Tax Relief, Unemployment Insurance Reauthorization, and Job Creation Act of 2010
ACTEC	American College of Trust and Estate Counsel
AMT	Alternative minimum tax
ATRA	American Taxpayer Relief Act of 2012
BEPS	Base erosion and profit shifting
CIT	Consumed-income tax (also known as cash-flow consumption tax)
Code	U.S. Internal Revenue Code of 1986, as amended (26 U.S.C.)
DSUE	Deceased spouse's unused exemption
EGTRRA	Economic Growth and Tax Relief Reconciliation Act of 2001
ERTA	Economic Recovery Tax Act of 1981
FASB	Financial Accounting Standards Board
GDP	Gross domestic product
GRAT	Grantor retained annuity trust
IASB	International Accounting Standards Board
IRA	Individual retirement account
I.R.C.	U.S. Internal Revenue Code of 1986, as amended (26 U.S.C.)
IRS	U.S. Internal Revenue Service
MNE	Multinational enterprise
OECD	Organization for Economic Cooperation & Development
OID	Original issue discount
QTIP	Qualified terminable interest property
R&D	Research and development
Treas. Reg.	Treasury Regulations (title 26, U.S. Code of Federal Regulations)
Treasury	U.S. Department of the Treasury
VAT	Value-added tax

Chapter 1
Introduction

Anthony C. Infanti

The Project

Despite beginning with the word "controversy," the title of this volume should itself be without any controversy whatsoever. After all, taxation has been a perennial source of debate and unrest in the United States—and it remains none the less so in the early twenty-first century. Historical examples are easily enumerated and include such pivotal events in American history as the Boston Tea Party, Shays's Rebellion, the Whiskey Rebellion, and the woman suffrage movement.

Though less momentous, early twenty-first century debates are no less consequential. Today's debates implicate such important questions as who should pay tax—think of Republican presidential candidate Mitt Romney's remarks during the 2012 campaign about the "47 percent" who pay no income tax at all (even if they do pay other federal, state, and local taxes). Today's debates also concern the important question of how much each of us should be asked to pay in tax—think of President Obama's insistence during that same presidential campaign that the Bush tax cuts for those with more than $250,000 of income should be allowed to expire.

So, when I was asked by the Centre for American Legal Studies at Birmingham City University School of Law to consider editing a tax volume for its "Controversies in … " series with Ashgate Publishing, I knew that there would be neither a dearth of material nor of individuals willing to contribute to the book. But I wanted to do something more than simply assemble a disconnected collection of opinions about the existing state or future direction of American tax law. Instead, I wished to approach contemporary tax controversies in a unique fashion—one that required scholars to actively engage with each other's viewpoints and writings in an attempt to gain a better understanding of why and how their perspectives differ.

The subtitle of the volume—"A Matter of Perspective"—reflects the fact that today's tax debates often turn on the differing *Weltanschauungen* of the participants in those debates. For instance, a central tension in the academic tax literature—which is filtering into everyday discussions of tax law—exists between "mainstream" and "critical" tax theorists. This tension results from a clash of perspectives: Is taxation primarily a matter of social science or a matter of social justice? In other words, should tax policy debates be grounded in economics or in critical race, feminist, queer, and other outsider perspectives?

Too often the two sides of these academic tax debates simply talk "at" or "past" each other rather than engage in a dialogue with each other. To capture and interrogate—and perhaps even to begin to bridge—what often seems like a chasm between the different sides of academic (and, increasingly, everyday) tax debates, this volume comprises six parts with each part containing a pair of chapters. Each pair of chapters approaches a general area of controversy in the tax laws from different perspectives. In most of these pairs, one chapter will approach the topic from a "mainstream" perspective while the other will approach the same topic from a "critical" perspective. In the other pairs, the perspectives on a given topic will differ in other ways.

In the preparation of this volume, I afforded the authors of each of the chapters in a given pair multiple opportunities to read and incorporate reactions to each other's chapters in the writing of their own. In the writing and rewriting of their chapters, I asked the authors to pay specific attention to the influence of perspective both on the issue that they address and on the writing of their own contributions to the debate. In this way, I tasked the contributors to the volume with being actively engaged with each other during the writing of the volume, producing what I hope is a series of chapters that you will find equally engaging.

The Chapters: A Preview

Tax, Gender, and History

Part I of this volume focuses on the intersection of tax with gender and history. A thorough and meaningful understanding of current tax law is difficult—if not impossible—without an understanding of both the history of the tax laws and the historical context within which those laws were created. The story only becomes richer—even if more troubling—when taxes and history are viewed through the lens of gender. Carolyn Jones and Stephanie McMahon have each contributed a chapter to this volume that views tax and history through the lens of gender, but they see very different things through that lens.

In Chapter 2, Carolyn Jones takes a critical approach in her attempt to retake home economics and demonstrate the discipline's relevance to current tax reform debates. She starkly contrasts the strong relationship between the work of (male) economists and the shaping of tax policy and administration with the complete failure of tax academics even to notice the relevance of home economics to tax policy and administration. In her contribution, Jones focuses particularly on the work of Hazel Kyrk and other pioneers in the home economics field, who all engaged in social and economic analyses of the home.

These home economists explored questions of ability to pay, control of income, and standards of living—all of which are relevant to contemporary tax reform debates about imputed income and tax incentives for families. In this way, Jones explains how early home economists ruminated about many issues that are (and long have been) of interest to tax academics and policy makers, but how their ideas and contributions were nonetheless overlooked or ignored. By retaking home economics, Jones asserts that tax academics and policy makers might not only learn something about tax policy and administration but also be pushed to think about these issues in a broader context as well.

In Chapter 3, Stephanie McMahon explains a different way in which women were overlooked in the formation of tax policy. She examines the failure, at the time, to grasp the gender dimensions of the tension that the Tax Reform Act of 1969 created between married and single taxpayers. Among other things, the Tax Reform Act of 1969 reduced the singles tax penalty by ensuring that a single taxpayer with the same income as a married couple would pay not in excess of 120 percent more than the married couple did in taxes. By reducing the tax penalty on singles, however, the Tax Reform Act of 1969 created a marriage penalty for couples in which both spouses worked and earned relatively equal amounts of income. (The Tax Reform Act of 1969 maintained the preexisting marriage "bonus" for couples with a single income earner.)

McMahon acknowledges that reinforcement of the traditional family norm likely influenced policy makers—whether consciously or unconsciously—when they were crafting the Tax Reform Act of 1969. But McMahon complicates this critique, which is often leveled by critical tax scholars against treating the married couple as a taxable unit, by exploring how divergent interests among various groups of women—coupled with co-optation of gender by those who simply wished to achieve tax reduction—limited the influence of women and women's interests on the shape of the taxable unit and the debate over the marriage penalty. Or, as McMahon puts it, "the marriage penalty [became] gendered but insufficiently so to force its repeal."

Taxation of Imputed Income

Picking up on a thread in Carolyn Jones's contribution, Part II concerns the taxation of imputed income—with a particular focus on the long-standing debate over whether to tax imputed income from owner-occupied dwellings. Henry Ordower and Steve Johnson provide a nice point–counterpoint in their contributions to this volume, with one taking a critical perspective and the other a mainstream perspective on this issue.

In Chapter 4, Henry Ordower takes a distinctly critical perspective and centers his attention on the fairness of the implicit exclusion from taxation of imputed income produced by owner-occupied dwellings. After examining the exclusion using the core tax policy principles of horizontal and vertical equity, Ordower concludes that the exclusion violates both of these principles. The exclusion violates horizontal equity because it treats similarly situated taxpayers dissimilarly; that is, homeowners are permitted to pay for occupancy of their homes with untaxed income while renters must pay for occupancy of their homes with taxed income. This differential treatment of homeowners and renters leads, in turn, to a violation of vertical equity because high-income taxpayers are much more likely to be homeowners than lower-income taxpayers.

Ordower then examines this class-based distinction through the lens of race, pointing out that racial minorities are overrepresented in the tax-disadvantaged lower-income groups (i.e., they are more likely to rent than to own their homes), which means that this violation of vertical equity also has discriminatory impact along racial lines. Ordower strenuously argues that this class- and race-based discrimination needs to be addressed, either through the inclusion of imputed income from owner-occupied dwellings in gross income or by providing a deduction for rental payments for residences. After weighing the costs and benefits of each approach, Ordower expresses his preference for taxing imputed income rather than providing a deduction to renters.

In Chapter 5, Steve Johnson takes a mainstream perspective of the implicit exclusion from taxation of imputed income produced by owner-occupied dwellings. Johnson is sympathetic to Ordower's fairness arguments; however, he believes that it is unwise and impractical to tax imputed income. Although he concedes that the arguments in favor of taxing imputed income do have some purchase, Johnson dissects those arguments and explains why their force has been overstated.

Countering these (now diminished) arguments in favor of taxing imputed income, Johnson maintains that (1) homeowners would encounter reporting and recordkeeping problems if imputed income were taxed; (2) the IRS would encounter difficulties policing the taxation of imputed income; and (3) valuation problems would bedevil both taxpayers and the IRS if imputed income were taxed. Compounding these problems, Johnson points out the political difficulty of taxing imputed income. Not only would taxing imputed income be unpopular, but, according to Johnson, its lack of acceptance among taxpayers would also put an undue strain on our already strained self-assessment system of taxation. For all of these reasons, Johnson opposes the taxation of imputed income from owner-occupied dwellings. If any steps are to be taken to redress the fairness issues that Ordower raises in Chapter 4, Johnson is of the view that a deduction for renters would be preferable to taxing the imputed income produced by owner-occupied dwellings.

Tax Accounting: Book–Tax Disparities

Turning from questions of imputed income to tax accounting, Part III addresses so-called book–tax disparities—in other words, disparities between the reporting of income and expense for financial accounting purposes versus their reporting for tax accounting purposes. Contrary to the expectations of those who think of accounting as staid and boring, Lily Kahng and Adam Chodorow engage in a lively and fascinating debate about book–tax disparities. While finding some ground for agreement, Kahng and Chodorow see book–tax disparities in quite different lights.

In Chapter 6, Lily Kahng undertakes a historical examination of the differing natures and perceived purposes of financial and tax accounting. She explains how financial accounting has historically been conservative in its approach and tended to understate income because of its focus on providing information to stakeholders (e.g., shareholders and creditors). In contrast, tax accounting has historically tended to overstate income in order to protect the public fisc. More recently, however, the tables have turned and businesses have reported greater income for financial accounting purposes than they have for tax purposes. Against this background of an increasingly troubling book–tax gap, Kahng considers the question of whether there should be greater conformity between financial and tax accounting.

Kahng accepts some divergence between financial and tax accounting and finds the arguments in favor of book–tax conformity unpersuasive. Nevertheless, she does find that tax accounting might benefit from conforming more closely to financial accounting in its treatment of intellectual capital. In this area, Kahng argues that financial accounting is moving in the right direction while tax accounting is moving in the wrong direction. In order for tax accounting to more accurately measure income from intellectual capital, Kahng argues that tax accounting should embrace the trend in financial accounting toward capitalization (rather than immediate expensing) of intellectual capital.

In Chapter 7, Adam Chodorow agrees with Kahng that tax accounting can learn some lessons from financial accounting. Nevertheless, he sees strong reasons not only for the extant divergence between the two accounting systems but also for pushing them further apart. In coming to this conclusion, Chodorow reexamines the historic justifications for the divergence between financial and tax accounting and comes away unconvinced. Instead, he proposes that the divergence between financial and tax accounting is most appropriately grounded in hewing to basic income tax principles.

In making this argument, Chodorow focuses in particular on the accrual method of accounting. He argues that Congress should eliminate that method of accounting and require all taxpayers to use the cash receipts and disbursements method of accounting. This argument flies in the face of the conventional wisdom that the accrual method provides a more accurate measure of income than the cash method. But Chodorow asserts that the purpose of tax accounting is not to obtain the most accurate measure of economic income; rather, it is to ensure that all income—including investment income—is taxed, and that it is taxed only once. By divorcing the receipt or payment of cash from the accrual of income and deductions, Chodorow contends that the accrual method of accounting violates the notion that returns on capital should be subject to tax and, as a result, turns the income tax into a consumption tax. If Congress is unwilling to rectify this problem by taking the drastic step of eliminating the accrual method of accounting, Chodorow argues in favor of increasing the IRS's ability to challenge taxpayers' methods of accounting when those methods result in exempting returns on capital from tax.

Entity Taxation

Shifting from questions of how to account for items of income and deduction, parts IV and V implicate the question of how to identify the appropriate taxpayer when taxpayers come together to operate a business. In a division that is natural to tax academics but in reality quite artificial, Part IV takes on the taxation of flow-through business entities while Part V takes on the taxation of corporations. Despite the division, the discussions in both of these parts share common (and perennial) themes regarding fairness and the potential for abusing the differing tax regimes applicable to different business entities.

Taxation of Flow-Through Entities

In addressing the taxation of flow-through entities, Part IV focuses in particular on the partnership tax regime found in subchapter K of the Internal Revenue Code (Code). Andrea Monroe and Bradley Borden make a notoriously arcane corner of an already arcane area of the law highly accessible with their debate over the future of subchapter K. Their differing perspectives—with Monroe focusing on the equity of subchapter K and Borden focusing on its efficiency—only make their contrasting contributions that much more interesting.

In Chapter 8, Andrea Monroe argues that subchapter K is broken and that the root of the problem lies in its focus on a small number of elite partnerships and attempts to combat their efforts to obtain undue tax advantages through abuse of the Code. This has led to the creation of a highly complex, technical tax regime that is nearly inaccessible to the more numerous "everyday" partnerships, which lack the resources to navigate subchapter K's complexity. Monroe highlights the partnership allocation and distribution rules as examples of the complexity of partnership tax. She asserts that the inordinate complexity of rules such as these creates a division between everyday and elite partnerships that undermines the rule of law, as everyday partnerships encounter a system designed for the wealthy under which they are relegated to merely guessing at the appropriate legal treatment of their operations.

Monroe contends that subchapter K could be made simpler and more accessible to everyday partnerships by refocusing the rules on governing ordinary transactions, essentially outsourcing the policing of abusive transactions to the general rules and tools for targeting tax abuse that are available outside of subchapter K and apply to the Code more generally. This shift in focus would permit the wholesale elimination of the many highly complex partnership tax rules that are designed to do no more than combat abuse. The overall result would not only be a simpler, more accessible partnership tax system but also one that would bolster the tax system's perceived legitimacy and, ultimately, the rule of law. In particular, Monroe makes a provocative proposal to begin taxing distributions of property from partnerships—in the name of achieving a system that, in the end, is simpler and more consistent with basic income tax principles.

In Chapter 9, Bradley Borden takes a different, more historical view of subchapter K. Borden examines the economic and historical origins of partnership taxation and concludes that complexity in the partnership tax rules stems not from staving off abusive taxpayer behavior but from grappling with the inherent complexity of the economic arrangements among even the simplest of partnerships. He also downplays the practical level of complexity encountered by everyday partnerships, asserting that they need not worry about complex antiabuse rules so long as they are not engaged in abusive behavior. For truly simple economic arrangements, Borden suggests the alternative of forming a small business (so-called "S") corporation, because the Code's subchapter

S does not permit the same level of flexibility in structuring economic arrangements as subchapter K does. Instead, subchapter S contemplates a simple, uniform sharing among co-owners.

Borden thus embraces the complexity of subchapter K. Where he suggests alteration is in deviations from the initial approach taken in crafting the rules that make up the partnership tax regime. In keeping with the nature of the economic arrangements among partners, Borden maintains that the crafting of partnership tax rules should be initially approached from the perspective that a partnership is really no more than an aggregate of its partners. Only where necessary for administrative convenience should the partnership be viewed as a separate entity. Borden explains the benefits of this approach using as examples the rules in subchapter K governing contributions to partnerships and transfers of partnership interests. In those rules, he asserts that Congress has mistakenly taken an entity-oriented starting point and added reparative aggregate rules, whereas an aggregate starting point would have resulted in rules that are more efficient and accurate—and possibly simpler. That his suggested approach might potentially lead to complexity in the partnership tax rules does not bother Borden because he sees complexity as inherent in the economic arrangements of all partnerships.

Taxation of Corporations

Part V addresses the taxation of corporations. Yariv Brauner and I each approach the question of whether corporations should be taxpayers from different perspectives. I approach the question from a critical perspective while Brauner approaches it from a mainstream perspective.

In Chapter 10, Yariv Brauner issues a call to repeal the corporate tax. By way of background, Brauner summarizes the policy rationales articulated in support of the corporate tax, traces the history of the corporation, summarizes research on the incidence of the corporate tax, and dissects the arguments that have traditionally been made in support of and against the corporate tax. Ultimately, Brauner concludes that there is no sound policy reason for keeping the corporate tax.

In coming to this conclusion, Brauner makes a move one might expect more from a critical tax scholar and argues that conservatives should support (rather than oppose) and liberals should oppose (rather than support) the corporate tax. Brauner argues that liberals should advocate repeal of the corporate tax (and its replacement by a mere withholding mechanism for the individual income tax) because it would lead to greater redistribution of income. Moreover, Brauner advocates abandoning the corporate tax because policy makers cannot effectively control the corporate tax as a tax policy instrument as a result of their inability either to determine the incidence of the tax or to evaluate its effects on natural persons.

In Chapter 11, I approach the corporate tax reform debate from a different perspective—more as an outsider than an insider, such as Brauner. I compare the tenor of the corporate tax reform debate with the tenor of the debate over reforming the taxation of the family. I explain how families and corporations are both sociolegal constructs that actually receive very similar treatment for tax purposes: Both families and corporations are sometimes ignored for federal tax purposes. At other times, families and corporations are treated as an aggregate of individual family members or of shareholders. And at yet other times, families and corporations are treated as real entities. Each of these different treatments comes with different tax consequences.

Yet, despite the strong similarities in the taxation of families and corporations, the debates over corporate tax reform and family tax reform widely diverge. The corporate tax reform debate tends to center on leveling down the taxation of corporations to approximate the taxation of partnerships and disregarded entities; that is, it focuses on eliminating the "double" taxation of corporations in favor of the single level of taxation that applies to flow-through entities. In contrast, the family tax reform debate tends to center on leveling out or up; that is, its focus is on reworking or expanding the special tax treatment of the family to better tailor it to economic reality and tax policy norms, all while addressing issues of gender equity that have historically plagued the institution of marriage. The basic purpose of my highlighting these similarities and differences is to draw attention to—and, I hope, erase—a portion of the public–private divide that pervades the tax laws by showing that those engaged in the corporate tax reform debate might actually learn some lessons from the debate over reforming the taxation of the family.

Transfer Taxation

Up to this point, the contributions to this volume have predominantly concerned varying aspects of the federal income tax. To close the volume, Part VI significantly changes course by focusing on the separate federal transfer tax system—that is, the federal estate and gift taxes. Joseph Dodge contributes a chapter that considers the design of the federal transfer tax system from a mainstream perspective. Bridget Crawford and Wendy Gerzog together contribute a chapter that considers from a critical perspective the advent of "portability" of the lifetime gift/estate tax exemption.

In Chapter 12, Joseph Dodge does a thorough job of disentangling the norms underpinning transfer taxation—both those internal to the tax system and those external to the tax system. The internal-to-tax norms that Dodge identifies are fairness and administrative efficiency. The external-to-tax norms that he identifies are economic efficiency and distributive justice. Against this background, Dodge posits that the primary rationales for transfer taxation are (1) to advance the fairness norm of ability to pay (whether generally or as an enhancement of the progressivity of the federal income tax); and (2) to act as a curb on excessive concentrations of wealth received by gift or inheritance.

Approaching the question of design of the federal transfer-tax system from a traditional academic perspective, Dodge maintains that, consistent with the above-mentioned rationales, a tax on gratuitous transfers ought to be imposed on transferees. The tax either could take the form of a separate accessions tax or could be folded into the federal income tax by including gratuitous transfers in gross income. Dodge contends that which form the tax takes depends on whether one is more concerned with ability to pay or with curbing excessive concentrations of wealth. To avoid sacrificing either end, Dodge suggests that the income-inclusion approach could actually be combined with an accessions tax (so long as the accessions tax had a large exemption amount and high rates).

In Chapter 13, Bridget Crawford and Wendy Gerzog pick up a thread of Dodge's discussion and focus on the distortions redressed and created by the advent of "portability" to the federal gift and estate taxes. Crawford and Gerzog provide helpful background by explaining the common estate planning mistakes that married couples made in the pre-portability era by failing to take full advantage of their lifetime gift/estate tax exemptions. They then explain how portability of the exemption may simplify estate planning and effectively remove the source of those common mistakes.

But Crawford and Gerzog then go beyond the typical academic discussion of tax rules by looking at the impact of portability on the economic and power dynamics in married couples, especially on women because they are statistically more likely to be the poorer spouse in a married couple. Crawford and Gerzog also critically examine the ways in which portability further reifies the married couple as a taxable unit and troublingly distributes tax benefits based on sexual relationships. Like Dodge, Crawford and Gerzog are concerned by the distortionary effects of the tax system; however, their focus is that of the critical tax scholar, as they interrogate the structure and function of the law, its privileging of certain (i.e., marital) relationships over others, and its impacts along lines of gender (as well as class, race, sexual orientation, etc.).

A Few Words of Thanks

Working on this book has been a pleasure. I would like to thank Anne Richardson Oakes for asking me to consider editing this volume on controversies in tax law and my editors at Ashgate for embracing the idea of a book that would ask contributors to actively engage with each other and their unique perspectives on U.S. tax law. I have thoroughly enjoyed working with all of the contributors to this volume, who have made my job of editing an exceedingly easy and pleasurable one. I appreciate their patience as they signed on to—and then diligently carried out—a project in which I asked them to produce three separate drafts of their chapters: an initial draft that they exchanged with each other early on so that they could begin to take each other's perspectives into account in producing the initial draft that I would review; a second draft for my review (and which was again exchanged); and then a final draft. Watching the chapters take shape through this process was exciting, and I am quite pleased with the end product. I hope that you will be as well.

PART I
Tax, Gender, and History

Chapter 2
Retaking Home Economics: Gendered Perspectives on Tax Equity

Carolyn C. Jones*

Mainstream accounts of the development of the design of the U.S. tax system focus on the establishment and professionalization of the economics profession as a shaping and legitimating force in tax policy and administration.[1] Central to these accounts are economic arguments and insights from the work of influential male economists. Most notable among this group was E.R.A. Seligman, known for his advocacy of a progressive system of taxation and for his seminal work on tax incidence—the question of who, ultimately, pays a tax.[2] But these mainstream accounts fail to mention and analyze another branch of economics which also examined issues at the heart of a mass tax system; namely, the branch of economics known as home economics. Scholars have not studied what professors in home economics departments thought about reforming tax laws and policies. They have even failed to notice the views of home economists teaching at prestigious universities such as the University of Chicago. Today we tend to think of home economics as an outmoded and sex-biased field of study concerned mainly with corporatist and trivial features of domestic life. And to some extent that is true.[3] But there is another side to home economics.

This chapter focuses on the "economic" side of home economics, showcasing the work of Hazel Kyrk and others who thought deeply about important issues relating to ability to pay and standards of living. To be sure, Kyrk and her associates had little influence in tax policy circles.[4] But revisiting their work decades later—retaking the course they offered in home economics—reveals the wisdom of their analysis, and it would provide valuable reading for today's tax students and scholars as they consider today's tax controversies.

Before turning to home economics and its relation to issues of taxation, I will provide a very brief overview of the tax system in the late nineteenth and early twentieth centuries—the time in which both economics and home economics arose as disciplines.

---

* I would like to thank Martha Chamallas for her comments on this piece and Olivia Rossi and Janice Kim for their research assistance.

1 Ajay K. Mehrotra, Making the Modern American Fiscal State: Law, Politics, and the Rise of Progressive Taxation, 1877–1929 (2013); W. Elliot Brownlee, *Economists and the Formation of the Modern Tax System in the United States: The World War I Crisis*, *in* The State and Economic Knowledge 401 (Mary O. Furner & Barry Supple eds., 2002).

2 Edwin R.A. Seligman, On the Shifting and Incidence of Taxation (1892).

3 *See* Megan J. Elias, Stir It Up: Home Economics in American Culture (2008); Carolyn M. Goldstein, Creating Consumers: Home Economists in Twentieth-Century America (2012); Rethinking Home Economics: Women and the History of a Profession (Sarah Stage & Virginia B. Vincenti eds., 1997).

4 Kyrk left academia in 1937 to join the U.S. Bureau of Human Nutrition and Home Economics in the Department of Agriculture. In 1943, she served as chair of the Consumer Advisory Committee to the Office of Price Administration.

The U.S. Tax System from Civil War to 1920s

The tax landscape looked much different in 1890 than it does today. As industrialization and urbanization accelerated after the Civil War, labor unrest and violence and a lively commentariat displayed a society riven by economic conflict. Some of that conflict was produced by arguments that the existing Republican system of taxation was inequitable and regressive. At the federal level in 1890, customs duties supplied 57 percent of federal revenues; alcohol, tobacco, and luxury taxes on such items as cosmetics and perfumes supplied 35 percent; and sales of public lands and other miscellaneous taxes supplied the remaining 8 percent.[5] The tariffs and sin taxes were regressive in incidence; however, this was not always apparent. Tariff opponents tried to overcome this cognitive problem. In 1912, before federal women's suffrage, the Democrats tried to bring the argument about tariffs home at the Wilson and Marshall Chamber of Tariff Horrors on Union Square in New York. The Woman's National Democratic League passed out samples of ratiné with Wilson buttons on them. As the *New York Times* explained in describing "housewives day," "[r]atine … is a soft, heavy wool material with a pebbly surface on the right side. It is a material which will lend itself to tight-fitting skirts, but it may not suit the woman with hips."[6] The fabric sample was accompanied by this message:

> "This All-Wool Ratine
> Costs the merchant in Paris 55 cents a yard.
> Costs the merchant in New York $2.05 a yard.
> The difference is caused by the tariff."[7]

During economic hard times in the 1890s, populists, westerners, and southerners increasingly objected to the high tariff regime, arguing that it encouraged monopoly and was socially unjust.[8] Henry George's single tax tract, *Progress and Poverty*, advocated a utopian world based upon a single tax on monopoly profits in land.

Things were no better at the state level. The states and localities were generally reliant on property taxes. For those holding real property, particularly farmers, assessment and enforcement of the property tax (with its often disputed valuations) was a dissatisfying feature of rural life. Those possessing intangibles (i.e., stocks, bonds, and the like) could avoid the property tax easily, and, the farmers noted, they were often the wealthiest people in the community. Again, the perception was that the wealthy were not paying their "fair share."[9]

Various groups began to advocate for a tax that would be more equitable—capturing those able to avoid the harsh effects of tariffs, sin taxes, and property taxes. A campaign for a progressive income tax, aimed at the rich, gathered strength among populists, farmers, Democrats, and those outside the Northeast. By 1913, federal income tax advocates had succeeded in overcoming constitutional impediments and created the modern federal income tax on individuals. The income tax, initially modest in its rates and covering only the wealthy because of its generous exemption levels, became a bit more widespread in its incidence with the arrival of World War I. The World

---

5 Mehrotra, *supra* note 1, at 3, 7.

6 *Wilson Women Use a Ratine Argument*, N.Y. Times, Sept. 21, 1912, at 11.

7 *Id.*

8 W. Elliot Brownlee, Federal Taxation in America: A Short History 43 (2d ed. 2004).

9 Paula Baker, The Moral Frameworks of Public Life: Gender, Politics, and the State in Rural New York, 1870–1930 (1991).

War I income tax covered 15 percent of the American population.[10] After the war, a series of Republican administrations cut back the progressive rates of the income tax but did not eliminate the tax.[11] It was not until World War II that the mass federal income tax, covering a majority of Americans, came into being.[12]

Today, one of the fundamental questions surrounding tax reform is the distribution of the tax burden and providing economic security for nonaffluent families. During the 2012 presidential campaign, former Governor Mitt Romney's statement that 47 percent of Americans do not pay income taxes focused this issue for fact-checking and for policy discussion. Romney connected failure to pay income tax with government dependency and a failure to "take personal responsibility and care for their lives."[13] The 47 percent figure is essentially correct. The Urban Institute-Brookings Tax Policy Center notes that 46 percent of Americans were expected to pay no federal income taxes in 2011.[14] Of those not paying federal income tax, 61 percent were paying Social Security and Medicare taxes. Twenty-two percent were retired. About 17 percent pay no federal taxes because they are unemployed, disabled, students, or the very poor.[15] As the twentieth century progressed and more Americans were required to pay federal income taxes, Social Security and Medicare taxes, and even Affordable Care Act individual insurance premiums or penalties, the effects of taxes and social insurance and socialized consumption on the lower and middle classes became worthy of attention.

For mainstream income tax economists working in the early part of the twentieth century, taxpayers were wealthy and relatively few in number. As the American fiscal system began to meld taxation and "insurance," an understanding of the effects, possibilities, and consequences of this system in the lives of less well-endowed citizens was needed. In the undervalued realm of home economics, these sorts of nuanced considerations were brought forward. This detailed look at American lives also exposed the inadequacy of incomes for many—inadequacies that could not have been addressed by greater economic efficiencies within the home. Some home economists exposed the need for family allowances and higher minimum wages and for socialized consumption and social insurance. It is to this discipline, new in the early twentieth century, that this chapter now turns.

Home Economics

As the federal fiscal regime was debated and changed in the early years of the twentieth century, some attention was paid to the effects of federal taxation in homes across the United States. The eventual adoption of the modern income tax coincided with the rise of the social sciences and the professionalization of those disciplines. Much has been written about the professionalization of economics, but very little has been written about its gendered nature as "new women" entered

10 Brownlee, *supra* note 8, at 63.

11 *Id.* at 74.

12 *Id.* at 108–19; *see generally* Carolyn C. Jones, *Class Tax to Mass Tax: The Rise of Propaganda in the Expansion of the Income Tax in World War II*, 37 Buff. L. Rev. 685 (1989).

13 *Full Transcript of the Mitt Romney Secret Video*, Mother Jones (Sept. 19, 2012), www.motherjones.com/politics/2012/09/full-transcript-mitt-romney-secret-video.

14 Rachel Johnson et al., Urban-Brookings Tax Pol'y Ctr., Why Some Tax Units Pay No Income Tax 1 (2011), *available at* http://www.taxpolicycenter.org/UploadedPDF/1001547-Why-No-Income-Tax.pdf.

15 Chuck Marr & Chye-Ching Huang, *Misconceptions and Realities About Who Pays Taxes*, Ctr. on Budget & Pol'y Priorities (Sept. 17, 2012), http://www.cbpp.org/cms/?fa=view&id=3505.

academia as social economists, as they developed the field of home economics, and as they advocated for social reform. Those involved in the creation of home economics did not view the subject as teaching domestic skills, but rather as a social and economic analysis of the home that embraced a broad spectrum of topics from psychology to finance.

These women, who have not really been noticed by tax scholars, had a variety of imaginative proposals. In the writings of these women, there is a surprising amount about women's unpaid work in the home, a critical tax design question even today. Some argued for wages for wives and for treating the home as a joint-stock company. As a way of increasing efficiency in domestic production in areas from housing to child care to food preparation, some home economists proposed moving these activities from private households to community cooperatives.

In retrospect, however, the most striking feature of the "economics" in home economics was the ways in which women economists and home economists developed sophisticated analyses of the question at the root of the federal income tax—taxing on the basis of ability to pay. How that ability could be measured by income and its nuances and complications were treated in courses offered in home economics departments.

The area in which one finds the most explicit treatment of taxation in the work of women economists is in the field of budget studies. Researchers, including Jessica Peixotto, examined the expenditures of a variety of families in cities across the country as they confronted the costs of living and the rising expectations fueled by consumerism.[16] Taxation—state, local, and federal—was a part of that picture. As states turned to new taxes, like sales taxes, the tie between taxation and consumerism became more obvious and robust.

The *Smith Alumnae Quarterly* urged that women have a responsibility to understand economic change as the world is driven largely by advancing consumerism.[17] The early twentieth-century social and home economists were not entirely successful in educating women about economics. Their ambitious and imaginative experiments may, however, enrich our understanding of current tax policies and draw attention to the gendered aspect of both professionalization and tax policies.

At the turn of the nineteenth century to the twentieth, the United States was in the midst of rapid change. Production was moving from homes to factories. People were moving from the countryside to cities. Urbanization, industrialization, and immigration were powerful forces. With these changes, women, especially middle-class women, were less involved in traditional production within the household, becoming consumers of material welfare for their families in an economy more controlled by exchange of money (as opposed to goods).

As the economy altered (more for some than for others) and as societal change accelerated, a new discipline, home economics, was created. Some historians trace the roots of the home economics movement to Catherine Beecher's 1841 publication of the *Treatise on Domestic Economy for the Use of Young Ladies at Home*.[18] With the Morrill Act of 1862 and establishment of land-grant colleges in each state, courses began to be offered to rural women through extension services.[19] What bound these efforts together was the notion of consumption and a consumer society.

---

16 Daniel Horowitz, The Morality of Spending: Attitudes Toward the Consumer Society in America, 1875–1940, at 134–47 (1992); Jessica B. Peixotto, Getting and Spending at the Professional Standard of Living (1927).

17 Chase Going Woodhouse, *Some Socializing Aspects of Education for Homemaking*, 17 Smith Alumnae Q. 146 (1925).

18 Emma Seifrit Weigley, *It Might Have Been Euthenics: The Lake Placid Conferences and the Home Economics Movement*, 26 Am. Q. 79 (1974). Beecher's 1869 *The American Woman's Home* was written with her sister, Harriet Beecher Stowe.

19 Elias, *supra* note 3, at 4.

In areas, like the East, less affected by land-grant developments, cooking schools emerged. During the 1870s and 1880s, home economics began to appear in curricula in high schools, women's colleges, and state universities.

The post-Civil War era, with its increased prosperity for some, also marked a distinct increase in demand for higher education for women. Despite much-rehearsed concerns that higher education would harm the (maternal) health and/or marriageability of young women, women reformers refused to accept such assertions. Women's colleges in the East sought to offer the classical and moral curriculum offered in elite men's colleges. In the West, however, at land-grant universities and at the newly reformulated University of Chicago, both the identity of students and the curricula available were quite different. In 1902, there were more women than men at the University of Chicago, with the number of women students almost equaling or sometimes exceeding men at public universities in California, Illinois, Iowa, Kansas, Michigan, Minnesota, Missouri, Nebraska, Ohio, Texas, Washington, and Wisconsin.[20] A backlash in some cases resulted in freezing the number of women or in their segregation (as in Chicago).[21]

Higher education itself was changing beyond coeducation. Some colleges, inspired by the German model of graduate education and research, altered the old emphasis on political and moral philosophy and began to change academia. The flowering of the social sciences ensued along with institutional battles over the placement and power of the new disciplines.

It is in this turn-of-the-century environment that a variety of disciplines were launched as professions—for example, economics, sociology, and anthropology. In some circumstances it was difficult to determine where home economics fit in. At the University of Chicago, home economics pioneer Marion Talbot was part of the social science department until she was "awarded" a department of her own—a step that could be seen as both status enhancing and deflating.

Some of the debate in higher education about the role and place of home economics was the perception that the discipline was trade school-like or, as it was put in the early days of the discipline, specializing in the three fundamental Cs—cooking, clothing, and cleaning.[22] When Isabel Bevier took over the Department of Home Economics at the University of Illinois, a dean asked about her bread-baking skills. She assured him that this had little to do with the department's purpose.[23]

For some home economists, science was the foundation for evaluating food, textiles, and sanitation. Psychology and its subspecialty of child development provided another respected disciplinary anchor for home economics. In the age of Taylorization,[24] home economists sought a new level of efficiency from homemakers who purchased rather than produced, who used new technologies and were subject to higher standards of homemaking.[25] An editorial in the *Journal of Home Economics* urged application of Taylor's principles to the home and more particularly in

20 Rosalind Rosenberg, Beyond Separate Spheres: Intellectual Roots of Modern Feminism 44 (1982).

21 *Id.*

22 Gwendolyn Stewart, *The Economics of the Family: A Suggested Course for the Department of Home Economics*, 2 J. Home Econ. 209, 212 (1910); *see also* Mabel L. Wellman, *Home Economics in a Liberal Arts College*, 15 J. Am. Ass'n U. Women 78 (1922).

23 Isabel Bevier, *Recollections and Impressions of the Beginnings of the Department of Home Economics at the University of Illinois*, 32 J. Home Econ. 291 (1940).

24 Taylorization was named for efficiency consultant Frederick Winslow Taylor, the "father" of scientific management. "That meant less autonomy, more surveillance, more quantified timing and measurement of output." Jackson Lears, Rebirth of a Nation: The Making of Modern America, 1877–1920, at 228 (2009).

25 *See* Ruth Schwartz Cowan, *The "Industrial Revolution" in the Home: Household Technology and Social Change in the 20th Century*, 17 Tech. & Culture 1 (1976).

the homes of the "well-to-do"—counting steps between stove, sink, and table; finding the optimal height for tables and sinks; considering the use of dumbwaiters—all designed to improve the home.[26]

As helpful as this could be, some home economists saw the discipline as tending to confine itself within the walls of individual homes and as failing to address larger questions of women's ambitions. Chase Going Woodhouse, in her 1926 essay in the *Journal of the American Association of University Women*, asked:

> The stay-at-home, devoted housewife of the past century did little to improve her methods. May it not be possible that with the right help and a bit of direction the present-day college woman with her wide interests, her ambition to continue her professional work, her refusal to be tied to a house, will make it a more desirable and efficient place in which to develop the coming generation?[27]

A few early home economists urged an understanding and advocacy of social reform outside the curtilage of the middle-class home. In the *Journal of Home Economics*' books and literature section were reviews of such Progressive Era writings. For example, B.R. Andrews,[28] in his essay on E.T. Devine's *Misery and Its Causes*, relates larger social issues to the home economics program:

> The concluding chapter is a striking presentation of practical Utopia for which all may work and in which the Home Economics student and teacher may feel he has a hand. The characteristics of this better time will be the provision for each individual of a sound, physical heredity; a protected childhood; a prolonged working period of both men and women; freedom from preventable disease; freedom from professional crime; a general system of insurance against contingencies of death, old age, accident, sickness, and unemployment; a system of elementary education adapted to the present day needs; a liberal relief system and a standard of living high enough to insure full nourishment, reasonable recreation, shelter and other elementary necessities. It is in such a program that Home Economics must largely express itself.[29]

And what of economics in home economics? It seemed not to get the attention that home décor and menu planning did. This was recognized early on:

> Pioneers in Home Economics in the early stages of its development did not undertake the economic study of the family or the home, but rather the activities of the home. Now students of Home Economics realize the importance of the principles of economics as applied to these activities and to the family as a whole.[30]

26 Editorial, *The New Gospel of Efficiency*, 3 J. Home Econ. 194, 197 (1911).

27 Chase Going Woodhouse, *Modern Home Making in Relation to the Liberal Arts College for Women*, 19 J. Am. Ass'n U. Women 7, 8 (1926).

28 B.R. Andrews was a professor of household economics at the Teachers College at Columbia University. *See* Benjamin R. Andrews, Economics of the Household (1923).

29 B.R. Andrews, *Misery and Its Causes*, 2 J. Home Econ. 109 (1910).

30 Stewart, *supra* note 22, at 211.

A 1910 proposal for a course on the economics of family urged that the course consider the family from the standpoint of the woman who controlled family funds and, thus, the family's status.[31] "Such a course would be essentially a study of the family as it may be controlled by woman."[32]

By 1925, the situation had not improved appreciably. Hildegard Kneeland of the Bureau of Home Economics in the U.S. Department of Agriculture had studied sociology, statistics, and the economics of consumption as a graduate student at the University of Chicago and later at Columbia University.[33] Kneeland wrote, "After jogging along comfortably for many years with little attention to this section of our field, we have suddenly become sensitive to the scanty amount of economics in our home economics and are bestirring ourselves to fill this gap."[34]

Hazel Kyrk

Probably the leading economist in home economics was Hazel Kyrk. Kyrk was born in 1886 and was self-supporting from the time of her high school graduation. She became a mother's helper in the household of Leon Carroll Marshall who became dean at the University of Chicago's College of Commerce and Administration. Kyrk followed the family, earning her B.A. in economics in 1910 from Chicago. She continued with graduate studies in economics, teaching and working as a statistician for the American Division of the Allied Maritime Transport Council during World War I.[35] In 1921, Kyrk's dissertation won the prestigious Hart, Schaffner & Marx Prize. It was later published in 1923 as *A Theory of Consumption*.[36] In 1925, Kyrk was able to secure a joint appointment in economics and home economics. It was this "borderland between economics and home economics to which she devoted the rest of her career," and which she encapsulated in her 1933 book, *Economic Problems of the Family*.[37] Kyrk was significant in tracking the largest trends in the early twentieth century, as the United States became a society devoted to consumption—one of her major scholarly topics. Because she was based in home economics, Kyrk explored the effects of this transformation on women and families—in areas including household production in a newly urbanized and industrialized economy, compensation for home work, control of income and its adequacy, and the need for social insurance for many families made vulnerable in the new shape of the economy. These themes are fundamental to the design of a fiscal and modern state. This chapter next turns to an exploration of each of Kyrk's themes and of their relevance to her time and to ours.

31 *Id.* at 212.

32 *Id.* There is a description of an economics course taught in household science at the University of Illinois by David Kinley. The first half of the year was an introduction to general economics with the second half focusing on the home. There is little attention to taxation—unless it can be tied to the brief description of "social consumption" (i.e., parks, libraries, etc.). David Kinley, *Aspects of Economics of Importance in Household Science*, 3 J. Home Econ. 253 (1911).

33 Carolyn M. Goldstein, Creating Consumers: Home Economists in Twentieth-Century America 75–76 (2012).

34 Hildegard Kneeland, *The Field of Research in the Economics of the Home*, 17 J. Home Econ. 15 (1925).

35 Susan Van Velzen, *Hazel Kyrk, and the Ethics of Consumption*, *in* Toward a Feminist Philosophy of Economics 39 (Drucilla K. Barker & Edith Kuiper eds., 2003); *see also* Charles F. McGovern, Sold American: Consumption and Citizenship 1890–1945 (2006).

36 Van Velzen, *supra* note 35, at 44; McGovern, *supra* note 35, at 154–62.

37 Van Velzen, *supra* note 35, at 44.

Household Production

Rather quickly in the design of the income tax, the question of imputed income is mentioned and rejected as part of the tax base.[38] Usually, a concern for privacy and the accuracy of valuation are cited as reasons. Imputed income is the economic benefit derived from consumption of services produced by the taxpayer or from the enjoyment and use of the taxpayer's property. A taxpayer-owned home could be rented to another to produce rental income (which could go into gross income). If instead the taxpayer uses the house herself, the foregone rental value is not added to gross income and is not taxed under the American system. (For differing perspectives on whether such imputed rental income ought to be included in the income tax base, see chapters 4 and 5 of this volume.)

As slight as the attention to imputed income may be in the tax literature, imputed income from household services was at the center of attention in the home economics curriculum. For the more typical focus "within four walls," the very aim of home economics was to make household production more valuable and efficient. In many ways, then, home economics was centered on imputed income from services.

Kyrk's *Economic Problems of the Family* went into some detail on the work of homemakers. Kyrk, however, recognized the intractable problems of data collection and valuation. She estimated that, in 1930, approximately 49 million people in the United States had a "gainful occupation" (a term resented by home economists) while about 25.5 million were engaged as "homemakers."[39]

Kyrk was quick to note difficulties in defining "household production." She asked how Thorstein Veblen's conspicuous consumption or conspicuous leisure of the upper-class wife would be classified. Would rest and beautifying regimes be time spent in household production so that a wife "may be [an] agreeable and entertaining companion to [her] husband and children?"[40] Margaret Reid, a student of Kyrk's and later a home economics professor at Iowa State University, limited the definition of household production to those activities done by household members that could be delegated to someone outside the household or purchased on the market.

Kyrk's treatment of household production then became a critique of household production itself. She doubted it could ever be particularly efficient in the business sense, given fixed overhead costs and the dispersion of efforts typical in a homemaker's day. Indeed, Kyrk saw the household as antithetical to business: "Household management like business management may strive to lower costs, but the aim of the one is thereby to maximize income and of the other to maximize the results of expenditure."[41] As Kyrk stressed the conversion to money incomes, she saw similar forces competing with household production in the future:

> There are certain pervasive, underlying forces that in the future as in the past will in so far as they come into operation tend to substitute commercial or cooperative production outside the home for production within the home. It is the productive efficiency of specialized machinery and

38 *See* Edwin R.A. Seligman, The Income Tax 20–21 (1914) ("A further difficulty arises as to whether income is to include only money income, or whether it also comprises the so-called enjoyable or psychic income, that is the pleasurable sensation or usufruct that flows in to the individual in the shape not of money, but of money's worth … . [I]t may therefore be said that income at least for purposes of taxation, signifies in general money income, with an occasional inclusion of such psychic income as is notorious and easily calculable.").

39 Hazel Kyrk, Economic Problems of the Family 42–43 (1933).

40 *Id.* at 47.

41 *Id.* at 58.

> labor utilized to full capacity under centralized management, and the power of associative effort functioning through exchange, which have drawn task after task from the unspecialized household worker's hands.[42]

Kyrk saw that much household production was the result of societal norms preferring independent private households with food and entertainment in the home. "The essential point," she wrote, "is that production takes place not only in order that we may live but that we may live as we desire."[43] At some level, then, production becomes indistinguishable from consumption.

From the beginning, home economists had been interested in some of these alternatives to home production. With the movement of much of household production out of the home, service businesses moved in to fill the gap. In their famous study *Middletown* from 1929, Robert and Helen Lynd expressed concern about the individual ownership of washing machines:

> This is an example of the way in which a useful new invention vigorously pushed on the market by effective advertising may serve to slow up a secular trend. The heavy investment by the individual family in an electric washing machine costing from $60 to $200 tends to perpetuate a questionable institutional set-up—whereby many individual homes repeat common tasks day after day in isolated units—by forcing back into the individual home a process that was following belatedly the trend in industry towards centralized operation.[44]

At the time of the development of home economics, there was not unanimity about the desirability of capital-intensive investments in each home. For women who lived in settlement homes, a common kitchen and living space provided an alternative way of living. Charlotte Perkins Gilman (of *Yellow Wallpaper* fame) devoted considerable energy to the development of a feminist housing complex. She described its object as professional women with families. The apartments would not have kitchens, meals being provided from a central kitchen or in a common dining room. Cleaning would be organized centrally and children would be provided with a roof-garden, day nursery, and kindergarten.[45] In home economics departments, cooperative arrangements for nurseries and for food were an important part of the discipline.[46] Gradually, however, interest fell off and the stress on "within the four walls" continued.[47] The failure to tax imputed income both exempts household services and the use value of household durables.

---

42 *Id.* at 74.

43 *Id.* at 75.

44 Robert Lynd & Helen Lynd, Middletown: A Study in American Culture 175 (1929).

45 Dolores Hayden, The Grand Domestic Revolution: A History of Feminist Designs for American Homes, Neighborhoods, and Cities 189 (1981).

46 *See* Ethel Puffer Howes, *How to Start a Coöperative Kitchen* (on file with Sophia Smith Archives, Smith College); Ethel Puffer Howes, *How to Start a Coöperative Nursery* (on file with Sophia Smith Archives, Smith College); Ethel Puffer Howes & Esther H. Stocks, *Co-operating Mothers*, Woman Citizen, Feb. 1921 (on file with Sophia Smith Archives, Smith College); Myra Reed Richardson, *How to Start a Coöperative Laundry* (on file with Sophia Smith Archives, Smith College).

47 Kneeland, *supra* note 34, at 18 ("How does the efficiency of the outside agency, commercial or coöperative, compare with that of the individual home, in money and time costs and in the quality of the product? What would be the effect upon family relationships if the laundry, the mending, the cooking, the serving of meals were taken out of the home? Such questions as these challenge the prevailing assumption that the work should remain in the home.").

While contemporary efforts at cohousing and other alternatives to single-family living do exist, the current situation is in many ways similar to the living models of the early twentieth century. Unpaid work within the home is not subject to federal income tax. The use of consumer durables is not taxed either. The early 1900s, according to Hazel Kyrk, were largely characterized by a shift to money incomes. As money incomes have become less than sufficient to support a family on the money income of one earner, women have entered the paid workforce in greater numbers. As Stephanie McMahon notes in Chapter 3, as of 2009, 59.1 percent of women are in the labor force. Our current tax system, although characterized by lower marginal rates than those in effect in the post-World War II era until 1986, still gives a marriage bonus to families with one earner and inflicts a marriage penalty upon spouses who are both in the paid workforce and earn roughly similar incomes. The untaxed value of household labor has never really received direct attention by tax policy makers, but it lurks in the background of a tax system that disincentivizes the increasingly necessary work of the "secondary worker," who is seeking the money income so crucial to modern middle- and lower-class life.

Wages for Wives

In her home economics textbook, Kyrk addressed the value of homemaker's services and the movement advocating "wages for wives." Examples of these proposals can be found in Doris Stevens's 1926 article for *The Nation* entitled "Wages for Wives: The Home as a Joint-Stock Company."[48] One proposed version of this program would require valuation of the wife's services. This could result in a wife receiving wages that may not correspond to her husband's standard of living, or, conversely, in a husband having very little in the way of income after paying his wife's wages. Alternatively, the wife's services could be valued by reference to her husband's income. "[I]n fact, all that the system would mean would be a recognition of her right to a percentage of his income."[49] While this proposal might address intrafamily issues of power and control, it would not necessarily add to the family's money income in the economy at large. Kyrk saw psychological benefit in the control and recognition "wages for wives" would give them, but as discussed below, she was a greater advocate of control by family council. Similarly, those urging a joint federal income tax return in 1948 based upon legal entitlements rather than arbitrary splitting of income were also interested in altering domestic economic control. This, indeed, leads to the next tax-related issue addressed by Kyrk.

Control of Income

Hazel Kyrk's 1933 home economics textbook included a chapter entitled "Control of the Purse."[50] This question was an important one in the field of home economics. If a college education in domestic consumption "within the four walls" constructed a professional identity for home economics graduates, power over expenditures provided a platform for realizing that role. Kyrk wrote that women were increasingly exercising control of money income just as wages and salaries

48 Doris Stevens, *Wages for Wives: The Home as a Joint-Stock Company*, 122 The Nation 81 (1926); *see also Shall We Place Wives on a Salary Basis?*, 53 Current Literature 413 (1912).

49 Kyrk, *supra* note 39, at 185.

50 *Id.* at 166.

were increasingly becoming the major sources of income. Kyrk viewed the trend with some concern. "Observation of the trend may even cause us to wonder if there is not danger of undue feminine influence and power over the disposition of the money income and over the standard of living."[51] After surveying traditional common law and civil law regimes, married women's property acts and the control of the community vested in the husband, Kyrk was ambivalent about which legal system was best. She displayed greater interest in actual as opposed to legal control. Her text seems to favor joint control through a family council in which even children have a say in spending decisions. Kyrk advocated for "weight in the family council … in proportion to age and special knowledge."[52] But, if actual arrangements are most salient, Kyrk noted the paucity of empirical data about family financial arrangements.[53]

Although taxes are not mentioned, this question of control within the family became critical with the adoption of the mass income tax during World War II with a very progressive rate structure. With automatic income splitting in community property states (despite control by the husband), assignment of property income to its legal owner in common law states, and reluctance by the Bureau of Internal Revenue to apportion income according to family partnership agreements, questions of contribution and control of marital income and assets became critical to the post-World War II revisions to the federal income tax. The desire to tax individuals with equal taxable incomes equally and couples with equal incomes equally has proved to be impossible in a progressive rate environment. That impossibility has led to an assortment of adjustments over time since the adoption of the joint return in 1948, which are admirably discussed by Stephanie McMahon in Chapter 3. Most recently, societal and legal changes in the definition of the "couple" to include same-sex married couples have come to the fore with the U.S. Supreme Court's 2013 decision in *United States v. Windsor*.[54]

Adequacy of Money Incomes

Some home economists who valued traditional norms believed that elimination of waste and a more energetic work ethic would help those in poverty to attain a middle-class standard of comfortable living. Ellen Richards, in her 1911 essay "The Social Significance of the Home Economics Movement,"[55] quoted C.R. Henderson:

> The architecture of a city tenement house is to blame for the silent but certain transformation of the home into a sty. Instead of accepting this condition as inevitable, like a law of nature, and accepting its consequences, all experience demands of those who believe in the monogamic family that they make a united and persistent fight on the evil which threatens the slowly acquired qualities secured

51 *Id.* at 181.

52 *Id.* at 182.

53 *Id.* at 185–86.

54 133 S. Ct. 2675 (2013); *see generally* Anthony C. Infanti, *LBGT Families, Tax Nothings*, 17 J. Gender Race & Just. 35 (2014); Anthony C. Infanti, *Tax ~~Equity~~*, 55 Buff. L. Rev. 1191 (2008); Carolyn C. Jones, *Split Income and Separate Spheres: Tax Law and Gender Roles in the 1940s*, 6 Law & Hist. Rev. 259 (1988); Marjorie Kornhauser, *Love, Money and the IRS: Family Income Sharing and the Joint Income Tax Return*, 45 Hastings L.J. 63 (1993); Stephanie Hunter McMahon, *To Save States' Residents: States' Use of Community Property for Federal Tax Reduction, 1939–1947*, 27 Law & Hist. Rev. 585 (2009).

55 Ellen H. Richards, *The Social Significance of the Home Economics Movement*, 3 J. Home Econ. 120 (1911).

> in the highest form of the family. It would be unworthy of us to permit a great part of a modern population to descend again to the animal level from which the race has ascended only through aeons of struggle and difficulty.[56]

Hazel Kyrk was less convinced. In her 1933 textbook, *Economic Problems of the Family*, Kyrk recognized that money income was "indispensable" in twentieth-century America.[57] Kyrk began her book with the question, "What Constitutes a Family?"[58] She started her analysis of this question with the nuclear family of parents and children (noting the less than comprehensive data available). But households also included other relatives. Day Monroe's study of white Chicago families in 1920 found 11.2 percent had boarders or lodgers; 20 percent of families in her study had households with other relatives.

Later in her text, Kyrk returned to the nuclear family and to the question, "Are the incomes received by the majority of married men today adequate for family support?"[59] The answer was made more difficult because of the lack, again, of comprehensive data. In trying to answer this question, Kyrk used statistics gathered from the newly restored federal income tax. She calculated that 3.77 million married men received $2,000 in income in 1922.[60] In 1927, the obligation to report kicked in at $3,500. Kyrk found that 658,472 returns showed income over $5,000. Kyrk, in trying to assess this question, noted problems in defining adequacy from the identification of those items that provide adequacy to the variable notions of sufficiency based on class. Kirk utilized four "levels of living":[61] minimum of subsistence; health and decency; comfort; and, finally, riches. Kyrk cautioned against class-based notions of adequacy: "Once the principle 'It is necessary that a group should not lose caste' is adopted, all objectivity is cast aside and every convention that marks existing social status is written into the standard of essentials."[62] Kyrk noted that, in addition to class, the concept of a minimum standard of money income could have racial and ethnic dimensions: "To Americans there is a minimum tolerable level for American families that is not only different but higher than one they might set up for 'foreigners.' What would be accepted as tolerable for Negroes might not be so accepted for white families and so on."[63] Kyrk was very clear-eyed regarding the socially constructed notions behind some of home economics' budgeting guidance.

Kyrk also noted the variation in earning over a married man's life and its relationship to parental responsibilities during the life cycle.[64] While data were inadequate, Kyrk concluded that poverty "is to a large extent the result of our own standard of essentials."[65] "Modern poverty is also an aspect of the increased demand upon money income as such, the decline in forms of income other than money."[66]

To Kyrk it was clear that there were inadequate incomes, despite the inadequacies of data on the matter. What could be done? First, homemakers could "increase … managerial efficiency" and

---

56 *Id.* at 124–25 (quoting C.R. Henderson).
57 *Id.* at 123–24.
58 *Id.* at 1.
59 *Id.* at 188.
60 *Id.* at 192.
61 *Id.* at 198.
62 *Id.* at 199.
63 *Id.* at 202.
64 *Id.* at 221.
65 *Id.* at 225.
66 *Id.*

make rather than buy.[67] Yet, Kyrk argued, there are limits to the ability to substitute the homemade for the purchased or, for that matter, to increase "managerial skill." The next possibility is a lowered standard of living. Although many mothers "did without," Kyrk was particularly concerned with the impact on children, especially those in families with three or more dependent children.[68] If that failed, mothers and children could go to work, a self-evidently bad result according to Kyrk.[69]

Kyrk linked this problem of inadequacy of income to risks of disability, unemployment, and old age—and to the more general discussion of social insurance in the 1920s and 1930s. She joined Eleanor Rathbone and Paul Douglas in rejecting a uniform minimum wage that some argued should be set at the cost of maintaining a family of five. Rathbone and Douglas argued for a variable family allowance, one that would vary according to the needs of the "worker and his family."[70] Kyrk did point out that such a system could be "organized on a national or local scale and according to a regional or trade basis," and she considered the possibility that the expense could "be borne by the state or industry."[71]

Kyrk referred to Paul Douglas's 1925 book *Wages and the Family*. Douglas surveyed family allowances in Europe and Australia. He endorsed the family allowance system:

> The allowances which are granted under an ideal system of family allowances should be adequate to meet the extra cost which dependents occasion a wage-earner. So far as possible, they should be so flexible that while all families, whatever their composition, will be assured of at least a minimum, yet at the same time no person or group will be paid any appreciable excess over the actual needs.[72]

The man most known for the study of tax incidence had a connection to Douglas's project. To complement a proposed investigation of the International Labour Office (ILO), the University of Chicago joined a research effort with Professor E.R.A. Seligman of Columbia University. Douglas made use of the ILO documents in his book.[73]

Douglas considered whether the expense of the allowance system should be borne by the state or by industry. Socialists and labor leaders in Australia and Europe as well as English feminists argued for state provision on the grounds that it would not lower the wages of workers to the same extent as an industrially based system and that the incidence of the cost of allowances could be shifted to the wealthy through income and inheritance taxes. Douglas disagreed with his fellow advocates for family allowances asserting that existing wages would be lowered. "There is no reason, however, why the single men should continue to enjoy a surplus over and above that which is necessary to maintain them."[74]

Douglas also disputed that the cost of a state system would fall upon the wealthy. If this were a national system, Douglas remarked that "it should be remembered that a portion of the national revenues is derived from tariff duties and internal-revenue taxes upon articles of consumption

67 *Id.* at 223.

68 *Id.* at 224.

69 *Id.* at 225.

70 *Id.* at 226 (providing as suggested reading Paul H. Douglas, Wages and the Family (1925), and Eleanor Rathbone, The Disinherited Family (1927)).

71 *Id.* at 226 n.28.

72 Paul H. Douglas, Wages and the Family 210 (1925).

73 *Id.* at x.

74 *Id.* at 215.

which are primarily paid for by the poorer and by the middle-class families."[75] If left to the states, which Douglas saw as "the logical bodies to grant such allowances," their revenues were largely derived from property taxes which failed to reach the intangible property of the wealthy.[76] Entrepreneurs could lower wages and gain a windfall, according to Douglas, while government payments would "open the way for extensive corruption and favoritism."[77] Douglas concluded that the administration of family allowances should be left to employers.

Today, far from adopting Douglas's proposal for employer-based family allowances, our federal income tax system provides a child tax credit and, more significantly, the earned income tax credit. It provides refundable tax credits that are mostly transfer payments rather than refunds of taxes paid. While there are limited benefits to childless taxpayers, the program is largely targeted at "working" taxpayers with children. It has been described as a wage subsidy, a work bonus, even as a negative income tax. It is the United States's "largest anti-poverty entitlement program."[78]

Social Insurance

In Kyrk's *Theory of Consumption*, her award-winning 1923 book, she recognized the problem of unequal distribution of wealth. She noted that in the United States in 1918, "ten percent of the population has the power to consume thirty-five percent of the product."[79] Kyrk reached the conclusion that "[t]he smaller number with the larger income have not only had more wants satisfied and all wants more fully satisfied, but less urgent needs are gratified, caprice and whim are met."[80] "When the discrepancy in purchasing power spells disease, premature death, ill-nourished children, ignorance, crime, pauperism, degradation, society is bound to have some realization of the wastes involved in the way its productive resources are utilized."[81]

Kyrk devoted considerable space to socialized consumption—taxpayer-provided parks, museums, schools, street cleaning, and extending to free medical clinics and free lunches for school children.[82] Her *Theory of Consumption* noted that there were "strong arguments" for provision of a "minimum standard of living" through minimum wage legislation and through provision of insurance for the "uncertainties of income."[83] Kyrk saw the incidence of such programs falling on the industries, as they employed workers.[84]

Later, as the Great Depression increased popular pressures for social insurance, Kyrk's 1933 home economics textbook, *Economic Problems of the Family*, included an entire chapter on social insurance. Even though the Bureau of Labor Statistics showed in 1918–1919 that 80 percent of the lowest income group carried life insurance, the payments were often sufficient only for funeral expenses. As Kyrk noted in the introduction to her social insurance chapter, "The theory upon

75 *Id.* at 217.

76 *Id.*

77 *Id.* at 218.

78 Richard Schmalbeck & Lawrence Zelenak, Federal Income Taxation 791–93 (3d ed. 2011); *see generally* Dennis J. Ventry, Jr., *Welfare by Any Other Name: Tax Transfers and the EITC*, *in* Critical Tax Theory: An Introduction 283 (Anthony C. Infanti & Bridget J. Crawford eds., 2009).

79 Hazel Kyrk, A Theory of Consumption 50 (1923).

80 *Id.*

81 *Id.* at 51.

82 *Id.* at 59.

83 *Id.* at 63.

84 *Id.*

which our society has been proceeding is that each family makes its own provision against the financial hazards to which it is exposed."[85] In reality, however, Kyrk concluded that none of the standard budgets for "health and decency" could make adequate provision for sickness, premature death, or old age.[86] A poorer family could purchase more insurance, but it might come at the cost of food or clothing.

Kyrk's text then provided a comparative survey of social insurance (both internationally and by reference to the states), citing I.M. Rubinow, who was its leading exponent in the United States.[87] "Social insurance," according to Rubinow, was "the policy of organized society to furnish protection to one part of its population which some other part may need less, or, if needing, is able to purchase voluntarily through private insurance."[88] As Kyrk concluded, "the costs of providing against certain risks should not fall upon those who are exposed to them, but upon others, and of the fact that many of the urban and wage-earning population cannot make provision for the future that is adequate without infringing on accepted standards of food, housing, education and similar essentials."[89]

Kyrk began with workers' compensation schemes ("the only part of a social insurance program that exists on any comprehensive scale in the United States today")[90] and then moved to discussions of social insurance against sickness, unemployment, and old age. Kyrk cited the work of University of California–Berkeley law professor Barbara Armstrong, who was instrumental in the development of the Social Security system.[91] Kyrk referred to potential financing methods, including "compulsory insurance," constitutionally characterized as a "tax" in our time.[92]

Conclusion

Hazel Kyrk and the economics of home economics were not particularly influential in the development of the modern federal income tax. Before World War II, the income tax was essentially a tax on the rich. The sex segregation of women economists into home economics foretold the degree of attention their arguments would receive in the larger tax world. We should, however, retake home economics.

The concerns of these early home economists proved to be central to the design of the overall tax structure we experience today. It was when the Social Security system began in 1935 and when the federal income tax became a mass tax that the issues of such interest to Kyrk and others came to the fore. While imputed income is not taxed directly, its existence and scale in the form of homemakers' labor required legislative recognition and, in some cases, adjustments in the development of the child-care credit and in efforts to deal with what became the marriage penalty. The question of "control of the purse" became a part of the messy application of the federal income tax to legal regimes before Congress "resolved" the issue with the enactment of a joint return that

85 Kyrk, *supra* note 39, at 272.

86 *Id.* at 279.

87 *Id.* at 281.

88 *Id.* (citing Isaac Max Rubinow, Social Insurance 3 (1913)).

89 *Id.* at 281–82.

90 *Id.* at 283.

91 Roger J. Traynor, *Barbara Nachtrieb Armstrong—In Memoriam: The Light-Years of Barbara Armstrong: 1890–1976*, 65 Cal. L. Rev. 920 (1977).

92 Nat'l Fed'n of Indep. Bus. v. Sebelius, 132 S. Ct. 2566 (2012).

did not require the transfer of legal control. The question of measuring ability to pay is still with us in all its gendered dimensions.

The early generation of home economists, who like Hazel Kyrk were focusing on economics, soon were replaced by those with a more corporatist and conservative agenda focused on middle-class homemakers. The discipline, as it evolved from settlement house workers to more conventional and traditional lifestyles, would have had little disagreement with the lifestyles of those enjoying a marriage bonus. While writers like Kyrk placed women and their concerns at the forefront, the narrative line in *Economic Problems of the Family* is less woman-centric than it is class-centric.

In the end, the vision that emerges from retaking home economics is attention to a problem larger than tax policy—the problem of adequacy of incomes for many poor and working-class households. As wages stagnate and unemployment is high, a progressive income tax that is highly redistributive and politically viable is not likely to emerge. The creation of entitlements like Social Security, Medicare, and Medicaid, supported in part by dedicated taxes, have done more to address the question of adequacy. The revenues and outlays connected with those programs have continued to grow in significance and to create questions of sustainability. These programs have gendered dimensions, but, as Stephanie McMahon notes in Chapter 3, the gendered focus may take the background as economic problems of families—the subject of Kyrk's home economics text—take the fore.

In many ways, McMahon and I share similar perspectives. I believe we are committed to the study of taxation as revelatory of society's values and priorities and of history as a way of illustrating the very complicated interactions among taxpayers, tax administrators, interest groups, and tax policy makers. Our chapters deal with different time frames, which necessarily provide different perspectives.

In the late nineteenth and early twentieth centuries, society was revolutionized by industrialization, urbanization, and larger-scale institutions. The small-scale community with family farms and tradesmen began to dwindle in importance. As a result of many social reform projects, women began to assert their desires for new opportunities and rights. Thus emerged the demand for higher education for women. Strong social norms, particularly the idea of separate spheres—a public domain for men and a private domestic world for women—shaped the higher education that a woman received. She may have been an economist, or may have studied economics within the new discipline of home economics, but, in the end, she would base her consideration of the economy on the family. Taxation itself was an epiphenomenon in that time—secondary to questions of power within the home and the adequacy of family income. These Progressive Era considerations, going explicitly to issues more foundational than tax unit or marginal tax rate suggest, I believe, the value of these unusual home economists' thinking to contemporary shifts in our economy and concomitant inequality of income and wealth.

Chapter 3
Gendering the Marriage Penalty

Stephanie Hunter McMahon

Introduction

Three days before turning over the reins of government to Richard Nixon, the Lyndon Johnson administration announced that 155 people with adjusted gross incomes over $200,000, including 21 individuals with incomes over $1 million, paid no federal income tax.[1] The public then demanded that the new Republican administration reduce this perceived tax avoidance by the wealthy. But economic worries and a Democratic Congress limited the ability to enact changes to the tax system. In a period of inflation, top economic advisers opposed tax cuts.[2] And enacting tax reform, not coupled with a tax reduction, would be nearly impossible with the split between Congress and the presidency. In this heated political environment, Congress enacted the Tax Reform Act of 1969.[3] Compromises linked some tax simplification, a bit of tax reduction, and a new alternative minimum tax—with only the latter directly responding to the initial provocation for changes to the tax system.

One change adopted in 1969 responded to inequities created by the Revenue Act of 1948.[4] In 1948, Congress permitted married couples to divide spouses' combined incomes by two for purposes of determining applicable income tax rates. The result of this income splitting was to decrease, sometimes substantially, the tax obligations of some married couples, providing them a "marriage bonus." The 1948 change to the tax unit (from the individual to the married couple) forced a greater relative proportion of the federal tax burden onto single taxpayers, which is referred to as the "singles penalty." With tax rates for single taxpayers higher under the Revenue Act of 1951 than during World War II, pressure grew for tax relief for certain "worthy" groups, such as widows and widowers who were raising dependent children.[5] Discussion continued throughout the 1950s and 1960s about the equity of denying single individuals equality with married couples.

It was not until 1969 that this disparity between singles and married couples was addressed in a bill instigated to address the public's concern about the progressivity of the tax laws. The 1969 legislation ensured that taxpayers filing individually would not pay more than 120 percent of the tax paid by joint filers with the same income. Capping single taxpayers' disadvantage was meant to restore equity between single and married taxpayers with the same combined incomes, but it had the effect of causing some spouses to face higher tax rates upon marriage.[6] When two relatively equal-earning people married, they often found their tax rates increased. This increased

1 *Treasury Secretary Warns of Taxpayers' Revolt*, N.Y. Times, Jan. 18, 1969, at 15.

2 *See* Edwin L. Dale, Jr., *To Brake Inflation—But Not Prosperity*, N.Y. Times, Jan. 19, 1969, at E3; Joseph R. Slevin, *Request for 10% Surtax Extension Expected*, Wash. Post, Feb. 16, 1969, at K2.

3 Tax Reform Act of 1969, Pub. L. No. 91-172, 83 Stat. 48.

4 Revenue Act of 1948, Pub. L. No. 80-471, 62 Stat. 110.

5 *See, e.g.*, George F. James, *The Income of Married Couples*, 26 Taxes 311, 366 (1948); F.M. Ryan, *Tax Treatment of the Family*, 33 Marq. L. Rev. 1 (1949).

6 Staff of S. Comm. on Finance, 91st Cong., Summary of H.R. 13270, at 101 (Comm. Print 1969).

rate of taxation on two-income married couples causes a "marriage penalty." The fact that this provision was added to a complex bill containing many different changes to the tax system has raised questions as to what motivated this particular 1969 change.

The marriage penalty created by using the married couple as the tax unit is only one of many marriage penalties in the Code. This chapter focuses on the tax unit because it has received a significant amount of attention for a long time. Although the marriage penalty affects both men and women, scholars tend to focus on the 1969 change's impact on wives, as the secondary earner within many families.[7] The concern is that wives are discouraged from earning taxable wages, or encouraged to perform untaxed work in the home, because their first dollar of income is taxed in their husbands' highest bracket as though the wives' income were stacked on top of their husbands'. Reviewing the 1969 marriage penalty within this gendered framework, the assumption that the change was intended to reinforce the stereotypical family with a male breadwinner and a stay-at-home mother is often given cursory attention. Although policy makers' biases were undoubtedly reflected, consciously or unconsciously, in the legislation, this ignores the larger story of this 1969 legislative change.

In this chapter, I argue that the creation of this marriage penalty can only be understood in the legislative context in which it arose; that is, as part of the evolution of the income tax system through the post-World War II period. In the midst of the Cold War, tax policy was seen as a tool to stimulate economic growth for the fight against communism. As discussed below, Congress and the various administrations were largely reacting to short-term needs, tinkering with the Code to

7 For law review articles published in the last 10 years, see Stephanie Hoffer, *Adopting the Family Taxable Unit*, 76 U. CIN. L. REV. 55 (2007); Martha T. McCluskey, *Taxing the Family Work: Aid for Affluent Husband Care*, 21 COLUM. J. GENDER & L. 109 (2011); Stephanie Hunter McMahon, *London Calling: Does the U.K.'s Experience with Individual Taxation Clash with the U.S.'s Expectations*, 55 ST. LOUIS U. L.J. 161 (2010); Stephanie Hunter McMahon, *To Have and to Hold: What Does Love (of Money) Have to Do with Joint Tax Filing?*, 11 NEV. L.J. 718 (2011); Shari Motro, *A New "I Do": Towards a Marriage-Neutral Income Tax*, 91 IOWA L. REV. 1509 (2006); Lora Cicconi, Comment, *Competing Goals Amidst the "Opt-Out" Revolution: An Examination of Gender-Based Tax Reform in Light of New Data on Female Labor Supply*, 42 GONZ. L. REV. 257 (2007); Wendy Richards, Comment, *An Analysis of Recent Tax Reforms from a Marital-Bias Perspective: It Is Time to Oust Marriage from the Tax Code*, 2008 WIS. L. REV. 611. Some academics focus their discussion of the joint return on women working in the home, the single taxpayer, or same-sex couples. *E.g.*, Stephen T. Black, *Same-Sex Marriage and Taxes*, 22 BYU J. PUB. L. 327 (2008); Patricia A. Cain, *Taxing Families Fairly*, 48 SANTA CLARA L. REV. 805 (2008); Anthony C. Infanti, *Decentralizing Family: An Inclusive Proposal for Individual Tax Filing in the United States*, 2010 UTAH L. REV. 605; Lily Kahng, *One Is the Loneliest Number: The Single Taxpayer in a Joint Return World*, 61 HASTINGS L.J. 651 (2010); Nancy J. Knauer, *Heretonormativity and Federal Tax Policy*, 101 W. VA. L. REV. 129 (1998); William P. Kratzke, *The Defense of Marriage Act (DOMA) Is Bad Income Tax Policy*, 35 U. MEM. L. REV. 399 (2005); James M. Puckett, *Rethinking Tax Priorities: Marriage Neutrality, Children, and Contemporary Families*, 78 U. CIN. L. REV. 1409 (2010); Theodore P. Seto, *The Unintended Tax Advantages of Gay Marriage*, 65 WASH. & LEE L. REV. 1529 (2008); Carlton Smith & Edward Stein, *Dealing with DOMA: Federal Non-Recognition Complicates State Income Taxation of Same-Sex Relationships*, 24 COLUM. J. GENDER & L. 29 (2012); Nancy C. Staudt, *Taxing Housework*, 84 GEO. L.J. 1571 (1996); Keeva Terry, *Separate and Still Unequal? Taxing California Registered Domestic Partners*, 39 U. TOL. L. REV. 633 (2008); Dennis J. Ventry, Jr., *Saving* Seaborn*: Ownership Not Marriage as the Basis of Family Taxation*, 86 IND. L.J. 1459 (2011). Not all scholars agree that wives should be categorized as secondary wage earners. Dorothy Brown, for example, argues that this perspective is held mainly by upper-income, white families. Dorothy A. Brown, *Race, Class, and Gender Essentialism in Tax Literature: The Joint Return*, 54 WASH. & LEE L. REV. 1469, 1508–11 (1997); *see also* Beverly I. Moran & William Whitford, *A Black Critique of the Internal Revenue Code*, 1996 WIS. L. REV. 751.

promote national growth without triggering additional inflation. By 1968, inflation had made an unpopular tax increase inevitable.[8] Once disclosure of massive tax avoidance was made public in 1969, the federal government had to shore up the progressivity of the income tax but without upsetting the nation's economy with another tax increase. The Revenue Act of 1969 was an attempt to meet these goals.

The economic story leaves unexplored the particular changes to the tax laws adopted in 1969, especially the creation of this marriage penalty.[9] What caused Congress to enact this specific change? And why did the marriage penalty become gendered but insufficiently so to force its repeal? For most of the federal income tax's history, the concern over the appropriate tax unit was a "genderless" issue, not because of the lack of effect on women but because of their lack of influence, as Carolyn Jones discusses in Chapter 2. Jones, in her chapter, explores what women's voices would have been on many tax-related topics, while this chapter shows how and why their voice was not heard on one issue. For a period during World War II and then after 1969, focusing on the effects of the tax unit on women became useful for political purposes, but less because of concern about equity toward women than about dominant groups' tax burdens. The small number of women in positions of power and influence foretold women's limited influence, and this chapter demonstrates one way in which women's lack of influence extends to the making of the current income tax. This lack of influence is due in part to differences in women's own interests with respect to taxation, as illustrated below. In the process of examining this history, it is important to remember that some women's arguments or achievements must not obscure the ways those with other agendas exploited women and women's issues in day-to-day politics. There is a risk that those who want tax reduction will co-opt social movements. In 1969, the tax unit had insufficient command as an issue of gender equity to prevent this co-opting of the issue.

1948—Using Gender

Between 1913 and 1948, the individual income tax changed radically. In 1913, the rates were low—only 1 percent with an additional surcharge ranging from 1 to 6 percent—with a high exemption of $3,000 (to put this figure in perspective, the mean adult male income of the time was $578 per year).[10] The vast majority of Americans thus had no need to file a tax return. It was on this limited foundation that the income tax grew so that, by 1948, it was a tax affecting the bulk of working Americans. Because of the tax's limited applicability in its early stages, the taxable unit, whether the individual or the family, mattered relatively little. By 1948, the issue of the taxable unit demanded congressional attention.

By 1948, after a period of tax litigation and widespread tax planning, couples with the same income but living in different states and with different types of family planning had different tax results. Spouses in the eight community property states defaulted to splitting their income between them for federal income tax purposes, whereas spouses in common law states found

8 Revenue and Expenditure Control Act of 1968, Pub. L. No. 90-364, 82 Stat. 251; *see* Julian E. Zelizer, Taxing America 255–82 (1998).

9 Although the 1951 adoption of the head-of-household status created the first marriage penalty in the rate brackets, it was not generally perceived as such or discussed in such terms. Therefore, because this chapter focuses on perceptions, it generally does not extend to the creation of the head-of-household status.

10 Robert Stanley, Dimensions of Law in the Service of Order 249 (1983).

it more difficult, but not always impossible, to accomplish the same result.[11] Splitting couples' income allowed them to double dip in low tax brackets. The resulting play on federalism violated the equitable norm of taxing similarly situated taxpayers similarly, and it confounded the New Deal's tax focus on soaking the rich. Removing this method for decreasing some wealthy married couples' collective taxes would equalize burdens among those with equal incomes and make the income tax more progressive.

During World War II, President Franklin Roosevelt urged reform of this and other tax issues; however, the need for revenue made it risky to alienate those who benefited from limited tax reduction. Roosevelt's Treasury Department twice recommended mandatory joint returns to force all married couples to file jointly and use the same rate structure as individuals, which would have created a large marriage penalty for dual-earning couples and would have eliminated the marriage bonus for one-earner couples. A Catholic bishop in a community property state opposed the change, introducing the phrase "marriage penalty" for its potential to dissuade people from marrying by increasing their taxes.[12]

Debate over the mandatory joint-filing proposal reflected less of a dialogue between aspiring feminists and their opponents than between class-based interests. Although some women had used federal tax reduction to further their state-based property rights, these efforts generally failed.[13] At the national level, women's groups were generally divided on this issue along socioeconomic lines. For example, the National Woman's Party, speaking largely for middle- and upper-class women, recognized that the Treasury's proposal would decrease most wives' liability for taxes, but opposed what would be a tax increase for many of its members' families.[14] On the other hand, groups representing lower-income women actively supported the mandatory joint-filing proposal because they perceived it more as class- rather than gender-based legislation.[15] Thus, women, as well as men, divided on the administration's proposal in predictable ways based on its economic impact.

---

11 *See* Stephanie Hunter McMahon, *To Save States' Residents: States' Use of Community Property for Federal Tax Reduction, 1939–1947*, 27 Law & Hist. Rev. 585 (2009).

12 87 Cong. Rec. A3688 (1941) (letter from Jules B. Jeanmard, Bishop of Lafayette, to Vance Plauché, Member of U.S. House of Representatives).

13 *See* Stephanie Hunter McMahon, *California Women: Using Federal Taxes to Put the "Community" in Community Property*, 25 Wis. J.L. Gender & Soc'y 35 (2010).

14 Wives' proportion of families' taxes would be lowered because liability was to be apportioned rather than joint and several. *Compulsory Joint Income Tax Returns*, Equal Rights, Sept. 1941, at 74; *Joint Income Tax Return*, Equal Rights, Aug. 1941, at 66; *Joint Income Tax Returns*, Equal Rights, July 1941, at 58; *see also Hearings on Revenue Revision of 1952 Before H. Comm. on Ways and Means*, 77th Cong. 1340 (1942) (testimony of Margaret Stone, representing National Women's Trade Union League); Dorothy D. Crook, *Not Guilty! (Legal Status of the Married Woman Worker)*, 20 Indep. Woman 179 (1941); *Women Plan to Fight Joint Tax Return*, N.Y. Times, June 4, 1942, at 16; Mary Anderson, *Dismissal of Married Women an Attack on Democracy*, May 17, 1939, Reel 22, Record of the Women's Bureau of the U.S. Dep't of Labor, 1918–1965 [hereinafter Women's Bureau Microfilm]; Mary Anderson, *Effect of So-Called Married Women Bill on Business in General*, Feb. 10, 1940, Reel 9, Women's Bureau Microfilm.

15 *Hearings on Revenue Revision of 1942 Before the H. Comm. on Ways and Means*, 77th Cong. 1946 (1942) (statement of Virginia League of Women Shoppers); *Revenue Act of 1941: Hearing on H.R. 5417 Before the S. Comm. on Finance*, 77th Cong. 328, 1413 (1941) (statement of Jane David, representing the National League of Women Shoppers and New Jersey League of Women Shoppers); *Labor Party Asks Tax Bill Revision*, N.Y. Times, July 6, 1942, at 11; *League Thinks Joint Tax Fair*, N.Y. Times, May 31, 1942, at 2; *Mrs. Roosevelt Backs Joint Income Return*, N.Y. Times, June 9, 1942, at 18; National Consumers League, Minutes of May 6, 1942, p. 4, *microfilmed on* Reel 2, Minutes to Meetings 1932–1949, Nat'l Consumers League Records, 1899–1972.

Congressional representatives from community property states sought to maintain their tax preference while the representatives of the other states dismissed as "more imaginary than real" the former's claim that mandatory joint returns would threaten women's rights.[16] The congressional majority, which in previous years had argued that allowing wives and mothers to *enter* the workforce would destroy the family, reversed course and argued that a tax provision that gave wives an incentive to *leave* the workforce was a threat to domestic peace.[17] Although not reflected in recorded congressional debates, the fact that the proposal might have discouraged wives from entering the labor market had to be particularly unattractive when there existed a large government effort to encourage them to enter it to help the war effort.[18] In this environment, the only politically viable option was to allow all couples to split income between spouses, equalizing the tax burden between states. This would not create a marriage penalty for two-earner couples but would create a large marriage bonus for single-earner families who were not already splitting their incomes.

As this debate unfolded, the financial demands of World War II changed the reach and purposes of the federal income tax, increasing the relevance of the tax unit. By the end of the war, nearly 90 percent of the workforce was required to submit federal income tax returns and 60 percent paid some amount of income tax.[19] Rates were raised and made more progressive, ranging from 22 to 94 percent.[20] Moreover, wartime changes altered the nation's perception of how best to stimulate the economy. Before the war, the nation saw federal spending as the primary means to encourage economic growth, while a federal tax cut was viewed as a benefit only to the wealthy, largely because of the limited reach and limited progressivity of the tax rates. With the expansion of the tax base and reduction of exemptions, tax policy was increasingly put ahead of spending policy to stimulate growth, both because it helped the middle class and because, in line with Keynesian theory, it contained greater built-in flexibility.[21]

The end of World War II and the resulting surplus in federal revenue brought demands for tax cuts to stimulate investment and to encourage consumer demand as the government decreased its demand for war materials. However, the government also confronted fears of inflation, and standard economic policy was that tax reduction would only exacerbate inflation.[22] Without theoretical agreement on tax policy, the president and Congress failed to agree on the most appropriate method to stimulate economic growth. Although most policy makers agreed that in times of inflation the country should maintain a surplus, no one agreed how large the surplus should be.

From the time Republicans took control of both houses of Congress in 1946, tax reduction to reduce the surplus was a high priority. They claimed that if taxes were not reduced, the combined

16 H.R. Rep. No. 77-1040, at 13–14 (1941); 87 Cong. Rec. 6617 (statement of Rep. Bertrand Gearhart), 6634 (statement of Rep. George Dondero), 6708 (statement of Rep. Harold Knutson) (1941); George E. Ray, *Proposed Changes in Federal Taxation of Community Property*, 30 Cal. L. Rev. 397, 413 (1942).

17 *Hearings on Revenue Revision of 1942*, *supra* note 15, at 276, 1295; H.R. Rep. No. 77-1040, at 12, 69; 87 Cong. Rec. 6617 (statement of Rep. Bertrand Gearhart), 6714 (statement of Leonard W. Hall), A3524 (statement of Rep. Wesley E. Disney), A3688 (statement of Rep. Vance Plauché) (1941).

18 Henry Dorriss, *Women Warn of More Divorces with Enforcing of Joint Returns*, N.Y. Times, Mar. 26, 1942, at 21; Stuart Piebes, *Joint Tax Returns Opposed*, N.Y. Times, July 23, 1941, at C18.

19 John F. Witte, The Politics and Development of the Federal Income Tax 126 (1985).

20 Individual Income Tax Act of 1944, Pub. L. No. 78-315, 58 Stat. 231.

21 Herbert Stein, The Fiscal Revolution in America (1990); *see also Hearings on Tax Changes for Shortrun Stabilization Before Subcomm. on Fiscal Policy of the J. Econ. Comm.*, 89th Cong. (1966).

22 Stein, *supra* note 21.

federal surplus for fiscal years 1948 and 1949 would be almost $16 billion.[23] These taxes would be "the crushing of initiative," "destroying of free enterprise," and possibly resulting in "socialistic and communistic" systems.[24] While the Republican Congress sought to use the budget surplus to cut taxes, Democratic President Harry Truman thought that the surplus would not last and could be put to better use, including funding new international obligations, and so resisted reductions beyond limited cuts made in 1946.[25]

The 1948 tax cut was passed only after overcoming a third presidential veto, with substantial changes made to garner more widespread congressional support.[26] The first two vetoed versions of the tax cut were across-the-board tax rate cuts.[27] The Democratic Party Whip proposed an amendment to the first bill that targeted tax reduction to low-income and disadvantaged groups, but the amendment failed to pass.[28] The third version of the tax cut incorporated many of the previously proposed amendments, gaining broader support in Congress by targeting divergent interest groups. For example, the 1948 Revenue Act increased personal and dependent exemptions, provided a special exemption for the blind and elderly, and cut tax rates more for lower-income groups but included some reduction for all taxpayers.

One of these politically motivated changes granted married taxpayers the option to split their combined income and double the tax owed on one-half of their total income, resulting in a marriage bonus for some that was sometimes called Uncle Sam's dowry.[29] But two-earner couples with relatively equal incomes enjoyed no tax reduction when they married.[30] Although argued to be a matter of fairness, the Republican chair of the Senate Finance Committee admitted after the fact that income splitting "was deliberately contrived in order to attract the votes, because we wanted to reduce taxes."[31] The timing of the cut was particularly politically advantageous: early enough to be noticed in paychecks before the November election but late enough not to noticeably affect that year's federal budget.

The Revenue Act of 1948 made income splitting, previously enjoyed by all couples only within community property states, a national privilege. One practitioner noted of income splitting, "The net effect will only be to shift some of the tax burden from married to single persons. Politically this should not be difficult."[32] Before its enactment, the new burdens inflicted on single taxpayers received scant attention.[33] Singles were raised only three times in official debate. The

---

23 *Reduction of Individual Income Taxes, Hearings Before the S. Comm. on Finance on H.R. 4790*, 80th Cong. (1948).

24 Randolph Paul, Taxation in the United States 488–89 (1954) (quoting with commentary).

25 Harry S. Truman, *Years of Trial and Hope*, *in* 2 Memoirs by Harry S. Truman 40–41, 117–19, 174–75 (1956).

26 Revenue Act of 1948, Pub. L. No. 80-471, 62 Stat. 110, 111–12.

27 93 Cong. Rec. 2637 (1947).

28 93 Cong. Rec. 3707, 5927–35 (1947).

29 H.R. 4970, § 301, 80th Cong. (1948); Philip M. Stern, The Rape of the Taxpayer (1973) (quoting Ludwig Hellborn, research economist with General Motors Corp.).

30 Throughout this chapter, references to two-earner couples who suffer the marriage penalty or fail to enjoy the marriage bonus are more accurately, but more cumbersomely, references to two spouses with relatively equal earnings.

31 97 Cong. Rec. 11,731 (1951).

32 George T. Atman, *Community Property and Joint Returns*, 19 Taxes 588, 590 (1941).

33 U.S. Dep't of Treasury, *The Tax Treasury of Family Income*, *in* H. Comm. on Ways and Means, 80th Cong., Revenue Revisions, 1947–48, at 857–58 (1947); *Individual Income Tax Reduction, Hearings on H.R. 1 Before S. Comm. on Finance*, 80th Cong. 526–28 (1947); Stanley S. Surrey, *Family Income and Federal Taxation*, 24 Taxes 980, 980–87 (1946).

Treasury emphasized the inequity of the income-splitting proposal as favoring wealthy married couples—$803.5 million of the tax cut would go to married taxpayers with incomes over $5,000, and it granted 97.5 percent of its benefits to less than 4 percent of all taxpayers—but even this argument did not sway many congressmen or the public.[34]

Thus, in 1948 the taxable unit was changed from the individual to married couples. The political justification was that it addressed inequities between married taxpayers with different tax-planning opportunities. However, a significant effect was to reduce the progressivity of the income tax for many couples. The 1948 Revenue Act also created new inequities between different types of married couples (those with two relatively equal earners versus one dominant earner) and between single and married taxpayers. The drive to make the Code apply uniformly between states and to promote economic efficiency by cutting tax rates to avoid a postwar recession thus drove changes to the tax system without a full awareness of the problems that would be created.

Those arguably most affected by the 1948 income-splitting joint return were working wives. The marriage bonus was reduced, or even completely lost, if wives entered the paid labor market, creating a significant disincentive for two-income families.[35] Nevertheless, this group remained silent. They were understandably preoccupied, particularly as their role in the economy was changing. As discussed in Chapter 2 with respect to home economists' studies, the issues facing women were broad and had many dimensions beyond tax policy. Struggling in the labor market, women lacked seniority in unions and, even in nonunionized businesses, faced high rates of layoffs. Forty-three states still regulated women's working hours in 1948.[36] Policy makers examining the changing economy assumed that women hired "for the duration" would willingly leave the employment market after the war. Women themselves were not of one mind as to their proper roles in postwar America.[37]

Without women's own intervention, the argument that joint returns without a marriage bonus would hurt women's rights had become an "iron petticoat" that income-splitting proponents hid behind in 1948.[38] Included with congressional arguments for economic incentives, inflation control, and national unity were arguments over working women. Lumped together as a means of securing lower taxes, Congress used gender to first fend off a tax increase and then secure a tax decrease. Through the years, these genderless goals were recognized as having a gendered impact.

Genderless in 1969

In the aftermath of World War II, the Democratic Party joined the Republican Party in using tax reduction to stimulate the postwar economy.[39] Taxation was largely abandoned as an instrument to mobilize class interests. Despite this agreement over broader objectives, there was little consensus

34 *Reduction of Individual Income Taxes, Hearings on H.R. 4790 Before H. Ways and Means Comm.*, 80th Cong. 36–37 (1948). Over 75 percent of respondents thought all married couples should be allowed to split income. George H. Gallup, The Gallup Poll 633, 686 (1972).

35 Douglas Thorson, *An Analysis of the Sources of Continued Controversy over the Tax Treatment of Family Income*, 18 Nat'l Tax J. 113 (1965).

36 U.S. Inter-Agency Comm., The American Family: A Factual Background 84 (1948).

37 Kathleen A. Laughlin, Women's Work and Public Policy 12–40 (2000); Ruth Milkman, Gender at Work (1987).

38 Alice Essler-Harris, In Pursuit of Equity 191 (2001); *see also* 88 Cong. Rec. A2473, A2476, 6367 (1942).

39 Stein, *supra* note 21.

on the most effective form of tax cuts, both between and within the parties. During the early 1950s, legislation widened loopholes, reducing taxes on the wealthy by approximately 25 percent even as top statutory rates rose.[40] Pressure for tax reduction mounted as the country experienced numerous minor recessions.[41] But inflation lurked, threatening to dampen economic gain. Active tax policy, meant to micromanage the economy, provided the backdrop for the 1969 tax reform. Politicians needed to support tax reform and progressivity, but the government did not want to overheat the economy by cutting taxes. Alleviating the singles penalty by reducing single taxpayers' rate brackets relative to joint filers had the allure of being framed as a tax cut for singles but, because the number of singles with significant incomes was relatively low, without the risk of meaningful inflation.

With the solidification of the Cold War, government officials worried that, "[t]o a very substantial extent, the conflict between the East and West today is an economic one, a struggle between conflicting economic ideologies."[42] Policy makers argued that the federal government needed to cut taxes to stimulate national economic growth to compete with the Soviet Union but faced an ever-present fear of inflation.[43] Economists coming of age under Keynesian tutelage pushed a new active tax policy. A professor at the Wharton School of Finance argued, "More and more, taxation is being related to the problems of the economy—to such objectives as increasing the national income, stabilizing the economy, maintaining high-level employment, encouraging investment, and increasing the flow of consumer purchasing."[44]

As part of this developing policy, many scholars attacked progressive taxation, so that it, as a concept, provided less of a constraining influence on tax policy after the war.[45] As scholars debated whether the system was in fact progressive,[46] Australian economist Colin Clark warned that high levels of taxation, often interpreted as requiring highly progressive taxation, would result in destructive inflation. According to his work, when taxation exceeds 25 percent of gross national product, inflation is inevitable.[47] The attack on progressivity was also at the theoretical level. In 1952, Walter Blum and Harry Kalven, Jr. published their article, "The Uneasy Case for Progressive Taxation." Although personally supporting progressivity, they concluded that support for this form of income taxation could only be made on the grounds of income redistribution.[48] Conservative political economist F.A. Hayek then argued that redistributive policies fostered class discrimination and threatened tyrannies of the majority.[49] These and other

---

40 W. Elliot Brownlee, *Historical Perspective on U.S. Tax Policy Toward the Rich*, *in* Does Atlas Shrug? 29, 61 (Joel B. Slemrod ed., 2000).

41 By 1962, there had been four postwar recessions: 1948, 1953, 1957, and 1960. Comm. for Econ. Dev., Fiscal and Monetary Policy for High Employment 6 (1962).

42 J. Econ. Comm., 84th Cong., Federal Tax Policy for Economic Growth and Stability, at ix (Comm. Print 1955).

43 Zelizer, *supra* note 8.

44 Alfred G. Buehler, *Taxation and the Economy*, 3 Nat'l Tax J. 121 (1950).

45 T.R. Beard, *Progressive Income Taxation, Income Redistribution, and the Consumption Function*, 13 Nat'l Tax J. 168 (1960); Roy Blough, *The Argument Phase of Taxpayer Politics*, 17 U. Chi. L. Rev. 604 (1950).

46 *See* James R. Beaton, *Family Tax Burdens by Income Levels*, 15 Nat'l Tax J. 14 (1962); R.A. Musgrave et al., *Distribution of Tax Payments by Income Groups*, 4 Nat'l Tax J. 1 (1951); R.S. Tucker, *Distribution of Tax Burdens in 1948*, 4 Nat'l Tax J. 269 (1951).

47 Colin Clark, *The Danger Point in Taxes*, 201 Harper's Mag. 67 (1950).

48 Walter J. Blum & Harry Kalven, Jr., *The Uneasy Case for Progressive Taxation*, 19 U. Chi. L. Rev. 417 (1952).

49 F.A. Hayek, *Progressive Taxation Reconsidered*, *in* On Freedom and Free Enterprise 265–84 (Mary Sennholy ed., 1956).

attacks on progressive taxation supported a new focus on growing the national economic pie instead of redistributing the slices.

Not everyone attacked progressivity, but the goal fell in political importance. For example, congressional hearings held in 1955 focused taxation on "enhanc[ing] the built-in stabilizing capacity of the Federal tax system" and "encourag[ing] the balanced growth of the economy." Congress did not agree that an objective of the tax laws was either to increase fairness or to redistribute income.[50] Some politicians used the accepted goals as justification to cut tax rates. Proposals circulated in Congress for a constitutional amendment to limit federal income and estate taxation to 25 percent.[51]

The political concern was with statutory rates, despite their limited applicability. For the people of plenty in the early 1960s, although rates included 70, 80, and 90 percent brackets, wealthy individuals were actually paying tax at an average rate of 48 percent.[52] Reformers argued that Congress enacted high surtaxes as a political necessity but then "deliberately [made] them ineffective."[53] The chair of the House Ways and Means Committee noted that the individual income tax is "borne principally by low and middle income groups because in most instances all their income is fully subject to tax."[54] Most middle- and low-income taxpayers remained in the dark about relative effective tax rates until alerted by the disclosure in 1969. Nonetheless, newly inaugurated President Nixon defended those taxpayers whom the outgoing Treasury Secretary attacked, contending that these "people are neither tax dodgers nor tax cheats."[55] And even with the public pressure caused by the revelations about wealthy individuals paying no income tax, the quickly convened House hearings discussed this issue for less than one day on the tenth day of 30 days of hearings.[56]

When income splitting was discussed, it was assumed that all married couples reduced their taxes with income splitting.[57] However, only couples with significant income and with a dominant income earner benefited. In 1951, there were close to 25 million taxable joint returns, less than one-third of which had lower tax liabilities because of income splitting. But the 29 percent who did benefit accounted for 49 percent of total taxable net income.[58] Thus, it was the wealthy who benefited the most from income splitting.

In the two decades after 1948, concern grew over the burden this new regime imposed on single taxpayers, but the concern remained mild. Senator Eugene McCarthy proposed legislation every year after 1962 (except, for an unknown reason, 1966) to extend favorable tax rates to "certain"

50 S. Rep. No. 84-1606, at 105–08 (1956).

51 The idea had been introduced to Congress in 1939, 1945, 1947, 1951, and 1953 with variations as to implementation and percentages. *See* Erwin Griswold, *Can We Limit Taxes to 25 Percent*, 190 Atlantic Monthly 76 (1952).

52 Stanley S. Surrey, *The Federal Income Tax Base for Individuals*, 58 Colum. L. Rev. 815, 816 (1958). In a study of the years from 1953 through 1961, effective rates declined at all but the lowest levels of income, with the decline greatest at the highest level of income. William V. Williams, *The Changing Progressivity of the Federal Income Tax*, 17 Nat'l Tax J. 426 (1964).

53 Randolph E. Paul, *Erosion of the Tax Base and Rate Structure*, 11 Tax L. Rev. 203, 216–17 (1955).

54 Wilbur Mills, *Preface*, 44 Va. L. Rev. 835, 836 (1958).

55 *Hearings on the Subject of Tax Reform Before the H. Ways and Means Comm.*, 91st Cong. 5047 (1969).

56 *Id.*

57 Arno Karlen, *The Unmarried Marrieds on Campus*, N.Y. Times, Jan. 26, 1969, at SM31.

58 J. Econ. Comm., *supra* note 42, at 333.

single taxpayers on the ground that they had similar expenses when maintaining a household.[59] McCarthy's and others' proposals generally limited the benefits to those over the age of 35 or some other arbitrary age threshold and imposed other limitations on income splitting. Instead of abolishing this form of tax reduction, opponents tried to nullify its impact by extending it to more taxpayers. Even with this attention, support was minimal. Neither Nixon nor his Treasury Department proposed changes addressing this issue.

With lukewarm support, the 1969 bill meandered through a Congress seeking to make some substantive change largely for political purposes but not wishing to alter federal revenue significantly. As passed by the House of Representatives, the bill permitted single persons 35 years of age or older (echoing McCarthy's earlier bills) and persons whose spouse had died access to income tax rates equal to those applicable to heads of household, a middle ground between individual reporting and income splitting.[60] This would have helped many women. Of the 18 million unmarried persons over age 35, 13 million were women.[61] The proposal was costly and the Secretary of the Treasury stressed to the Senate the need to reduce the revenue loss.[62] Treasury's response was to revise single tax rates relative to married rates.[63] The 20 percent differential the Treasury proposed "reflect[ed] a reasonable judgment of the additional costs of living of married couples and their ability to pay as compared to single persons."[64] The Treasury's process allowed more artful adjusting of the rates to minimize revenue loss while addressing the concerns of singles. The resulting Senate bill was also significantly cheaper than its House counterpart.[65]

Thus, in 1969 the tax cut went to single taxpayers, although not enough to please everyone.[66] Almost 60 percent of people polled thought their taxes were too high.[67] In this period, and arguably today, tax cuts were popular as long as they were framed as such. It was important that the introduction of the marriage penalty was framed as a tax cut for singles rather than a tax increase for two-earner couples. Once in place, affected taxpayers began to recognize the change as an increase, a politically unpopular result.

Women were noticeably lacking as a separate interest group in the pre-1969 debates. In discussions of tax revision, women were frequently grouped with children or the elderly and not treated separately.[68] This conceptualization with respect to taxes was sometimes self-imposed. In 1968, the President's Commission on the Status of Women considered the relative equities of the married, single, and head of household filing statuses to be outside its purview because this was

59 108 CONG. REC. 7198 (1962).

60 H.R. REP. NO. 91-413, at 3–4, 17 (1969).

61 110 CONG. REC. 2093–94, 2135 (1964) (statement of Eugene McCarthy). Senator Russell Long was worried that the rate cut for singles would place a premium on bachelorhood at a time when divorce rates were rising. *Id.* at 2314–15, 2140.

62 S. COMM. ON FINANCE, 91ST CONG., TAX REFORM ACT OF 1969: H.R. 13270: STATEMENT OF HON. DAVID KENNEDY 1 (Comm. Print 1969).

63 *Id.* at 4.

64 *Id.* at 13–25 (statement of Edwin Cohen).

65 S. COMM. ON FINANCE, 91ST CONG., TAX REFORM ACT OF 1969: H.R. 13270: SENATE OPENING DEBATE STATEMENT 8 (Comm. Print 1969).

66 The same day the House voted favorably on the revised tax bill, McCarthy introduced legislation to extend full income splitting to all unmarried taxpayers. 115 CONG. REC. 22,859–60 (1969).

67 GALLUP, *supra* note 34.

68 Gail Beckman, *Do Our Tax Laws Satisfy the Needs of the Working Woman?*, 53 WOMEN LAW. J. 5 (1967); Mary W. Smelker, *The Impact of Federal Income and Payroll Taxes on the Distribution of After-Tax Income*, 21 NAT'L TAX J. 448, 451 (1968).

not a female-specific issue.[69] Instead of being perceived as a gendered issue, the impact of the tax unit and income splitting was generally discussed as affecting "singles" in a gender-neutral way and along class lines. Representative of this approach, the Association of National Manufacturers and the Chamber of Commerce fought the American Federation of Labor and American Taxpayers Association over income splitting.[70] Women's groups, such as the National Organization for Women, also focused on the tax treatment of singles and not of women.[71] Vivien Kellems, who later lost a lawsuit over the singles penalty,[72] complained that members of Congress discussed "people" as though everyone were married; notably, she did not say as though everyone were male.[73] For these advocates of singles, the 1969 change was a success, although an incomplete one. "Congress has finally recognized the inequity of taxing single taxpayers—including the formerly married—at much higher rates than their married contemporaries."[74]

Gendering the Story

Before passage of the Revenue Act of 1969, the Treasury Department warned of the marriage penalty—that two single persons could find their income taxes increased if they married. The Treasury's report also explained that this "tax on marriage" was "a necessary result of changing the income-splitting relationship between single and joint returns."[75] Congress does not appear to have read the report, as politicians claimed to be surprised when complaints were made public. Because the backlash was moderate, some policy makers dismissed the consequence as a "mistake."[76] One member of Congress considered it "the result of an oversight in the drafting of the Tax Reform Act of 1969,"[77] while another explained it was "more the result of caprice than deliberation."[78] Contemporaries argued with more or less credibility that the adverse effects for some married

69 Citizens' Advisory Council on the Status of Women, Task Force on Social Insurance and Taxes 120 n.5 (1968).

70 J. Econ. Comm., *supra* note 42, at 85.

71 Jean McVeety, *Law and the Single Woman*, 53 Women Law. J. 10 (1967); Letter from Ester F. Johnson, National Secretary-Treasurer of National Organization for Women, to Eugene McCarthy, U.S. Senator, Apr. 28, 1967, Folder 6, Taxes, 1967–1973, Box 18, MC 478, Marguerite Rawalt, Schlesinger Library; Legislative program, 1969, Folder 56, Legislative Conference, 1969, Box 26, Nat'l Org. for Women, MC 496, Schlesinger Library.

72 Kellems v. Comm'r, 58 T.C. 556 (1972), *aff'd*, 474 F.2d 1399 (2d Cir. 1973).

73 *Hearings on Tax Reform Act of 1969 Before the S. Comm. on Finance*, 91st Cong. 290, 295 (1969).

74 Robert Metz, *A Guide to the Mysteries of Form 1040*, N.Y. Times, Feb. 4, 1973, at 16.

75 Staff of J. Comm. on Internal Revenue Taxation, 91st Cong., General Explanation of the Tax Reform Act of 1969, at 10, 222–24 (Comm. Print 1969). Treasury acknowledged again in 1972 that it had known of the marriage penalty and that Congress had been warned. *Hearings on Tax Treatment of Single Persons and Married Persons Where Both Spouses Are Working Before H. Comm. on Ways and Means*, 92d Cong. 75 (1972) (statement of Edwin Cohen) [hereinafter *Hearings on Tax Treatment of Single Persons*].

76 *Hearings on Tax Treatment of Single Persons*, *supra* note 75, at 35 (statement of Sen. George Murphy).

77 118 Cong. Rec. 16,117 (1972) (statement of Rep. Bella Abzug).

78 *Hearings on Tax Treatment of Single Persons*, *supra* note 75, at 174 (statement of Rep. Seymour Halpern).

couples were unintended; they continued to focus their attention on relative tax burdens based on marital status.[79]

Women shared the generally slow recognition of the marriage penalty that disproportionately affected working wives, in part because few were affected. As of 1969, fewer than 10 percent of married couples had wives earning relatively equal amounts as their husbands. Among those couples, over 70 percent had a combined taxable income of less than the $12,000 floor at which marriage penalties began. Thus, fewer than 3 percent of all married couples suffered a marriage penalty.[80] Possibly as a result, in the immediate aftermath of 1969, women's groups that were focused on national taxation remained primarily concerned with the taxation of single taxpayers relative to married couples. For example, in 1970 the Women's Equity Action League considered the Revenue Act of 1969 a triumph for single taxpayers.[81]

As the number of singles continued to grow, there was even demand for additional tax reduction for singles.[82] In 1970 and 1971, members of Congress introduced 17 and 59 pieces of legislation, respectively, to equalize the income tax treatment of married and single taxpayers by creating one rate schedule for all taxpayers.[83] If married couples were allowed to continue income splitting under these proposals, the change would have removed the marriage penalty but at the cost of increasing the marriage bonus (in other words, providing an additional tax cut) for families with a single breadwinner. If income splitting were abolished, two-earner couples would suffer an increased marriage penalty. Ignoring those potential consequences, the attractiveness of tax reduction continued. But more telling, on the first day of hearings in 1972 on the tax treatment of single persons and dual-earner married couples, the chair of the House Ways and Means Committee said that family taxation was simply not a top priority.[84]

Each year the traditional family with a single breadwinner became less prevalent, the percentage of couples who were affected by the marriage penalty increased. Throughout the 1960s, the Secretary of Labor had often referred to women as "secondary workers," as a means of minimizing their role in the economy and in families.[85] That sentiment became increasingly dated. In 1970, 50 percent of college freshmen and 30 percent of women agreed that the "activities of married women are best confined to the home and family."[86] By 1975, only 30 percent of men and less than 20 percent of women took that position.[87] In 1979, dual-earner married couples outnumbered single-earner couples for the first time.[88]

---

79 *See id.* at 35, 174 (statements of Sen. George Murphy and Rep. Seymour Halpern); 118 Cong. Rec. 16,117 (1972) (statement of Rep. Bella Abzug); Michael W. Betz, Comment, *Federal Income Tax Discrimination Between Married and Single Taxpayers*, 7 U. Mich. J.L. Reform 667, 690 (1974); George Dullea, *"Marriage Tax" Has Couples in Rage—And Even Divorcing*, N.Y. Times, Mar. 27, 1975, at 51.

80 *Hearings on Tax Treatment of Single Persons*, *supra* note 75, at 73–95.

81 Jean Faust, Report of the National Legislative Committee, March 20–22, 1970, at 3, Folder 5, Legislative Committee Report, 1970, Box 51, Nat'l Org. for Women, MC 496, Schlesinger Library.

82 118 Cong. Rec. 32,285, 35,988 (1972); 117 Cong. Rec. 3037–38 (1971); 116 Cong. Rec. 36,634–35 (1970).

83 Dennis Joseph Ventry, Jr., The Treatment of Marriage Under the U.S. Federal Income Tax, 1913 to 2000, at 436 (September 2001) (unpublished Ph.D. dissertation, University of California–Santa Barbara).

84 *Hearings on Tax Treatment of Single Persons*, *supra* note 75, at 2.

85 Kathleen A. Laughlin, Women's Work and Public Policy 114 (2000).

86 Steve Gillon, Boomer Nation 79–80 (2004).

87 *Id.*

88 Pamela Gann, *Abandoning Marital Status as a Factor in Allocating Income Tax Burdens*, 59 Tex. L. Rev. 1, 33 (1980).

But women did not effectively seek the elimination of the marriage penalty. At first, the women's movement was too weak. It was not until the mid-1970s that membership of all feminist groups combined surpassed 100,000.[89] And in July 1969, when four congresswomen sent President Nixon a memorandum asserting his administration had done nothing for women, he shelved his Task Force's response.[90] Women's legal groups, which might have recognized the import of the marriage penalty before the law's enactment, were formed after 1969.[91] By the peak of the second wave of feminism, women as a group did not have a coherent position on this issue.

In part, women's inability to gender the tax unit was because of their divergent economic interests. Stay-at-home wives often benefited from income splitting while working wives should have preferred individual filing. In other words, there was not a single, natural feminist position for the women's movement to coalesce behind because women do not compose a single interest group with respect to taxes.[92] On this issue, women actually comprised three groups—singles, those in one-earner marriages, and those in two-earner marriages.[93] Because their interests diverged, there was no way for the tax system to please all women all of the time.

In the 1970s, some women's groups began to focus on two-earner couples. The National Organization for Women dropped the issue of tax equality for singles from their 1970 platform and, later in the 1970s, urged that Congress "[a]mend the Internal Revenue Act [sic] so that married working couples do not pay a higher tax than if they had remained single."[94] The Women's Equity Action League, although focused primarily on the tax treatment of child care, also admonished Congress to revise "the tax code so that families with two wage-earners [sic] are not penalized."[95] The focus remained on the relative tax treatment of the various marital statuses as it had before, but there was an evolving understanding that not all married couples were the same.[96] Even into the 1980s, the focus was often on marital status, as opposed to its gendered consequences. During that period, one couple, the Boyters, gained notoriety by divorcing each December only to remarry the following January in their failed attempt to file as single taxpayers.[97] The publicity they actively sought fueled a national debate regarding the taxation of married couples versus single taxpayers.[98]

---

89 Susan M. Hartmann, From Margin to Mainstream 209 (1989).

90 *Id.* at 61–69.

91 Legal challenges to the marriage penalty failed. *See, e.g.*, Johnson v. United States, 422 F. Supp. 958 (N.D. Ind. 1976), *aff'd*, 550 F.2d 1239 (7th Cir. 1977); Mapes v. United States, 217 Ct. Cl. 115 (1978).

92 Anne L. Alstott, *Tax Policy and Feminism: Competing Goals and Institutional Choices*, 96 Colum. L. Rev. 2001 (1996).

93 Arguably heads of households are a fourth group because their interests may diverge from the other groups. However, their separate interests are beyond the scope of this chapter.

94 Folder 43, Marriage, Divorce, and Family Relations, Box 47, Nat'l Org. for Women, MC 496, Schlesinger Library; From Ann Scott and Betty Berry to Legislative Task Force, "Legislative Recommendations from the Task force on Marriage and Divorce," Eastern Regional Conference; Folder 8, Bd. Minutes, 1970, Nat'l Org. for Women, MC 496, Schlesinger Library.

95 Report of the Organizing Conference of National Women's Political Caucus, July 10–11, 1971, Washington D.C., Nat'l Legislative Program 1977, Box 45, Folder 18, Legislative Program, Women's Equity Action League, MC 500, Schlesinger Library.

96 Dullea, *supra* note 79.

97 Boyter v. Comm'r, 74 T.C. 989 (1980), *rev'd*, 668 F.2d 1382 (4th Cir. 1981).

98 *See* Note, *The Haitian Vacation*, 77 Mich. L. Rev. 1332 (1979); David Carr Kelly, Note, *Income Tax—Tax Motivated Divorce and the Sham Transaction Doctrine*, 18 Wake Forest L. Rev. 881 (1982); Karen De Witt, *The Tax-Saving Divorce Goes to Court*, N.Y. Times, Nov. 9, 1979, at A24; *Marriage Penalty Foes Say 'Tax Reform' Wasn't*, Chi. Trib., Oct. 16, 1981, § 5, at 3; *Md. Couple, IRS Exchange Vows*, Wash. Post,

But the shift to gendered arguments regarding the marriage penalty developed slowly. Grace Ganz Blumberg's seminal article "Sexism in the Code: A Comparative Study of Income Taxation of Working Wives and Mothers,"[99] published in 1972 just three years after enactment of this marriage penalty, argued that when filing a joint return the spouse who earns the lesser amount of income, more frequently the wife, is psychologically taxed at higher rates than the primary earner because of the stacking of the spouses' incomes. Thereafter, several articles noted that the marriage penalty applied if a wife worked and earned an amount roughly equal to her husband.[100] By the 1980s, the Women's Equity Action League noted, "The penalty on two earner couples may discourage second earners, who are primarily women, from participating in the work force."[101]

For a time these concerns were partially addressed in another attempt at tax reduction. In 1981, as in 1948, congressional Republicans proposed across-the-board tax rate cuts, and the political process resulted in a broader bill that dispersed tax reduction among different groups. One such group was two-earner couples. In 1981, Congress passed a deduction for 10 percent of the income of a lower-earning spouse, capped at $3,000, which was targeted at reducing the tax burden on two-earner couples.[102] The proposal was one of many adopted "at the last minute to cement the victory in the House."[103] Congress chose this option over eliminating joint filing because its primary concern was secondary earners.[104] Nevertheless, there was academic concern that the two-earner deduction did not address the marriage penalty for all couples and increased the marriage bonus for others.[105] Despite being a step in addressing inequities for two-earner couples, the earned-income deduction was eliminated with little fanfare in 1986.[106] According to Congress, across-the-board tax rate cuts reduced the marriage penalty to the point of eliminating the need for the two-earner deduction.[107] Tax reduction trumped gender equity.

Other than the 1981 two-earner deduction that focused on working wives, politics has been apt to use the marriage penalty for the same reason as the singles penalty was used in 1969—namely, tax reduction. In a study of the politics of this issue, Ann Thomas examined legislative proposals targeting the marriage penalty in the 105th and 106th Congresses.[108] Defying academic prescriptions,

---

July 7, 1986, at D3; *Pair Finds Marriage Too Taxing—Again*, L.A. Times, Oct. 13, 1976, at CC2; William Raspberry, *Divorce from the Marriage Tax*, Wash. Post, Sept. 12, 1979, at A15.

99 21 Buff. L. Rev. 49 (1972).

100 Dullea, *supra* note 79; Edward Burks, *Mrs. Fenwick Sees Marriage Tax's End*, N.Y. Times, Mar. 1, 1981, at NJ1; *Marriage Tax*, N.Y. Times, Apr. 3, 1980, at 71; Deborah Rankin, *The Marriage Penalty Eased*, N.Y. Times, Mar. 6, 1979, at D2; Deborah Rankin, *Plans to Ease Marriage Tax*, N.Y. Times, Sept. 9, 1980, at D2; Leonard Sloane, *Personal Finance: Does It Pay for a Wife to Work?*, N.Y. Times, Mar. 11, 1976, at 63.

101 May 8, 1981 WEAL's Legislative Program, Folder 29, WEAL Facts, Box 78, Folder 9, Tax Packet, Jan. 1987, Women's Equity Action League, MC 500, Schlesinger Library.

102 Economic Recovery Tax Act of 1981, Pub. L. No. 97-34, 95 Stat. 172.

103 Tax Found., Special Report: The Economic Recovery Act of 1981, at 3 (1981).

104 S. Rep. No. 97-144, at 29–30 (1981) (previously proposed in S. Rep. No. 96-940, at 34–35 (1980)).

105 Pamela Gann, *The Earned Income Deduction: Congress's 1981 Response to the "Marriage Penalty" Tax*, 68 Cornell L. Rev. 468 (1983); Nancy E. Shurtz, *Marital Status Discrimination: A Problem Not Solved by the Economic Recovery Tax Act of 1981*, 59 Den. U. L. Rev. 767 (1982).

106 Tax Reform Act of 1986, Pub. L. No. 99-514, 100 Stat. 2085.

107 *See* Staff of J. Comm. on Taxation, 100th Cong., General Explanation of the Tax Reform Act of 1986, at 15 (Comm. Print 1987).

108 Ann F. Thomas, *Marriage and the Income Tax Yesterday, Today, and Tomorrow: A Primer and Legislative Scorecard*, 16 N.Y.L. Sch. J. Hum. Rts. 1 (1999); *see also* Amy C. Christian, *Legislative Approaches to Marriage Penalty Relief: The Unintended Effects of Change on the Married Couple's Choice of Filing Status*, 16 N.Y.L. Sch. J. Hum. Rts. 303, 329 (1999).

all proposals sought to retain the joint return and most would have significantly increased the marriage bonus, in addition to reducing the marriage penalty.[109] Republicans predominated in proposals for relief as they did in proposals for tax cuts in general.[110] Representatives in the 105th Congress even passed a resolution that "the federal government should acknowledge the importance of stay-at-home parents and should not discriminate against families who forgo a second income in order for a mother or father to be at home with their children."[111] Notably, women's groups did not participate in these two Congresses' hearings on the issue.

The political process in 1998 and 1999 was reminiscent of 1948 but for its failure. Anticipating a presidential veto because President Bill Clinton felt that tax burdens were sufficiently low and that there were more pressing needs for the revenue surplus, congressional proposals sought wider support for a $792 billion tax cut bill by giving targeted tax cuts to many.[112] Congress still could not override the veto. As a presidential candidate, George W. Bush once campaigned on a deduction for two-earner couples,[113] but by the 2000 election he had changed his focus to across-the-board tax cuts.[114] The form of marriage penalty relief he signed into law was rate reductions that not only provided such relief but also increased marriage bonuses because the relief came in the form of cutting taxes for all married couples.[115] The percentage of relief was the same across all incomes but, in absolute dollars, more relief went to the wealthiest taxpayers and, of those, the most relief went to couples with a single earner.[116] Those who lost in this political compromise were single taxpayers whose relative tax burdens increased and two-earner couples who were ineligible for the growing marriage bonus. Despite this, President Barack Obama twice signed into law extensions of the pro-bonus tax rate cuts.[117]

Politicians continue to debate the marriage penalty in ways that signal a desire for tax reduction more than tax reform. Some complain of the marriage penalties imposed on the wealthy, using the two-earner family as a reason for tax reduction.[118] Others criticize tax increases for married couples, forgetting to distinguish between one- and two-earner couples.[119] Some argue that taxpayers should have a choice over their filing status, with the implicit assumption that everyone should be able to reduce their taxes as much as possible.[120] Conflating concern for secondary earners with a desire

---

109 Thomas, *supra* note 108, at 3.

110 *Id.* at 63.

111 H.R. Res. 202, 105th Cong. (1998), *quoted in* Thomas, *supra* note 108, at 93.

112 Thomas, *supra* note 108, at 64–65.

113 *A Tax Plan Paid for with the Budget Surplus*, N.Y. Times, Dec. 1, 1999, at A20.

114 Alison Mitchell, *Bush Returning Tax-Cut Plan to Center Stage*, N.Y. Times, Oct. 2, 2000, at A1.

115 Economic Growth and Tax Relief Reconciliation Act of 2001, Pub. L. No. 107-16, §§ 101(a), 301(b), 115 Stat. 38, 41. The Jobs and Growth Tax Relief Reconciliation Act of 2003, Pub. L. No. 108-27, 117 Stat. 752, accelerated the 2001 relief. The Working Families Tax Relief Act of 2004, Pub. L. No. 108-311, § 101, 118 Stat. 1166, 1167–68, extended this acceleration.

116 Tax Policy Ctr., Urban Inst. & Brookings Inst., T07–0028, Extend Marriage Penalty Relief (Jan. 19, 2007), http://www.taxpolicycenter.org/numbers/displayaTablecfm?DocID=1431.

117 American Taxpayer Relief Act of 2012, Pub. L. No. 112-240, 126 Stat. 2313; Tax Relief, Unemployment Insurance Reauthorization, and Job Creation Act of 2010, Pub. L. No. 111-312, 124 Stat. 3296.

118 Tom McClusky, *"Fiscal Cliff" Deal Penalizes Married Couples*, Wash. Times, Jan. 9, 2013, *available at* http://www.washingtontimes.com/news/2013/jan/8/fiscal-cliff-deal-penalizes-married-couples/.

119 Tami Luhby, *Marriage Penalty Could Make Costly Return*, CNN Wire, Dec. 24, 2012, *available at* http://money.cnn.com/2012/12/26/news/economy/marriage-penalty-fiscal-cliff/.

120 Jason Fichtner & Jacob Feldman, *Eliminate the Marriage Penalty*, U.S. News & World Rep. (Sept. 18, 2012), http://www.usnews.com/opinion/blogs/economic-intelligence/2012/09/18/eliminate-the-marriage-tax-penalty.

to reduce taxes demonstrates that, although the story has changed, it is far from fully transformed into a gendered one.

Conclusion

The marriage penalty has a counterpart in the marriage bonus. While the former is given rather extensive attention both within the government and by commentators, the latter is often ignored. The marriage penalty imposes higher taxes on relatively equal earning spouses who marry. The marriage bonus reduces taxes for married couples with a dominant income earner. Most proposals to reduce or eliminate the marriage penalty have the effect of increasing the marriage bonus. Thus, all couples, even those who do not suffer the penalty, share tax reduction through most forms of marriage penalty relief.[121] That marriage penalty relief can be a politically acceptable form of tax reduction has often influenced how people see, and use, the gendering of the marriage penalty. Looking at its political usage, the gendered imagery surrounding the tax unit is largely for the purpose of securing targeted tax reduction or to prevent a targeted tax increase without particular benefit for women.

The genderlessness of the marriage penalty is surprising because one group is disproportionately affected—working wives.[122] That policy makers and the public did not appreciate in 1969 the cost of the marriage penalty to working wives should be less surprising than the effect today. Today, most couples have two earners, and increasingly this is true for wealthier couples.[123] As of the 2009 census, 59.1 percent of women are in the labor force.[124] Throughout the 1980s and 1990s, married women became less likely to reduce their work effort following tax increases, signaling a growing inelasticity of their labor, and their willingness to work is no longer as dependent on their

121 I have argued elsewhere that single-earner couples could maximize benefits to the extent they can adopt pre-1948 tax planning devices. McMahon, *To Have and to Hold*, *supra* note 7.

122 This is possible because of the unknown extent to which the marriage penalty affects wives' choices. *See* Cong. Budget Office, For Better or For Worse: Marriage and the Federal Income Tax 12 (1997); Francine D. Blau & Lawrence M. Kahn, *Changes in the Labor Supply Behavior of Married Women: 1980–2000*, 25 J. Labor Econ. 393 (2007); Paul J. Devereux, *Changes in Relative Wages and Family Labor Supply*, 39 J. Hum. Res. 696 (2004); Nada Eissa & Hilary Williamson Hoynes, *Taxes and the Labor Market Participation of Married Couples: The Earned Income Tax Credit*, 88 J. Pub. Econ. 1931 (2004); Claudia Goldin, *The Quiet Revolution that Transformed Women's Employment, Education, and Family*, 96 Am. Econ. Ass'n Papers & Proc. 1 (2006); Bradley T. Heim, *The Incredible Shrinking Elasticities: Married Female Labor Supply, 1979–2003*, 42 J. Hum. Res. 881 (2007); Chinhui Juhn & Kevin M. Murphy, *Wage Inequality and Female Labor Supply*, 15 J. Labor Econ. 72 (1997); Audrey Light & Yoshiaki Omori, *Can Long-Term Cohabitating and Marital Unions Be Incentivized?*, *in* Research in Labor Economics 241 (Solomon Polachek & Konstantinos Tatsiromos eds., 2012); Thomas Mroz, *The Sensitivity of an Empirical Model of Married Women's Hours of Work to Economic and Statistical Assumptions*, 55 Econometrica 765 (1987); Robert K. Triest, *The Effect of Income Taxation on Labor Supply in the United States*, 25 J. Hum. Res. 491 (1990). Women penalized by the marriage penalty potentially do not recognize it because taxes are not withheld disproportionately.

123 U.S. Census Bureau, Percent of Married-Couple Families with Both Husband and Wife in the Labor Force (2007), *available at* http://factfinder.census.gov/servlet/ThematicMapFramesetServlet?_bm=y&-geo_id=01000US&-tm_name=ACS_2007_3YR_G00_M00661&-ds_name.

124 U.S. Census Bureau, Table 599: Employment Status of Women (2012), http://www.census.gov/compendia/statab/2012/tables/12s0599.pdf.

husbands' earnings.[125] But in 1969, only one person—a man—spoke out in congressional hearings on the issue.[126] His concern was not with the negative incentive the proposed change had on two-income families, and especially not with wives, but with the loss of a tax advantage some married couples enjoyed.

The 1969 Tax Reform Act created this marriage penalty because policy makers who wanted tax reduction proved better at framing the issue. Because economic growth was perceived as dependent upon low tax rates, income splitting served the function of allowing the wealthy to avoid highly progressive tax rates while keeping those rates on the books. As Congress was forced to eat away at this privilege, it did so in the smallest politically acceptable bites. The marriage penalty turned out to be a good way to cut taxes in 1969, without hurting traditional families and without generating significant dissent in a piece of legislation that tried to give something to everyone cloaked in the mantle of tax reform. The only ones who suffered were those married couples who earned relatively equal amounts and then only when compared with single taxpayers. This group was politically insignificant in 1969.

But even today the marriage penalty is used for many purposes other than gendered ones. This is partly because women do not visibly respond to taxation. Although one scholar warned in the early 1990s that the income-splitting joint return might make the traditional single-earner family self-perpetuating,[127] even in the face of the negative tax consequences wives are increasingly entering the paid labor force and with little complaint regarding the tax cost of doing so. Their entry into the market despite the marriage penalty does not make this redistribution of tax burdens, and subsequently this tax on an isolated group, less egregious.

As does Chapter 2, this chapter explores women's lack of influence. However, Carolyn Jones's and my focus differ: Jones examines the women themselves whereas this chapter looks at the political and economic environment in which they operated. In Chapter 2, Jones tells the history of one group of women, home economists, who succeeded in entering academia and grappled with society's problems. Thus, Jones depicts active and vocal (at least in writing) women. Nevertheless, even the notable Hazel Kyrk failed to influence policy. On the other hand, this chapter has largely voiceless women who acted as though unaware of their deeper interests with respect to a particular tax issue and were co-opted for a political cause that was more class-focused than gender-focused. The relative silence of my chapter was partly because not all women shared the same interests so that, at times, women were speaking against each other. Additionally, the silence of my chapter was because, as Jones aptly points out, women experienced many different issues that demanded their time and attention.

The difference in our approaches stems in some measure from our desire to convey different messages with these gendered stories. In Chapter 2, Jones develops the voice of a largely forgotten subgroup of women, both giving them credit for developing valuable ideas and directing today's policy makers to alternative choices to address continuing problems. In contrast, I examine the topic's political development in order to examine why women failed to influence what is now recognized as a gender issue. In my opinion, focusing on what women wrote or said tells an incomplete story until we examine why their message was not heard. Thus, although I agree that these home economists have many ideas that are as important today as when written, the

125 *See* Cicconi, *supra* note 7, at 263–64; Staudt, *supra* note 7, at 1600; *see also supra* note 123 and accompanying text.

126 *Hearings on H.R. 13270 before S. Comm. on Finance*, 91st Cong. 1055 (1969) (statement of Richard Edwards).

127 Edward J. McCaffery, *Taxation and the Family: A Fresh Look at Behavioral Gender Biases in the Code*, 40 UCLA L. Rev. 983, 1000 (1992).

disconcerting issue to me is why they failed to change the way that policy makers understood taxation. I would argue the reasons the message was ignored are relatively more important than the message itself, although that is not to suggest the latter is not worthy of study. By framing the issue around the reasons for the failure to influence policy, this chapter shows how women played at least a small role in their own failure by their indifference to the issue or their preference for tax reduction over gender equity.

Although Jones and I both focus on gender issues in history, we part company in the weight we give to individual women's voices in the past. In Chapter 2, Jones makes female economists her principal actors; whereas this chapter shows women as divided. At some point a group of women is not indicative of the whole. The difficulty is delineating the differences between groups, as this chapter hopefully shows that working wives bear a tax cost not borne by other women. A risk in our pleasure at finding home economists' voices is that we may forget to investigate the relation of the smaller subset of women to the whole of womanhood. As Jones notes in her conclusion, these economists were "less woman-centric than … class-centric," implying the natural divisions found within the larger group of women that is also shown in this chapter.

This chapter explores how divisions between women partially explain the lack of gender power in tax policy. And if, as this chapter shows, women are largely passive with respect to tax issues, Jones's group is all the more special for its interest in tax-related issues. Focusing on a handful of successful and thoughtful women, conversant in issues of taxation, may make these women's lack of influence more tragic. However, if tax policy was simply not a significant concern for most women, their relative indifference to their own co-opting might be less surprising. Perhaps most importantly, the perspective one chooses changes the prescriptive response from trying to encourage policy makers to hear women's message to fostering women's awareness of tax issues.

Despite our different focuses and likely political responses, Jones and I agree that women's influence on tax policy has historically been limited. Jones and I also agree that as a result women's interests are not satisfied in the current system. For working wives to gain control over the limited issue of the marriage penalty, I fear that it must be reframed away from gender and marriage to one of tax reduction. In the past, gender has too often been a tool used against these women's interests. The costs of working for two-earner couples are higher than for one-earner couples and, therefore, a relative tax reduction is warranted. This argument might be successful as demographics continue to change, especially if men continue to become the secondary earner within families.[128] The risk, however, is from those who would not benefit from this reframing and who have quietly entrenched the marriage bonus—one-earner couples. Although most commentators note that the marriage penalty is coupled with a marriage bonus, the bonus has never received the same political attention. Without a fully gendered (and therefore un-gendered) understanding of this issue, the economic and social cost of tax policy will likely continue to be, as it has been in the past, shifted disproportionately onto a subset of women.

128 Richard Fry & D'Vera Cohn, Pew Research Ctr., Women, Men, and the New Economics of Marriage 1–2 (2010).

PART II
Taxation of Imputed Income

Chapter 4
Income Imputation: Toward Equal Treatment of Renters and Owners

Henry Ordower*

This chapter argues that fundamental fairness principles demand changes in U.S. tax law to place those who rent on an equal tax footing with those who own their residences. The disparity in tax treatment of owners and renters results primarily from the failure of the tax law to include the use value from investment of capital in a personal residence in the incomes of owners. While the yield from investment in a personal residence is not cash, the yield is valuable as it replaces an outlay for dwelling use the owner otherwise would have to make. That occupancy right as an investment yield remains undiminished by any income tax. Renters, on the other hand, may not deduct what they pay for their dwelling use.[1] Renters pay for residence occupancy with what they have left after their income from all sources, including alternative investments of capital, has been taxed.

The mortgage interest deduction[2] exacerbates the disparity between owners and renters and encourages owners to incur excessive debt[3] but is not primarily responsible for the tax advantage of owner occupancy of housing. Failure to impute income from owner occupancy is a tax benefit to all owners—and not just to those who borrow to acquire their residences, as the mortgage interest deduction is.

To illustrate this proposition, assume taxpayers *A* and *B* each have $100,000 to invest. Taxpayer *A* buys a $100,000 dwelling for personal use. A comparable dwelling would rent for $10,000 annually but taxpayer *A* neither pays rent nor includes the $10,000 of use value from capital invested in the dwelling in income. The $10,000 imputed income from use of one's own property is not taxable.

Taxpayer *B* invests $100,000 at a taxable yield of 10 percent and has taxable investment income annually of $10,000. Assuming that taxpayer *B*'s marginal rate of tax is 25 percent, taxpayer *B* will have only $7,500 remaining from the return on the $100,000 capital each year after tax.[4] Despite starting with the same amount of capital as taxpayer *A*, taxpayer *B* will not have sufficient funds from the investment of the $100,000 capital to rent a dwelling comparable to *A*'s dwelling. If rent paid were deductible, *B* would be able to use the full investment yield, undiminished by tax, to rent a dwelling comparable to the dwelling *A* purchased, because *B* would have income of $10,000 and

* Thank you to Lindsay Johnson, a law student research assistant, and Margaret McDermott, law librarian, for research assistance.

1 Rent is a personal, living, or family expense expressly made nondeductible by Code § 262.

2 With limitations, home mortgage interest is deductible under Code § 163(h)(3) notwithstanding the general disallowance of personal interest under Code § 163(h)(1).

3 Benjamin H. Harris et al., *New Perspectives on Homeownership Tax Incentives*, 141 Tax Notes 1315, 1318 (2013) (arguing that the mortgage interest deduction and exclusion of gain do not encourage homeownership but "induce people to take on more debt to buy bigger homes").

4 $10,000 draws a tax of $2,500, leaving the taxpayer with $7,500 after tax.

a deduction of $10,000 for a net inclusion of zero.[5] But because rent is not deductible, if taxpayer *B* wishes to rent a $10,000-per-year dwelling comparable to taxpayer *A*'s, *B* must devote an additional $3,333 of pre-tax income to rent. At a 25 percent marginal rate of income tax, $13,333 will leave $10,000 available for rent after the 25 percent income tax has been paid.[6]

To eliminate this disparity in treatment of owners and renters, this chapter concludes that either residential rent should be deductible or the use value of owner-occupied dwellings should be includable in gross income. For several administrative and tax collection reasons, the chapter expresses a preference for inclusion of use value in income.

In Chapter 5, Steve Johnson agrees generally that the disparate treatment of renters and owners is unfair but disagrees with much of my analysis. Johnson concludes that practical and administrative considerations render taxing the use value of owner-occupied dwellings impractical and politically unacceptable. I contend here that technological advances in large database management make the determination of the use value of owner-occupied dwellings possible with reasonable accuracy, so that inclusion in income is practical. Further, following a transition period in which there is likely to be an increase in litigation challenging valuation and inclusion, inclusion will be a routine matter little different from the current inclusion of income from bank deposits and mutual funds supported by an information reporting requirement for financial institutions.[7]

In this chapter, I first briefly discuss the general rules governing the taxation of income and gain from capital investment and position home ownership in the context of investment of capital. Next, I explore the fundamental, fairness-based tax principles of horizontal equity—treating like taxpayers alike—and vertical equity—progressive rates based on ability to pay—in the context of home ownership and observe that exclusion of use value violates both principles. Then, I focus on the discriminatory impact of the exclusion of use value because people of color disproportionately rent rather than own their homes. Finally, I suggest ways to level the tax treatment of renters and owners and discuss the advantages and drawbacks of each. I conclude with a recommendation to include use value in owners' incomes and identify technological advances that facilitate implementation of the recommendation.

Taxation of Income from Capital: Investment Choice

An individual need not place her money into productive use. She may bury her money, hide it under her mattress, or swim in it like Scrooge McDuck does.[8] Uninvested money yields no income and attracts no income tax. If a taxpayer chooses to invest, she need not seek to maximize her

5 *A* and *B* may be dissimilar in that *A* may be taking an investment risk that *B* is not. *A*'s dwelling may depreciate economically in value while *B*'s investment may preserve *B*'s capital. In the case of owner-occupied dwellings, *A*'s risk seems small in as much as the housing value trend in the United States since 1945 has been appreciation in residential value not depreciation. For example, the Standard & Poor's Case-Shiller home price index for the period 1988–2010 displays general, but varying, price increases throughout most of the period. Press Release, S&P Indices, Home Prices in the New Year Continue the Trend Set in Late 2009 According to the S&P/Case-Shiller Home Price Indices (Mar. 30, 2010), http://www.standardandpoors.com/spf/CSHomePrice_Release_033056.pdf.

6 If the individual pays a 25 percent tax on each dollar she earns, it requires $13,333.33 to leave $10,000 after tax. This computation does not take Social Security and Medicare taxes into consideration, nor does it consider state and local income and wage taxes.

7 For example, Code § 6049 relating to interest payments.

8 Scrooge McDuck was Donald Duck's uncle in the Donald Duck comic book series. Scrooge was, as

return on investment.[9] Even if the taxpayer could have invested her money productively or more efficiently but does not, she does not become taxable on the income she forgoes in failing to invest or in investing inefficiently.[10] Ongoing theoretical discussion addresses the role of income maximization under a taxation system reflecting ability to pay. A system that pegs the tax rate to ability to pay is likely to include potential earnings.[11] Taxing potential earnings would, however, undermine taxpayers' freedom to choose to invest their capital inefficiently or not at all.

Nevertheless, if the individual does place her capital into productive use, she becomes taxable on any return the money yields unless the income tax exempts the specific investment return. Statutes expressly exempt various types of investment income from the income tax.[12] With exceptions,[13] an individual may choose freely among investments for her money and is only taxable on the actual return from the investment she chooses rather than some idealized return she could have received had she chosen an investment with a greater yield.[14] Also, with some exceptions,[15] if the investment return takes the form of capital appreciation, under the U.S. realization-based income tax system, the individual is not taxable until she sells or exchanges the investment,[16] and possibly not even then if the taxpayer received the investment from a decedent.[17]

Some productive uses of capital remain exempt from tax even absent a statutory exclusion. Homeownership is probably the most prominent of those untaxed productive uses. Imputed income from use of one's owned dwelling is neither notional nor "measured by the income forgone when the taxpayer chose not to put the item involved into the stream of commerce," as Professor Johnson argues.[18] Imputed income is not potential income from uninvested capital but rather actual return on investment in the form of use rather than money. The dwelling is very much in the stream of commerce since the owner is both owner and occupant. As occupant, the owner is using the dwelling for its intended purpose rather than keeping it empty and hence out of the stream of

---

his name suggests, wealthy and stingy. He kept his money in a vault and spent countless hours counting and swimming around in it.

9 Although someone with control over another person's wealth (e.g., a trustee) may have an obligation to invest that wealth productively. While Code § 7872 imputing a minimum interest rate to lending transactions between taxpayers in certain relationships such as parent–child or employer–employee would seem an exception to this taxpayer choice rule, it is not. Its purpose is not to limit taxpayers' investment choices but to prevent avoidance of tax otherwise payable. A below-market interest rate in those loans otherwise enables the parties to transfer the below-market amount without paying gift tax in the parent–child context or income tax on compensation in the employer–employee context.

10 Similarly, an individual need not enter the labor market or maximize her earnings in the labor market.

11 For a discussion of endowment taxation, see Chris William Sanchirico, *Progressivity and Potential Income: Measuring the Effect of Changing Work Patterns on Income Tax Progressivity*, 108 Colum. L. Rev. 1551, 1552–54 (2008).

12 *E.g.*, 26 U.S.C. § 103 (excluding interest on state and local obligations from gross income).

13 *E.g.*, *id.* § 7872 (imputing a market-based interest rate to certain low-interest or no-interest loans and including that interest in the taxpayer's income); *see supra* note 9.

14 26 U.S.C. § 61 (defining gross income as "all income from whatever source derived" and forming the point of departure for computation of taxable income).

15 *Id.* §§ 475 (marking to market certain dealer-held securities and including the appreciation or depreciation in the value of those securities annually in determining taxable income), 1256 (imposing similar treatment on certain commodities positions).

16 *Id.* § 1001 (determining gain from the sale or exchange of property).

17 *Id.* § 1014 (giving property acquired from a decedent a new basis equal to the fair market value of the property at the decedent's death).

18 Johnson, *infra* ch. 5, text accompanying note 3.

commerce. Use without payment is a valuable receipt and is income,[19] just as the receipt of goods without payment for which one otherwise would have paid is valuable and is income.[20]

Fundamental Fairness Principles and Taxation of Housing

The horizontal and vertical equity principles inform the structure and development of taxation rules in the United States, and the exclusion of imputed use value of owner-occupied dwellings from income violates both principles.

Horizontal Equity and Homeownership

Underlying the federal income tax is the fundamental tax principle of horizontal equity. Horizontal equity is a basic fairness notion postulating that like taxpayers should be taxed alike.[21] However, what makes taxpayers alike is the subject of debate—for instance, should it include only the amount and types of a taxpayer's income or should it also include taxpayers' differing family sizes and living circumstances? Perhaps a better formulation of the horizontal equity principle might be that taxpayers with like family sizes living under substantially identical cost of living circumstances and receiving equal amounts of income should pay equal amounts of tax.

Whatever the formulation of the principle, often like taxpayers with like incomes pay different amounts of tax. For example, one taxpayer's income might consist of income exempt from tax[22] or net capital gain eligible for preferential tax rates,[23] while another taxpayer might select investments that yield ordinary income[24] subject to the higher ordinary income tax rates.[25] Insofar as taxpayers freely make their own investment decisions and can select among favored (i.e., capital-gain- or exempt-income-producing) and disfavored (i.e., ordinary-income-producing) investments, the selection of disfavored investments often is a matter of individual preference.[26] Where taxpayers' informed investment decisions result in dissimilar treatment of equal amounts of income, a violation of horizontal equity might not be troubling. The taxpayer who has the knowledge and power to alter the deployment of her capital in a way that would establish horizontal equity with other taxpayers should not complain of unequal tax treatment. If, however, the difference in treatment results not from taxpayers' investment decisions but from unalterable structural characteristics of their income, a taxpayer might be unable to establish tax parity. For instance, a taxpayer with income

19 For example, an employee must include in income the value of the personal use of an employer-provided car. I.R.S. Pub. No. 15-B, Employer's Tax Guide to Fringe Benefits, at 22 (2014).

20 *Cf.* 26 U.S.C. § 83 (taxing a service provider on the value of property received in payment for services).

21 William A. Klein, Policy Analysis of the Federal Income Tax: Text and Readings 7 (1976). *But see* James R. Repetti & Diane M. Ring, *Horizontal Equity Revisited*, 13 Fla. Tax Rev. 135 (2012) (arguing that horizontal equity has no normative content and is only part of vertical equity).

22 26 U.S.C. § 103.

23 *Compare id.* § 1(a)–(d), *with id.* § 1(h).

24 *See id.* § 65 (defining ordinary income).

25 *Id.* § 1(a)–(d).

26 The choice may be a matter of risk. The capital-gain-producing investments may be riskier than investments that yield ordinary income.

from services, which is subject to tax at the higher ordinary income rates[27] plus the additional wage-based Social Security and Medicare taxes,[28] generally cannot transform her income mix to achieve tax parity with a taxpayer having an equal amount of income that comes from investments taxed at favorable rates.

The U.S. federal income tax is replete with schedular features that cause identical amounts of income differing in form,[29] use,[30] or source[31] to be subject to differing rates of tax.[32] I have argued elsewhere that these schedular features violate the principles of horizontal and vertical equity.[33] Schedularity renders the achievement of horizontal equity an elusive goal. While one might argue that only taxpayers with incomes equal both qualitatively and quantitatively should be treated alike, qualitative form, use, or source differences do not alter amounts and ought not impact the rate of tax. Qualitative differences often introduce uncertainty into determination of value. Fixing the value of nontransferable or nonexchangeable types of income such as meals and lodging may be challenging,[34] but once one establishes the monetary value of a nonmonetary receipt, quantity alone ought to be pertinent to tax imposition. Income is indeed measured in money and money is fungible.

In many instances, the tax law provides a tax benefit to one group of taxpayers while another group gets no benefit even though both groups engage in similar activities. Students on scholarship, for example, may exclude their scholarships from gross income,[35] but students without scholarships may not reduce their incomes by the amount of tuition they pay.[36] In addition, life insurance premiums paid by an employer are not included in the employee's gross income,[37] but employees who must pay for their own life insurance premiums may not reduce their gross income through a deduction for the premiums that they pay. Yet, even if such imbalances in tax benefits are commonplace, each imbalance violates the horizontal equity principle and generates winners and losers. In many instances, the taxpayer is unable to choose the tax benefit by voluntarily altering her circumstances, as she might do with her investment decisions.[38] If the winners and losers routinely belong to different societal groups, the imbalance discriminates unfairly in favor of or against specific groups. In those instances, the imbalance is particularly troubling even if not impermissible.[39]

27 26 U.S.C. § 1(a)–(d).

28 *Id.* § 3101 (imposing Social Security and Medicare taxes).

29 *Id.* § 132(a)(1) (travel benefits received in kind excludable—that is, subject to a zero percent rate—in some instances).

30 *Id.* § 117 (qualified scholarships excludable—that is, subject to a zero percent rate).

31 *Id.* § 1(h) (net capital gain from the sale or exchange of capital assets taxed at a reduced rate).

32 *See generally* Henry Ordower, *Schedularity in U.S. Income Taxation and Its Effect on Tax Distribution*, 108 Nw. U. L. Rev. 905 (2014) (arguing that schedularity causes unfair distribution of tax burdens in the United States).

33 *Id.* at 910.

34 *See* 26 U.S.C. § 119 (excluding from gross income certain meals and lodging provided to employees on the employer's business premises for the convenience of the employer).

35 *Id.* § 117.

36 *See id.* § 262 (no deduction for "personal, living or family expenses").

37 *Id.* § 79.

38 *See supra* text accompanying note 24.

39 *See infra* text accompanying notes 57–59.

Exclusion of the use value of a personal residence from the income tax base is just such a troubling violation of the horizontal equity principle. Homeowners pay for occupancy of their dwellings with untaxed investment income while renters pay for their dwellings with taxed investment or labor income. To argue, as Steve Johnson does,[40] that purchase and occupancy of a dwelling is simply consumption and deferred consumption of already-taxed dollars, just as renting is consumption of already-taxed dollars, conflates dissimilar expenditures for tax purposes. Purchase of the dwelling is investment, not consumption or deferred consumption.[41] Occupancy of a dwelling neither diminishes its value nor uses the dwelling up.[42]

Other instances in which the income tax does not reach imputed income are not nearly as troubling as the case of imputed use value of a dwelling. Most consumer goods that a taxpayer owns and uses do get used up over time. Steve Johnson's observation that purchase is simply deferred consumption thus seems more accurate with respect to items such as cars, clothing, and televisions.[43] Those items, unlike housing, do get used up in the course of the owner's use of them. Goods like artwork that give pleasure but do not deteriorate over time and with use are more troubling but, unlike housing, the enjoyment of art is not a necessity of life. In that respect, enjoyment of artwork one owns differs from enjoyment of the dwelling one owns. Everyone must live somewhere.

Devotion of one's uncompensated time to performance of services for oneself or members of one's family (e.g., cooking meals or cleaning one's house) is indeed outside the line of commerce. In many instances, the services do not replace items for which the taxpayer otherwise would pay. This makes them different from housing, which everyone must consume.

Occupancy, whether by the owner or a tenant, is consumption of the dwelling's use. The renter pays for consumption of occupancy with after-tax dollars. The owner pays for consumption of occupancy with the tax-free yield from investment in the dwelling. Both the renter and the owner consume only temporal occupancy of the dwelling. Neither consumes the dwelling itself. If the tax law permitted renters to deduct their rent, they also would pay for their dwellings with the equivalent of untaxed income and the treatment of renters and owners would be comparable.[44] But the tax law does not allow that deduction. Lest taxpayers eliminate much of the income tax base

---

40 Johnson, *infra* ch. 5, text accompanying note 56.

41 Since 2007, EU Statistics on Income and Living Conditions include implicit rents on owner-occupied dwellings as income. Eurostat, Eur. Comm'n, *European Union Statistics on Income and Living Conditions*, http://epp.eurostat.ec.europa.eu/portal/page/portal/microdata/eu_silc (last visited July 22, 2014). For a discussion of the impact of imputed rent on income distribution, see Veli-Matti Törmälehto & Hannele Sauli, *The Distributional Impact of Imputed Rent in EU-SILC* (2010), *available at* http://epp.eurostat.ec.europa.eu/cache/ITY_OFFPUB/KS-RA-10-023/EN/KS-RA-10-023-EN.PDF. On the relationship between the failure of tax systems to impute income from owner-occupied dwellings and increasing income disparities between rich and poor, see Joachim R. Frick & Markus M. Grabka, *Accounting for Imputed and Capital Income Flows in Income Inequality Analyses* (IZA Discussion Paper Series, Discussion Paper No. 4634, 2009), *available at* http://ftp.iza.org/dp4634.pdf, and Joachim R. Frick & Markus M. Grabka, *Imputed Rent and Income Inequality: A Decomposition Analysis for the U.K., West Germany, and the U.S.A.*, 49 Rev. Income & Wealth 513 (2003).

42 *See supra* note 5.

43 Johnson, *infra* ch. 5, text accompanying notes 45–63.

44 The deduction would have to be an adjustment to gross income deductible under Code § 62 rather than an itemized deduction under Code § 63 in order for the deduction not to be limited as itemized deductions are.

with deductions for their living expenses, the Code expressly denies deductions for "personal, living and family expenses," including rental of a dwelling.[45] Yet, the income tax does not treat current use of a dwelling as the owner's residence as an investment yield includable in gross income.[46] The absence of parallel treatment—that is, the pairing of an exclusion for owner-occupiers with a deduction for renters[47]—leaves owner-occupiers with a significant tax benefit unavailable to renters.[48]

Like statutory exemptions, the nonstatutory exemption from tax of imputed income from use of an owner-occupied dwelling appears taxpayer neutral. Because anyone owning a dwelling may

45 26 U.S.C. § 262(a).

46 The Code is silent on the exclusion. It does not expressly exclude that current use from gross income. *See* Bruce Bartlett, *Taxing Homeowners as if They Were Landlords*, N.Y. Times Economix (Sept. 3, 2013), http://economix.blogs.nytimes.com/2013/09/03/taxing-homeowners-as-if-they-were-landlords/?_php=true&_type=blogs&_r=0 (arguing that imputed rent is income). According to the Joint Committee on Taxation, the exclusion of imputed use or rental value of owner-occupied dwellings is not a tax expenditure because the exclusion is not within the definition of tax expenditure because there is no statute applicable to it. Staff of J. Comm. on Taxation, 113th Cong., Estimates of Federal Tax Expenditures for Fiscal Years 2012–2017, at 2 (Comm. Print 2013). Tax expenditures are "revenue losses attributable to provisions of the Federal tax laws which allow a special exclusion, exemption, or deduction from gross income or which provide a special credit, a preferential rate of tax, or a deferral of tax liability." Congressional Budget and Impoundment Control Act of 1974, Pub. L. No. 93-344, § 3(3), 88 Stat. 297, 299. Despite not falling within the statutory definition, the Joint Committee on Taxation observes about imputed income: "The individual income tax does not include in gross income the imputed income that individuals receive from the services provided by owner-occupied homes and durable goods. However, the Joint Committee staff does not classify this exclusion as a tax expenditure. The measurement of imputed income for tax purposes presents administrative problems and its exclusion from taxable income may be regarded as an administrative necessity." Staff of J. Comm. on Taxation, *supra*, at 5. *Compare* Bureau of Econ. Analysis, U.S. Dep't of Commerce, Survey of Current Business: An Introduction to the National Income and Product Accounts: Methodology Papers: U.S. National Income and Product Accounts 3 (2007) (including estimates of this imputed income in the National Income and Product Accounts), *and* James R. Follain et al., *The Preferential Income Tax Treatment of Owner-Occupied Housing: Who Really Benefits?*, 4 Housing Pol'y Debate 1 (1993) (arguing that nonimputation is a major tax expenditure distributed primarily to high-income taxpayers, but distributional effect depends on how the tax gets redistributed among households), *and* Harris et al., *supra* note 3, at 1315, 1317 (acknowledging imputed use value as income but finding it too difficult to tax and recommending other tax credits to enhance progressivity despite the exclusion), *with* Joseph M. Dodge et al., Federal Income Taxation: Doctrine, Structure, and Policy 293–300 (2012) (arguing imputed income is not income).

47 Excluding from gross income items that some taxpayers receive in kind without providing a comparable deduction to taxpayers who pay for the same items themselves occurs with regularity in the Code. *See supra* note 35 and accompanying text.

48 Unless landlords discount the rental prices they charge so that the tenant pays only the tenant's after-income-tax rental value. In the example in the text below, the renter paying $10,000 in rent would rent a dwelling having a fair rental value of $13,333 but only pay $10,000 in rent. Steve Johnson, *infra* ch. 5, text accompanying notes 23–27, correctly points out that there are various rental housing tax benefits that may inure to renters in the form of lower-than-market rents. However, whether this actually occurs is uncertain because those benefits are indirect for renters, while the owners of the residential rental properties, who directly receive these benefits, are likely to pass on to renters as little of the value of the benefits as possible in order to rent the property successfully. Even a deduction for rent might not reach renters, as landlords might capture the benefit with increased rents. *See infra* note 81 and accompanying text.

exclude the use value of the investment from her income, failure to tax the imputed income does not seem to favor any group of taxpayers over any other group. Homeowners enjoy a tax benefit that follows from homeownership just as owners of qualifying state or local obligations enjoy the benefit of tax-exempt interest that follows from ownership of those obligations.[49] Although others who do not own homes enjoy no compensating benefit, no law limits home ownership to any identifiable group of taxpayers. In theory, anyone may become a homeowner. Yet, despite the tax advantage, not everyone does.[50]

If it is a simple choice to own or rent, the decision to forego the tax benefit by renting makes owners and renters sufficiently dissimilar to justify taxing them differently because of their voluntary investment choices.[51] In the United States, however, many taxpayers who rent may not choose freely between owning and renting and people of color are overrepresented in the class of renters.[52] In the absence of a choice to own or rent, more favorable tax treatment of owners is troubling.

Vertical Equity and Home Ownership

Excluding use value of owner-occupied housing from income violates the principle of horizontal equity because the tax law fails to treat renters and owners alike when they have equal economic incomes.[53] Taxation separates taxpayers into a tax-advantaged owner class and a tax-disadvantaged renter class. Distribution of membership in the tax-advantaged owner class of taxpayers is not proportional at different levels of income. Higher-income taxpayers are far more likely to become homeowners than are lower-income taxpayers.[54] In 2011, for example, fewer than half of households with incomes under $20,000 owned their own dwellings while more than 90 percent of households with incomes of $120,000 or more owned their own dwellings.[55] That distributional inequality in homeownership causes the exclusion of imputed income from the use of owner-occupied housing to violate the principle of vertical equity in taxation.

Vertical equity is a more nuanced concept than horizontal equity but equally fundamental to incomc taxation in the United States.[56] The historical preference for progressive income taxes in most developed economies, like the United States, emerges from the vertical equity principle.[57] Vertical equity, like horizontal equity, is a basic fairness notion that follows an ability-to-pay principle. Vertical equity assumes that as a taxpayer's income increases, the taxpayer should contribute an increasing percentage of her incremental income to taxes. Application of vertical equity tends to

49 26 U.S.C. § 103.

50 Including Steve Johnson. Johnson, *infra* ch. 5, note 87.

51 *Cf.* discussion *supra* text accompanying note 24.

52 *See infra* note 74 and accompanying text.

53 *See supra* text accompanying note 47.

54 *See* Harris et al., *supra* note 3, at 1318 (indicating that current homeownership incentives favor higher-income taxpayers).

55 Census Bureau, U.S. Dep't of Commerce, American Housing Survey, at tbl.C-09-AO (2011).

56 *But see* Repetti & Ring, *supra* note 21 (arguing that horizontal equity is not separate from vertical equity).

57 Ajay K. Mehrotra, *Making the Modern American Fiscal State: Law, Politics, and the Rise of Progressive Taxation, 1877–1929*, at 1–7 (Ind. Legal Studies Research Paper No. 267, 2013), *available at* http://ssrn.com/abstract=2320767 (describing the rise of progressive taxation in the United States and the influence of European thought).

redistribute income from higher- to lower-income taxpayers, as higher-income taxpayers pay for disproportionately larger shares of governmental services that all taxpayers consume.[58]

Acceptance of some form of progressivity is substantially universal, as even the most fervent proponents of proportional, rather than progressive, income taxation include a zero rate for some income, rendering even a proportional system minimally progressive.[59] Exclusion of income (e.g., the imputed use value of homeownership) from the tax base undermines vertical equity. The exclusion prevents the tax system from measuring owners' total economic income accurately, leaving the progressive rate schedule to apply only to the owners' remaining income. The exclusion results not only in a failure to tax the excluded income but also a failure to tax the owners' remaining income at the correct rate.

While subprime lending during the 1990s and into the twenty-first century rendered homeownership accessible to a broadening group of lower-income individuals, the subprime lending market contracted and nearly disappeared following the 2007 financial crisis as credit availability tightened. Homeownership has slipped out of reach for much or even most of the lower-income community.[60] Increasing income and wealth disparities in the United States,[61] leaving the United States with the greatest such disparities among developed nations,[62] render the exemption of imputed income from owner-occupied dwellings even more insidious as higher-income taxpayers tend to own their dwellings while lower-income taxpayers do not.[63] Although the exclusion of imputed income from homeownership is theoretically available to all taxpayers, only those taxpayers who own their homes, generally higher-income taxpayers, avail themselves of the exclusion.

---

58 The classic work cataloging arguments for progressive taxation is Walter J. Blum & Harry Kalven, Jr., The Uneasy Case for Progressive Taxation (1953); *see also* Sanchirico, *supra* note 11, at 1563 (asserting that, when potential income is taken into account, progressivity in labor income distribution from 1989 to 2000 declined while statutory progressivity increased; with potential income being an income-maximization concept).

59 Any system that has a zero rate on small income amounts and at least one positive rate on incomes in excess of the zero rate amount is progressive because it takes a larger share of higher incomes than of the lowest incomes. A perfectly progressive system would increase the rate in possibly infinitely small increments with each dollar of increased income, so that the taxpayer with the very greatest income might pay 99.999 … 9 percent on her last dollar, while the taxpayer with a dollar less income might pay 99.999 … 8 percent on his last dollar. But Germany's progression reaches its maximum rate at relatively low income levels. Einkommensteuergesetz [EStG] § 32a(1) (rates of income tax including a linear progression in the range of incomes from €8,131 to €52,881, with a maximum 45 percent rate at taxable incomes of €250,731 and more).

60 Interagency Statement, Office of the Comptroller of Currency, U.S. Dep't of Treasury, et al., Statement on Subprime Mortgage Lending, *available at* http://www.federalreserve.gov/newsevents/press/bcreg/bcreg20070629a1.pdf.

61 Peter Dreier et al., Place Matters: Metropolitics for the Twenty-First Century 18–27 (2d ed. 2004) (addressing the increasing income disparity from the 1970s to 2000 in the United States).

62 *Id.* at 19.

63 *Id.* at 122–23 (discussing the mortgage interest and property tax deductions and observing that the top 10 percent of earners claim 59 percent of mortgage interest deductions, and that there is similar regressivity in the state and local property tax deduction). Imputed income amounts would correlate roughly with the distribution of the mortgage interest deduction.

In her study of the increasing size of single-family homes, Rachel Dwyer[64] observes that ownership of big houses[65] in the United States grew at all income levels but much more rapidly at the highest income levels. Dwyer's study uses census data throughout the period 1960–2000 and observes the trend toward larger housing. Based on the work of other scholars, Dwyer attributes the trend at middle- and lower-income levels in part to the availability of credit in the form of subprime loans and reverse mortgages.[66] Dwyer concludes that "housing consumption inequality increased with income inequality,"[67] observing that "the historical trend in the income stratification of big house ownership was most consistent with divergence theories that expected rising income inequalities would be reflected in increasing disparities in living standards as well."[68] Dwyer further observed that "the striking divergence in big house ownership between the top and bottom of the income scale illustrates one more important way that the experiences of the affluent became less similar to those of the rest of the population."[69] Dwyer's study illustrates that higher-income taxpayers disproportionately own larger houses that tend to be more valuable than smaller houses, so they exclude disproportionately larger amounts of imputed income from use of their owned dwellings.[70]

The exclusion of imputed income is only one of the factors undermining both horizontal and vertical equity in taxation. More broadly affecting these fairness notions is the current split between the treatment of income from investment, of which homeownership is part, and income from the performance of personal services. The U.S. federal income tax frequently applies lower tax rates to investment income than it applies to income from services. Higher-income and wealthier taxpayers generally have the resources to invest, while lower-income and less wealthy taxpayers general consume the bulk of their incomes. Where lower rates of tax routinely apply to the incomes of higher-income taxpayers than apply to the incomes of lower-income taxpayers, the effect is regressive and a violation of vertical equity. Even if discriminating among taxpayers based on their voluntary investment choices might be acceptable,[71] routinely treating lower-income taxpayers less favorably than higher-income taxpayers because they have neither investments nor investment choices is an unacceptable form of discrimination. A variety of policy decisions that are neutral as to classes of taxpayers and that involve no discriminatory intent may result in the favoring of investment income for tax purposes; however, the resulting discrimination in favor of higher-income taxpayers and against lower-income taxpayers is still pernicious.

---

64 Rachel E. Dwyer, *The McMansionization of America: Income Stratification and the Standard of Living in Housing, 1960–2000*, 27 Res. Soc. Stratification & Mobility 285, 293 (2009) (analyzing housing trends in relationship to stratification).

65 *Id.* (defining a big house as seven or more rooms without regard to square footage).

66 *Id.* at 289.

67 *Id.* at 298.

68 *Id.* at 294.

69 *Id.*

70 Interesting as well is that the study discloses that by the year 2000, income became more important than family size as a determinant of big house ownership. *Id.*

71 *See supra* note 23 and accompanying text.

Discrimination in the Imputed Income Exclusion

Much commentary has focused on the imputation of income from owner-occupied dwellings.[72] Frequently those discussions of homeownership include the mortgage interest deduction.[73] Some of those discussions highlight the discriminatory impact of the exclusion of imputed income and the mortgage interest deduction insofar as these tax benefits from homeownership favor higher-income whites over lower-income people of color.[74] More recently, Lily Kahng has argued that the exclusion of gain on the sale of a personal residence is also discriminatory.[75]

Provisions of the Code that have a discriminatory impact for or against specific groups are not uncommon. There is a rich scholarly literature identifying many of those often-subtle instances of inadvertent (and occasionally intentional) discrimination against people of color. If, for example, the distribution of scholarships were substantially proportional to the relative numbers of students in various racial, ethnic, sex, and national-origin groups, the tax exclusion itself might be neutral

---

72 *Compare* Hugh J. Ault & Brian J. Arnold, Comparative Income Taxation: A Structural Analysis (2d ed. 2004) (arguing that the undertaxation of housing expenditures results from nonimputation of income plus the mortgage interest deduction causing overinvestment in owner-occupied dwellings and underinvestment in rental housing, and discussing other countries' approaches to the issue, including the Netherlands' imputation of hypothetical rent), *and* Richard Goode, *Imputed Rent of Owner-Occupied Dwellings Under the Income Tax*, 15 J. Fin. 504 (1960) (arguing that not imputing income favors owners over renters and higher income over lower income), *and* Donald B. Marsh, *The Taxation of Imputed Income*, 58 Pol. Sci. Q. 514 (1943) (arguing imputed income is income and should be taxed), *and* Francesco Figari et al., *Taxing Home Ownership: Distributional Effects of Including Net Imputed Rent in Taxable Income* (IZA Discussion Paper Series, Discussion Paper No. 6493, 2012), *available at* http://ftp.iza.org/dp6493.pdf (providing recommendations for imputing use-value income—an opportunity cost approach, a capital market approach, and self-assessment—and finding a 5 percent change in taxable income in Germany and as much as an 8 percent change in Greece if imputed rent were includable in income), *with* Dodge et al., *supra* note 46 (not income), *and* Jane G. Gravelle & Thomas L. Hungerford, Cong. Research Serv., R42435, The Challenge of Individual Income Tax Reform: An Economic Analysis of Tax Base Broadening (2012) (dismissing imputation to broaden the tax base on administrability, especially valuation, grounds), *and* Steven C. Bourassa & William G. Grigsby, *Income Tax Concessions for Owner-Occupied Housing*, 11 Hous. Pol'y Debate 521 (2000) (finding that imputing income is undesirable due to administrative difficulties and because it would amount to a tax on wealth, but favoring repeal of the mortgage interest deduction), *and* Steve R. Johnson, *Don't Tax Imputed Income from Owner-Occupied Houses*, ABA Sec. Tax'n NewsQuarterly, Winter 2013, at 17 (opposing imputation on administrability grounds and due to a lack of political acceptability).

73 *See* Jerome Kurtz, *The Interest Deduction Under Our Hybrid Tax System: Muddling Toward Accommodation*, 50 Tax L. Rev. 153, 154 (1995) (arguing for imputation partially to make the interest deduction more rational); Roberta F. Mann, *The (Not So) Little House on the Prairie: The Hidden Costs of the Home Mortgage Interest Deduction*, 32 Ariz. St. L.J. 1347, 1350 (2000) (arguing against ownership incentives insofar as they promote urban sprawl); William T. Mathias, *Curtailing the Economic Distortions of the Mortgage Interest Deduction*, 30 U. Mich. J.L. Reform 43 (1996) (arguing against the mortgage interest deduction as it exacerbates income inequalities resulting from the exclusion of imputed rental income).

74 *E.g.*, Census Bureau, *supra* note 55, at tbl.C-08-AO (disclosing that whites are disproportionally represented among homeowners); Dorothy A. Brown, *Teaching Civil Rights Through the Basic Tax Course*, 54 St. Louis U. L.J. 809, 813–15 (2010) (blacks receive fewer tax benefits from homeownership because they tend to be renters).

75 Lily Kahng, *Path Dependence in Tax Subsidies for Home Sales*, 65 Ala. L. Rev. 187 (2013).

even though the numbers of students in each group is not proportional to that group's representation in the community at large. On the other hand, if white students were to receive a disproportionate number of scholarships, the scholarship exclusion itself would favor the class of white students over students of color.

Further analysis of the composition of the lower- and higher-income groups of taxpayers discloses that racial minorities are overrepresented in lower-income groups. Income distribution tables reveal that approximately 21.4 percent of whites and only 9.3 percent of blacks had incomes in excess of $100,000 in 2009, while 11.6 percent of whites and 15.4 percent of blacks had incomes in the $15,000–$25,000 range. In that year, median income for blacks was approximately $32,500 but median income for whites was nearly $52,000.[76] Dwyer's study of the ownership of big houses discloses that "all non-white racial groups … became less likely to own big houses over time. This result is particularly striking given other evidence of (slightly) lessening racial stratification in housing after passage of Fair Housing legislation."[77] Also significant here is that the larger—and, therefore, more valuable—the home, the greater the amount of tax-free imputed income received by the owner.

Leveling the Owner/Renter Playing Field: Recommendations

In Chapter 5, Steve Johnson argues forcefully that imputation of income from owner-occupied housing is neither practical nor politically acceptable nor administrable.[78] Yet, despite those powerful arguments, the existing difference between the tax treatment of owners and renters with respect to living expenses should be unacceptable in the United States. The preceding discussion illustrates how that difference violates fundamental principles of horizontal and vertical equity; provides a tax benefit to higher-income individuals that is largely unavailable to lower-income individuals; and, owing to overrepresentation of people of color in the lower-income group, tends to affect people of color unfavorably relative to whites. Changes in the tax law that would eliminate the unequal treatment of owners and renters could be made on either the renter or the owner side of the rules.[79] Both approaches to the issue are imperfect and neither is more desirable than the other. On balance, I recommend changes in the tax treatment of owners, but that recommendation does not express a compelling preference for one approach over the other.

Renters

On the renter side, the simplest fix to level the tax treatment of owners and renters is to provide renters an above-the-line deduction for rent.[80] With a deduction for rent, both renters and owners would pay for their dwellings with pretax income. Despite the simplicity of this solution, it is

76 Census Bureau, U.S. Dep't of Commerce, Statistical Abstract of the United States, at tbl.690 (2012), *available at* http://www.census.gov/compendia/statab/cats/income_expenditures_poverty_wealth/household_income.html.

77 Dwyer, *supra* note 64, at 294.

78 Johnson, *infra* ch. 5, text accompanying notes 112–56.

79 *See* Goode, *supra* note 72, at 520–24 (suggesting similar solutions to level the playing field between renters and owners).

80 That is, to provide an adjustment to gross income under Code § 62.

unclear that the deduction would inure to the benefit of renters. More likely, landlords will capture part or all of the benefit intended for renters by increasing rents.[81]

In addition, a deduction for rent will result in the loss of a substantial amount of tax revenue, which the government might have to replace.[82] Increasing taxes elsewhere to replace the lost revenue—for example, by broadening the tax base or increasing marginal rates of tax—might prove challenging. Thus, the collateral impact of the deduction might not be significantly more acceptable than taxing imputed income from the use of owner-occupied dwellings. Substituting a different tax (e.g., a value-added tax) might be possible. But a value-added tax is generally regressive and adversely affects the same taxpayers who are disadvantaged by the disparate tax treatment of owners and renters (i.e., lower-income taxpayers). Accordingly, a reduction in government services might be the most likely outcome following the reduction in tax revenue. Moreover, a deduction for rents is inconsistent with the long-standing policy that personal, living, and family expenses should not be deductible for income tax purposes.[83]

A targeted tax credit for renters might limit the loss of revenue if it phases out with increasing income. Those higher-income taxpayers who have an effective choice between renting and owning and who choose to rent would not receive the credit. Lower-income taxpayers would get the credit so that the credit would diminish or eliminate the disparate treatment of high- and low-income taxpayers with respect to housing. Similarly, an increased standard deduction for renters that phases out at higher income levels would also target the group that is subject to disparate treatment and does not have a realistic choice to own rather than rent. Whether either targeted approach would limit the ability of landlords to capture the renters' tax savings is doubtful, although a phased-out credit or increased standard deduction might result in some leveling of rents as lower-end rents increase to capture the tax benefit while higher-end rents do not. Alternatively, a phase-out structure might drive some higher-income renters into the ownership market in order to avoid becoming the only disadvantaged renter class.

Owners

A number of countries (but not the United States) at one time or another in their income tax histories have taxed imputed income from owner-occupied homes. And some continue to do so.[84] The approaches have varied from country to country but most have imputed a much smaller amount

81 Misdirection of targeted tax benefits often has plagued taxation in the United States. The tax-shelter industry sought to capture various development tax incentives and redirect them to a passive investor group with economically unsound projects. *See generally* Henry Ordower, *The Culture of Tax Avoidance*, 55 St. Louis U. L.J. 47, 57–58 (2010). Similarly, the exemption for interest on state and local obligations tends to misdirect a portion of the subsidy to investing taxpayers whose maximum marginal rate of tax is higher than the bracket the bonds target in setting their interest rate. *Id.* at 67; Victor Thuronyi, *Tax Expenditures: A Reassessment*, 1988 Duke L.J. 1155, 1161–62. On the tax expenditures concept generally, see Stanley S. Surrey, Pathways to Tax Reform: The Concept of Tax Expenditures (1974).

82 Omnibus Budget Reconciliation Act of 1990, § 13204, Pub. L. No. 101-508, 104 Stat. 1388 (including pay-as-you-go rules (Paygo) requiring tax legislation that reduced revenue to include an offsetting revenue increase).

83 26 U.S.C. § 262.

84 The Netherlands and Switzerland, for example.

of income than the value of the dwelling might predict.[85] All countries that have imputed income have found the imputation difficult and imperfect. Valuation problems have led to many failures in tax collection, ranging from the early failure to tax employer-provided meals and lodging[86] to the more recent failure to tax the income from partnership interests received by managers of private equity funds as compensation.[87] Similar valuation uncertainties plague attempts to impose wealth taxes and estate taxes.[88]

As Steve Johnson emphasizes,[89] imposing a tax on imputed rent is a formidable task. Nevertheless, it closely resembles the task that county tax assessors routinely perform throughout the United States as they assess and collect local *ad valorem* property taxes critical to funding schools and other government services. While disagreements as to rental value undoubtedly would arise and litigation to establish value would ensue, the United States should not permit valuation difficulties to impede a fair distribution of tax burdens based on sound tax policy considerations. Technological tools in the form of advanced computing capacity, including large database management, could aid in making determinations of value that are accurate, predictable, and uniform. Those making valuations could mine vast amounts of data with ease and would be able to determine and track changes in value with greater certainty than has been possible in the past. Given the relationship between rental value and property value,[90] imputation would encourage cooperation between federal and local taxing authorities with respect to value determinations. Resulting improvements in valuation methodologies for local property taxes, estate and gift taxes, and the federal income tax would follow, as the three tax bases could operate from a single, extensive database. In fact, development of the database for dwellings might address Johnson's reporting concerns.[91] The IRS could send each taxpayer a statement of imputed rental value from that database to include in the

85 Similarly, local real property taxes in the United States customarily assess property at amounts significantly lower than fair market value, often using a portion of fair market value as the amount on which to impose the *ad valorem* tax.

86 Benaglia v. Comm'r, 36 B.T.A. 838 (1937) (holding meals and lodging provided for the convenience of the employer not includable in the taxpayer's income). Exclusion was inappropriate under any consistent tax theory because the employee clearly received some benefit. Valuation of that benefit may have been sufficiently difficult to encourage the Board of Tax Appeals to avoid the valuation issue. Congress later codified the outcome in *Benaglia*. 26 U.S.C. § 119.

87 *See* Rev. Proc. 93-27, 1993-2 C.B. 343 (treating the value of a partnership profits interest as zero). Private equity fund managers receive a portion of their compensation in the form of profits interests and become taxable under customary partnership rules on their shares of partnership profits—including long-term capital gain. *See* 26 U.S.C. § 702(b) (determining the character of a partner's distributive share of partnership income as if the partner had directly realized the income herself). Failure to tax the receipt of the profits interest enables the managers to receive much of their compensation as long-term capital gain. *See generally* Victor Fleischer, *Two and Twenty: Taxing Partnership Profits in Private Equity Funds*, 83 N.Y.U. L. Rev. 1 (2008) (addressing the capital gain/fee issue for private equity funds); Henry Ordower, *Taxing Service Partners to Achieve Horizontal Equity*, 46 Tax Law. 19 (1992) (arguing that profits interests should be valued upon receipt or taxed as open compensation transactions).

88 Valuation difficulty—and especially out-of-date values—resulted in the German Constitutional Court finding the German wealth and estate taxes unconstitutional. BVerfGE 93, 121 (June 22, 1995, 2d Senate) (holding the wealth tax, as applied, to violate the equality principle); BVerfGE 93, 165 (June 22, 1995, 2d Senate) (likewise the inheritance tax).

89 Johnson, *infra* ch. 5, text accompanying notes 112–56.

90 The value of property is simply equal to the present value of the rents it will produce over its useful life (or, forever in the case of real property).

91 Johnson, *infra* ch. 5, text accompanying notes 144–49.

taxpayer's self-reported income in the same manner that financial institutions and government agencies now report interest income on Form 1099.[92] Ownership of real property is a matter of public record throughout the United States, so matching ownership records with taxpayers should prove far less difficult than determination of value.

A change in the law regarding imputed income might disrupt the housing market. Housing values are likely to decline in response to the change.[93] The economic displacement from the tax law change might be no worse than the impacts on real estate values that accompanied other tax law changes. In 1981, the introduction of the accelerated cost recovery system of depreciation with 15-year useful lives for real property caused a significant increase in commercial and residential rental property values.[94] This tax law change created an opportunity for large gains for many owners of commercial and rental real estate, whose buyers could recover their investments (made primarily with borrowed funds) rapidly. Those values retreated several times as Congress extended useful lives through subsequent changes to the accelerated cost recovery provisions.[95]

A second level of economic displacement relates to liquidity, as the increased income tax may compromise some owners' liquidity. Taxpayers voice similar concerns with respect to *ad valorem* real property taxes. For new purchases, liquidity should not be problematic. Buyers will select dwellings with respect to which they can afford the periodic payments of mortgage interest and principal, real estate taxes, and the increased income tax. A few existing owners may have to sell their homes and buy less expensive dwellings. But the economic displacement from the change in the tax laws would be short-lived. Once the real estate market assimilated the change in law and housing prices have adjusted accordingly, the market would stabilize as long as there were no reason to anticipate any further change in the law.

Because the dwelling becomes income-producing property, additional deductions accompany imputation and ameliorate the adverse impact of the imputed income. Expenses of operating income-producing property, including maintenance costs and insurance premiums landlords customarily pay, become deductible.[96] The owner may claim a depreciation allowance[97] and both real estate taxes and mortgage interest change from itemized deductions, limited in deductibility,[98] to adjustments to gross income that are always deductible.[99] Expenses a tenant normally pays (e.g., utilities) remain nondeductible personal living expenses.[100]

If the imputed income is less than 4 percent of a dwelling's purchase price, depreciation allowances and additional deductible expenses such as maintenance might even equal or exceed the

92 *See* 26 U.S.C. § 6049 (interest payment reporting to the recipient and IRS). Anyone familiar with the struggle to build information reporting into current tax rules will view objections as minor political barriers in contrast to the more serious resistance to withholding on interest and dividends. *See* Lily Kahng, *Investment Income Withholding in the United States and Germany*, 10 Fla. Tax Rev. 315, 325–26 (2010) (discussing the failure to implement withholding on interest and dividends).

93 *See* Harris et al., *supra* note 3, at 1323 (discussing housing price reactions to their recommendations).

94 Economic Recovery Tax Act of 1981, § 209, Pub. L. No. 97-34, 95 Stat. 172.

95 Marcus & Millichap, Research Review Trends Report: Commercial Real Estate Review (2011) (discussing the impact of tax law changes on commercial real estate), *available at* http://vitorinogroup.com/wp-content/uploads/2012/02/CommercialREReview.pdf.

96 26 U.S.C. §§ 62(a)(4), 212.

97 *Id.* § 168.

98 *Id.* § 63.

99 *Id.* § 62.

100 *Id.* § 262.

imputed income because of the short depreciable life under current rules.[101] The short useful life for residential rental real estate is a tax expenditure designed to subsidize investment in, and encourage development and operation of, rental housing.[102] The subsidy was not directed to owner-occupied housing. The subsidy seems unnecessary and inappropriate to owner-occupied housing insofar as the depreciation allowances in excess of economic depreciation[103] that reduce the owner's adjusted basis in the dwelling[104] may never generate taxable gain to counterbalance the excess deduction.[105] Rental housing owners, on the other hand, eventually will become subject to tax on gain measured from depreciated basis when tax depreciation exceeds economic depreciation.[106] A longer and more economically realistic useful life for depreciation purposes is appropriate to complement the imputation even if market rents usually exceed 4 percent of the purchase price.[107]

In addition, some temporary assistance to homeowners who were adversely impacted could be funded with the additional revenue yielded by taxing the imputed rental value of owner-occupied dwellings. Various ways of softening the impact suggest themselves. On several occasions, an income-averaging provision has enabled taxpayers to spread extraordinary income over several years. Similarly, the imputation of income might be phased in over a number of years, so that there would not be a spike in owners' incomes in a single year.

Despite some added administrative complexity in taxing imputed income,[108] change in the law is critical to eliminate the long-standing disparity in treatment of owners and renters. Unlike a deduction for renters, the imputation structure does not afford an opportunity for a group not intended to benefit from the change—namely, landlords—to capture part or all of the benefit. It is possible that the legal change would drive owners into the renter group,[109] but the homeownership preference in the United States surely is sufficiently well-embedded in Americans' psyches to withstand any overreaction to the tax law change. Renting does not become more attractive as a result of income imputation because rent remains nondeductible.

Johnson overstates the political risk of taxing imputed income from owner-occupancy of a dwelling.[110] Taxpayers do accept changes in long-standing practice without significant resistance.[111]

101 Under Code § 168(c), the useful life of residential real estate for depreciation purposes is 27.5 years, so the annual deduction for depreciation is approximately 4 percent of the purchase price for the first 27.5 years of ownership.

102 Thuronyi, *supra* note 81, at 1184.

103 *See supra* note 5.

104 26 U.S.C. § 1016(a)(2).

105 Owners often may exclude gain under Code § 121.

106 Subject to elimination of gain for all taxpayers holding property at death under Code § 1014.

107 Single family homes, however, tend not to depreciate in value at all. *See supra* note 5.

108 Matters of definition and valuation, as Steve Johnson notes *infra* ch. 5, text accompanying notes 128–43, certainly add administrative complexity; however, the development of a uniform valuation standard that will follow enactment and information reporting of the includable amount of income will eliminate the added complexity quickly.

109 *See* Steven C. Bourassa & Martin Hoesli, *Why Do the Swiss Rent?*, 40 J. REAL ESTATE FIN. & ECON. 286 (2010) (attributing the high rate of rental rather than ownership in Switzerland to the taxation of imputed use value and high purchase prices of owned property).

110 Johnson, *infra* ch. 5, text accompanying notes 157–67.

111 For example, while not as broad a change as taxing imputed income, changes to Code § 104(a)(2) eliminated exclusions for nonphysical injuries and (possibly) punitive damages in personal injury awards. Small Business Job Protection Act of 1996, § 1605, Pub. L. No. 104-188, 110 Stat. 1755. And Code § 469 limited the deductibility of passive activity losses to passive activity income, thereby shutting down many traditional tax shelters.

Widespread tax evasion is unlikely to accompany enactment because most failures to report will trigger automatic matching notices such as those that are generated by taxpayer underreporting of interest or dividends (as compared to the amount reported to the IRS by the payor of the interest or dividends). Imputation is not high on taxpayers' lists of sensitive tax issues. The bulk of public discussion, as opposed to scholarly literature, long has emphasized the mortgage interest deduction as the key benefit of homeownership. The availability of that deduction would not change.

In addition, even taking additional deductions into account,[112] imputation would increase tax revenues.[113] The increase in taxes would fall primarily on higher-income taxpayers who pay tax at high marginal rates, which would support the progressivity of the income tax. Increased revenue and more progressive taxation are more attractive than the decreased tax revenue that would follow a deduction for renters. Thus, there would be no need for other changes in the tax law to replace lost revenues. Imputation of income might provide Congress flexibility in tailoring taxes and tax benefits to provide other desirable tax benefits or to reduce tax rates at all income levels, just as it might do with any broadening of the tax base.

Steve Johnson and I reach opposite conclusions on imputation. Johnson is wrong but makes a strong argument nonetheless. He views imputation as administratively impractical and politically unacceptable. He sees owner-occupied housing as outside of commerce and not income. He supports the long-standing, nonstatutory error of failing to tax imputed income from owner-occupied dwellings. I view use of owner-occupied housing as a replacement for an expenditure the taxpayer otherwise would make in cash. More important, however, is that imputation is necessary to help rebalance sadly out-of-balance taxation in the United States. Imputation would reinvigorate the historically sound, fundamental tax principles of horizontal and vertical equity in taxation. Imputation would eliminate part of tax discrimination against people of color. I conclude that imputation is both administratively feasible and, while difficult to sell to the public, politically manageable. It is the right thing to do.

112 See discussion of deductible expenses *supra* text accompanying notes 96–105.

113 Estimating the minimum value of the owner-occupied housing stock by multiplying the number of owner-occupied units (i.e., 71 million) by the median price (i.e., $110,000) yields a total value of U.S. owner-occupied housing of approximately $8 trillion. The median price, however, leaves an unlimited price range over the median for half the units but only a range of less than $110,000 for the lower half, so the total value is likely to be much greater than $8 trillion. Census Bureau, *supra* note 55, at tbl.C-13-OO. If the net imputed income from that value is as little as 1 percent after deductible expenses and depreciation and the 1 percent is subject to a 20 percent annual rate of tax, then the additional tax revenue will be $16 billion annually. Rent to house price ratios have tended to be greater than 8 percent, which suggests that increased revenue would be substantial. Kamilla Sommer et al., *The Equilibrium Effect of Fundamentals on House Prices and Rents*, 60 J. Monetary Econ. 854, 860 (2013) (studying the effects of fundamentals on equilibrium house prices and rents).

Chapter 5
Imputed Rental Income: Reality Trumps Theory

Steve R. Johnson*

It is a personality flaw, no doubt, but I often feel uncomfortable when I find myself on the side of orthodoxy. The conventional view is that there are weighty policy reasons in favor of including in homeowners' taxable incomes the imputed rental value of their residences but that practicality overrides these reasons.[1] In this case, alas, I must swallow my usual discomfort and ally myself with the majority.[2] Despite substantial theoretical arguments for taxing imputed rental income, administrative and political realities confirm the wisdom of the great majority of countries around the world in forgoing taxation of imputed rents.

Fortunately for my carefully nurtured self-image, there is one aspect of my view of the imputed rents issue that allows me to maintain a claim of unconventionality. Consistent with the notion that administrative and political exigencies are the barriers to taxation, it usually is believed or assumed that imputed rents are "income" and thus should be taxed under a conceptually pure income tax—or at least could be taxed were Congress to so choose. The accuracy of those propositions is not clear to me. There are substantial arguments that imputed rents are not income at all in conceptual, statutory, or constitutional senses. Although my principal objections to imputation and taxation of rental values remain administrative and political, the "it's not income to begin with" dimension also has some cut.

The first section of this chapter is foundational. It defines imputed rental income, notes its relation to other features of U.S. tax law favorable to housing, and sketches the history of taxation of imputed rental values in the United States and other countries. The second section then discusses whether imputed rents constitute "income." It describes reasons to believe that imputed rents are not income, as the concept of income has developed for U.S. tax purposes.

The ensuing sections of the chapter address policy. The third section acknowledges the arguments most frequently advanced in favor of taxing imputed rental values. It concedes that some of these arguments have force but maintains that the degree of force they possess sometimes is overstated.

---

* I thank Mary McCormick for research assistance.

1 "If … imputed income [from consumer durables, self-performed services, and enjoyment of leisure] is not taxed, [the] received wisdom says, it is only because of the practical difficulties involved." Thomas Chancellor, *Imputed Income and the Ideal Income Tax*, 67 Or. L. Rev. 561, 561 (1988).

2 The question "majority of whom?" needs to be addressed. Most public finance scholars and economists have long supported taxing imputed rents, certainly from houses and, less often, from other consumer durables and even self-performed services. *E.g.*, Richard Goode, *Imputed Rent of Owner-Occupied Dwellings Under the Income Tax*, 15 J. Fin. 504, 504 (1960); Jorge Onrubia et al., *How Do Services of Owner-Occupied Housing Affect Income Inequality and Redistribution?*, 18 J. Housing Econ. 224, 230 (2009). However, as seen in the first section of the chapter, throughout fiscal history only a minority of jurisdictions have actually gone this route, and the minority has shrunk in recent decades. Thus, in saying that I stand with the majority, I mean the majority of policy makers.

The fourth and fifth sections develop the policy ripostes. The fourth section notes the powerful considerations of administrability at work. These include serious problems of reporting and recordkeeping for homeowners; enforcement for the IRS; and valuation for taxpayers, the IRS, and the courts.

The fifth section examines the political difficulties that taxing imputed rents would entail. My argument is more than a simple "it would be unpopular with citizens and voters." Instead, the argument is based on the self-assessment character of the U.S. income tax. At the low rates of audit that currently exist (and foreseeably will exist) in the United States, taxpayer commitment to (or at least grudging acceptance of) the tax system is a necessity. That allegiance is strained whenever taxpayers believe the system to be unfair. Taxpayers would neither understand nor accept the fairness of taxation of imputed rental values. That being so, stretching for the brass ring of theoretical purity would entail an unacceptably high risk of falling off the horse.

Definition and History

Definition

Imputed income is notional rather than actual, reflecting what the taxpayer putatively could have made rather than what she actually did make. Thus, the concept is related to opportunity cost, with the amount imputed being measured by the income forgone when the taxpayer chose not to put the item involved into the stream of commerce.[3]

According to Donald Marsh's widely quoted definition, "[i]mputed income may be defined provisionally as a flow of satisfactions from durable goods owned and used by the taxpayer, or from goods and services out of personal exertions of the taxpayer on his own behalf."[4] But this description is underinclusive: it omits imputed income from the taxpayer's leisure. That is, a taxpayer has forgone income if she uses her home or other durables herself rather than renting them out, if she performs services for herself (like a lawyer writing her own will) rather than for paying customers, or if she consumes her time in recreation or contemplation rather than working longer hours.

However, the debate between this chapter and Chapter 4—mirroring the debate in tax circles generally—centers on imputed rental income from owner-occupied residences. Theoretical consistency would suggest that the tax system should treat alike all types of imputed income, taxing all or taxing none. But consistency would have to border on zealotry before one would insist on universal taxation of imputed income regardless of type. Decisions as to leisure, self-performed services, and consumer durables of every stripe are so numerous, ubiquitous, and various that universal imputation would intrude severely on personal privacy and would fling open a Pandora's box of bureaucratic complication. Accordingly, very few advocate taxing imputed income from leisure or self-performed services, and only a minority advocate taxing imputed income from consumer durables other than houses.[5]

---

3 Onrubia et al., *supra* note 2, at 226.

4 Donald B. Marsh, *The Taxation of Imputed Income*, 58 Pol. Sci. Q. 514, 514 (1943). For this purpose, "taxpayer" is taken "in a broad sense, including those who are grouped with the taxpayer proper as part of the underlying unit, e.g., his wife and dependents." *Id.* at 514 n.2. For examples of other kinds of imputed income from goods and services, see Onrubia et al., *supra* note 2, at 225–26.

5 *E.g.*, Goode, *supra* note 2, at 507 (consumer durables other than housing); Marsh, *supra* note 4, at 521 (leisure).

Public finance luminaries have proposed taxing imputed residential real property rents for generations.[6] However, as discussed below, such proposals have been rejected in the United States and have gained only limited purchase in other countries.

Three recent events and trends have coalesced to spark renewed interest in the idea of taxing imputed income from owner-occupied housing. First, concerns about the extent to which tax policies contributed to the U.S. housing bubble—and thus the 2008–2012 financial crisis—prompted reconsideration of those policies.[7] Second, pervasive budget deficits have spawned renewed interest in curbing tax expenditures.[8] Third, because capital is now more globally mobile than labor, international tax competition has been driving down taxation of capital relative to taxation of labor.[9] Against this trend, "housing taxation is holding the spotlight as one of the few practicable ways of raising tax revenues while lowering the tax wedge on labour income."[10]

United States

The United States has long afforded favorable tax treatment to residential real estate. The four major current benefits to homeowners are the exclusion of imputed rental income, the deductibility of interest on home mortgages,[11] the deductibility of real property taxes,[12] and the exclusion of gain from the sale of principal residences.[13] These are "big ticket" items. Estimates of their cost vary, but the U.S. Office of Management and Budget assesses their cost as approximately $51 billion, $187 billion, $16 billion, and $16 billion, respectively.[14]

---

6 *E.g.*, William Vickery, Agenda for Progressive Taxation 19–22 (1947); Richard A. Musgrave, *In Defense of an Income Concept*, 81 Harv. L. Rev. 44, 56 (1967); Joseph A. Pechman, *What Would a Comprehensive Individual Income Tax Yield?*, *in* 1 H. Comm. on Ways & Means, 86th Cong., Tax Revision Compendium: Compendium of Papers on Broadening the Tax Base 251, 261–62 (Comm. Print 1959).

7 *E.g.*, Edward Glaeser, *Housing Policy in the Wake of the Crash*, 139 Daedalus 95 (2010). *See generally* Katie Jones et al., Cong. Research Serv., R43367, Housing Issues in the 113th Congress (2014); Benjamin H. Harris et al., *New Perspectives on Homeownership Tax Incentives*, 141 Tax Notes 1315 (2013); Lily Kahng, *Path Dependence in Tax Subsidies for Home Sales*, 65 Ala. L. Rev. 187 (2013).

8 The U.S. Department of the Treasury considers nontaxation of imputed rents to be a tax expenditure. Office of Mgmt. & Budget, Exec. Office of the President, Analytical Perspectives: Fiscal Year 2013 Budget of the U.S. Government, at 250 (2012). Deeming the exclusion to be warranted by administrative necessity, the Joint Committee on Taxation does not consider the exclusion to be a tax expenditure, nor does the Congressional Budget Office. Staff of J. Comm. on Taxation, 112th Cong., Estimates of Federal Tax Expenditures for Fiscal Years 2011–2015, at 6 (Comm. Print 2012); Steven C. Bourassa & William G. Grigsby, *Income Tax Concessions for Owner-Occupied Housing*, 11 Housing Pol'y Debate 521, 522 n.2 (2000).

9 Reuven Avi-Yonah, *Globalization, Tax Competition, and the Fiscal Crisis of the Welfare State*, 113 Harv. L. Rev. 1573, 1577–78 (2000); Henry Ordower, *Utopian Visions Toward a Grand Unified Global Income Tax*, 14 Fla. Tax Rev. 361, 365 (2013).

10 Francesco Figari et al., *Taxing Home Ownership: Distributional Effects of Including Net Imputed Rent in Taxable Income* 3 (IZA Discussion Paper Series, Discussion Paper No. 6493, 2012), *available at* http://ftp.iza.org/dp6493.pdf.

11 I.R.C. § 163(a), (h)(2)(D), (h)(3)–(4).

12 *Id.* § 164(a)(1), (c)(1).

13 *Id.* § 121. For discussion of Code § 121 and other tax benefits for home sales, see Kahng, *supra* note 7.

14 Office of Mgmt. & Budget, *supra* note 8, at 250.

Several less expensive provisions also favor homeowners. These provisions include the exclusion of interest on bonds for owner-occupied housing,[15] the tax credit for mortgage credit certificates,[16] the exemption from an additional tax for qualified first-time homebuyer distributions from individual retirement plans,[17] the exclusion of the rental value of parsonages[18] and military housing allowances, the exclusion of discharge of indebtedness income from qualified principal residence indebtedness,[19] and the deductions available to tenant stockholders of cooperative housing corporations.[20] In addition, responding to the sharp 2008–2012 recession, both federal and state governments enacted a variety of ad hoc tax relief measures for housing, including temporary homebuyer tax credits.[21]

Why do these provisions exist? The well-funded political action committees of the real estate industry may have something to do with it, but policy reasons also have been advanced (whether sincerely or pretextually). They include (1) the hope that tax subsidies encourage homeownership, a highly valued priority; (2) the fear that removing the incentives would cause home values to drop sharply; and (3) suspicion that elimination of the provisions might increase rather than reduce distortions caused by the tax laws.[22]

Federal tax law also has provisions favorable to renters, although they are not of the same magnitude as the provisions favoring homeowners. The pro-renter provisions include: (1) the low-income housing credit;[23] (2) the rehabilitation credit;[24] (3) the exclusion of interest on state or local qualified private activity bonds for rental housing;[25] (4) accelerated depreciation for rental housing;[26] and (5) exceptions from the passive activity loss disallowance rules for rental real estate activities.[27]

The United States has never taxed imputed rental income even though subnational experimentation has occurred.[28] The Union's Civil War income tax expressly excluded "the rental value of any homestead used or occupied" by the taxpayer.[29]

No such express exclusion exists in the current Code. The existence of the current exclusion has been described variously as "a matter of administrative practice, but no less firmly established for

15 I.R.C. § 143.

16 *Id.* § 25.

17 *Id.* § 72(t).

18 *Id.* § 107. In late 2013, a federal district court invalidated part of Code § 107, but that decision was vacated on appeal for lack of standing. Freedom from Religion Found., Inc. v. Lew, 983 F. Supp. 2d 1051 (W.D. Wis. 2013), *vacated*, 114 A.F.T.R.2d 2014-6570 (7th Cir. 2014).

19 I.R.C. §§ 108(a)(1)(E), 1017(b)(2).

20 *Id.* § 216. For a discussion of these tax benefits, see Staff of J. Comm. on Taxation, 113th Cong., Present Law, Data, and Analysis Relating to Tax Incentives for Residential Real Estate 2–14 (Comm. Print 2013).

21 *See* Karen Dynan et al., Brookings Inst., An Evaluation of Federal and State Homebuyer Tax Incentives (2013).

22 *See, e.g.*, Bourassa & Grigsby, *supra* note 8, at 524 (citing studies).

23 I.R.C. § 42.

24 *Id.* § 47.

25 *Id.* § 142(d).

26 *E.g.*, *id.* § 168(e)(6)–(8).

27 *E.g.*, *id.* § 469(i). For discussion of the pro-renter provisions, see Staff of J. Comm. on Taxation, *supra* note 20, at 15–23.

28 During the heyday of populism, Wisconsin included estimated rental value of owner-occupied residences in its state income tax base—from 1911 to 1917. *See* State v. Frear, 134 N.W. 673, 693 (1912) (upholding the constitutionality of this provision).

29 Act of June 30, 1864, ch. 173, § 117, 13 Stat. 223, 281.

that reason";[30] as "an implicit understanding that these benefits are not subject to the income tax";[31] or as established by case law.[32] Regardless of which foundation it rests on, the exclusion is firmly anchored in American tax law.

Other Countries

The clear majority of other countries have taken the same tack as the United States; that is, they have excluded imputed rental values from gross income. Moreover, some countries that once included such values in the income tax base have abandoned the effort, in name or in fact. However, as seen below, identifying precisely which countries fall on which list can be difficult. Many tabulations or assertions have been made of how many countries tax imputed income, and they do not always agree.

The high-water mark among the studies was reported in Paul Merz's 1977 article, which found that over one-third of the national tax systems then in existence (42 out of 115) taxed imputed income from owner-occupied housing.[33] However, there were two major caveats. First, at the time of Merz's writing, "[m]any of [the countries on the list were] small and at an earlier stage of economic development."[34] Accordingly, "there [was] little published or otherwise readily available information on the experiences of most of the countries" on the list, which necessitated reliance on comments from knowledgeable individuals.[35]

Second, "the majority of the countries [on the list] were either affiliated with Britain, retain[ed] some affiliation, or ha[d] personal income taxes similar to the British income tax model."[36] Britain ceased taxing imputed rental values in 1963.[37] Presumably, many or most of the British-inspired countries subsequently abandoned imputation either by actually repealing their provisions or by ceasing to enforce them.

A 2010 article drawing on work done in the 1980s and 1990s found that 10 OECD countries "tax at least some imputed income."[38] In contrast, a 1990 report listed only seven—Denmark, Finland, Greece, Luxembourg, the Netherlands, Spain, and Sweden[39]—while a 2005 article stated that the enterprise had been abandoned in all but Belgium and the Netherlands.[40]

The different results reflect both timing and design differences. Because of low rates, generous exclusions, and liberal valuation rules, some countries' regimes are so porous that imputation under

30 J. Martin Burke & Michael K. Friel, Taxation of Individual Income 28 (10th ed. 2012). Other tax exclusions by administrative practice also exist, such as the general welfare exception. *See, e.g.*, William D. Popkin, Introduction to Taxation 59–60 (5th ed. 2008).

31 Chancellor, *supra* note 1, at 567 n.281 (further adding that, "[i]n this, it is similar to other implicit exclusions (e.g., a gift of appreciated property is not a recognized event)").

32 Helvering v. Indep. Life Ins. Co., 292 U.S. 371, 379 (1934); Morris v. Comm'r, 9 B.T.A. 1273, 1278 (1928), *acq.*, VII-2 C.B. 2 (1928).

33 Paul E. Merz, *Foreign Income Tax Treatment of the Imputed Rental Value of Owner-Occupied Housing: Synopsis and Commentary*, 30 Nat'l Tax J. 435, 435–37 (1977).

34 *Id.* at 438.

35 *Id.* at 435.

36 *Id.*

37 *See generally* G.S.A. Wheatcroft, *The Death of Schedule A*, 1963 British Tax Rev. 223.

38 Bourassa & Grigsby, *supra* note 8, at 525.

39 Gavin A. Wood, *The Tax Treatment of Housing: Economic Issues and Reform Measures*, 27 Urban Stud. 809, 811 (1990). *Cf.* Bourassa & Grigsby, *supra* note 8, at 525 (adding Switzerland, Belgium, and Italy).

40 Paul van den Noord, *Tax Incentives and House Price Volatility in the Euro Area: Theory and Evidence*, 101 Economie internationale 29, 36 (2005) (Fr.).

them is more nominal than real,[41] leading to reasonable differences as to inclusion or omission of particular countries from the tabulation.

In addition to such backdoor "repeals by insignificance," many countries that once attempted to tax imputed residential housing income have formally repealed their regimes, typically because of administrability and other policy concerns. Australia, perhaps the first country to tax such imputed income, did so only between 1915 and 1923. Britain ceased taxing such income in 1963, as did France in 1965 and West Germany in 1987.[42] Some other countries decided after study to eschew income taxation from this source.[43]

As noted above, most economists endorse the desirability of taxing imputed rental values from owner-occupied residences (or would do so if administrability concerns could be overcome). But most countries have chosen not to go down this path or have retraced their steps. This raises the question: Where does the presumption lie, with theory or with history?[44]

Is it Income?

Early attempts to define "income" were largely the province of economists.[45] Work done from the 1890s through the 1940s by Georg von Schanz, Robert M. Haig, and Henry C. Simons came to be melded into what has become "a gold standard of income tax theory and public discussion."[46] After some flirtation with defining income in terms of the flow of satisfactions, they and those following them came to see income as the sum of the taxpayer's consumption and the increase in her wealth over a given period.

In those terms, there are grounds for seeing imputed rental value as income. "Imputed rent enhances homeowners' consumption ability because they benefit from housing services they would otherwise need to pay for, depleting cash resources."[47] Housing represents a flow of satisfaction—the value thereof is measurable, and the use of the property is in the nature of consumption. The owner's choice to occupy the home rather than rent it out suggests that the value of the occupancy to her at least equals the forgone rent.[48] Alternatively, the owner-occupied home can be seen as an investment yielding an implicit rate of return. The homeowner could have chosen instead to

41 *See* Hugh J. Ault & Brian J. Arnold, Comparative Income Taxation: A Structural Analysis 181–83 (2d ed. 2004); Figari et al., *supra* note 10, at 9; Onrubia et al., *supra* note 2, at 225.

42 *See, e.g.*, Merz, *supra* note 33, at 438; Wood, *supra* note 39, at 811 (also listing Ireland as a country abandoning imputation); Judith Yates, *Imputed Rent and Income Distribution*, 40 Rev. Income & Wealth 43, 49–50 & n.9 (1994). The principal reasons for such abandonment are practical, involving serious administrative obstacles.

43 Such as Canada. *See* 3 Report of the Royal Commission on Taxation 41, 56 (1966) (popularly known as, and hereinafter, the Carter Report).

44 *See* Bourassa & Grigsby, *supra* note 8, at 524 ("an old tax concession is a good tax concession, unless the arguments for eliminating it are especially compelling").

45 *See, e.g.*, Chancellor, *supra* note 1, at 575–78 (discussing the contributions of Adam Smith, Thomas Hobbes, Irving Fisher, and Nicholas Kaldor, among others).

46 Joseph M. Dodge, *Deconstructing the Haig-Simons Income Tax and Reconstructing It as Objective Ability-to-Pay "Cash Income" Tax* 1 (Fla. State Univ. Coll. of Law, Pub. Law Research Paper No. 633, 2013), *available at* http://ssrn.com/abstract=2245818; *see also* George Cooper, *The Taming of the Shrewd: Identifying and Controlling Income Tax Avoidance*, 85 Colum. L. Rev. 657, 660–62 (1985) (describing the three phases or "waves" of influence of Schanz-Haig-Simons in American tax policy discussion).

47 Figari et al., *supra* note 10, at 4.

48 Goode, *supra* note 2, at 504.

invest her capital in other assets. The investment in the home will be used up in consumption over the years.[49]

But just as "[t]he 14th Amendment does not enact Mr. Herbert Spencer's Social Statics,"[50] the Code does not enact the Schanz-Haig-Simons definition of income. "[A] neutral, scientific measure of taxable income is a mirage" because "the income tax structure cannot be discovered, but must be constructed; it is the final result of a multitude of debatable judgments."[51] The very name "income tax" is misleading. The U.S. federal income tax is a hybrid, embracing income tax and consumption tax principles in roughly equal measure.[52]

The U.S. Supreme Court has stated: "The rental value of the building used by the owner does not constitute income within the meaning of the Sixteenth Amendment."[53] Several arguments support such a view. First, imputed rent "is not a coming-in from the outside. The service is provided by the homeowner to herself. Intra-taxpayer transfers (moving economic value from one pocket to another) do not count in taxation."[54] Similarly, taxing imputed rents would traduce the "basic principles" that tax should be imposed on "what was actually done … as opposed to what *might* have been done" and that "self-help (or fortuitous) 'avoided cost' (such as reducing consumption …) are not income."[55]

Second, buying and using a house is consumption, not income. The funds used to make the purchase presumably already had been subject to tax. The tax system usually controls expenditures by disallowing deductions rather than through inclusions in income, and neither the initial purchase price nor the subsequent imputed rents paid to oneself are deductible.[56]

Third, "single taxation of current and deferred consumption can legitimately be viewed as a core income tax principle," and the current system meets that principle. Buying a house entails deferred consumption because the price of the house reflects the present discounted value of future imputed rents. The current system treats deferred personal expenses and current personal expenses the same: "taxing" both only once by disallowing deduction of the expenses. Taxing imputed rents would break this equality of treatment by imposing a second level of tax on the deferred consumption of the housing.[57]

Fourth, taxing imputed rents ignores part of the housing transaction. People buy houses in part to live in them (deferred consumption) but also in part to sell later at a higher price (investment). Indeed, "[f]or many people their home is their largest investment. Taxation based on full fair market value would be equivalent to taxing unrealized appreciation due to the investment rather

49 Chancellor, *supra* note 1, at 602.

50 Lochner v. New York, 198 U.S. 45, 75 (1905) (Holmes, J., dissenting).

51 Boris I. Bittker, *A Comprehensive Tax Base as a Goal of Income Tax Reform*, 80 Harv. L. Rev. 925, 925, 985 (1967).

52 *E.g.*, William D. Andrews, *A Consumption-Type or Cash Flow Personal Income Tax*, 87 Harv. L. Rev. 1113, 1117 (1974); Don Fullerton, *The Consumption Tax: An Idea Whose Time Has Come?*, 27 Tax Notes 435, 438 (1985).

53 Helvering v. Indep. Life Ins. Co., 292 U.S. 371, 379 (1934); *see also* Morris v. Comm'r, 9 B.T.A. 1273, 1278 (1928) ("the rental value of a private residence … has never been regarded as income"), *acq.*, VII-2 C.B. 2 (1928).

54 Dodge, *supra* note 46, at 10.

55 Joseph M. Dodge et al., Federal Income Tax: Doctrine, Structure, and Policy 300 (4th ed. 2012).

56 Chancellor, *supra* note 1, at 562, 610; Dodge, *supra* note 46, at 2, 3, 9.

57 Dodge et al., *supra* note 55, at 298, 300.

than the consumption element of the home."[58] This would violate the realization requirement that is fundamental to income taxation in the United States.[59]

Fifth, imputed income from a house can be expressed as a percentage of the asset's value. From this standpoint, a tax on imputed income is a tax on the value of property and could be challenged as being a direct tax that is unconstitutional because of not being apportioned among the states in accordance with population.[60]

I offer the constitutional point for completeness but not as a matter of advocacy. In the *Pollock* case, the Supreme Court held unconstitutional the 1890s federal income tax, which led to the adoption of the Sixteenth Amendment on which the modern U.S. federal income tax is based.[61] The constitutional objection to taxing imputed residential real estate rents is consistent with *Pollock*,[62] but most doubt that the constitutional objection would prevail today. More modestly, this can be recast as a subconstitutional, prudential concern. "[A]ny tax on imputed income could be considered a tax on wealth, and vice versa. Except in the case of estate taxes, the federal government does not tax wealth, because that is a state and local prerogative in the present federal system."[63]

Arguments for Taxing Imputed Rents

Henry Ordower and others criticize the imputed rents exclusion on a number of grounds. I respond here to three of the main criticisms: (1) depletion of the federal fisc; (2) encouraging economically inefficient behavior; and (3) producing unfair outcomes. The discussion below finds that the force of these criticisms sometimes has been overstated.

Revenue

The U.S. Treasury Department estimates that the imputed rents exclusion depletes federal revenues by over $50 billion a year.[64] That can't be right. As discussed above, the trend has been toward eliminating or subverting imputed rental regimes in other countries. Countries usually do not abandon fiscally successful regimes.

---

58 Jerome Kurtz, *Comments*, *in* COMPREHENSIVE INCOME TAXATION 197, 201 (Joseph A. Pechman ed., 1977).

59 *E.g.*, Comm'r v. Glenshaw Glass Co., 348 U.S. 426, 431 (1955) (identifying realization as one of the three key attributes of items included in gross income).

60 DODGE ET AL., *supra* note 55, at 299. *See generally* Joseph M. Dodge, *What Federal Taxes Are Subject to the Rule of Apportionment Under the Constitution?*, 11 U. PA. J. CONST. L. 839 (2009).

61 Pollock v. Farmers' Loan & Trust Co., 157 U.S. 429, *aff'd on rehearing*, 158 U.S. 601 (1895). *See generally* Erik M. Jensen, *The Taxing Power, the Sixteenth Amendment, and the Meaning of "Incomes,"* 33 ARIZ. ST. L.J. 1057 (2001).

62 The initial *Pollock* opinion held that a tax on rents from real estate is a tax on the real estate itself and thus a direct tax, which rendered the tax unconstitutional because it was not apportioned among the states in proportion to their populations. *Pollock*, 157 U.S. at 580–81, 583; *see* U.S. CONST. art. I, § 9, cl. 4 (setting out the apportionment requirement).

63 Bourassa & Grigsby, *supra* note 8, at 528.

64 OFFICE OF MGMT. & BUDGET, *supra* note 8, at 250.

Indeed, "revenue yield tends to be low" in countries taxing imputed rents,[65] and that likely would be the experience in the United States as well. First, scoring needs to consider dynamic effects.[66] As described below, the economic effects of ending the exclusion are hard to predict. One possible outcome could be weakening the housing market. Thus, some economists suggest that revenue actually produced by taxing imputed rents would be less than predicted because of general equilibrium effects, including reduction of housing consumed by owner-occupants.[67]

Second, as described below, eliminating the exclusion would adversely affect elderly and lower-income homeowners. Thus, some countries partly or entirely exempt such groups from the taxation of imputed rents. The United States could do so too, but such measures "would blunt the efficiency gains and reduce tax revenues" from the change.[68]

Third, proposals to end the exclusion usually would allow homeowners to deduct mortgage interest, property taxes, depreciation, repairs, and other expenses. But in many cases, the deductions would exceed the imputed income, turning the change from a revenue winner into a revenue loser.[69]

Several characteristics of mortgage borrowing reinforce this prospect. One: "Generally, new homeowners have large mortgages and relatively little equity, making for large interest deductions and small imputed rents."[70] Two: "[E]specially when borrowing has been made at a high interest rate, [the prospect exists that] the imputed rent will be a negative figure."[71]

Three: "Even when homebuyers have other financial assets, they often take out mortgages for a higher percent of value due to the high visibility of the mortgage interest deduction, the greater ease of selling with a large mortgage, and the reluctance to liquidate other assets."[72] To the extent mortgages are kept high for such reasons, net imputed income (and thus revenue from taxing it) will be reduced.

Economic Efficiency

Some of the housing-friendly provisions in the Code—especially the deduction for mortgage interest—are justified (or rationalized) on the ground that they contribute to the socially desirable goal of promoting homeownership. I see the exclusion of imputed rents as resting mainly on other foundations.[73] Nonetheless, the effect on housing stock—whether intended or accidental—merits consideration.

---

65 Merz, *supra* note 33, at 435 (reporting that, in other countries, taxation of imputed rents produces "negligible amounts of revenue relative to [other taxes] … and remain[s] a matter of great vexation to the tax authorities"); Wood, *supra* note 39, at 811.

66 As to dynamic scoring in tax generally, see Alan J. Auerbach, *Dynamic Scoring: An Introduction to the Issues*, 95 Am. Econ. Rev. 421 (2005); Patrick Driessen, *What Conditions Tax Distribution and Dynamic Scoring Are in*, 141 Tax Notes 425 (2013).

67 *E.g.*, James R. Follain et al., *The Preferential Income Tax Treatment of Owner-Occupied Housing: Who Really Benefits?*, 4 Housing Pol'y Debate 1 (1993).

68 Bourassa & Grigsby, *supra* note 8, at 528.

69 *E.g.*, Dodge et al., *supra* note 55, at 299; Kurtz, *supra* note 58, at 199.

70 William F. Hellmuth, *Homeowner Preferences*, *in* Comprehensive Income Taxation, *supra* note 58, at 163, 191.

71 Taxation Review Comm., Commonwealth of Austl., Full Report 67 (1975).

72 Hellmuth, *supra* note 70, at 190.

73 Such as conceptual concerns regarding whether imputed rents are "income" as understood for U.S. federal income tax purposes, *see supra* text accompanying notes 60–63, and practical concerns regarding whether taxing imputed rents is administratively feasible and democratically acceptable, *see* discussion *infra*.

Such consideration has two dimensions: the factual (does the exclusion actually cause more houses to be built?) and the normative (if it does, is such increase good or bad for the economy and society?). Both of these questions, to be addressed responsibly, would require analysis beyond the scope of this chapter, especially since reputable economists can be found on both sides of both dimensions. Accordingly, I will here record only some general observations.

As to the factual dimension, some studies have concluded that the exclusion does increase housing supply and homeownership. One U.S. study found that about one-quarter (that is, four percentage points) of the growth in the homeownership rate since World War II was due to the combined effect of the exclusion of imputed income and the deductions for mortgage interest and property taxes.[74] Another study concluded that the exclusion accounted for at least two percentage points of the rate of homeownership.[75]

Experience abroad also is pertinent. Switzerland has the lowest rate of homeownership in Western Europe. One study concluded that the fact that Switzerland taxes imputed rental income is one of the two principal causes of this phenomenon.[76] Australia ended imputation eight years after creating it, in part because it seemed to discourage homeownership.[77]

On the other hand, there is considerable evidence that housing tax breaks have been capitalized into housing prices.[78] As a result, the tax breaks have caused home prices to rise, and the higher prices discourage homeownership as much as tax benefits encourage them.[79]

As to the normative dimension, it may well be that too much of the wealth of the United States is concentrated in our housing stock, particularly single-family residences.[80] This is a plausible concern, but not an absolute one. Many issues in life reduce to the question "compared to what?" and this question is unanswered in this context. In other words, possible overconsumption of housing

> is a problem only to the extent that the spending diverted to housing would have contributed to the efficiency and productivity of the U.S. economy. If, instead, the spending would have been mainly on other luxuries, such as imported cars or international vacations, then the misallocation of resources to housing consumption and investment may not matter or may even be desirable.[81]

---

74 Harvey S. Rosen & Kenneth T. Rosen, *Federal Taxes and Homeownership: Evidence from Time Series*, 88 J. Pol. Econ. 59 (1980).

75 Kenneth T. Rosen, *The Mortgage Interest Tax Deduction and Homeownership* (Univ. of Cal., Ctr. for Real Estate & Urban Econ., Working Paper No. 89-159, 1989).

76 Steven C. Bourassa & Martin Hoesli, *Why Do the Swiss Rent?*, 40 J. Real Est. Fin. Econ. 286 (2010). Unsurprisingly, the other main cause is high housing prices caused in part by limited land suitable for building.

77 Barry F. Reece, *The Income Tax Incentive to Owner-Occupied Housing in Australia*, 51 Econ. Rec. 218 (1975).

78 *E.g.*, Tommy Berger et al., *The Capitalization of Interest Subsidies: Evidence from Sweden*, 32 J. Money Credit & Banking 199 (2000); Steven C. Bourassa et al., *Determinants of the Homeownership Rate: An International Perspective* 12 (Swiss Fin. Inst., Research Paper No. 11–49, 2013), *available at* http://ssrn.com/abstract=1953196.

79 *E.g.*, Taxation Review Comm., *supra* note 71, at 66; Bruce Bartlett, *The Sacrosanct Mortgage Interest Deduction*, N.Y. Times Economix (Aug. 6, 2013), http://economix.blogs.nytimes.com/2013/08/06/the-sacrosanct-mortgage-interest-deduction/.

80 Single family homes account for 94 percent of all owner-occupied housing. Hellmuth, *supra* note 70, at 190 (citing U.S. Bureau of the Census data).

81 Bourassa & Grigsby, *supra* note 8, at 537.

It might be the case that, in the long run, decreased consumption of single-family houses would be in the national interest, but, like going "cold turkey" on any addiction, the short-term consequences could be unpleasant.[82] Economic efficiency is certainly one piece of this puzzle, but where it fits and how large a piece it is are debatable.

Fairness

The exclusion of imputed rents from owner-occupied real estate often is said to discriminate in favor of homeowners (and against renters) and in favor of high-income (and against low-income) taxpayers. There is something to these charges, but less perhaps than may seem to be the case at first blush. The two charges are considered below, after which I note that ending the exclusion could create new inequities.

Owners versus Renters

At first glance, the discrimination seems obvious. But five considerations undercut the concern. First, for a variety of reasons, not all Americans are legally required to pay federal income tax. Some sources of income—such as gifts, unemployment compensation, Social Security, and welfare payments[83]—are partly or wholly excluded from taxation. Taxable receipts are offset by itemized deductions or the standard deduction as well as by personal exemptions.[84] And a variety of refundable and nonrefundable credits can reduce or eliminate income tax liability and sometimes can even produce a refund.[85] "[M]any renters do not pay income tax, so they cannot be said to be treated inequitably in the Internal Revenue Code with respect to households that do pay taxes."[86]

Second, when individuals and families are unrestricted in their choice between renting and owning, it cannot be said that they have been discriminated against when they choose to rent. Henry Ordower acknowledges this in Chapter 4. Of course, this is only a partial answer to the discrimination concern. For a variety of reasons—such as discriminatory practices, inability to amass the funds for a downpayment, or a shaky credit history—some do not have effective choice. But some who do have freedom of choice exercise it in favor of renting. Such people need not be protected against the "discriminatory" effects of their own freely made choices.[87]

Third, not just homeowners but renters too receive tax advantages.[88] Indirectly, renters benefit from tax breaks going to developers and landlords. For example, accelerated depreciation deductions for owners of, and investors in, rental complexes lead to creation of more rental housing, which in theory reduces the cost of such housing relative to prices of other consumer goods and services.[89] Tax benefits for owners do exceed those for renters, but a possible response

---

82 *See, e.g., id.* at 524 ("removing [the] tax concessions without causing a significant reduction in the market value of owner-occupied homes is thought to be difficult and problematic").

83 I.R.C. §§ 85(c), 86, 102; Rev. Rul. 57-102, 1957-1 C.B. 26.

84 I.R.C. §§ 63, 151.

85 *E.g., id.* §§ 21–32.

86 Bourassa & Grigsby, *supra* note 8, at 536.

87 I am an example. I always have rented and never have owned, and I hope to keep that record intact for the remainder of this incarnation. In my personal constellation of values, the psychological benefit of freedom of mobility far outweighs the psychological benefits of stability and the financial advantages of ownership.

88 *See supra* text accompanying notes 23–27.

89 Hellmuth, *supra* note 70, at 190; *see* I.R.C. § 168.

to disparate treatment could be to provide a federal deduction for renters rather than withdraw federal benefits for owners.[90]

Fourth, in a vast economy and a vastly complicated tax system, disparate effects are inevitable. Disparities that are troublesome are those that violate the principle of horizontal equity, which is the notion that similarly situated taxpayers should be treated similarly. But it is not clear that renters and homeowners should be seen as similarly situated for this purpose. For one thing, "a case can perhaps be made for treating homeownership specially favourably on the ground that widespread ownership is socially desirable and good housing benefits the whole community."[91] Perhaps more compellingly, owners and renters arguably are not similarly situated because their risks, rewards, and responsibilities differ. Numerous differences exist between owning and renting. Some—like the impermanence of a lease and the hazards of depending on another (i.e., the landlord)—favor owners. Others favor renters. Specifically:

> [t]he owner pays for future use in advance; the renter makes periodic payments. The owner has to attempt to cover costs of recovering his investment and maintaining the property; the renter does not. The owner bears higher transaction costs of disposing of the property than the renter does in allowing a lease to lapse. The owner bears the risk (both ways) of future changes in underlying value; the renter's downside risk (of non-habitable premises) is protected by landlord-tenant law, and there is little or no upside risk.[92]

Fifth, such discrimination as may exist in any one year often is mitigated over the life of the taxpayer. "[A] large percentage of current renters have been or will be owners at some point during their lifetime, so any tax inequity they now suffer as renters will be partially or fully offset by their favored position later when they are owners."[93]

Rich versus Poor

It is often observed that exclusions and deductions are more valuable to high-bracket than to low-bracket taxpayers. That is true, but it is not especially illuminating. It is an inevitable consequence of having progressive rates. If one believes that rates should be progressive, any allowed exclusions and deductions will be regressive.[94] Thus, to raise a substantial question, more than the above is needed. The "more" in our context is the idea that the affluent acquire owner-occupied housing at a higher rate than the nonaffluent.

Even so refined, however, this concern is not overwhelming. First, as noted above, there is a significant possibility that tax breaks have been capitalized into housing prices.[95] If the result of the

90 Some states provide income tax deductions for renters. *E.g.*, Ind. Code § 6-3-2-6 (2014).

91 Taxation Review Comm., *supra* note 71, at 66 (but questioning whether the exclusion is the best way to advance this policy); *see also* Figari et al., *supra* note 10, at 8.

92 Dodge, *supra* note 46, at 9 n.54.

93 Bourassa & Grigsby, *supra* note 8, at 536. This possibility has been enhanced by the growth of lower-cost ownership alternatives such as manufactured housing and condominiums.

94 Lawrence Zelenak, *Taking Critical Tax Theory Seriously*, 76 N.C. L. Rev. 1521, 1569 (1998).

95 *See supra* text accompanying notes 78–79. Some have addressed the question whether such capitalization has equal effects on different types of homeowners. *E.g.*, Dorothy A. Brown, *Tales from a Tax Crit*, 10 Pitt. Tax Rev. 47, 55–56 (2012); *see* Dorothy A. Brown, *Shades of the American Dream*, 87 Wash. U. L. Rev. 329 (2009) (offering proposals to cause the tax benefits of homeownership to be distributed more equitably among class and racial groups).

exclusion is that wealthier taxpayers just pay more for their homes, they have gained little.[96] Indeed, considering the capitalization effect, eliminating the exclusion could create its own inequity. It "might lead to some bona fide inequality for those who had bought heavily in housing … after the tax differential had been capitalized, that is to say, at high prices relative to imputed rental value."[97]

Second, and more importantly, this concern chases form at the expense of substance. Imputing rental income will make at best small inroads on economic inequality; in fact, it may make economic inequality worse. The rich live in more expensive houses, no doubt. But that does not always mean that they would have higher imputed incomes. A study of the United States, Britain, and Germany found that "[t]he income position of owner-occupiers who are still paying off mortgages is considerably higher than for those who own outright." Indeed, "[t]his result is very pronounced for the U.S., where outright owners appear to live on below-average income."[98] Imputed income proposals usually allow deduction of mortgage interest paid. To the extent the affluent carry bigger mortgages, incomes imputed to them will be lower.

In addition, "housing consumption rises less than proportionately with income."[99] Thus, numerous studies of both the United States and other countries show that both income inequality and poverty rates decline when imputed rents are included in the computation of incomes.[100] In addition, elderly households benefit from imputed income more than younger households.[101]

For these reasons, taxing imputed rents may or may not enhance progressivity. One study concluded that eliminating the exclusion and both the mortgage interest and property tax deductions would raise the average tax rate for all homeowners by 11 percent. For nonitemizers (who would be affected only by ending the exclusion), the increase would be only 4 percent while the increase for itemizers would be 12.8 percent. Although "[t]he absolute increase in the effective rate would be smaller in the lower income brackets … the relative increase would be larger in [the lower] brackets."[102]

Moreover, overall calculations of relative effects can be deceiving, depending on where one draws the line between the affluent and nonaffluent. Thus, in the view of one commentator, "taxing net imputed income from homes would actually undermine progressivity where it would count the

96 Marsh, *supra* note 4, at 534 ("It is often argued, with some justice, that old taxes are good taxes. It may also be urged, in the [imputed income] case, that old inequities are good inequities, because in fact inequity disappears over time due to the capitalization of differential tax advantages."). On the other hand, this is not exactly a ringing endorsement of the housing breaks. To the extent capitalization occurs, the real beneficiaries are real estate developers, agents, and banks—not everyone's image of the most deserving beneficiaries of federal largesse.

97 *Id.* at 535.

98 Joachim R. Frick & Markus M. Grabka, *Imputed Rent and Income Inequality: A Decomposition Analysis for Great Britain, West Germany and the U.S.*, 49 Rev. Income & Wealth 513, 525 (2003); *see also* Benjamin H. Harris & Amanda Eng, *The Benefits of Mortgage Interest and Property Tax Deductions*, 140 Tax Notes 947 (2013) ("Older homeowners, especially those with relatively low income … carry less mortgage debt."). *See supra* text accompanying notes 70–72.

99 Donald L. Lerman & Robert I. Lerman, *Imputed Income from Owner-Occupied Housing and Income Inequality*, 23 Urban Stud. 323, 325 (1986).

100 *E.g.*, Timothy M. Smeeding et al., *Poverty, Inequality, and Family Living Standards Impacts Across Seven Nations: The Effect of Noncash Subsidies for Health, Education, and Housing*, 39 Rev. Income & Wealth 229, 246 (1993); *see also* Figari et al., *supra* note 10, at 3–4.

101 *E.g.*, Thesia I. Garner & Kathleen Short, *Accounting for Owner-Occupied Dwelling Services: Aggregates and Distributions*, 18 J. Housing Econ. 233, 247 (2009); Yates, *supra* note 42, at 55.

102 Hellmuth, *supra* note 70, at 184.

most, as it would disproportionately burden the middle class, for which home ownership constitutes a principal vehicle for 'investment,' relative to the very wealthy."[103]

Further, because imputed rent produces no cash, even a finding of enhanced progressivity would "not imply anything about ability to pay."[104] The truly wealthy could afford to pay extra tax as a result of imputed income. Homeowners of modest means often could not, without suffering hardships. A study offered these examples:

> In times of high interest rates, annual imputed rent on a house with a capital value of $40,000 may amount to $4,000. If this is added to a retired persons investment income of, say, $6,000 and the total amount of $10,000 is taxed, hardship may result … One could visualize similar difficulties arising for other classes of taxpayers: for example, a widow with young children may have been left the family home, now freed of mortgage by the proceeds of an insurance policy taken out by her husband, but she may have only modest cash income and few other assets.[105]

It is possible to design features that mitigate the effect of imputation on the aged, the poor, and the middle class. But careful attention would have to be paid to such issues. Moreover, enactment of any such features would add to the complexity of the tax system and would diminish its benefits. As one commentator observed, "[p]erfunctory taxation of imputed rental income will not produce equity, efficiency, or meaningful revenue in the tax system."[106]

Other Fairness Effects

We have seen that differential effects on renters versus owners and on affluent versus other taxpayers are not as powerful arguments against the exclusion as might at first appear. As described below, ending the exclusion would also create new inequities of its own.

First, implementation of the new tax would entail design choices. Inevitably, there would be imprecisions, with resultant inequities. For instance, one possible approach would be to impute a net rate of return on only the equity in the home. But that would be inaccurate because it would disregard differences in rates of mortgage interest paid by different homeowners and differences in expenses for repairs, maintenance, and other items paid by different homeowners. Simplicity would have been purchased at the price of ignoring relevant differences. The approach would often be arbitrary, inequitable, and unjust.[107] Alternative approaches would breed their own inequities, as described below.

Second, no matter how well-designed the system, it would have to be effectively enforced. One advocate of imputation noted: "In accordance with the American tradition of self-assessment … the procedure for including imputed net rent in taxable income would probably begin with the taxpayer's estimate of gross rental value and allowable costs … Unless the taxpayers' estimates

---

103 Dodge, *supra* note 46, at 9.

104 Bourassa & Grigsby, *supra* note 8, at 528 n.16.

105 Taxation Review Comm., *supra* note 71, at 67; *see also* Andrews, *supra* note 52, at 1157–58 (indicating that "we may feel we do not want our income tax to impair" the ability of "older people to live in houses that are more expensive than they could afford to move into now").

106 Merz, *supra* note 33, at 438.

107 *See* Kurtz, *supra* note 58, at 200.

were subject to careful review and equalization, serious inequities would no doubt arise."[108] Given current IRS audit rates and resources, such careful review is far from assured.[109]

Third, as discussed above, imputed rents on owner-occupied residences are only one type of imputed income, but, because of administrative difficulties, it typically is the only type theorists are willing seriously to propose should be subjected to tax.[110] But "people invest large sums in antiques, art, and collections of various kinds. To exclude the imputed income from such assets—while including the imputed income from consumption assets owned through the scale of incomes—may not improve equity."[111]

Nor, one may add, will it necessarily improve economic efficiency. Taxpayers are now supposed to overinvest in houses because of the exclusion of imputed income. If this theory holds, elimination of the exclusion for imputed income from housing—but not for imputed income from other assets—presumably would cause capital to flow from houses to such other assets. Economic inefficiency would not be ended, merely shifted.

Administrative Objections

Practicality is unglamorous, but it has an important role to play. Unclipped, the wings of fancy often carry us to unpleasant destinations.

For over a century, the Supreme Court has reminded us that "[t]axation is eminently practical."[112] More recently, in a constitutional context, Chief Justice Roberts observed: "To an economist, perhaps, there is no difference between activity and inactivity … . But the distinction … would not have been lost on the Framers who … were not mere visionaries, toying with speculations or theories, but practical men, dealing with the facts of political life."[113]

The same is, or should be, true for the men and women who craft our tax laws. Three of Adam Smith's four maxims as to taxation and two of Henry George's four principles involve practicality.[114] Joseph Sneed, a professor and later federal circuit court judge, saw practicality as one of the seven pervasive purposes shaping federal income tax rates and structure.[115] He accorded practicality and equity the two highest positions among seven macrocriteria of taxation, and he ventured: "Of the two, Practicality frequently must be granted more weight than Equity."[116]

That priority should, I believe, control as to our issue. Henry Ordower forcefully argues in Chapter 4 that the failure to tax imputed residential real estate rents is unfair in several dimensions. He is right to a significant degree (although, as maintained above, perhaps to a somewhat lesser degree than might at first appear). However, the practicality objections to the proposal outweigh the equity and other arguments in favor of it. In writing provisions of the Code, Congress has often

108 Goode, *supra* note 2, at 521.

109 *See infra* text accompanying notes 150–56.

110 *See supra* text accompanying notes 4–5.

111 Kurtz, *supra* note 58, at 198.

112 Nicol v. Ames, 173 U.S. 509, 516 (1899); *cf.* United States v. Midwest Oil Co., 236 U.S. 459, 472 (1915) ("government is a practical affair, intended for practical [people]").

113 Nat'l Fed'n of Indep. Bus. v. Sebelius, 132 S. Ct. 2566, 2589 (2012) (punctuation and citations omitted).

114 Adam Smith, The Wealth of Nations 777–79 (Mod. Lib. 1937) (1776); Henry George, Progress and Poverty 414–18 (4th ed. 1929).

115 Joseph T. Sneed, *The Criteria of Federal Income Tax Policy*, 17 Stan. L. Rev. 567, 601–02 (1965).

116 *Id.*

compromised equity, efficiency, and other goals in order to promote practicality.[117] That is also the right course in the area at issue in this debate.

The United States and a number of other countries compute imputed housing rental values and include them in macroeconomic calculations of national income and wealth distribution.[118] But wide is the gulf between macro and micro. The fact that imputed rental values can be estimated on aggregate bases does not mean that they can be feasibly ascertained for particular individuals and families nor that fair and administrable taxes can be levied on such values.[119]

I consider now the formidable practical challenges attending the attempt to administer taxation of imputed rents as to owner-occupied residences. I first give examples of the discouraging experiences of other countries. Then I explore the reasons for such disappointing results.

Experience

The historical record is hardly one of unblemished success as to experiments with taxing imputed income. A number of countries, initially ensorcelled by the siren song of theory or the lure of revenue, later abandoned imputation or so watered it down as to reduce it virtually to insignificance. Typically, they did so because of the cold realities of administration, "problems clustering around enforcement, compliance, income measurement, invasion of privacy, and taxpayer liquidity."[120]

Australia abandoned the attempt to tax imputed rents in 1923. A half century later, a comprehensive study of Australia's tax system recommended that the enterprise not be exhumed. The study "recognize[d] the arguments for including imputed rent in the tax base; but having regard especially to the administrative difficulties it [was] not prepared to recommend a change in the law to this end."[121]

The United Kingdom, France, and West Germany followed suit, discarding taxation of imputed rents in 1963, 1965, and 1987, respectively, "because of difficulties in applying the tax on a realistic basis."[122] West Germany, for instance, based rental value "on either the assessed value of the real estate, which was seldom an accurate measure of the market value, or on comparable rentals which also presented some valuation problems."[123] Repeal in the United Kingdom also was based on the difficulty of accurately, fairly, and consistently valuing properties.[124]

Tax on imputed values is retained principally by countries much smaller than the United States in area and population and which are characterized by less geographic variation and workforce mobility. But practicability problems can be significant even in such countries. Sweden is a case in point. Because of valuation difficulties, the attempt to use fair market value gave way to a system using standardized amounts. Cooperative apartment houses (common in Sweden) were subjected

117 Among numerous possible examples, see I.R.C. §§ 63(c), 102(e), and 152(e). *See also* Steve R. Johnson, *The E.L. Wiegand Lecture: Administrability-Based Tax Simplification*, 4 Nev. L.J. 573, 582–84 (2004) (arguing that conceptual purity should yield to practicality even more often).

118 This is part of a long-term, multilateral effort to improve the coherence of macro and micro statistics and to facilitate transnational comparisons. *See, e.g.*, Peter Saunders & Peter Siminski, *Home Ownership and Inequality: Imputed Rent and Income Distribution in Australia*, 24 Econ. Papers 346 (2005); Yates, *supra* note 42.

119 *E.g.*, Hellmuth, *supra* note 70, at 170. *See generally* Garner & Short, *supra* note 101.

120 Dodge et al., *supra* note 55, at 299.

121 Taxation Review Comm., *supra* note 71, at 68.

122 Ault & Arnold, *supra* note 41, at 181.

123 *Id.*

124 *Id.* at 182.

to lower taxation than owner-occupied houses. Nonetheless, the system remained contentious, especially in areas with rapidly rising housing prices but low-income owners. This led to caps on the taxes and reduced rates of tax, all of which produced complexity, lack of uniformity, and reduced revenue.[125] The experience in Finland generally parallels that in Sweden: below-market valuations, substantial deductions and expenses, and limited effect.[126]

Similarly, in Italy and Belgium available deductions almost entirely offset imputed income. In the Netherlands, only a small fraction of residential market value enters taxable income. In Greece, "only part of the imputed rent of larger dwellings is taxed [thus affecting] relatively few households."[127]

Reasons

We explore here four categories of administrability concerns: definition, valuation, reporting, and enforcement. By themselves, individual concerns may be controllable—although often at the cost of complexity or unfairness. Taken together, though, the concerns are daunting.

Definition

Definition is the least problematic of the four categories. Nonetheless, careful attention would have to be paid to specification of the imputed income base.[128] Former U.S. Commissioner of Internal Revenue Jerome Kurtz identified some of the definitional issues. The most fundamental question "is that of defining a home, and that will involve difficult problems of drawing a line."[129] As examples:

- Farmers are a powerful political bloc. How would we treat farmers and ranchers who live on self-owned farms and ranches producing very small income compared to the values of the property? "Presumably they tolerate low rates of return on their assets because they like to live on a farm or a ranch. [Arguably] additional income should be imputed to them for living on the farm rather than elsewhere."[130]
- "Mobile homes should clearly be included [in the imputed income tax base]; if so, campers, houseboats, and recreational land cannot be excluded. If a summer home is included, why not a hunting preserve?"[131]
- Would long-term leases be treated as functionally equivalent to ownership? The Code's like-kind exchange rules treat 30-year leaseholds as equivalent to fee simple ownership.[132] Even a shorter lease term may count. Commissioner Kurtz gives the example of a taxpayer who leases a house for 10 years at a flat rental. Does this taxpayer "have imputed income

125 *Id.* at 182–83.

126 Wood, *supra* note 39, at 811.

127 Figari et al., *supra* note 10, at 9.

128 Kurtz, *supra* note 58, at 198 (definitional issues "may appear to be fringe matters, but in this area the fringes are important").

129 *Id.*

130 *Id.*

131 *Id.*

132 Treas. Reg. § 1.1031(a)-1(c); *see also* Rev. Rul. 78-72, 1978-1 C.B. 258.

if, toward the end of the lease term, the current rental value is higher than that which he committed himself to pay in the beginning?"[133]

- "How should living in rent-controlled housing be treated? They may be the beneficiaries of as much imputed income by reason of governmental controls as those who own their own homes."[134]

Clarifying what constitutes owner-occupied housing would not be the end of the definitional effort. One would then need to ask questions like: Should any items that clearly are conceptually part of the base be excluded on equity, efficiency, or other grounds? If not wholly excluded, should any categories be granted a preferential valuation or rate rule? And what, if any, deductions should be allowed? As discussed above, such questions have proved thorny in other countries.

Valuation

As noted by a major Australian report, there are two principal alternatives for calculating the amount to be taxed under an imputed income regime:

- The first way involves the determination of the gross rental value of the home. From this repairs, depreciation, and [state and local taxes] are deducted to arrive at a figure representing net rental value. A further deduction of interest on money borrowed and invested in the home is then made in order to establish the net rental of the owner's equity. This is the amount subject to tax.
- The second way avoids some of the complexities of the first, though, in the result, it involves elements of arbitrariness. A percentage of the capital value of the home is assumed to be the net rental value. Interest on money borrowed is then deducted and the residual is the amount subject to tax.[135]

A 2012 congressional report describes the same two alternatives. It finds the first alternative to be the more precise, "but [that alternative] is difficult to implement because it requires estimates of rental values for homes, complex recordkeeping by homeowners, and additional monitoring responsibilities for the Internal Revenue Service."[136]

The report notes that the second alternative "requires less recordkeeping but would still require the IRS to take on more administrative responsibilities, such as verifying whether taxpayers owned or rented the home in which they reside and what they reported as house values." In addition, the second approach would be more challenging than verifying the current law deduction for

---

133 Kurtz, *supra* note 58, at 199.

134 *Id.*

135 Taxation Review Comm., *supra* note 71, at 67.

136 Larry Ozanne, *Taxation of Owner-Occupied and Rental Housing* 28 (Cong. Budget Office Working Paper Series, Working Paper No. 2012-14, 2012). Other approaches also are possible, including ones with elective aspects. An approach recommended 40 years ago failed to catch fire. Under it: (1) the taxpayer would report a value for her home on her return (subject to the possibility of IRS review); (2) the IRS would create regional guideline rates, either gross or net (or both); (3) the taxpayer would apply the rate to the reported value to compute the annual rate; and (4) if gross basis were chosen, deductions for interest and taxes would be allowed. Comm'n to Revise the Tax Structure, Reforming the Federal Tax Structure 39 (1973).

mortgage interest because all filers—including those who do not currently itemize or who do not have mortgages on their homes—would be affected."[137]

Depending on which of the two alternatives were chosen, the following would be among the valuation-related challenges: First, there is no fully satisfactory candidate for measuring the value of the house. The initial purchase price "is a less acceptable proxy for use value in the case of very longlife items like housing, because tax rates may change and property may go up or down in value for reasons not anticipated at the time of purchase."[138] Assessed values for local property taxes usually are below-market values, often substantially so.[139] Moreover, assessment practices are notoriously variable, thus imperiling horizontal equity on a national basis. And the problem remains widespread despite improved procedures in some jurisdictions: "In many communities, real estate assessment practices are so poor that the taxes homeowners pay do not accurately reflect the value of their properties."[140]

Second, to move from gross value to net value, various deductions typically are allowed, but they would entail their own complications. Current depreciation rules are more complicated than many homeowners could readily navigate. Moreover,

> [t]he problems of estimating the cost of repairs and maintenance boggle the mind. It is an extraordinarily difficult problem in business just to distinguish between repairs and capital additions. In addition, in an owner-occupied home, it would be necessary to distinguish between normal repairs and repairs that are incurred solely because the property is a home. One may paint every two years rather than every four. One may keep the property in a condition that would be uneconomical if one were renting the property. Such excess maintenance is really current consumption rather than repairs that are related to the imputed rent. Separating these items seems impossible.[141]

Third, instead of trying to measure the value of a house, the system could attempt to estimate potential rent. Since the houses in question are not being rented, however, this effort would not have the benefit of being directly referable to market transactions. The system would thus be forced to search for comparables, but this too would be problematic. Rents are affected by duration. Is imputation to be based on one-year leases (because of the length of a tax year) even though homeownership is of indefinite duration? More significantly, the more expensive the house, the more unique it is. In many areas, "there is no active single-family rental market in the middle and upper price ranges that could provide comparative data on prices and rents."[142] Most importantly,

> both current and long-term net rates of real return vary substantially from one property to another, depending on location and time of purchase. This variation makes it grossly inaccurate to apply a

---

137 Ozanne, *supra* note 136, at 28–29.

138 Andrews, *supra* note 52, at 1157; *see also* Goode, *supra* note 2, at 522 (deeming use of the original cost minus current mortgage debt as the owner's equity to be "seriously objectionable").

139 Figari et al., *supra* note 10, at 8; Wood, *supra* note 39, at 811.

140 Bourassa & Grigsby, *supra* note 8, at 538; *see also id.* at 529 ("The large number of local property-tax jurisdictions in the United States, with their wide range of valuation standards and methods, makes it extremely difficult and expensive to develop a common basis for assessment across jurisdictions.").

141 Kurtz, *supra* note 58, at 200.

142 Bourassa & Grigsby, *supra* note 8, at 528 n.14.

> single imputed rate of return across all properties ... To assume a constant rate of net rental returns across properties would ignore the wide disparity in rates of appreciation or depreciation.[143]

The inequities would be even worse were taxation to reflect some nonhousing actual or assumed rate of return, such as bank account interest rates, government securities rates, or the like. The theory would be that, by "investing" in the house rather than in alternative vehicles, the homeowner evinces her expectation that the rate of return on the housing will at least equal the forgone rate of return on alternative investments. This might work were we all the *homo economicus* posited by law-and-economics pundits. But real human beings tend to view their homes through rather different lenses.

Reporting

Some homeowners—especially the aged and those with relatively low incomes—do not itemize;[144] indeed, some are not required to file federal income tax returns at all. But, unless exemptions were crafted into the system, all homeowners would have imputed rental income and, depending on the alternative chosen, might have to compute the associated deductions for interest, repairs, taxes, and other expenses.[145]

This would have several unwelcome effects on taxpayers. Some who now do not have to file returns would have to. Others would have to wrestle with much more complicated returns than they normally would. Michael Graetz has advanced an interesting tax reform proposal to replace the income tax with a consumption tax for most Americans, thereby eliminating 100 million unnecessary income tax returns.[146] Taxing imputed rental incomes would march in the opposite direction, burdening taxpayers and the system with more returns than are already unnecessary under current law.

An additional complication is the fact that imputed rents would be a different kind of income, without the usual alarms to warn taxpayers of the need to deal with them. When a taxpayer receives wages, federal income tax is prepaid through withholding and the taxpayer receives a year-end Form W-2. When the taxpayer receives interest or dividends, she receives a Form 1099.

But, in the imputed rent situation, there would be no withholding, no Form W-2, and no Form 1099—let alone actual receipt of some item. In bilateral transactions, there is something to remind the taxpayer. In the unilateral, imputed-income situation, many taxpayers would be unaware until too late that they had to file estimated tax returns, report the imputed income on their Forms 1040,

143 *Id.* at 529; *see also* Hellmuth, *supra* note 70, at 172 ("Given the difficulties of obtaining comparable and accurate property tax valuations on residences within local assessing districts and under statewide equalization programs, the administration of an income tax including both imputed rent and annual changes in the net value of owner-occupied homes on a national basis seems impractical.").

144 Seventy-eight percent of households in the top income quintile itemize; 22 percent of middle-income households itemize; 1 percent of households in the bottom quintile itemize. Harris & Eng, *supra* note 98, at 947.

145 *See* Emil M. Sunley, Jr., *Summary of the Conference Discussion*, *in* COMPREHENSIVE INCOME TAXATION, *supra* note 58, at 261, 269 ("Businesses may be able to handle the complexities of income measurement; the average homeowner cannot, and he may have difficulty understanding why income is being imputed to him.").

146 Michael J. Graetz, *100 Million Unnecessary Returns: A Fresh Start for the U.S. Tax System*, 112 YALE L.J. 261 (2002).

and put aside enough money to satisfy the additional tax liability. The scenario is pregnant with possibilities of taxpayer surprise, frustration, anger, and hardship.[147]

The complications would involve the alternative minimum tax (AMT) as well as the regular income tax. Those homeowners with substantial imputed income would have higher alternative minimum taxable incomes, pushing some beyond the exemption amount and thus into taxation under the AMT.[148] The AMT already is notorious for its "traps of the unwary."[149] Taxing imputed rental incomes would create another such trap.

Enforcement

The IRS, as well as homeowners, would be substantially stressed by the attempt to administer imputed income taxation. As even a prominent early advocate of imputation acknowledged: "The estimation of imputed rent would involve the federal income tax authorities in a new kind of problem, and it would be necessary to deal with a large number of cases."[150] Other commentators have put the matter more starkly. One offered that the IRS "does not have the resources to treat homeowners as landlords and process 65 million Schedule C income and expense statements … . [E]ven [a] streamlined approach is too cumbersome to adopt here."[151]

The additional burdens on the IRS would stress yet further an organization already under severe pressure. Congress continues to expand the duties of the IRS while cutting its budget.[152] Between fiscal years 2010 and 2013, the number of tax filers grew by 4 percent while the IRS budget dropped by 8 percent. This caused a 9 percent decrease in permanent IRS employees, an 83 percent reduction in IRS training expenditures, reduction of taxpayer and practitioner services, and "the prospect of [the IRS] having to make very critical performance tradeoffs."[153] And all of this preceded full implementation of the enormous new responsibilities imposed upon the IRS by the Affordable Care Act (i.e., "Obamacare").[154] In light of the already acute demands on the time and resources of the IRS, it would risk fracture to add to the camel's back the considerable additional straws that taxing imputed income would entail.

One further concern is that taxpayers do not always respond to tax changes, especially unpopular ones, with Merovingian supineness. They and their advisors often devise creative schemes through which they hope to blunt the effects of revenue-enhancing measures. The exertions of taxpayers to find, and of the government to control, tax shelters and other tax-minimization arrangements will hardly have escaped the notice of those interested in fiscal administration. Various types of trusts, family partnerships, and other arrangements have been used to attempt to minimize taxes attending the transfer of houses and other assets or to protect them from the reach of governmental

---

147 *See* Taxation Review Comm., *supra* note 71, at 67 (noting that there would be administrative problems in attempting to link imputed income to an installment system but that the system "would be seriously weakened" by not doing so).

148 *See* I.R.C. § 55(b)(2), (d).

149 *See, e.g.*, Popkin, *supra* note 30, at 387–88.

150 Goode, *supra* note 2, at 521.

151 Bourassa & Grigsby, *supra* note 8, at 529.

152 *See generally* Steve R. Johnson, *The 1998 Act and the Resources Link Between Compliance and Tax Simplification*, 51 U. Kan. L. Rev. 1031 (2003).

153 Danny Werfel, Acting Comm'r of Internal Revenue, Remarks Before the American Institute of Certified Public Accountants 8–11 (Nov. 5, 2013) (on file with author).

154 Patient Protection and Affordable Care Act, Pub. L. No. 111-148, 124 Stat. 119 (2010), *amended by* Health Care and Education Reconciliation Act of 2010, Pub. L. No. 111-152, 124 Stat. 1029.

or private creditors. Can there be any doubt that, upon adoption of a tax on imputed income that many homeowners would attempt to develop creative, sometimes collusive, schemes manipulating use, ownership, and value of their houses? This would spawn a new dimension of tax sheltering.

The precise nature of the weeds that would sprout in the garden of imputed income is hard to predict, of course, and would depend on the particulars of the regime enacted. But that much manipulation would be attempted is quite a safe bet.

For example, some imputed interest approaches would allow deduction of mortgage interest. The availability of such deductions "would open up avenues of tax planning for the well-advised who will consolidate their debts into the borrowing for home finance."[155]

Similarly, other approaches would allow depreciation deductions. Such deductions would also create juicy opportunities. For instance:

> If the precedent of rental housing is followed, losses rather than gains will be generated on imputed income [from owner-occupied residences]. Much … rental housing … shows no taxable income for eight to ten years. The accounting losses are rather substantial. Since houses turn over every eight years on average, this may be a roundabout way of giving tax shelters to middle-income people.[156]

Political Objections

In a democracy, no feature of a fiscal system can long be maintained without the approval, or at least the acceptance, of the people. Moreover, the attempt to maintain that feature in the face of deep public disapproval poses risks to the viability of the whole tax system. Even prominent supporters of imputation sometimes acknowledge that "[t]he public would no doubt find the new provisions complicated and distasteful."[157]

This is a major reason why policy makers in the United States, Canada, and other countries have refrained from taxing imputed rent[158] and why, as discussed above, policy makers in countries that nominally tax imputed rents have often kept exemptions and deductions so high and rates and valuations so low that the regime produces little revenue, or even negative revenue. Their caution is well placed. As discussed above, the details of imputation are challenging even for experts. Also as discussed above, the U.S. Department of the Treasury does include some imputed income in "family economic income," for macroanalytical purposes. "But even this limited use of imputed income is not well understood by the media, politicians, or the public."[159] Both the Supreme Court and the predecessor of the Tax Court have doubted that imputed rents are income.[160]

The citizenry at large would have even greater difficulty understanding and embracing the new regime. They might think, "It's my home, not my business. I paid for it with money already taxed,

155 Taxation Review Comm., *supra* note 71, at 68.

156 Kurtz, *supra* note 58, at 523; *see also* Dodge, *supra* note 46, at 9 ("Enacting a complex [imputation] scheme that creates tax shelters for homeowners is worse than pointless.").

157 Goode, *supra* note 2, at 523.

158 *E.g.*, Dodge et al., *supra* note 55, at 299; Melville L. McMillan, *A Residential Interest Approach to Taxing Imputed Rent*, 5 Can. Pub. Pol'y 195, 196 (1979).

159 Michael J. Graetz & Deborah H. Schenk, Federal Income Taxation: Principles and Policies 133 (6th ed. 2009).

160 *See supra* note 53 and accompanying text.

so it's double taxation. And how can it be income when I'm not getting any money!?!"[161] During periods of rapidly rising home prices, homeowners could face sharp year-to-year increases in their tax bills without corresponding cash in their wallets to pay those bills.[162] During periods of free fall of home prices, homeowners would find it more than ironic that they would be paying income tax on the use of their "underwater" residences. In short, one may doubt "the political wisdom of a rule [taxing imputed income] that no one would understand or accept."[163]

The attempt to maintain such an unpopular feature would pose risk to the whole system. The U.S. federal income tax is a self-assessment system.[164] Taxpayers make the first determination of their liabilities on the returns they file, and that first determination often is the final determination because of inaction by the IRS. Audit rates in the United States are low,[165] a big reason for the currently estimated gap of $450 billion between federal taxes that should be paid and federal taxes that are paid.[166] In such an environment, it is critical that the returns taxpayers file bear at least reasonable correspondence to reality. Public confidence in, and support for, the tax system are crucial to the viability of the U.S. tax system.[167] The stakes are too high—and, as shown above, the net benefits are too low—to pursue theoretical purity in the face of widespread public dissatisfaction and alienation.

Conclusion

In this chapter, I have suggested that there are substantial reasons for thinking that imputed rents are not income as that term is understood for U.S. federal income tax purposes. But, even if that is so, that reason would not alone be dispositive. Barring a constitutional barrier (which most do not see here), Congress can always write statutes that change definitions and trump received concepts.

I have also acknowledged here that force exists in the criticisms of the exclusion advanced by Henry Ordower in Chapter 4 of this volume and by other commentators elsewhere. However, the discussion above minimizes these criticisms sufficiently, I believe, that they should not control the resolution of this controversy either.

Instead, the minimized criticisms should, in my estimation, yield to the practicability and democratic acceptability considerations developed above. Supporters of taxing imputed rents from owner-occupied housing admit that there would be administrative challenges but believe (at

161 Similar notions have had traction in other tax contexts. The "double tax" mantra is one reason the estate tax is unpopular and, indeed, was repealed for one year (i.e., 2010). And the fact that the transaction yields no cash to pay the resulting tax is part of the rationale behind a number of nonrecognition provisions, such as the like-kind-exchange rules of Code § 1031.

162 In part, the problem is one of hardship. In part, it is political. A consideration not to be ignored "is the importance of the taxpayers' perception of the equity. Taxpayers generally think in terms of money income, or things that are essentially equivalent to money income; they would have great difficulty in understanding why imputed rent should be taxed." Kurtz, *supra* note 58, at 198.

163 Graetz & Schenk, *supra* note 159, at 131.

164 *E.g.*, United States v. Middleton, 246 F.3d 825, 840 (6th Cir. 2001).

165 The IRS now audits about one in every 100 returns filed, about one-fifth of the audit rate in the 1960s. David M. Richardson et al., Civil Tax Procedure 95 (2d ed. 2008).

166 *See* Internal Revenue Serv., U.S. Dep't of Treasury, *Tax Gap "Map": Tax Year 2006* (2011), *available at* http://www.irs.gov/pub/newsroom/tax_gap_map_2006.pdf.

167 *E.g.*, U.S. Dep't of Treasury, The Problem of Corporate Tax Shelters: Discussion, Analysis and Legislative Proposals, at iv (1999); Thomas F. Field, *The Emperor Has No Clothes*, 102 Tax Notes 1125, 1125 (2003).

least some of them do) that such challenges "do not appear to be insuperable or even intrinsically very difficult."[168]

Based on the historical experience and the particular difficulties described above, however, I believe such supporters are looking at this issue through rose-colored glasses. Canada's Carter Report had a clearer view of the issue when it concluded: "In most circumstances … the valuation and administrative problems are insuperable … . Because of the administrative difficulty of properly and equitably determining the amount of gain, we suggest that imputed rent [from owner-occupied homes] continue to be omitted from the tax base."[169]

It may be that, some day, Schanz-Haig-Simons or others will inspire us to ascend to a self-luminous realm of theoretical tax purity. For the reasons developed in this chapter, however, I join a former Commissioner of Internal Revenue in believing "that in building the stairway to the paradise of a comprehensive tax base, imputed rent should be one of the last steps" we lay.[170] This conventional view is, alas, the better view.

Let me close on a personal note, not because the eccentricities of my mind are of any great significance but because these remarks are in keeping with the theme of this book. The paired chapters in this volume seek to illuminate the clash of perspectives between "mainstream" and "critical" tax theorists, to move past the two sides talking "at" or "past" each other instead of engaging in genuine dialogue.

As our chapters reveal, Professor Ordower and I differ as to some matters of detail, but we share considerable common ground as to the factual record and identification of the core issues. I acknowledge that there is force in his fairness and other concerns about the exclusion, and he acknowledges that my administrability concerns should receive serious consideration. The main difference between us, I think, relates to the background values and assumptions against which one weighs facts.

The Roman maxim *fiat justitia ruat caelum*[171] is aspirationally beautiful, but applying it rigorously would engender practical problems of unacceptable magnitude. That is why neither Rome nor any other polity has lived up to the aspiration. Law, like art, demands the exquisitely difficult challenge of balancing the classical (i.e., rules, order, and practical consequences) and the romantic (i.e., freedom, flexibility, and equality). Tilting too much in either direction can lead to doleful consequences.[172]

On the issue addressed in this pair of chapters I am on the side of retaining the exclusion because I see abolition as likely to produce greater practical harms than theoretical benefits.[173] More broadly, I am in the "mainstream" rather than "critical" camp as to most tax issues. No tax

168 Goode, *supra* note 2, at 523.

169 Carter Report, *supra* note 43, at 41, 49; *see also* Bourassa & Grigsby, *supra* note 8, at 526 (concluding that the pros of the exclusion outweigh the cons and that the "[a]dministrative infeasibility of accurately taxing net imputed income makes it undesirable").

170 Kurtz, *supra* note 58, at 197.

171 "Let justice be done even though the heavens fall."

172 Indeed, excess in either direction contains the seeds of its own destruction. Full-bore laissez-faire capitalism in Europe and America created miserable conditions for workers that necessitated relief legislation. On the other hand, the radical egalitarianism of the French Revolution soon gave way to the reign of terror, despotism, and imperialism.

173 *See* William A. Klein, *The Deductibility of Transportation Expenses of a Combination Business and Pleasure Trip—A Conceptual Analysis*, 18 Stan. L. Rev. 1099, 1102 (1966) (noting that the residential imputed income exclusion and some other "exclusions may be bothersome to one who seeks perfect equity in the tax system, but they nonetheless seem quite wise").

system ever has or ever will operate with perfect fairness.[174] That is no warrant for turning a blind eye to tax unfairness whose correction can be accomplished without excessive costs. But it should remind us that there are multiple desiderata of a functioning, effective tax system. These goals often are in conflict, and sometimes the goal of fairness must yield. To repeat part of the title of this chapter, "Reality Trumps Theory."

174 *E.g.*, Railroad Comm'n of Ala. v. Cent. of Georgia Ry. Co., 170 F. 225, 232 (5th Cir. 1909) ("[L]aws imposing taxes … cannot be so made and enforced as to always insure perfect equity.").

PART III
Tax Accounting: Book–Tax Disparities

Chapter 6
Perspectives on the Relationship Between Financial and Tax Accounting

Lily Kahng*

Introduction

This chapter analyzes similarities and differences between financial and tax accounting with a view toward understanding how financial accounting might inform and improve tax accounting and vice versa. It begins with a brief overview of the historical relationship between the two and discusses how lawmakers and scholars have traditionally thought about that relationship—one in which financial accounting tends to understate income out of a reflexive conservatism, while tax accounting, ever protective of the fisc, tends to overstate income. The chapter then turns to what I call the "modern era," in which the traditional values and policies promoted by each system have reversed, with financial accounting overstating income and tax accounting understating it. It considers whether the two systems can benefit by requiring greater conformity or disclosure of the differences between them.

The final part of the chapter explores how the financial and tax accounting systems treat intellectual capital, a vital and growing driver of global economic productivity. It finds that the two systems are relatively aligned at this time but are trending in opposite directions. Financial accounting is poised to make significant changes that will more accurately measure income from intellectual capital while tax accounting has regressed to a less accurate treatment of intellectual capital. The chapter argues that tax accounting for intellectual capital can and should be informed by the research and reforms taking place in financial accounting.

My endorsement of a close relationship between financial and tax accounting differs markedly from Adam Chodorow's perspective in Chapter 7. Chodorow proposes to widen further the divergence between financial and tax accounting with respect to the timing of inclusions and deductions. He argues that lawmakers erred when they conformed tax accounting with financial accounting in the adoption of accrual method taxation, and advocates a return to the cash method. Alternatively, he proposes that the courts and the IRS aggressively apply antiavoidance standards to prevent abuses under the current law accrual method.

Historic Similarities and Differences

Financial and tax accounting systems share a common ancestry. Ajay Mehrotra documents how the rise of large-scale, hierarchically managed, industrial corporations in the early twentieth

* I am grateful to Adam Chodorow, Mary Louise Fellows, Anthony Infanti, Calvin Johnson, Marjorie Kornhauser, and the participants of the Seattle University Law School faculty workshop and the 2014 Law and Society Annual Meeting for their helpful comments. I also thank Seattle University law librarian Kelly Kunsch for his invaluable assistance.

century created a managerial class of corporate executives who "needed and craved precise and systematic quantitative information about the everyday operations of their enterprises."[1] This led to the development of modern accounting, with its sophisticated and systematic consolidation of cost, capital, and financial accounting,[2] which in turn "facilitated—inadvertently perhaps—the development of the modern income tax by giving government organizations ample opportunities to assess and collect corporate profits and personal incomes."[3] The tax law explicitly acknowledges its common ancestry with financial accounting: "Taxable income shall be computed under the method of accounting on the basis of which the taxpayer regularly computes his income in keeping his books."[4]

In addition to their shared ancestry, financial and tax accounting systems share a fundamental purpose: to state some economic "truths" about a business—the amount of revenue it generates from the sale of good or services, the costs it incurs in the production of that revenue, and thus the net profits of the business. However, the two systems also have widely divergent functions.[5] The primary function of financial accounting is to provide information to current and prospective stakeholders including investors, creditors, and employees to allow them to monitor and make decisions about their stakes in a firm.[6] The primary function of tax accounting is to help ensure the collection of revenue.[7] Furthermore, tax accounting does not aim exclusively to achieve an

1 Ajay K. Mehrotra, *American Economic Development, Managerial Corporate Capitalism, and the Institutional Foundations of the Modern Income Tax*, 73 Law & Contemp. Probls. 25, 56 (Winter 2010). For a historical overview of the evolution of financial accounting, see Deborah A. Geier, *The Myth of the Matching Principle as a Tax Value*, 15 Am. J. Tax Pol'y 17, 75–84 (1998).

2 Mehrotra, *supra* note 1, at 56–57.

3 *Id.* at 57. Mehrotra further describes how financial accounting and the tax law entered into what he calls a "virtuous feedback cycle," in which, for example, government research bureaus adopted corporate accounting practices, while at the same time, corporations enhanced their accounting methods to comply with tax law reporting requirements. *Id.* at 57–59.

4 26 U.S.C. § 446(a). This provision of the tax law does not require conformity of tax and financial accounting. Rather, the "books" of the taxpayer refers to internal records, which provide the raw data for both financial and tax accounting. *See* Alvin D. Knott & Jacob D. Rosenfeld, *Book and Tax (Part Two): A Selective Exploration of Two Parallel Universes*, 99 Tax Notes 1043, 1044 (2003). Nor does the provision require conformity between internal books and tax accounting; taxpayers can choose or may be required to use different methods. Linda M. Beale, *Book–Tax Conformity and the Corporate Tax Shelter Debate: Assessing the Proposed Section 475 Mark-to-Market Safe Harbor*, 24 Va. Tax Rev. 301, 316–17 (2004).

5 Thor Power Tool v. Comm'r, 439 U.S. 522, 542–43 (1978); Gil Manzon, Jr., & George A. Plesko, *The Relation Between Financial and Tax Reporting Measures of Income*, 55 Tax L. Rev. 175, 178–82 (2002); John McClelland & Lilllian Mills, *Weighing Benefits and Risks of Taxing Book Income*, 114 Tax Notes 779, 779 (2007); Douglas A. Shackelford et al., *Financial Reporting, Tax, and Real Decisions: Toward a Unifying Framework*, 18 Int'l Tax & Pub. Fin. 461, 463–64 (2011); Daniel Shaviro, *The Optimal Relationship Between Taxable Income and Financial Accounting Income: Analysis and a Proposal*, 97 Geo. L.J. 423, 430–45 (2009). *But see* Wolfgang Schon, *The Odd Couple: A Common Future for Financial and Tax Accounting?*, 58 Tax L. Rev. 111, 126–39 (2005) (questioning the assumption that financial and tax accounting systems have divergent aims and concluding that "there is no fundamental antagonism between the goals of tax accounting and financial accounting that would render the task of aligning financial and taxable income impossible from the start").

6 *Thor Power*, 439 U.S. at 542; Manzon & Plesko, *supra* note 5, at 178–79; Celia Whitaker, Note, *Bridging the Book–Tax Accounting Gap*, 115 Yale L.J. 680, 688 (2005).

7 *Thor Power*, 439 U.S. at 542; *see* Manzon & Plesko, *supra* note 5, at 18; Whitaker, *supra* note 6, at 688–89.

accurate measure of economic income. Other objectives such as ease of administration, achieving a predictable stream of revenues, or promoting economic or social policies also animate the tax laws.[8]

Depreciation is a good example of the divergence between financial and tax accounting that arises by reason of the multiple objectives of the tax system.[9] Consistent with financial accounting, tax accounting seeks to measure economic depreciation—that is, the decline in value of the asset as it is used productively in a trade or business.[10] However, tax depreciation also employs simplifying assumptions to make the computation of depreciation more administrable.[11] Furthermore, tax depreciation is more accelerated than is warranted under pure economic depreciation in order to stimulate investment.[12] As a result, depreciation reported on financial statements differs significantly from depreciation allowed as a deduction for tax purposes.[13]

The U.S. Supreme Court highlighted the differences between tax and financial accounting in its 1978 decision in *Thor Power Tool Co. v. Commissioner*,[14] observing that financial and tax accounting systems have "vastly different objectives," a "diversity, even contrariety, of objectives."[15] According to the Court, "financial accounting has as its foundation the principle of conservatism, with its corollary that 'possible errors in measurement [should] be in the direction of understatement rather than overstatement of net income and net assets'"[16] in contrast to "the major responsibility of the Internal Revenue Service … to protect the public fisc."[17]

In light of the divergent purposes of financial and tax accounting systems, the Court stated, "the accountant's conservatism cannot bind the Commissioner in his efforts to collect taxes."[18] The Court upheld the power of the IRS to disallow a loss deduction on unsold inventory even though the loss had been reported by the taxpayer in its financial statements, and rejected the taxpayer's argument that the tax loss was presumptively valid by reason of its financial accounting treatment.

Thor Power was a victory for the government in its quest to disallow loss deductions, and it established that financial accounting does not determine the proper tax treatment of a transaction. However, in keeping with Martin Ginsburg's famous observation that "every stick crafted to beat on the head of a taxpayer will metamorphose sooner or later into a large green snake and bite the commissioner on the hind part,"[19] the wall between tax and financial accounting has sometimes been used to the government's detriment.[20] The discontinuity of financial and tax accounting reached its apotheosis in *Cottage Savings Ass'n v. Commissioner*,[21] which involved the swap of devalued mortgages for other similar mortgages. The Court upheld the taxpayer's loss deduction,

8 *Thor Power*, 439 U.S. at 542–44; Beale, *supra* note 4, at 355–59; Manzon & Plesko, *supra* note 5, at 180–81; Shaviro, *supra* note 5, at 434–35; Whitaker, *supra* note 6, at 686.

9 *See* Staff of J. Comm. on Taxation, 112th Cong., Present Law and Background Relating to the Interaction of Federal Income Tax Rules and Financial Accounting Rules 10–19 (Comm. Print 2012).

10 *See* Staff of J. Comm. on Taxation, 112th Cong., Present Law and Background Relating to Cost Recovery and Domestic Production Activities 2–3 (Comm. Print 2012).

11 *See id.* at 3.

12 *See id.* at 3–12.

13 *See id.* at 13–19; Michelle Hanlon & Terry Shevlin, *Book–Tax Conformity for Corporate Income: An Introduction to the Issues*, 19 Tax Pol'y & Econ. 101, 105 (2005).

14 439 U.S. 522 (1978).

15 *Id.* at 542–43.

16 *Id.* at 542 (footnote omitted).

17 *Id.*

18 *Id.* at 543.

19 Martin D. Ginsburg, *Making Tax Law Through the Judicial Process*, 70 A.B.A. J. 74, 76 (1984).

20 *See* Whitaker, *supra* note 6, at 689–90.

21 Cottage Sav. Ass'n v. Comm'r, 499 U.S. 554 (1991).

finding that the swapped mortgages were "materially different"[22]—despite a decree by federal bank regulators that the mortgages were "substantially identical" and that the loss did not need to be reported on the taxpayer's financial statements.[23] Without even bothering to cite *Thor Power* or discuss the relationship between financial and tax accounting, the Court dismissed the anomaly that property could be both "materially different" and "substantially identical" as "merely semantic."[24]

The Modern Era

Despite the U.S. Supreme Court's insistence that financial and tax accounting belong in separate silos, lawmakers, policy makers and academics continue to puzzle over the disparities in the two systems and ways to reconcile them.[25] One striking development that has prompted heightened interest is that the "contrariety" of objectives that concerned the Court has been turned on its head.[26] As exemplified by Enron and other high profile cases, financial accounting appears to have abandoned its conservative tendency to understate income and instead aggressively overstates income.[27] Tax accounting no longer protects the fisc but rather undermines it through aggressive tax planning, as evidenced by the explosion of corporate tax shelters.[28]

In recent years, the magnitude of the difference between financial income and taxable income has been substantial and worrisome. In 2007, the U.S. Department of the Treasury estimated that "book income"—that is, income reported in financial statements—had exceeded taxable income by 20 to 30 percent in prior years.[29] The "book–tax gap" became negative for a brief period during the 2008 recession—that is, book income was *less* than taxable income.[30] But in the years since then, the book–tax gap has resurged and grown to unprecedented amounts.[31] Many posit that corporate tax shelters have contributed substantially to the increase in the book–tax gap.[32]

---

22 *Id.* at 556.

23 *Id.* at 558.

24 *Id.* at 567.

25 For a detailed account of the financial and tax accounting disparities and efforts to conform them, see Beale, *supra* note 4, at 314–54, and Alvin D. Knott & Jacob D. Rosenfeld, *Book and Tax (Part One): A Selective Exploration of Two Parallel Universes*, 99 Tax Notes 865, 876–86 (2003). *See also* David I. Walker, *Financial Accounting and Corporate Behavior*, 64 Wash. & Lee L. Rev. 927, 971–93 (2007) (discussing the disparity between financial and tax accounting and the proposals for requiring greater conformity).

26 *See* Knott & Rosenfeld, *supra* note 4, at 1057 (noting that prior to the 1980s, financial accounting tended to understate income as compared to tax accounting but that beginning in the 1980s, financial accounting income tended to exceed tax accounting income).

27 *See* Olufunmilayo B. Arewa, *Measuring and Representing the Knowledge Economy: Accounting for Economic Reality Under the Intangibles Paradigm*, 54 Buff. L. Rev. 1, 81–92 (2006); Whitaker, *supra* note 6, at 694–97.

28 *See* Shaviro, *supra* note 5, at 425–27.

29 Office of Tax Pol'y, U.S. Dep't of Treasury, Approaches to Improve the Competitiveness of the U.S. Business Tax System for the 21st Century, at 100 (2007).

30 John R. Graham et al., *Research in Accounting for Income Taxes*, 53 J. Acct. & Econ. 412, 416 (2012).

31 *Id.* at 416–17.

32 *See Penalty and Interest Provisions in the Internal Revenue Code: Hearing Before the S. Comm. on Finance*, 106th Cong. 234–35 (2000) (statement of John Talisman, Acting Assistant Treasury Secretary (Tax Policy)); Shaviro, *supra* note 5, at 426; Martin A. Sullivan, *Shelter Fallout? Corporate Taxes Down, Profits Up*, 84 Tax Notes 653, 654–56 (1999); Joann M. Weiner, *Minding the Book–Tax Gap*, 53 Tax Notes

However, whether and to what extent that is true is unclear, and will likely require years of additional research to ascertain.[33]

Although the specific causes of the book–tax gap have yet to be fully understood, the new and extreme contrariety of financial and tax accounting systems is both irksome and intriguing to lawmakers, policy makers, and academics. It is irksome because businesses often seem to enjoy the "best of both worlds"—that is, they report a rosy account of their financial results to their investors, while at the same time reporting a much gloomier account of their results to the IRS. The contrariety is intriguing because it presents the opportunity to exploit the competing incentives that businesses have with respect to financial and tax accounting—what Daniel Shaviro calls the "Madisonian tension" between wanting to overstate income for financial purposes and understate it for tax purposes.[34] Requiring greater conformity could help rein in excesses under both systems and ensure that both financial and taxable income more closely approximate economic income.[35]

On the tax side, this might be accomplished through an alternative minimum tax based on income reported on financial statements, although the one attempt to do this, in effect from 1987 to 1989, was widely criticized and short-lived.[36] Some scholars have proposed partial conformity between financial and tax accounting, with some allowance for differences between the two.[37] Alternatively, a more targeted approach would be to identify certain disparities in the financial and tax treatment of specific items or transactions ("book–tax disparities") and disallow tax deductions in those cases.[38] Another proposal is to require taxpayers to disclose book–tax disparities to help the IRS identify tax avoidance behavior.[39] In 2004, the IRS adopted this last proposal with the introduction of Schedule M-3, which requires large corporate taxpayers to disclose in their returns detailed information about book–tax disparities.[40]

INT'L 371, 372 (2009); George K. Yin, *Getting Serious About Corporate Tax Shelters: Taking a Lesson from History*, 54 SMU L. REV. 209, 225 (2001).

33 *Compare* Mihir A. Desai, *The Divergence Between Book and Tax Income*, *in* 17 TAX POLICY AND THE ECONOMY 200 (James M. Poterba ed., 2003) (finding changes in book–tax disparities suggestive of an increase in sheltering activity), *with* Manzon & Plesko, *supra* note 5, at 211–12 (finding a predictable and consistent book–tax disparity over time, which is inconsistent with an increase in sheltering activity). *See* Weiner, *supra* note 32, at 372.

34 Shaviro, *supra* note 5, at 484.

35 *Id.* 428–29, 484.

36 *See* Knott & Rosenfeld, *supra* note 4, at 1057, Beale, *supra* note 4, at 351.

37 *See* Shaviro, *supra* note 5, at 472–82 (proposing an adjustment to taxable income equal to 50 percent of the difference between financial and taxable income); Whitaker, *supra* note 6, at 719–24 (proposing to conform taxable income to financial income with exceptions for certain tax preferences that promote important social or economic policies).

38 *See* Mitchell L. Engler, *Corporate Tax Shelters and Narrowing the Book/Tax "GAAP,"* 2001 COLUM. BUS. L. REV. 539, 559–81 (proposing a targeted approach that would deny deductions for certain book–tax disparities); David I. Walker & Victor Fleischer, *Book–Tax Conformity and Equity Compensation*, 62 TAX L. REV. 399, 415–42 (2009) (proposing a targeted solution for the treatment of stock options). These proposals are reminiscent of prior law Code §§ 452 and 462, which allowed taxpayers to defer prepaid income or deduct accrued but unpaid expenses only if they also reported the items in the same way on their financial statements. The provisions, enacted in 1954, were repealed retroactively in 1955. *See* Beale, *supra* note 4, at 335–43; Knott & Rosenfeld, *supra* note 4, at 1048–49.

39 Lillian F. Mills & George A. Plesko, *Bridging the Reporting Gap: A Proposal for More Informative Reconciling of Book and Tax Income*, 56 NAT'L TAX J. 865 (2003).

40 In 2004, the IRS began to require corporations with assets of $10 million or more to file Schedule M-3, a detailed reconciliation of book and tax disparities. Rev. Proc. 2004-45, 2004-2 C.B. 140. Schedule

On the financial side, the proposals to address the book–tax gap mirror those on the tax side: (1) require some greater degree of conformity between financial and taxable income; or (2) require more disclosure about the differences between the two. Disclosure of book–tax disparities has long been part of the financial reporting process, given its focus on providing information to stakeholders.[41] It is therefore not surprising that proposals to increase disclosure about book–tax disparities have gained more traction than proposals to require conformity between financial and taxable income. Indeed, the principal objection to greater conformity is that it would result in the loss of valuable information to financial markets.[42] In 2007, the Financial Accounting Standard Board (FASB) adopted a new financial reporting standard that requires firms to disclose uncertain tax positions.[43]

To summarize, there has been a great deal of interest in "doing something" about the book–tax gap in recent decades, fueled by accounting scandals such as Enron and the explosion of corporate tax shelters. As a result, both the FASB and the IRS implemented additional disclosure of book–tax disparities on financial reports and tax returns. However, the book–tax gap has continued to grow, except for brief pauses during the dot-com crash of 2001 and financial crisis of 2008. Since 2008, it has increased exponentially. Today, financial accounting and tax accounting have never been farther apart, as measured by the dollar amount of the book–tax gap.

Should financial and tax accounting be required to conform more than they do? In the modern era of book–tax disparities, there are two possible reasons why greater conformity might be desirable: (1) to rein in bad behavior by corporate managers—so-called earnings management—on the financial side and tax avoidance on the tax side; and (2) to achieve a measure of income, for both financial and tax purposes, that more closely reflects economic income.

As a mechanism to rein in bad behavior, requiring conformity between financial and tax accounting seems a relatively crude tool.[44] To be sure, in cases where a business carries out both bad behaviors with the same transaction, conformity would restrain both sets of bad behavior simultaneously. Some of Enron's activities and other well-publicized corporate tax shelters were

---

M-3 essentially adopts the proposal of Lillian Mills and George Plesko. Mills & Plesko, *supra* note 39; *see* Charles Boynton & William Wilson, *A Review of Schedule M-3: The Internal Revenue Service's New Book–Tax Reconciliation Tool*, Petroleum Acct. & Fin. Mgmt. 1, 2–3 (2006).

In addition, in 2000, the IRS implemented disclosure reporting specifically aimed at corporate tax shelters. Treas. Reg. § 1.6011-4. Among the identifying characteristics of a reportable transaction was a "significant book–tax difference." *Id.* § 1.6011-4(b)(6)(i). In 2006, the IRS removed this characteristic, explaining that new Schedule M-3 would pick up such transactions. I.R.S. Notice 2006-6, 2006-5 I.R.B. 385; AJCA Modifications to the Section 6011 Regulations, 71 Fed. Reg. 64,488 (proposed Nov. 2, 2006) (to be codified at 26 C.F.R. pt. 1).

41 *See* Knott & Rosenfeld, *supra* note 25, at 887. For a comprehensive survey of finance and economics research relating to the financial reporting of information about income taxes, see Graham et al., *supra* note 30.

42 *See* Hanlon & Shevlin, *supra* note 13, at 117–22; Michelle Hanlon et al., *Evidence for the Possible Information Loss of Conforming Book Income and Taxable Income*, 48 J.L. & Econ. 407, 414–15, 436–37 (2005); McClelland & Mills, *supra* note 5, at 782–83.

43 *Accounting for Uncertainty in Income Taxes*, FASB Interpretation No. 48 (Fin. Accounting Standards Bd. 2006).

44 *See* Shaviro, *supra* note 5, at 463 (observing that "[i]t would be quite fortuitous if the Madisonian approach succeeded in eliminating income manipulation. Such an outcome would require perfect equipoise between the advantages that managers attributed to increasing book income on the one hand and reducing taxable income on the other, such that they were actually indifferent to matched changes").

of this nature.[45] Whether conformity would restrain each of the bad behaviors enough or too much, and at what cost, are questions that have been explored at length.[46] Furthermore, there are also cases where only one bad behavior is involved—that is, a firm overstates earnings on its financial statements without a corresponding understatement of income on its tax return or vice versa. In these cases, requiring conformity not only raises the question of whether the bad behavior would be appropriately restrained, but it also creates the possibility that perfectly legitimate financial or tax reporting would be penalized. The fact that both the finance and tax sides have adopted heightened disclosure regimes rather than greater conformity bespeaks these concerns about conformity.

If the goal of conformity is to achieve a better measure of economic income for financial and tax purposes, the assumption is that the two systems seek to measure the same thing. However, almost all scholars agree with *Thor Power* that this is not always the case.[47] Financial reporting, with its primary focus on accurate information, probably aligns more closely with the measure of economic income than tax reporting, which not only seeks to measure economic income but also must take into account revenue needs, ease of administration, and tax expenditures.[48] Therefore, to the extent that the two systems diverge in their purposes, the goal of conformity is unsupportable.

The principal rationales for financial and tax accounting conformity are unpersuasive. However, this does not mean that financial and tax accounting should be segregated. At their foundations, both systems seek to measure economic income. To be sure, the tax system reflects other concerns and objectives, but a well-designed tax system must strive to begin with the most accurate possible measure of economic income. The final part of this chapter examines the treatment of intellectual capital to demonstrate how much financial accounting can contribute to this endeavor.

Accounting for Intellectual Capital

Current Financial and Tax Treatment of Intellectual Capital

Intellectual capital, sometimes called knowledge-based capital or intangibles, encompasses all "nonphysical sources of value (claims to future benefits) generated by innovation (discovery), unique organizational designs, or human resources practices."[49] It includes a broad array of intangibles including (1) legally protected intellectual property such as patents, trademarks, and copyrights; (2) information systems, administrative structures and processes, market and technical knowledge, brands, and trade secrets; and (3) organizational "know-how," culture and strategic capabilities, and customer satisfaction.[50]

45 *See* Gary A. McGill & Edmund Outslay, *Did Enron Pay Taxes?* 96 TAX NOTES 1125, 1136 (2002) (noting that most tax shelter products at that time both reduced tax liability and increased financial earnings).

46 *See* McClelland & Mills, *supra* note 5, at 782–85; Shaviro, *supra* note 5, at 462–73; Walker, *supra* note 25, at 971–92; Walker & Fleischer, *supra* note 38, at 422–41.

47 *See supra* notes 5–8 and accompanying text.

48 *See* Shaviro, *supra* note 5, at 444; Hanlon et al., *supra* note 42, at 413–14.

49 BARUCH LEV, INTANGIBLES: MANAGEMENT, MEASUREMENT, AND REPORTING 5 (2001).

50 JUERGEN H. DAUM, INTANGIBLE ASSETS AND VALUE CREATION 16–17 (2002); LEV, *supra* note 49, at 5–7; Farok J. Contractor, *Intangible Assets and Principles for Their Valuation*, *in* VALUATION OF INTANGIBLE ASSETS IN GLOBAL OPERATIONS 3, 7 (Farok J. Contractor ed., 2001).

Intellectual capital can be observed and measured by reference to either *inputs* or *outputs*.[51] *Inputs* focus on resources expended to develop intellectual capital, and include expenditures such as research and development (R&D), strategic planning, and worker training. *Outputs* focus on the end result of the inputs. For example, patents and copyrights are outputs that are the product of R&D inputs. Outputs can either be acquired from third parties or self-created. On the output side, it is sometimes difficult to identify specific assets created, and as discussed below, both financial and tax accounting systems sometimes designate nonspecific intellectual capital as goodwill.

Theoretically, to reflect properly the value of intellectual capital for financial accounting purposes, intellectual capital inputs should be capitalized (i.e., reported on the asset side of a firm's balance sheet) rather than expensed (i.e., immediately subtracted from income).[52] The assets should then be amortized—that is, expensed over a period of time that corresponds to the useful life of the assets. If an asset has no finite life, it should not be amortized. Similarly, for tax purposes, investments in intellectual capital should be capitalized—that is, reflected as tax basis in the asset rather than deducted immediately. Assets with finite lives should then be amortized in much the same fashion as under financial reporting.

Current FASB guidance and tax law depart from this theoretical ideal in their treatment of most intellectual capital. Instead, most investments in intellectual capital are expensed for financial reporting purposes and deducted for tax purposes.[53] In the limited situation where intellectual capital is acquired from a third party (rather than self-created), some components of intellectual capital are capitalized and amortized. In contrast, where intellectual capital is self-created, it is for the most part expensed for financial reporting purposes and deducted for tax purposes.

Acquired Intellectual Capital

When acquired from a third party, goodwill and other intangible assets are generally capitalized for both financial reporting and tax purposes.[54] Where a specific intangible asset is acquired, the buyer reflects the asset at its cost on the balance sheet and takes a tax basis in the asset equal to its cost.[55] In cases where an entire business is acquired, the purchase price must be allocated among specific

51 Carol A. Corrado et al., *Intangible Capital and Economic Growth*, 55 Rev. Income & Wealth 661, 666 (2009).

52 *See id.* at 674.

53 *See* Calvin H. Johnson, *The Effective Tax Ratio and the Undertaxation of Intangible Investments*, 121 Tax Notes 1289, 1291 (2008); Lily Kahng, *The Taxation of Intellectual Capital*, 66 Fla. L. Rev. (forthcoming) (manuscript at 17–19, 34–41) (on file with author).

54 *Business Combinations*, Statement of Fin. Accounting Standards No. 141 (Fin. Accounting Standards Bd. 2001); *Goodwill and Other Intangible Assets*, Statement of Fin. Accounting Standards No. 142 (Fin. Accounting Standards Bd. 2001); 26 U.S.C. §§ 338, 1012, 1060; *see generally* Martin D. Ginsburg et al., Mergers, Acquisitions, and Buyouts ¶¶ 403.4.1.2–.4.2 (2012); Benjamin P. Foster et al., *Valuing Intangible Assets*, 73 CPA J. 50 (2003); Ronald J. Huefner & James A. Largay III, *The Effect of the New Goodwill Accounting Rules on Financial Statements*, 73 CPA J. 30 (2004); Jack S. Levin & Donald E. Rocap, *A Transactional Guide to New Code Section 197*, 61 Tax Notes 461 (1993); Jennifer M. Mueller, *Amortization of Certain Intangible Assets*, 198 J. Acct. 74 (2004); Xuan-Thao Nguyen & Jeffrey A. Maine, *Equity and Efficiency in Intellectual Property Taxation*, 76 Brook. L. Rev. 1 (2010); Michael L. Schler, *Basic Tax Issues in Acquisition Transactions*, 116 Penn St. L. Rev. 879 (2012); Mark Silverman, *Purchase Price Allocation Rules: Sections 1060, 338, and 197, in* Corporate Tax Practice Series (PLI 2013).

55 26 U.S.C. § 1012(a).

assets in order to capitalize the cost of each asset.[56] For both financial and tax purposes, the general approach is to allocate the purchase price first to specific and identifiable assets in accordance with their relative fair market values, and then to allocate any residual purchase price to goodwill.[57]

For financial accounting purposes, acquired intangible assets other than goodwill are amortized over their useful lives.[58] Acquired goodwill is deemed to have an indefinite life and therefore is not amortized over any fixed period for financial accounting purposes.[59] Instead, firms must make an annual assessment to determine whether goodwill has been impaired and expense the amount, if any, of such impairment.[60] For tax purposes, goodwill and other intangibles acquired as part of a business are generally amortized over 15 years.[61] Separately acquired intangibles are amortized over periods ranging from 3 to 15 years depending on the type of asset.[62]

---

56 *Business Combinations*, Statement of Fin. Accounting Standards No. 141 (Fin. Accounting Standards Bd. 2001); 26 U.S.C. §§ 338, 1060; Treas. Reg. § 1.338-6.

For tax purposes, this allocation method applies only to a taxable purchase of a business. If a tax-free acquisition is involved, the acquiring taxpayer generally takes a carryover (i.e., historic) basis for all assets of the business and amortizes that carryover basis. Generally, an acquisition is tax-free when equity (as opposed to cash or other property) is the sole or primary consideration for the acquisition. *See* Schler, *supra* note 54, at 882. Historically, financial accounting made a similar distinction between equity- and non-equity-based acquisitions, with the former treated under "pooling" accounting and the latter under "purchase" accounting. In pooling accounting, assets were reported at historic values on the acquiring company's financial statements. Under purchase accounting, assets were reported at their cost. *See* Christine Andrews et al., *SFAS 141(R): Global Convergence and Massive Changes in M&A Accounting*, 7 J. Bus. Econ. Research 125, 125–26 (2008); Stephen R. Moehrle & Jennifer A. Reynolds-Moehrle, *Say Good-Bye to Pooling and Goodwill Amortization*, 192 J. Acct. 31, 31 (2001). In 2001, the FASB eliminated pooling accounting and also changed the treatment of goodwill. *Business Combinations*, Statement of Fin. Accounting Standards No. 141 (Fin. Accounting Standards Bd. 2001); *Goodwill and Other Intangible Assets*, Statement of Fin. Accounting Standards No. 142 (Fin. Accounting Standards Bd. 2001); *see infra* note 62.

57 The methodology for identifying types of intangible assets and allocating purchase price among them differs somewhat for financial and tax purposes. For financial purposes, to be treated separately from goodwill, an intangible asset must be legally or contractually protected or be separable and capable of being monetized. *See Business Combinations*, Statement of Fin. Accounting Standards No. 141, app. A (Fin. Accounting Standards Bd. 2001) (providing a list of intangibles that may be separable). The tax law does not apply an overarching protectability or marketability standard to differentiate goodwill from other types of intangible assets. *See* Treas. Reg. § 1.338-6; Silverman, *supra* note 54, at 7–11.

58 *Goodwill and Other Intangible Assets*, Statement of Fin. Accounting Standards No. 142 (Fin. Accounting Standards Bd. 2001); Foster et al., *supra* note 54, at 51–52; Mueller, *supra* note 54, at 74–78.

59 *Goodwill and Other Intangible Assets*, Statement of Fin. Accounting Standards No. 142 (Fin. Accounting Standards Bd. 2001). Prior to 2001, goodwill was amortizable over a maximum of 40 years. *Intangible Assets*, APB Opinion 17 (Accounting Principles Bd. 1970), *superseded by Goodwill and Other Intangible Assets*, Statement of Fin. Accounting Standards No. 142 (Fin. Accounting Standards Bd. 2001); *see* Andrews et al., *supra* note 56, at 125–27; Huefner & Largay, *supra* note 54, at 30.

60 *Goodwill and Other Intangible Assets*, Statement of Fin. Accounting Standards No. 142 (Fin. Accounting Standards Bd. 2001); *see* Huefner & Largay, *supra* note 54, at 31–32.

61 Levin & Rocap, *supra* note 54, at 463–67. Some intangibles are excluded from this 15-year amortization rule and are amortizable over shorter time periods or deducted. *Id.*

62 *Id.* at 465–67; Nguyen & Maine, *supra* note 54, at 19–21; Silverman, *supra* note 54, at 45–53. Prior to 1993, goodwill and other intangibles were treated for tax accounting purposes similarly to their current treatment for financial accounting purposes; that is, goodwill was assumed to have an indefinite life and was therefore not amortizable and other intangible assets were amortized over their expected lives. *See*

Self-Created Intellectual Capital

Self-created intellectual capital comprises a much greater proportion of the total stock of intellectual capital than acquired intellectual capital. This is because only a small proportion of intellectual capital changes hands within a given time period.[63] The costs of most self-created intellectual capital are expensed for financial accounting purposes and deducted for tax accounting purposes.[64] FASB guidance and tax law explicitly provide this treatment for certain expenditures such as R&D costs.[65] More broadly, as discussed below, financial reporting rules and tax laws reflect an assumption that expenditures related to intellectual capital provide no future benefits.[66]

For tax purposes, expenditures for self-created intellectual capital theoretically ought to be capitalized under Code § 263 and the U.S. Supreme Court's 1992 decision in *INDOPCO, Inc. v. Commissioner*,[67] which set forth an expansive view of the types of expenditures that are capitalized rather than currently deducted.[68] However, subsequent administrative and judicial interpretations of *INDOPCO*, as well as subsequent legislation, have all operated to constrain this expansive capitalization principle.[69] Notably, in 2004, the IRS issued regulations that require capitalization of intangibles for a relatively narrow and rigid set of expenditures and presume all other expenditures are to be deducted.[70]

The Ascendance of Intellectual Capital and the Reform Movement in Financial Reporting

Intellectual capital is not a new concept. Mid-nineteenth-century economists recognized that knowledge is valuable and that human resources are a key input into economic productivity.[71]

---

generally Levin & Rocap, *supra* note 54 (describing and comparing pre- and post-1993 tax treatment of acquired intangibles).

63 The estimated volume of mergers and acquisitions has averaged 6.5 percent of total global market capitalization over the last 30 years. Stefano Gatti & Carlo Chiarella, M&A in Uncertain Times: Is There Still Value in Growing? 1 (2013).

64 *See* Leslie A. Robinson & Richard Sansing, *The Effect of "Invisible" Tax Preferences on Investment and Tax Preference Measures*, 46 J. Acct. & Econ. 389, 390–92 (2008).

65 *Accounting for Research and Development Costs*, Statement of Fin. Accounting Standards No. 2 (Fin. Accounting Standards Bd. 1974); 26 U.S.C. § 174; *see* Joseph Oliver, *Accounting and Tax Treatment of R&D: An Update*, 73 CPA J. 46, 46–48 (2003); Nguyen & Maine, *supra* note 54, at 15–19.

66 *See* Robinson & Sansing, *supra* note 64, at 391 (noting that both financial accounting and tax accounting disregard the future benefits of firm-specific human capital of the workforce and organizational capital such as Walmart's computerized supply chain).

67 503 U.S. 79 (1992).

68 *See* Kahng, *supra* note 53, at 30–34.

69 *See* Calvin H. Johnson, *Destroying the Tax Base: The Proposed INDOPCO Capitalization Regulations*, 99 Tax Notes 1381, 1382–94 (2003); Kahng, *supra* note 53, at 34–41; *see* John W. Lee, *Transaction Costs Relating to Acquisition or Enhancement of Intangible Property: A Populist, Political, but Practical Perspective*, 22 Va. Tax Rev. 273 (2002) (describing the audit and litigation challenges faced by the IRS in attempting to implement a broad capitalization principle, the congressional and judicial resistance to such efforts, and the IRS's capitulation).

70 Treas. Reg. § 1.263(a)-4; *see* James L. Atkinson, *The Final INDOPCO Regulations: A Primer*, Tax Exec., May–June 2004, at 222 (describing the treatment of intangibles as "a dramatic departure from 'capitalization is the norm' … to establish deductibility as the default rule").

71 *See* Peter Hill, *Tangibles, Intangibles and Services: A New Taxonomy for the Classification of Output*, 32 Can. J. Econ. 426, 428–37 (1999).

However, intellectual capital was historically undervalued.[72] It is only at the turn of the twenty-first century, due to the increasing dominance of technology and knowledge production in the global economy, that the ascendance of intellectual capital has become undeniable.[73]

Economists and finance scholars had been studying intellectual capital for decades[74] when Thomas Stewart's 1991 *Fortune* article introduced the concept into the mainstream U.S. business community.[75] Stewart highlighted the importance of intellectual capital and popularized the idea of "knowledge management":

> Every company depends increasingly on knowledge—patents, processes, management skills, technologies, information about customers and suppliers, and old-fashioned experience. Added together, this knowledge is intellectual capital .... [I]t's the sum of everything everybody in your company knows that gives you a competitive edge in the marketplace. Such collective knowledge is hard to identify and harder still to deploy effectively. But once you find it and exploit it, you win.[76]

Since then, catalyzed by the technology boom of the 1990s and the growth of the "knowledge economy,"[77] research on intellectual capital and knowledge management has exploded.[78] Businesses have implemented internal systems to identify intellectual capital, monitor its productivity, and allocate resources to its development.[79]

One burgeoning area of research focuses on financial reporting of intellectual capital. Economist Baruch Lev is one of the leading proponents of reforms in financial reporting better to reflect investment in intellectual capital.[80] Lev argues that the financial accounting rules—which generally require investments in intellectual capital to be reported incorrectly as expenses rather than as

---

72 *See id.* at 436–47, 444–45.

73 *See generally* ORG. FOR ECON. COOPERATION & DEV., NEW SOURCES OF GROWTH: KNOWLEDGE-BASED CAPITAL (2013) [hereinafter 2013 OECD REPORT] (documenting the global increase in business investment in intellectual capital and the increasing productivity gains therefrom).

74 *See generally* Leire Alcaniz et al., *Theoretical Perspectives on Intellectual Capital: A Backward Look and a Proposal for Going Forward*, 35 ACCT. F. 104 (2011); Leandro Canibano et al., *Accounting for Intangibles: A Literature Review*, 19 J. ACCT. LIT. 102 (2000).

75 Thomas A. Stewart, *Brain Power: How Intellectual Capital Is Becoming America's Most Valuable Asset*, FORTUNE, June 3, 1991, at 44 [hereinafter Stewart, *Brain Power*]; *see generally* THOMAS A. STEWART, BRAIN POWER (1997); Thomas A. Stewart, *Your Company's Most Valuable Asset: Intellectual Capital*, FORTUNE, Oct. 3, 1994.

76 Stewart, *Brain Power*, *supra* note 75, at 44.

77 Peter Drucker first used the term "knowledge economy" in 1969 to describe the shift in the U.S. economy from manufacturing to services and technology. PETER F. DRUCKER, THE AGE OF DISCONTINUITY 263–96 (1969).

78 For two influential and pathbreaking books on knowledge management, see THOMAS H. DAVENPORT & LAURENCE PRUSAK, WORKING KNOWLEDGE (1998); IKUJIRO NONAKA & HIROTAKA TAKEUCHI, THE KNOWLEDGE-CREATING COMPANY (1995). There are several peer-reviewed journals dedicated to research on intellectual capital and knowledge management including the *Journal of Intellectual Capital*, the *Journal of Knowledge Management*, and *Knowledge and Process Management*. In addition, there are innumerable books, policy briefs, and reports and articles on the subject.

79 *See* Nick Bontis, *Assessing Knowledge Assets: A Review of the Models Used to Measure Intellectual Capital*, 3 INT'L. J. MGMT. REVS. 41 (2001) (describing knowledge-management systems of Skandia, Dow Chemical, and other companies); Leif Edvisson & Patrick Sullivan, *Developing a Model for Managing Intellectual Capital*, 14 EUR. MGMT. J. 356 (1996) (describing management systems of several companies).

80 LEV, *supra* note 49; *see* MARGARET M. BLAIR & STEVEN M.H. WALLMAN, UNSEEN WEALTH (2001).

assets—have many undesirable consequences, including higher costs of capital, a systematic undervaluation of intangible assets, an increased risk of insider trading, and a degraded usefulness of financial reports.[81]

In response to calls for reform of financial accounting of intellectual capital, the FASB began a research project to study whether to require quantitative disclosure about intangible assets. But the project languished, and in 2004, the FASB withdrew it from its research agenda.[82] The FASB renewed its interest in intellectual capital in 2007, considering whether to undertake a joint project with the International Accounting Standards Board (IASB) to expand disclosure guidelines for intangibles.[83] Both the FASB and the IASB acknowledged the importance of the project but decided not to move forward with it due to lack of resources,[84] and the ensuing financial crisis of 2008 brought other concerns to the fore.[85] However, the last few years have seen a reaffirmation of intellectual capital as a global driver of economic productivity and growth, along with renewed calls for financial reporting reforms.[86]

National accounting is another area that has made significant advances in the measurement of intellectual capital. National accounting quantifies macroeconomic indicators of investment and productivity, as distinguished from financial accounting, which quantifies individual businesses' investment and productivity. Economists have argued that intellectual capital should be incorporated into macroeconomic measures of national productivity and wealth, finding that the failure to do so

---

81 Lev, *supra* note 49, at 79–103; *see generally* Wayne S. Upton, Jr., Business and Financial Reporting: Challenges from the New Economy (2001).

82 Fin. Accounting Standards Bd., *Project Updates, Disclosure About Intangible Assets* (2004), http://www.fasb.org/intangibles.shtml. The FASB's decision to abandon the project was likely influenced by events of the early twenty-first century including Enron, the bursting of the dot-com stock bubble, and the economic downturn precipitated by the September 11 terrorist attack. As a result of these events, intellectual capital temporarily lost some of its cachet. *See* Perry D. Quick & Mary T. Goldschmid, *FASB Statements 141/142 and the Business Economist—Where, Oh Where Have My Intangibles Gone?* 37 Bus. Econ. 61, 61 (2002). The high-profile Enron case, which involved fraudulent reporting of intangible assets (e.g., synthetic leases), contributed to the unease about whether intangibles should be reported as valuable assets. *See id.*; Arewa, *supra* note 27, at 66–79 (describing the challenges and uncertainties arising from attempts to account for intangibles in financial reporting, which facilitated fraudulent overstatement of the value of intangible assets by Enron and other corporations).

83 This was part of a broader and ongoing convergence project between the FASB and the IASB initiated in 2002. *See* Am. Inst. Certified Public Accountants, International Financial Reporting Standards (IFRS): An AICPA Backgrounder 5–6 (2011). The current FASB and IASB standards for R&D differ substantially in that the IASB standards provide for the capitalization of development costs. *See Intangible Assets*, International Accounting Standard 38 (Int'l Accounting Standards Bd. 2004); Baruch Lev et al., *An Accounting Perspective on Intellectual Capital, in* Perspectives on Intellectual Capital 42, 46–49 (Bernard Marr ed., 2005).

84 *See* Fin. Accounting Standards Bd., Action Alert No. 07-52 (2007).

85 The book–tax gap may also provide insights into the 2008 financial crisis. *See* Weiner, *supra* note 32, at 372 (noting that IRS data show that many of the largest book–tax gaps were reported by financial institutions that made use of structured financing and special purpose entities; positing that financial and tax reporting disparities may have contributed to the 2008 financial crisis). In contrast to the Enron/corporate tax shelter era, the book–tax gap has not featured prominently in the postmortem of the financial crisis.

86 *See* 2013 OECD Report, *supra* note 73; *see* Emily Chasan, *FASB's Future Priorities Start to Take Shape*, Wall St. J. CFO J. (Sept. 17, 2013) (noting that accounting for intangible assets is among the top reform priorities in a 2013 FASB survey), http://blogs.wsj.com/cfo/2013/09/17/fasbs-future-priorities-start-to-take-shape/.

understates U.S. national wealth by as much as $1 trillion.[87] As a result of this research, in 2013, the U.S. Bureau of Economic Analysis made a major change to its methodology for measuring gross domestic product: for the first time, it counted businesses' R&D outlays as investments rather than expenses and it also counted artistic creations such as films, music, and books as investments.[88] In 2013, these additions increased the size of the U.S. economy by $560 billion, or 3.6 percent.[89]

Financial and Tax Accounting for Intellectual Capital: An Assessment

This brief overview of the financial and tax treatment of intellectual capital has a number of implications for the ways in which financial reporting can inform the taxation of intellectual capital. Consistent with the modern trend regarding financial and tax accounting, the two systems have "flipped" in their treatment of intellectual capital, particularly self-created intellectual capital. Financial accounting is becoming less conservative, moving away from a system of expensing intellectual capital outlays and toward recognizing them as investments.[90] This change is largely inchoate, but according to the OECD, "[t]here is a growing consensus among practitioners and policymakers that better reflection of intangibles in corporate reporting is required to improve the functioning of capital markets and private finance."[91] At the same time, the tax law is becoming less protective of the fisc, moving away from capitalizing self-created intellectual capital and toward a regime of immediate deductibility.[92]

The incipient divergence between the financial and tax treatment of intellectual capital bears a superficial resemblance to the divergence observed during the Enron era, when corporations

87 *See* Corrado et al., *supra* note 51, at 669–70; Leonard Nakamura, *Investing in Intangibles: Is a Trillion Dollars Missing from GDP?*, Fed. Reserve Bank of Phila. Bus. Rev., Q4 2001, at 27, 36; *see also* Carol A. Corrado et al., *Measuring Capital and Technology*, *in* Measuring Capital in the New Economy 11, 22–29 (Carol A. Corrado et al. eds., 2005).

88 *See* Peter Coy, *The Rise of the Intangible Economy: U.S. GDP Counts R&D, Artistic Creation*, Businessweek, July 18, 2013, at 6. The Bureau of Economic Analysis restated gross domestic product for each year retroactive to 1929, the first year of measurement. *Id.*

89 Jared Bernstein & Dean Baker, *What Is 'Seinfeld' Worth?*, N.Y. Times, Aug. 1, 2013, at A21.

90 The trend away from conservatism in financial accounting of intellectual capital is part of a larger trend. In 2010, the FASB explicitly rejected conservatism as a principle of financial accounting. *See* George Mundstock, *Tax Accounting Myths*, 22 U. Miami Bus. L. Rev. 27, 28–30 (2013).

91 Org. for Econ. Cooperation & Dev., Corporate Reporting of Intangible Assets: A Progress Report 4 (2012). *But see* Inst. of Chartered Accountants in Eng. & Wales, Developments in New Reporting Models 15–22 (2009) (arguing that a new approach to the financial reporting of intangibles is not necessary or appropriate).

92 Johnson, *supra* note 69, at 1382–83; *see* David A. Weisbach, *Measurement and Tax Depreciation Policy: The Case of Short-Term Intangibles*, 33 J. Legal Stud. 199, 205 (2004) (noting a broad trend that most intangibles are deducted). The trend is a bit muddied by the treatment of intangibles under Code § 197. On the one hand, goodwill went from being nonamortizable to being amortizable over 15 years, which trends toward deductibility. On the other hand, some intangible assets subject to Code § 197 had a shorter amortization period under prior law, which trends away from deductibility. *See* Walter G. Antognini & Mitchell J. Kassoff, *Section 197: Congress and the IRS Attempt to Settle Disputes Involving Amortization of Intangibles*, 46 Tax Exec. 281, 281 (1994); *see* Israel Blumenfrucht, *Section 197: Intangible to Assess*, 75 Mgmt. Acct. 22 (1994) (noting that Code § 197 was scored as a revenue raiser because many intangible assets would be amortized over a longer period than under prior law). With respect to self-created intangibles, the INDOPCO regulations are a "radical departure" from capitalization to deductibility. Atkinson, *supra* note 70, at 229. This shift is likely much greater than the shift for acquired intangibles under Code § 197.

both overstated income on their financial reports and understated it on their tax returns. However, I would argue that the shift in financial accounting for intellectual capital is not indicative of the type of overly aggressive financial accounting that characterized the Enron era.[93] Rather, today's movement to reform financial accounting of intellectual capital to require increased capitalization reflects a growing consensus, supported by decades of research, that intellectual capital is inaccurately reported in financial statements.

The reasons why tax accounting is moving in the opposite direction—toward greater deductibility of self-created intellectual capital—are unclear, but I suspect they are less benign than on the financial accounting side. Some scholars assume that the current tax law deduction for self-created intellectual capital is an intentional legislative or administrative decision based on the ground that it is too difficult to value.[94] While concerns about administrability are clearly a dominant theme throughout the long and tortured history of capitalization,[95] there is scant direct evidence of a deliberate decision that intellectual capital should be deductible because it is too difficult to value.[96] Another rationale sometimes given for R&D deductions is that they are tax expenditures intended to subsidize activities that generate positive social externalities and offset the riskiness of investing in them.[97] However, this rationale fails to explain why the tax law also allows deductions for intellectual capital outlays such

93 On the other hand, there are still concerns about earnings management and Enron-type fraud. *See* Arewa, supra note 27, at 66–79 (describing the challenges and uncertainties arising from attempts to account for intangibles in financial reporting, which facilitated fraudulent overstatement of the value of intangible assets by Enron and other corporations); Gretchen Morgenson, *Earnings Without the Bad Stuff*, N.Y. Times, Nov. 9, 2013, at BN1 (describing how "non-GAAP reporting" under SEC Regulation G allows companies like Twitter to inflate earnings by removing goodwill amortization).

94 *See* Jane Gravelle & Jack Taylor, *Tax Neutrality and the Tax Treatment of Purchased Intangibles*, 45 Nat'l Tax J. 77, 81 (1992) (stating that the "tax treatment of created intangibles is largely due to administrative considerations, since it would be difficult in practice to identify those costs which are creating an intangible"); Weisbach, *supra* note 92, at 200 (stating that "because of [valuation] problems, the tax law often does not even try to measure depreciation for intangibles. Instead, it allows an immediate deduction, effectively choosing not to tax the return to these activities at all"). *But see* Johnson, *supra* note 53, at 1291 (stating that "there is no indication of [sic] a reasoned balance between convenience and a level economic playing field was ever under consideration. The expensing of intangible investments is not part of a deliberate decision to punish the disfavored tangible investments … or to subsidize intangible investments … .").

95 *See* Joseph Bankman, *The Story of* Indopco*: What Went Wrong in the Capitalization v. Deduction Debate*, *in* Tax Stories 225 (Paul Caron ed., 2d ed. 2009); John W. Lee et al., *Restating Capitalization Standards and Rules: The Case for Rough Justice Regulations (Part One)*, 23 Ohio N.U. L. Rev. 631 (1996–1997).

96 The only evidence of legislative purpose to this effect is from a Joint Committee on Taxation report studying the impact on small business of replacing the federal income tax: "Under present law, many expenditures by a business that may contribute to the creation of intangible assets are currently deductible as expenses of doing business. Thus, for example, salaries of employees, advertising, and other operating expenses generally are currently deductible, even though these expenditures may create or enhance the goodwill, going concern value, reputation, or customer base of the business. Expensing generally is allowed under present law because of the administrative difficulty of ascertaining the extent to which these expenditures contribute to the value of the intangible asset." Staff of J. Comm. on Taxation, 104th Cong., Impact on Small Business of Replacing the Income Tax 83 (Comm. Print 1996). This excerpt is a passing observation in a 100-page report about the impact on small business of replacing the income tax with a national sales tax, a value-added tax, or a consumption tax. The report devotes only a handful of pages to the taxation of intangibles.

97 Don Fullerton & Andrew B. Lyon, *Tax Neutrality and Intangible Capital*, *in* 2 Tax Policy and the Economy 63, 82 (Lawrence H. Summers ed., 1988); Robinson & Sansing, *supra* note 64, at 391; Martin A. Sullivan, *Will International Tax Reform Slow U.S. Technology Development?*, 141 Tax Notes 459, 459 (2013); Ethan Yale, *When Are Capitalization Exceptions Justified?*, 47 Tax L. Rev. 549, 573–74 (2004).

as advertising and strategic planning, which entail neither positive social externalities nor investment risk.[98] Another possible theory is that the trend toward greater deductibility is the result of industry capture and/or judicial ineptitude.[99] A third theory is that the income tax is moving toward a de facto consumption tax by allowing all capital investments to be deducted.[100]

This trend in tax accounting, toward greater deductibility of intellectual capital outlays, is cause for serious concern. It results in the loss of hundreds of billions of dollars in tax revenues, costly misallocations of resources, and a grave deviation from the accurate measurement of income.[101] The opposing trend in financial accounting can and should be enlisted to help reverse the tax trend. Financial accounting research and reform proposals advance a more accurate measurement of economic income from intellectual capital, which in turn can strengthen the foundations of both the financial and tax systems.

This is not to say that the financial and tax accounting systems should conform, nor is it to say that financial accounting has solved all the challenges of measuring intellectual capital accurately.[102]

The government currently takes an ambivalent stance on whether the R&D deduction is a tax expenditure (i.e., an explicit tax subsidy). On the one hand, the R&D deduction, along with the Code § 41 research and expenditure credit, is listed as a tax expenditure in the congressional and Treasury Department tax expenditure budgets. Staff of J. Comm. on Taxation, 113th Cong., Estimates of Federal Tax Expenditures for Fiscal Years 2012–2017, at 30 (2013); Office of Mgmt. & Budget, Exec. Office of the President, Fiscal Year 2013 Budget of the U.S. Government, at 254 (2012). On the other hand, the Treasury Department explanation states that while the deduction is considered a tax expenditure under the "normal tax method," it is considered not to be one under the "reference law baseline":

> Research and experimentation (R&E) projects can be viewed as investments because, if successful, their benefits accrue for several years. It is often difficult, however, to identify whether a specific R&E project is successful and, if successful, what its expected life will be. Because of this ambiguity, the reference law baseline tax system would allow of [sic] expensing of R&E expenditures. In contrast, under the normal tax method, the expensing of R&E expenditures is viewed as a tax expenditure.

Office of Mgmt. & Budget, *supra*, at 266.

98 In fact, some have argued the exact opposite—that advertising has negative externalities. *See* Fullerton & Lyon, *supra* note 97, at 83; Mona Hymel, *Consumerism, Advertising, and the Role of Tax Policy*, 20 Va. Tax Rev. 347 (2000–2001).

99 *See* Lee et al., *supra* note 95.

100 *See* Johnson, *supra* note 53, at 1291–92; Robinson & Sansing, *supra* note 64, at 391; *see also* Ethan Yale, *The Final* INDOPCO *Regulations*, 105 Tax Notes 435, 436 (2004) (stating that the INDOPCO regulations "resolve many capitalization questions in a manner that will defeat rather than promote a clear reflection of income, and move us closer to a consumption tax base").

101 *See* Kahng, *supra* note 53, at 41–44 (estimating the revenue loss resulting from intellectual capital deductions to be as high as $1 trillion over 10 years and describing the allocative inefficiencies that result from undertaxing the income from intellectual capital).

102 To better measure and report firm-specific intellectual capital investments such as worker training and strategic planning is an enormous challenge that has yet to be met by either financial or tax accounting. Because this type of investment does not produce separable and marketable assets, it is difficult to observe and value. (In cases where it does change hands—where an ongoing business is transferred—firm-specific investments are aggregated into a residual asset category—goodwill—after value is first assigned to other separate and identifiable assets.) *See supra* note 56 and accompanying text. In addition, there are long-held biases against considering human capital inputs to be valuable to economic productivity. *See* Hill, *supra* note 71, at 428–37 (describing how economists such as Adam Smith treated labor as "unproductive" in the sense that it did not increase the stock of material wealth).

As discussed above, each system has objectives that may warrant differing treatments of intellectual capital.[103] For example, some scholars argue that financial reporting of intellectual capital should not be quantified on the balance sheet but rather should be reported in qualitative, narrative form.[104] While this approach might be an effective way to provide information to investors, it obviously will not work for tax purposes, where the treatment of intellectual capital expenditures must be expressed in quantitative terms (i.e., either deducted or capitalized).

A more promising model for tax accounting of intellectual capital is the national accounting approach of economists Carol Corrado, Charles Hulten, and Daniel Sichel. To quantify the extent to which intellectual capital contributes to national economic productivity and growth, Corrado, Hulten, and Sichel estimate investments in various categories of intellectual capital such as R&D and advertising. They then apply a depreciation rate to each category based on empirical estimates of the expected useful life of the investments. Thus, for example, they assume an annual depreciation rate of 20 percent for R&D and 60 percent for advertising. This approach to accounting for intellectual capital was adopted by the 2014 tax reform proposals of the U.S. Senate Committee on Finance and the U.S. House Committee on Ways and Means, both of which would require intellectual capital expenditures such as R&D, advertising, and intangible drilling costs to be amortized over five years.[105]

Perspectives on the Relationship Between Financial and Tax Accounting

My purpose in discussing the financial and tax accounting treatment of intellectual capital is to demonstrate how much tax accounting can learn from financial accounting in this vitally important area. Contrary to the views of both the U.S. Supreme Court in *Thor Power* and Adam Chodorow in Chapter 7,[106] I contend that financial accounting should be highly relevant to tax accounting and vice versa. Both systems should be guided by a principle that prioritizes the accurate measure of economic income, and each should be informed by the other to help implement that principle.

---

103 Disclosure of financial and tax accounting differences may also be useful. In 2010, the IRS revised Schedule M-3 to require large corporations to disclose information about book–tax disparities regarding R&D. The new disclosure is likely intended to help the IRS identify income shifting through transfer-pricing and cost-sharing agreements. However, the new information will also highlight the differences in the treatment of intellectual capital outlays.

104 *See, e.g.*, Alcaniz et al., *supra* note 74, at 112–15 (describing the narrative and critical accounting approaches to reporting intellectual capital and noting that quantitative measures often disadvantage workers); Robin Kramar et al., *Accounting for Human Capital and Organizational Effectiveness*, *in* The Oxford Handbook of Human Capital 382, 393–95 (Alan Burton-Jones & J.C. Spender eds., 2011) (arguing that quantitative approaches to reporting financial capital are inadequate and must be broadened to include nonfinancial indicators through the use of narratives).

105 *See* Staff of S. Comm. on Finance, 113th Cong., Summary of Staff Discussion Draft: Cost Recovery and Accounting 8 (2013); Majority Staff of H. Comm. on Ways & Means, 113th Cong., 2014 Tax Reform Act Discussion Draft Section-by-Section Summary 54–56 (2014); *see also* Calvin H. Johnson, *Capitalize Costs of Software Development*, 124 Tax Notes 603 (2009) (proposing to repeal the deduction for software development costs and require their amortization over 15 years); Kahng, *supra* note 53, at 53–56 (proposing a unitary, five-year amortization period for self-created intellectual capital including computer software, scientific and nonscientific R&D, advertising, employee training, and organizational innovation).

106 *See supra* notes 14–18 and accompanying text; *see also* Geier, *supra* note 1 (arguing that financial accounting principles ought not to govern tax, as exemplified by the financial accounting matching principle).

I want to emphasize that this guiding principle should be a starting point for financial and tax accounting rules, not the end point. In the case of tax accounting, rules might diverge from an accurate measure of income to accommodate other goals of the tax system such as ease of administration, protection of the fisc, and the implementation of social and economic policies through the use of tax expenditures. But in the pursuit of these other goals, we should not lose sight of economic income as the foundation of the income tax.

With respect to his proposal to abandon accrual accounting in favor of cash accounting for tax purposes, Chodorow argues that financial accounting's reliance on accrual accounting mismeasures economic income and that a cash-based method of accounting would bring tax accounting into closer alignment with economic income.[107] Chodorow's argument is consistent with my methodological claim that tax accounting ought to start with economic income as its foundation. However, I disagree with Chodorow's view that cash accounting measures economic income more accurately than accrual accounting. Instead, I subscribe to David Hasen's view that cash accounting rules do not embody a coherent concept of economic income, although they may be justifiable on administrative or revenue raising grounds.[108] Hasen argues the rationales in favor of cash accounting conflate these secondary goals with the accurate measure of income.[109]

A similar conflation of goals occurs with respect to the tax treatment of intellectual capital. The tax accounting deduction for intellectual capital outlays severely understates income from intellectual capital. The mismeasurement is justified on the grounds of administrative ease or promoting R&D, but these casually offered rationales are inadequate to justify the extreme undertaxation of self-created intellectual capital. When we lose sight of the fact that economic income is the foundation of the income tax, it becomes all too easy for unreasoned arguments and specious rhetoric about administrability or tax expenditures to undermine the income tax. As the case of intellectual capital demonstrates, financial accounting can and should be used to bring tax accounting more closely into alignment with the accurate measure of income.

As a less radical alternative to the adoption of cash-based tax accounting, Chodorow proposes a more vigorous administrative and judicial oversight of abuses under accrual taxation pursuant to the IRS's authority to impose accounting rules that "clearly reflect income." I am highly skeptical of the efficacy of administrative and judicial oversight. The case of intellectual capital is again instructive. The IRS and courts have enabled and even promoted an inaccurate measure of income by allowing deductions for most self-created intellectual capital outlays—a stark illustration of their inability or unwillingness to ensure that the tax accounting rules measure income accurately. Only Congress has managed to defend the tax base with the enactment of Code § 197, although that provision applies to the limited universe of acquired intellectual capital. Congress should also act to ensure the accuracy of tax accounting rules with respect to self-created intellectual capital. To achieve this goal, it should capitalize on the wealth of research and advances in financial accounting, while remaining cognizant of the unique objectives, needs, and design constraints of the tax system. The 2014 legislative proposals described above adopt this approach.

---

107 Chodorow asserts that financial accounting's reliance on accrual accounting stems in part from its fundamental conservatism, which is inconsistent with the values of the tax system. *See* Chodorow, *infra* ch. 7, at text accompanying notes 37–38 and 64–65. I argue that financial accounting has abandoned its conservatism with respect to its treatment of intellectual capital, as part of a broader, explicit move away from conservatism in financial accounting. *See supra* notes 26–33, 90–91, and accompanying text.

108 *See* David M. Hasen, *The Tax Treatment of Advance Receipts*, 61 Tax L. Rev. 395, 397–99, 442–55 (2007).

109 *See id.*

Conclusion

Financial and tax accounting have much to say to each other, although their languages are not identical. At the root level, each system strives to measure economic income accurately, but each has constraints and secondary goals that necessitate departures from this ideal. While the systems should not be forced into conformity, their differences and similarities should be exploited to improve and enhance both. The case of intellectual capital is an important example of how financial accounting can lead the way in improving tax accounting.

Chapter 7

Is It Time to Abandon Accrual Accounting for Tax Purposes?

Adam Chodorow*

Introduction

Every few years, an outcry arises over the fact that large companies report billions of dollars of income on their financial statements yet pay little or nothing in taxes. This outcry is typically followed by calls to (1) require greater disclosure of differences between financial, sometimes referred to as book, and tax accounting; (2) impose a tax on the difference between book and tax income; or (3) align book and tax accounting so that firms must report the same income figures to investors and the IRS. This chapter focuses on the debate over book–tax alignment.

Those opposed to alignment have identified a number of problems with aligning book and tax accounting. Some are practical, such as the impact such a move might have on Congress's ability to use the tax laws for social policy objectives.[1] Others are more theoretical, focusing on the different roles these two accounting regimes serve. For instance in *Thor Power Tool Co. v. Commissioner*, the U.S. Supreme Court justified its refusal to require alignment by noting that financial accounting serves to provide information to investors, while tax accounting is aimed at raising revenue.[2] As a result of these different purposes, the former permits significant flexibility and even estimates, while the latter requires uniform treatment and precision, thus precluding alignment.

I argue here that a far more fundamental difference in purpose warrants keeping the two accounting systems separate. Accrual accounting, which lies at the heart of most financial accounting regimes, is routinely hailed as the most accurate way to measure income because it matches anticipated revenues and expenses regardless of when cash is actually received or spent. However, separating income inclusion or deductions from cash receipts or expenditures can seriously undermine an income tax. What distinguishes income taxes from consumption taxes is that income taxes reach both consumption and returns on capital, while consumption taxes reach only consumption. Accrual accounting's disconnect between cash receipts and expenditures and the reporting of income or deductions permits taxpayers to take advantage of the time value of money and can turn a nominal income tax into a de facto consumption tax by functionally excluding returns on capital from taxation.

The need for a tax-specific income definition and accounting system can also be seen in the early history of the income tax, in which tax authorities struggled to differentiate tax accounting rules from the trust and financial accounting rules that had been imported into the tax laws. In particular, they had to develop a system for tracking previously taxed dollars to ensure that all income was

* I would like to thank Lily Kahng, Tony Infanti, Deborah Geier, Joseph Dodge, and participants at the University of Seattle Faculty Workshop for comments on earlier drafts.

1 *See* Reuven S. Avi-Yonah, *The Case for Retaining the Corporate AMT*, 56 SMU L. Rev. 333, 334 (2003) (defending the traditional corporate AMT against claims that it should be abolished).

2 439 U.S. 522, 540 (1979).

taxed and that it was taxed only once. Aligning book and tax accounting would potentially reopen long-settled matters.

In light of this history and the more recent insights into the impact accounting rules can have on an income tax, I argue that efforts to align financial and tax accounting are misguided. Indeed, in some cases the two regimes should deviate more than they already do. Specifically, Congress should consider returning to the original income tax rules, which required taxpayers to use the cash method of accounting, to avoid the problems posed by accrual accounting.[3] If requiring all taxpayers to use the cash method of accounting is a bridge too far, Congress and the courts should make clear that the IRS's authority to challenge a taxpayer's accounting method under Code § 446(b) extends to any situation where timing effects permit income to go untaxed.[4]

To be clear, I do not mean to suggest that financial and tax accounting should deviate in all regards. Both systems attempt to measure income, and there is much tax accounting can learn from financial accounting, especially when it comes to income definition and capitalization. Financial accounting eschews the social and economic policy provisions that distort the Code's income definition and create unnecessary complexity and higher rates. And, as Lily Kahng describes in Chapter 6, financial accounting experts are seriously considering rules to require capitalization of expenditures that create intellectual capital. However, where fundamental tax principles and goals conflict with financial accounting rules, tax accounting should forge its own path.

The Book–Tax Disparity "Problem" and the Debate over Book–Tax Alignment

The Problem

Reports that wealthy Americans and American companies pay little or no income tax periodically bubble to the surface, creating significant impetus for reform. For instance, in 1969, Treasury Secretary Joseph Barr revealed that 155 individuals with annual incomes over $200,000 (including 20 earning over $1 million per year) paid no income taxes in 1967.[5] In response, Congress enacted the alternative minimum tax (AMT) to ensure that wealthy individuals pay some income tax.[6]

Fifteen years later, in 1984, Robert McIntyre issued a report for Citizens for Tax Justice, revealing that 128 out of the 250 large companies he studied, including General Electric (GE), Boeing, Dow Chemical, Lockheed, and W.R. Grace & Company, paid no federal income tax.[7] This report was seen as one of the important catalysts for the 1986 tax reform, which included a corporate AMT.[8]

3 Revenue Act of 1913, ch. 16, 38 Stat. 114, 167.

4 Code § 446(b) currently states that the IRS may challenge a taxpayer's accounting method where such method does not "clearly reflect income."

5 *See* J. Econ. Comm., 91st Cong., Economic Report of the President: Hearings Before the Joint Economic Committee, Congress of the United States 6 (Comm. Print 1969).

6 Tax Reform Act of 1969, Pub. L. No. 91-172, 83 Stat. 487.

7 *See* Jeffrey H. Birnbaum & Alan S. Murray, Showdown at Gucci Gulch 12 (1987). Ironically, W.R. Grace & Company's chairman headed a federal commission that concluded that wasteful spending was a huge threat to America's solvency.

8 Tax Reform Act of 1986, Pub. L. No. 99-514, 100 Stat. 2085. Corporations were required to include in income 50 percent of the difference between book and tax income for purposes of calculating the AMT. This provision was replaced in 1990 with one that required corporations to include 75 percent of the difference between adjusted current earnings and taxable income. Andrew B. Lyon, *Tax Topics: Alternative Minimum Tax,*

About 15 years later, the financial markets were rocked by a series of accounting scandals, in which a number of companies, including Enron, Worldcom, and Adelphia Communications, Inc., manipulated accounting rules to report inflated income, hide off-balance sheet debt, or smooth out income to show steady increases year over year. At the same time, these companies were able to report relatively low earnings to the IRS, thus avoiding the tax hit that would have otherwise accompanied their fraud. This crisis led to increased disclosure requirements both for tax and financial reporting purposes.[9]

More recently, the news has been dominated by reports that a number of companies, including GE (again) and Apple, have found ways to manipulate the international tax rules so as to pay little or no income tax anywhere.[10] The companies insist that they have followed all the rules and are doing nothing improper,[11] but the revelations have once again generated calls for reform. Assuming that this current outcry follows the pattern above and Congress is motivated to act, the question of what it should do arises.

The Debate over Book–Tax Alignment

Scholars have proposed three main types of responses to the problem of book–tax disparity. The first two track the reforms already implemented, including taxing the difference between book and tax income, either independently[12] or through a revised AMT, and requiring even greater disclosure whenever book and tax diverge, whether through the tax or financial accounting systems[13] or through some new format.[14] The third, and most radical, suggestion is that Congress align book and tax accounting,[15] requiring companies to report the same income figures for both tax and book purposes, perhaps subject to express, congressionally approved deviations.[16] Although accounting typically refers to the *timing* of income inclusion and deductions, in this context, alignment would require income definition conformity. This could significantly curtail Congress's ability to use the Code for social or economic policy purposes, assuming, as most do, that the tax rules would conform to those found in financial accounting.

Corporate, TAX POL'Y CTR., http://www.taxpolicycenter.org/taxtopics/encyclopedia/alternative-minimum-tax-corporate.cfm (last visited July 25, 2014).

9 Taxpayers had been required since 1990 to report certain differences between book and tax income on a Schedule M-1. This was replaced by Schedule M-3 in 2004, which among other things required taxpayers to explain the differences between their financial and tax accounting. Rev. Proc. 2004-45, 2004-2 C.B. 140. On the accounting side, the Financial Accounting Standards Board (FASB) enacted provisions, such as Financial Interpretation Number (FIN) 48, which required companies to report uncertain tax positions.

10 *See, e.g.*, Megan Greene, *Apple's Tax Dodge Should Prompt Rethink in Ireland*, BLOOMBERGVIEW (May 26, 2013), http://www.bloomberg.com/news/2013-05-26/apple-s-tax-dodge-should-prompt-rethink-in-ireland.html.

11 *See Apple CEO Rejects "Tax Evasion" Charges*, ALJAZEERA (May 21, 2013), http://www.aljazeera.com/business/2013/05/201352165831522483.html.

12 *See* Daniel Shaviro, *The Optimal Relationship Between Taxable Income and Financial Accounting Income: An Analysis and a Proposal*, 97 GEO. L.J. 423 (2009).

13 *See* Anthony J. Luppino, *Stopping the Enron End-Runs and Other Trick Plays: The Book–Tax Accounting Conformity Defense*, 2003 COLUM. BUS. L. REV. 35 (2003).

14 *See* Peter C. Canellos & Edward D. Kleinbard, *Disclosing Book–Tax Differences*, 96 TAX NOTES 999 (2002).

15 *See* Celia Whitaker, Note, *Bridging the Book–Tax Accounting Gap*, 115 YALE L.J. 680 (2005).

16 *See* George K. Yin, *Getting Serious About Corporate Tax Shelters: Taking A Lesson From History*, 54 SMU L. REV. 209 (2001).

It is hard to argue against increased disclosure, which would allow interested parties to identify issues with either the tax or accounting rules and propose changes when appropriate.[17] However, it is not clear how effective it would be. Some differences between book and tax are intended,[18] and book–tax disparity may not reflect sheltering activity.[19] Accordingly, significant gaps between book and tax income, and the outcry they engender, may persist. In addition, disclosure will not deter tax shelters that do not depend on book–tax disparity.[20]

Imposing a tax on book–tax disparity ensures that companies cannot avoid more tax than Congress intended[21] and preserves Congress's control over the tax rules, including its ability to use the Code to promote social and economic policy.[22] However, this solution retains two sets of accounting rules, which continues the current complexity. Indeed, it adds to that complexity because taxpayers may not be able to predict the tax consequences of their transactions until they determine their tax and financial accounting income at the end of the tax year.[23]

For these reasons, among others, a number of would-be reformers are drawn to the apparently simple solution of aligning tax with financial accounting. Those calling for book–tax alignment cite a number of benefits, including (1) simplifying the accounting process by having one set of books; (2) eliminating the incentive to search for arbitrage opportunities;[24] (3) constraining both financial fraud and tax evasion by "setting ambition against ambition," that is, by pitting the desire to report high earnings to regulators, investors, and lenders against the desire to minimize tax liabilities;[25] and (4) adopting a broader and more accurate measure of income, which should permit lower rates.[26]

Nevertheless, calls for tax to follow financial accounting have not been widely embraced, either from the tax or financial accounting side of the aisle. Concerns range from the practical to the theoretical. Some are concerned that Congress would have to give up its ability to implement social and economic policy through the tax laws.[27] Others are concerned that Congress will not

---

17 *See* Canellos & Kleinbard, *supra* note 14.

18 For example, the deferral of foreign earned income and the treatment of stock options.

19 *See* Linda M. Beale, *Book–Tax Conformity and the Corporate Tax Shelter Debate: Assessing the Proposed Section 475 Mark-to-Market Safe Harbor*, 24 Va. Tax Rev. 301, 352 (2004).

20 *See* George K. Yin, *The Problem of Corporate Tax Shelters: Uncertain Dimensions, Unwise Approaches*, 55 Tax L. Rev. 405 (2002) (discussing the Compaq and UPS cases).

21 *See* Avi-Yonah, *supra* note 1, at 334.

22 A tax on the difference between book and tax income will constrain Congress's ability to use the Code to provide benefits to some degree, because it might recapture some of the benefits conferred. Nonetheless, Congress can take this into account when designing benefits and increase them to account for this possibility. *Id.*

23 *See* Terrence R. Chorvat & Michael S. Knoll, *The Case for Repealing the Corporate Alternative Minimum Tax*, 56 SMU L. Rev. 305, 313 (2002) (arguing that the corporate AMT should be eliminated because it is inefficient).

24 *See* Luppino, *supra* note 13, at 184–85.

25 *See* Shaviro, *supra* note 12, at 446–47.

26 One study suggested that a switch from tax to book income would allow rates to drop from 35 percent to 28 percent. *See* Calvin H. Johnson, *GAAP Tax*, 83 Tax Notes 425, 425 (1999) (citing Kenneth Wertz, *A Book Income Tax*, Proceedings of 91st Annual Conference on Taxation, 1998).

27 For instance, the exclusion of municipal bond interest from income under Code § 103, understood to be a subsidy to bond issuers, would have to be abandoned. Similarly, accelerated depreciation would no longer be allowed. This is one of the largest corporate tax expenditures, costing an estimated $274 billion over a 10-year window. *See* Memorandum Regarding Revenue Estimates from Thomas A. Barthold, Joint Comm.

give up such power and instead will interfere with the financial accounting rules.[28] This could distort the information provided and transfer the rule-making process from accounting experts to a political body, a possibility accountants abhor.[29] Still others worry that aligning book and tax would decrease the amount of information available to investors.[30]

Others question whether the growth in book–tax disparity is actually a problem[31] or whether alignment will adequately address it.[32] Moreover, the financial accounting rules have their own problems,[33] which alignment would not solve. In addition, setting ambition against ambition may not actually curtail aggressive tax planning or financial reporting, especially for private companies, which have no incentive to report high earnings. Even public companies may not feel constrained because they might be able to find other ways to communicate value to investors,[34] allowing them to report low earnings to reduce tax burdens, without suffering any downside.[35] Managers may also be willing to pay higher taxes or report lower earnings if the detriment is outweighed by the benefit.[36]

In *Thor Power Tool Co. v. Commissioner*, the U.S. Supreme Court focused on the different purposes the two accounting regimes serve and the design features that flow from those differences in deciding that tax accounting need not follow financial accounting. Financial accounting is designed to provide management and investors with useful information, while the tax system is designed to collect revenue and ensure that similarly situated taxpayers bear similar burdens.[37] As

---

on Taxation, to an unnamed recipient (Oct. 27, 2011), *available at* http://democrats.waysandmeans.house.gov/sites/democrats.waysandmeans.house.gov/files/media/pdf/112/JCTRevenueestimatesFinal.pdf.

28 *See* Shaviro *supra* note 12, at 465.

29 *Id.* As noted above, a possible solution to these problems would be to use book income for tax purposes but to allow Congress to craft explicit deviations. *See* Yin, *supra* note 16, at 224. However, assuming Congress were to retain the number of different preferences now in the Code, the gains from simplification would likely be lost.

30 *See* Michelle Hanlon et al., *Evidence for the Possible Information Loss of Conforming Book Income and Taxable Income*, 48 J.L. & Econ. 407 (2005) (arguing that tax information that differs from financial accounting information may provide insights to investors that would be lost if book and tax were aligned).

31 For instance, two of the key drivers of book–tax disparity are the different treatment of options and foreign earned income under financial and tax accounting rules, neither of which involves improper sheltering.

32 *See* Yin, *supra* note 20, at 419.

33 For example, the Enron, Worldcom, and Adelphia accounting scandals.

34 For instance, taxpayers are now permitted to use the last-in, first-out (LIFO) method of inventory accounting for tax purposes only if they use LIFO for financial accounting purposes. Many companies do so but also report their financial results using the first-in, first-out (FIFO) method through a variety of means, including footnotes in the financial balance sheets and through press releases.

35 Some empirical evidence suggests that managers care about the cosmetics of their accounting, even when there is no cash-flow consequence. Efficient market theory suggests that this should not be so because the market will ferret out and account for information from whatever source available. Scholars have posited that external constraints, such as loan covenants, account for this behavior, though pride may also come into play. *See* David I. Walker & Victor Fleischer, *Book/Tax Conformity and Equity Compensation*, 62 Tax L. Rev. 399, 408–09 (2009); *see also* Shaviro, *supra* note 12, at 460 (noting that the accounting treatment of stock options appears to have affected behavior, despite having no impact on cash flow).

36 The short-lived version of the AMT that existed from 1986 until 1989, which keyed off of book–tax differences, has been referred to as a "bragging tax" that some companies were apparently willing to pay. *See* Johnson, *supra* note 26, at 426. Indeed, a recent study of companies forced to restate their earnings for financial accounting purposes revealed that they paid up to 11 cents on the dollar for their overstated earnings. *See* Shaviro, *supra* note 12, at 449.

37 439 U.S. 522, 543–44 (1979).

a result, financial accounting rules permit a wide range of options for reporting transactions as well as estimates and guesses. At its core, it is supposed to be conservative. In contrast, tax principles require consistent treatment and precision. Conservatively stating income is not an income tax value. The court noted that requiring tax accounting to follow financial accounting would cede significant power to companies to decide, within the limits their accountants set, how much tax they wanted to pay.[38] In other words, the flexibility inherent in financial accounting could be abused to the detriment of the public fisc.

As described below, both the early history of the income tax—in which tax authorities struggled to disentangle the tax accounting rules from financial and trust accounting terms and concepts—and the more recent insights into the effects timing can have on an income tax offer a much more compelling justification for keeping tax and financial accounting separate than that provided by the Supreme Court in *Thor Power Tool*. The goal of an income tax is not simply to measure income, but to ensure that all income is subject to tax. Alignment would undermine this important goal by permitting taxpayers to use accrual accounting to escape tax on returns on capital by virtue of the time value of money.

Income Tax Fundamentals and the Development of a Tax-Specific Income Definition and Accounting Regime

Before adopting the modern income tax in 1913, the U.S. government depended largely on import duties and excise taxes, both classic consumption taxes, to raise revenue. Policy makers at the time understood that this regime was regressive and permitted significant accumulations of wealth to go untaxed. Accordingly, they pushed for an income tax to fix this problem, which would impose a tax on both consumption and returns on capital.[39] By reaching the significant wealth that was generated but not currently consumed, the income tax would ensure that the tax burden was apportioned based on ability to pay.

Early authorities struggled with the question of just what constituted income for tax purposes,[40] eventually adopting a broad definition that encompassed most accessions to wealth.[41] In the process, they developed a tax-specific income definition and accounting system to ensure that all income was included in the tax base and was subject to tax only once. More recently, scholars have come to understand that the timing inherent in an accounting system can convert a nominal income tax into a de facto consumption tax. Both this early history and modern insights are directly relevant to the question of whether tax and financial accounting should be aligned.

---

38 The Court's arguments regarding variation among taxpayers is not as clear-cut as the Court suggests. Similarly situated taxpayers currently use a variety of accounting methods, which affects their tax liability.

39 *See* Erik M. Jensen, The Taxing Power: A Reference Guide to the United States Constitution 17 (2005); *see also* Ajay K. Mehrotra, *Forging Fiscal Reform: Constitutional Change, Public Policy, and the Creation of Administrative Capacity in Wisconsin 1880–1920*, 20 J. Pol'y Hist. 94 (2008) (describing efforts in Wisconsin to implement an income tax to address the regressive effect of property taxes, which did not reach the significant intangible wealth being created); Ajay K. Mehrotra, *"More Mighty than the Waves of the Sea": Toilers, Tariffs, and the Income Tax Movement, 1880–1913*, 45 Lab. Hist. 165 (2007) (describing the perceived problems of the tariff system and labor's support of an income tax).

40 Eisner v. Macomber, 252 U.S. 189 (1920).

41 Comm'r v. Glenshaw Glass Co., 348 U.S. 426 (1955).

Early Efforts to Disentangle Financial, Trust, and Tax Accounting

Early tax authorities borrowed heavily from other accounting systems, including trust and financial accounting. While many of the concepts and rules worked well in the tax arena, some did not. In particular, the trust and financial accounting notion of capital and the distinction between capital and income did not work well in the tax system. Accordingly, the early authorities developed a tax-specific income definition and accounting rules.

Capital Gains

One of the first issues to arise under the income tax was whether capital gains, which were clearly distinguished from income under the trust accounting regime, could be considered income for tax purposes. Trust law differentiates between the corpus or capital (i.e., amounts put into a trust) and the income produced by the capital. The distinction matters because trusts often permit access to the income to lifetime beneficiaries, while reserving the capital for remaindermen.

The question of whether capital gains (i.e., gains on the sale of capital assets) should be considered income for tax purposes first arose in England. As Calvin Johnson has explained, the British excluded capital gains from their first income tax in 1799.[42] The British income tax (like the American income tax) was based on the notion that those with a greater ability to pay should pay more to support government. However, at that time most real property in Britain was either entailed or held in trust.[43] Current owners were only entitled to the income generated by the land, usually in the form of agricultural produce or rents. Any gains that accrued to the trust property (i.e., the capital) were not available for current consumption and therefore did not increase a life beneficiary's ability to pay. Accordingly, they were not considered income for tax purposes.

The possibility of taxing capital gains in Britain was raised during major tax reform efforts in 1920 and 1955, but the idea was rejected both times. The British finally decided to tax capital gains in 1965, when it became apparent that such gains *were* available for current consumption thus increasing the recipient's ability to pay. Excluding capital gains from income under such circumstances created significant fairness issues because taxpayers with considerable capital gains were able to live largely income-tax free, while low-paid wage earners were subject to the tax. The decision to include capital gains in income rectified this inequity and brought the tax base closer to the underlying ability-to-pay justification for an income tax.

In the United States, this question was decided in *Merchants' Loan & Trust Co. v. Smietanka*,[44] in which the plaintiff argued that gain on the sale of trust property (i.e., stock in a company) was not taxable under the recently enacted income tax because it was not treated as income under the terms of the trust. The U.S. Supreme Court quickly disposed of this argument, holding that trust accounting rules distinguishing capital gains from income did not control in the income tax setting and that such gains were indeed subject to the income tax. The Court pointed out that the tax laws clearly contemplated a tax on gains from the sale of property,[45] and it would be problematic if private parties could remove such gains from the tax base by simply placing property in trust and restricting the use of capital gains.

42 Calvin H. Johnson, *Taxing the Consumption of Capital Gains*, 28 VA. TAX REV. 477, 488–98 (2009).

43 *Id.* at 490–94. Entailed property was deemed to be owned by the current owner and his heirs, which prevented the current owner from selling it.

44 255 U.S. 509 (1921).

45 *Id.* at 516 (citing Revenue Act of 1916, ch. 463, § 2(a), 39 Stat. 756, 757).

In fact, as noted above, subjecting returns on capital to taxation was precisely the goal of the income tax. Nonetheless, Congress quickly acted to reduce the tax rates on capital gains,[46] leaving the income tax rule unchanged but moving the treatment of capital gains closer to the trust accounting practice of excluding such gains from the definition of income. While there has been much debate since then over the appropriate treatment of capital gains under the income tax,[47] the notion that the income definition and associated accounting regimes for tax and trust or financial purposes should differ has gone unchallenged.

Basis, Damages, and Gifts

Another example of early efforts to develop a tax-specific income definition and disentangle tax accounting from other accounting systems can be seen in efforts to develop the concept of basis, especially as applied to damages and gifts. As Joseph Dodge and Deborah Geier have explained, the notion that income should be taxed only once is one of the key tenets of an income tax.[48] Thus, tracking previously taxed dollars is of utmost importance.[49] This tracking is accomplished through the now-familiar concept of basis. Thus, property purchased with after-tax dollars is given a basis equal to cost,[50] which is subtracted when the asset is sold to determine gain or loss.[51]

The tax-free return of basis is often referred to as a recovery of capital, a phrasing that derives directly from the trust and financial accounting concepts initially imported into the tax laws. As described below, using trust and financial accounting concepts led early administrators to issue tax rulings regarding both damages and gifts that were unworkable from a tax perspective. When the difficulties of using uniform rules for tax and other accounting systems became apparent, tax authorities developed tax-specific accounting rules to accomplish the income tax's goals.

One of the early issues raised was whether the proceeds of accident insurance received as a result of personal injuries should be included in income. Borrowing from trust law, the U.S. Attorney General issued an opinion holding that such proceeds were not taxable.[52] The opinion relied heavily upon *Doyle v. Mitchell Bros. Co.*, a U.S. Supreme Court case construing the corporate excise tax of 1909,[53] in which the Court was asked to decide whether the sale of capital should produce income and, if so, how much. The Court borrowed from trust and financial accounting principles to distinguish income from capital, and it held that amounts paid to replace capital should be received tax free. Only the *gain* on the sale of capital—that is, amounts received above

---

46 Revenue Act of 1921, Pub. L. No. 67-98, § 206(b), 42 Stat. 227, 233.

47 The capital gains rate has been changed numerous times over the 100-year history of the income tax, including a brief time from 1986 to 1990 when capital gains were taxed at the same rate as other income. For a discussion of the rationales offered for taxing capital gains at lower rates, see Walter J. Blum, *A Handy Summary of the Capital Gains Arguments*, 35 Taxes 247 (1957).

48 *See* Joseph M. Dodge, The Logic of Tax: Federal Income Tax Theory and Policy 20 (1989); Deborah A. Geier, Murphy *and the Evolution of "Basis,"* 113 Tax Notes 578 (2006).

49 Equally important is the idea that expenses should be deducted once. Thus, a system for tracking deductions to prevent a double benefit is necessary.

50 26 U.S.C. §§ 1011, 1012.

51 *Id.* §§ 61, 165, 1001. For example, if Chloe purchases a vacation home for $100,000, she gets a basis of $100,000 under Code §§ 1011 and 1012. When she later sells it for $120,000, her taxable gain is the amount realized (i.e., $120,000) less her basis (i.e., $100,000), or $20,000. *Id.* § 1001(a). She receives the remaining $100,000 tax free.

52 *See* Income Tax—Proceeds of Accident Insurance Policy, 31 Op. Att'y Gen. 304, 308 (1918).

53 247 U.S. 179, 182 (1917).

and beyond the original value of that capital—should be taxed.[54] Based on this reasoning, the Attorney General opined that insurance proceeds received on account of personal injury could not be considered income because they simply replaced capital lost in the accident. Later that year, the U.S. Department of Treasury issued a decision adopting this position.[55] Congress quickly followed suit.[56]

Missing from this analysis was the *reason* capital should be recovered tax free, namely because it has already been subject to tax. This notion was implicit in the idea that only the gains in the value of capital were properly considered income for tax purposes,[57] but early authorities missed that idea. Both the original value of capital and its increase were capital in the hands of the corporation in *Doyle*. The reason only the gain was subject to tax was that it had not previously been taxed, whereas the original value was deemed to have been taxed as of December 31, 1908, the day before the corporate excise tax went into effect. In other words, it had basis. Applying this reasoning to damages, recovery should be tax free only if a taxpayer had basis in the amounts recovered. People do not typically have basis in their reputations, bodies, or labor (sometimes referred to as human capital), and therefore the entire amount of most personal injury damage recoveries should be considered gain.[58]

By the time the tax authorities understood this concept, the tax-free recovery of damages for certain personal injuries was enshrined in statute, and there was nothing they could do to alter this treatment.[59] However, in other contexts, the tax authorities quickly moved away from these trust and financial accounting concepts to develop basis accounting rules that carried out income tax objectives. Thus, in 1944, when the U.S. Court of Appeals for the First Circuit considered the question of damage recovery in *Raytheon Production Corp. v. Commissioner*, it easily found that Raytheon's recovery of damages for a destroyed subsidiary—a clear recovery of its capital—should be subject to tax because Raytheon had no basis in the destroyed company.[60]

A similar progression can be seen in the treatment of gifts. Consistent with the trust and financial accounting notion of capital, the early tax rules permitted the basis of gifts to be recorded as the fair market value at the time of the gift.[61] This was, after all, the value of the capital the donee received. Tax authorities quickly recognized that this rule permitted taxpayers to avoid tax on the sale of appreciated assets by simply giving them to someone else, who could sell them immediately with no gain. The proceeds could then be given back as a gift or spent as directed by the donor.

In 1921, Congress amended this rule to require that the donee take the donor's cost as his basis, thus preventing this gambit.[62] This new rule was immediately challenged on the ground that it was unconstitutional. In particular, the taxpayer argued that the gift "became a capital asset of the donee to the extent of its value when received and, therefore, when disposed of by her no part

---

54 For an in-depth discussion of this case, see Joseph M. Dodge, Murphy *and the Sixteenth Amendment in Relation to the Taxation of Non-Excludable Personal Injury Awards*, 8 FLA. TAX REV. 369, 407–18 (2007).

55 T.D. 2747, 20 Treas. Dec. Int. Rev. 457 (1918).

56 *See* Revenue Act of 1918, ch. 18, § 213(b)(6), 40 Stat. 1057, 1066.

57 *Doyle*, 247 U.S. at 185.

58 Some have suggested that people should have a basis in their human capital equal to its fair market value. *See* Elizabeth A. Rose, Note, Murphy*'s Mistakes: How the Circuit Court Should Analyze Section 104(a)(2) upon Rehearing*, 60 TAX LAW. 533 (2007). However, such a result would mean that exchanging labor for wages would yield little or no income.

59 *See supra* note 56.

60 144 F.2d 110 (1st Cir. 1944).

61 Taft v. Bowers, 278 U.S. 470, 471–72 (1929) (argument for petitioner).

62 Revenue Act of 1921, ch. 136, § 202(a), 42 Stat. 227, 229.

of that value could be treated as taxable income in her hands."[63] The U.S. Supreme Court noted that adhering to trust and business accounting practices would be inconsistent with enforcing the general scheme of taxation. It upheld the new rule as constitutional, essentially recognizing both the need for, and Congress's right to craft, special accounting rules for taxation consistent with a tax-specific income definition.

Capitalization, Depreciation, Accrual Accounting, and the Income Tax

Accountants insist that accrual accounting is the most accurate measure of income because it takes income and expenses into account when they are earned or incurred as opposed to when cash is received or spent.[64] Under this system, a company that spends $100,000 in Year 1, but which is then scheduled to receive a $110,000 payment in Year 2, will be seen to have $10,000 of income in Year 1, and not a $100,000 loss in Year 1 and a $110,000 gain in Year 2, as would be the case for a company using the cash method. Accrual accounting effectively matches expenses incurred with the income they generate.[65] From the perspective of one seeking to assess a company's financial health, the former seems a far more accurate depiction than the latter. Similarly, the capitalization and depreciation rules ensure that expenses that generate future income (e.g., those used to acquire an income-producing asset) are matched with the income they generate, thereby minimizing distortions caused by timing differences in outlays and receipts.

In 1916, Congress permitted companies that used the accrual method for financial accounting purposes to do so for tax purposes as well.[66] In the years since, it has required an increasing number of companies to use the accrual method.[67] However, advances in the understanding of the time value of money and the effects it can have on a tax system suggest that accrual accounting can seriously distort the amount of tax paid in present-value terms, yielding results consistent with a consumption tax.[68] As Deborah Geier notes, to ensure that income—and not just consumption—is taxed: (1) investments must be made with after-tax dollars; *and* (2) the income generated by such investments must be subjected to tax.[69] Disassociating income inclusion and deductions from cash receipts and outlays violates the first of these two requirements and therefore can convert a nominal income tax into a de facto consumption tax. This insight has significant implications when considering aligning book and tax accounting.

Capitalization and Depreciation

Before turning to accrual accounting, it may help to discuss these concepts in the context of the capitalization and depreciation rules, which apply to both cash method and accrual accounting regimes. Under financial accounting rules, companies are not entitled to a deduction when they purchase an asset. With regard to the balance sheet, when a company purchases an asset, its cash balance declines, but it adds an asset of the same value to its balance sheet, leaving total assets,

---

63 *Taft*, 278 U.S. at 481.

64 For a discussion of the matching principle and the central role it plays in accrual accounting, see Deborah A. Geier, *The Myth of the Matching Principle as a Tax Value*, 15 AM. J. TAX POL'Y 17, 29–30 (1998).

65 *Id.* at 27–29.

66 Revenue Act of 1916, ch. 463, § 13(b), 39 Stat. 756, 770.

67 *See, e.g.*, 26 U.S.C. § 448 (requiring most C corporations to use the accrual method of accounting).

68 *See* Geier, *supra* note 64, at 25–26.

69 *See* DEBORAH A. GEIER, AN INTRODUCTION TO THE U.S. FEDERAL INCOME TAXATION OF INDIVIDUALS 34 (2014).

liabilities, and owner's equity unchanged. The purchase merely effects a change in the form of wealth, like changing a single $20 bill into four $5 dollar bills. For this same reason, the company would not be entitled to a deduction on its income statement.

Nonetheless, financial accounting permits businesses to take depreciation deductions both on the balance sheet and against income. On the balance sheet, the deduction reflects the presumed decline in value of the asset; on the income statement, the deduction is consistent with the matching principle, a core accounting concept that motivates many of financial accounting's rules.[70] Under this principle, a portion of an asset's cost should be deducted each year against income over the asset's useful life to paint an accurate picture of the business's income.[71] Otherwise, timing differences between expenditures and income will distort the picture of the business's overall income.

Tax accounting has capitalization and depreciation rules similar to financial accounting. Amounts spent to acquire or create assets are not deductible.[72] Instead, they are recorded as basis, which, in turn, is used to calculate both depreciation deductions (where appropriate) and the gain or loss realized on the asset's disposition.[73] It would be tempting to conclude that the ideas that motivate financial accounting justify the tax rules, and indeed, some of the key tax cases appear to endorse the matching principle as the justification for capitalization and depreciation in the tax system.[74] However, a deeper look at tax principles reveals that capitalization and depreciation serve a different and important function in an income tax that may justify significant deviations between tax and financial accounting in other contexts, such as the propriety of accrual accounting.

One way to get at the role of capitalization in an income tax is to compare similarly structured income and consumption taxes. The income tax measures income by tracking cash inflows (or in the case of accrual accounting, income earned), allowing deductions for most income-producing expenditures (or in the case of accrual accounting, obligations undertaken). In contrast, a cash-flow consumption tax measures consumption indirectly by tracking a taxpayer's cash inflow and permitting a deduction for income-producing expenditures and savings.[75] One of the key differences between the two taxes is capitalization and depreciation, which have no place in a cash-flow consumption tax.

So, what do capitalization and depreciation do in an income tax? The financial accounting answer would be that they match spending with income, so that net income can be properly determined and then taxed, and, indeed, some courts have suggested that this is their purpose.[76] Another possibility, and one more firmly grounded in tax theory, is that they are consistent with the Haig-Simons-Schanz income definition, which posits that income is the sum of consumption and change in wealth.[77] Capital expenditures should not lead to current deductions because they do not

70 *See* Geier, *supra* note 64, at 27.

71 Otherwise, the company that purchases a machine for $100,000 might report a $100,000 loss on the purchase and $10,000 per year of income from the machine over the next 15 years, as opposed to a net $50,000 gain. If the amount must be capitalized and no depreciation deductions are allowed, the result would be $10,000 of income each year and then a $100,000 loss when the spent asset is abandoned.

72 26 U.S.C. §§ 263, 263A.

73 *Id.* §§ 167, 168, 1001, 1011, 1012, 1016.

74 *See, e.g.*, INDOPCO, Inc. v. Comm'r, 503 U.S. 79, 83–84 (1992) ("[T]he Code endeavors to match expenses with revenues of the taxable period to which they are properly attributable, thereby resulting in a more accurate calculation of net income for tax purposes.").

75 *See* William D. Andrews, *A Consumption-Type or Cash Flow Personal Income Tax,* 87 Harv. L. Rev. 1113 (1974).

76 *See supra* note 74.

77 *See* Geier, *supra* note 64, at 42.

reflect consumption or a decrease in wealth. Depreciation deductions arguably reflect decreases in wealth as assets subject to wear and tear decline in value over time.[78] Yet another answer is that disallowing deductions for capital expenditures prevents taxpayers from taking advantage of the time value of money to turn a nominal income tax into a de facto consumption tax. It is this third answer that has broader implications for arguments to align financial and tax accounting and to which we now turn.

Income and consumption taxes that impose the same tax rate typically produce different after-tax results because the income tax covers both consumption and returns on capital, while consumption taxes only impose a tax on consumption. E. Carey Brown demonstrated in the 1940s that income and cash-flow consumption taxes yield identical after-tax results when taxpayers are permitted to deduct amounts used to purchase income-producing assets.[79] Allowing a current deduction for asset purchases violates one of the core requirements for an income tax; namely, that returns be earned on after-tax dollars.[80] Permitting a deduction for asset purchases is economically equivalent to excusing the income that the asset will produce from taxation;[81] that is, it produces results equivalent to consumption taxation.

This insight has implications for depreciation. Depreciation can be justified under income tax principles only if it is seen as an attempt to account for an irretrievable loss in wealth occasioned solely by the passage of time, similar to the way the value of an original issue discount bond increases solely with the passage of time.[82] While deducting losses in value absent a realization event is typically not allowed, losses occasioned *solely* by virtue of the passage of time are arguably realized because they are irretrievable.[83]

This justification for depreciation has significant implications for the appropriate amount of depreciation under income tax principles. Under the accounting system's matching principle, the appropriate depreciation amount is proportional to the income the asset will earn in a given year.[84] In contrast, the amount of depreciation appropriate under the income tax principle described above should be the diminution in value due solely to the passage of time; that is, it is a function of

---

78 Typically, changes in asset value are not included in the tax base until there has been a realization event (i.e., an asset has been sold or otherwise disposed of). However, exceptions do exist (e.g., the mark-to-market rules for certain assets), and the argument could be made that depreciation deductions warrant an exception as well. *See* Geier, *supra* note 64, at 58–60.

79 E. Cary Brown, *Business-Income Taxation and Investment Incentives*, *in* Income, Employment and Public Policy: Essays in Honor of Alvin H. Hansen 300, 300–16 (1948).

80 *See* Geier, *supra* note 69, at 35.

81 For a numeric example, see Geier, *supra* note 64, at 44. This is precisely the insight that led to the creation of Roth IRAs. Allowing a deduction for traditional IRA contributions and then taxing the money when withdrawn is economically equivalent to disallowing the deduction on contribution and not taxing the gains.

82 This is often referred to as Samuelson depreciation. *See* Paul A. Samuelson, *Tax Deductibility of Economic Depreciation to Insure Invariant Valuations*, 72 J. Pol. Econ. 604 (1964). While Samuelson depreciation works well for financial assets with fixed lives and income streams, it is virtually impossible to calculate for other assets.

83 *See* Joseph M. Dodge et al., Federal Income Tax: Doctrine, Structure, and Policy 663–708 (4th ed. 2012) (discussing theories of depreciation).

84 For a numeric example, see Geier, *supra* note 64, at 60–61. This is a "straight-line" approach. The accounting rules are flexible and permit a range of approaches, so long as they are consistently applied. That a number of approaches are acceptable reinforces the view of many that GAAP accounting rules are not suitable for tax purposes.

expected cash flows[85] and less than would be appropriate under financial accounting.[86] Allowing a depreciation deduction greater than appropriate under income tax principles violates the same income tax principle as the failure to capitalize in that it permits a taxpayer to earn returns using deducted, or pre-tax, dollars. The result is that some of the return will functionally be exempted from tax. Such a result is antithetical to a true income tax.[87]

Accrual Accounting

The insights described above have significant implications for the propriety of using accrual accounting in an income tax regime. As Daniel Halperin and others have explained, permitting taxpayers to deduct amounts that they have not yet paid or to exclude from income amounts that they have received but not yet earned has the same effect as allowing immediate expensing of capital expenditures or overgenerous depreciation deductions—it effectively exempts returns on capital from tax and undermines one of the core values of an income tax.[88]

For instance, the accrual of expenses in cases where the taxpayer has yet to actually incur the cost allows an investment return to be earned on pre-tax dollars (the tax savings created by the deduction), producing the same consumption-tax result that occurs with the premature deduction of capital expenditures.[89] Similar concerns arise regarding prepaid income, which effectively presents a mirror image of accelerated deductions. Accounting rules permit companies to exclude up-front, lump-sum payments for future services from income until they are earned. The difficulty with this practice from a tax perspective is that the taxpayer would have tax-free use of the money until it is earned.[90] While the interest earned on this prepaid income is subject to tax, excluding the initial payment from tax until it is earned violates the rule that investments be made with after-tax dollars. The result is economically equivalent to including the initial payment in income and excluding from tax the interest earned on it. In other words, it yields consumption-tax treatment.[91]

As originally enacted, the Code required taxpayers to use the cash method of accounting.[92] Congress first permitted accrual accounting in 1916.[93] Early court decisions held that accrual

---

85 *See* Christopher H. Hanna, *Tax Theories and Tax Reform*, 59 SMU L. Rev. 435, 445 (2006) (citing Marvin Chirlestein, Federal Income Taxation ¶ 6.09 (10th ed. 2005)).

86 For a numeric example, see Geier, *supra* note 64, at 61.

87 To be clear, the current income tax rules are also inconsistent with income tax principles. For instance, Code § 179 permits the immediate deduction of some amounts used to purchase certain types of assets. Code § 168(k) permits bonus depreciation under certain circumstances in the year an asset is put into service. The accelerated depreciation (and even the straight-line amounts) permitted in Code § 168(b) allows more depreciation to be deducted than would be justified under strict income tax principles. From an income tax perspective, these provisions can only be justified as tax expenditures or efforts to simplify the tax system to make it more administrable.

88 *See, e.g.*, Daniel I. Halperin, *Interest in Disguise: Taxing the "Time Value of Money,"* 95 Yale L.J. 506 (1986); Daniel I. Halperin, *The Time Value of Money—1984*, 23 Tax Notes 751 (1984).

89 For a numerical example, see Geier, *supra* note 64, at 93–95.

90 As discussed below, the courts have limited this possibility in some cases, but the problem persists.

91 The opposite problem arises in cases where taxpayers accrue income long before it is received. Current inclusion requires that taxes be paid today on money taxpayers do not have, resulting in overtaxation. As with accrued deductions of future expenditures, the worst of these problems are dealt with by findings that the future payment is somehow contingent, thus permitting deferral until payment is received. *See* I.R.S. Tech. Adv. Mem. 97-15-004 (Dec. 16, 1996).

92 *See supra* note 3.

93 *See supra* note 66.

accounting for tax purposes should follow the financial accounting regime.[94] Nonetheless, the courts established a test—eventually evolving into the all-events test—that did not require that result in all cases. For instance, courts permitted deductions of unpaid amounts where it seemed certain that the expense would ultimately be paid.[95] However, they drew the line at contingent liabilities.[96] In some cases they even deemed future liabilities to be contingent to avoid allowing a deduction.[97] Finally, in 1984, Congress enacted Code § 461(h), which precluded deductions absent economic performance. This rule effectively requires payment before deductions are allowed, which is consistent with income tax principles, and functionally put accrual method taxpayers on the cash method with regard to their deductions.

Conversely, with regard to prepaid income, where the dates on which prepaid income will be earned are certain, the U.S. Court of Appeals for the Seventh Circuit has permitted deferral until such amounts are earned, consistent with the financial accounting rules.[98] However, where the time at which the income will be earned is uncertain, the U.S. Supreme Court has required immediate inclusion, consistent with income tax principles.[99] The inquiry into when income is earned is critical from an accrual accounting perspective but less so from a tax perspective. As demonstrated above, if taxpayers are allowed to receive money and invest it without first paying tax, the amounts earned on such money will effectively be exempted from tax, and the very purpose of the income tax will be thwarted.

Income Tax Theory and the Book–Tax Alignment Debate

The foregoing should give considerable pause to those arguing that tax accounting should be aligned with financial accounting. The decision to adopt an income tax in the late nineteenth and early twentieth centuries reflected a clear understanding that consumption alone should no longer be subjected to tax. Rather, reformers believed that the tax base should also include changes in wealth, including returns on capital. Such a system would better align tax burdens with the ability to pay, a core value underlying the income tax.

Accrual accounting works well for financial accounting purposes precisely because it considers a business's rights to income and expenditure obligations independent of cash flows. The matching principle helps ensure that timing differences between income and expenses do not distort the picture of overall income. This is exactly the type of information an investor or corporate manager would want. Cash flow is not irrelevant; however, what matters most when assessing the financial health of a business is a complete picture of anticipated income and expenses.

By disassociating income inclusion and deductions from cash flow, accrual accounting can convert a nominal income tax into a de facto consumption tax by excusing returns on capital from tax. Early tax authorities spent significant effort developing a tax-specific income definition and the

---

94 *E.g.*, United States v. Anderson, 269 U.S. 422 (1926).

95 *Id.* at 441.

96 *E.g.*, Lucas v. Am. Code Co., 280 U.S. 445 (1930) (company prevented from deducting damages in year when final amount had not yet been set and was not reasonably predictable).

97 *E.g.*, Mooney Aircraft, Inc. v. United States, 420 F.2d 400 (5th Cir. 1969) (company prevented from taking a current deduction for bonds due far into the future, with the court straining to classify the expenditures as contingent to avoid the result the taxpayer wanted).

98 Artnell Co. v. Comm'r, 400 F.2d 981 (7th Cir. 1968).

99 Schlude v. Comm'r, 372 U.S. 128 (1963); Am. Auto. Ass'n v. United States, 367 U.S. 687 (1961); Auto. Club of Mich. v. Comm'r, 353 U.S. 180 (1957).

accounting rules that would make it possible to tax *all* components of income and make sure that it was taxed only once. Despite the rules permitting taxpayers to use accrual accounting, Congress and the courts crafted tax-specific accounting rules, such as Code § 461(h), that permitted and indeed required deviation from financial accounting norms where those norms would lead to improper reductions in taxes owed. Many of these changes serve to ensure that income is included upon receipt of cash and deductions disallowed until actual payment is made.[100] Aligning book and tax accounting would undo these important rules and significantly increase a taxpayer's ability to use the financial accounting rules to lower their tax liabilities.

Accrual accounting also deviates from the ability-to-pay principle that underlies the income tax. A promise to pay someone five years into the future does not diminish one's current ability to pay taxes. Conversely, a right to receive income in the future does not increase one's ability to pay taxes now, unless the right is somehow negotiable. Such concerns motivate the installment sales rules found in Code § 453, which impose tax liability only when money is actually received. Aligning book and tax accounting to allow full accrual accounting would thus undermine this important value as well.

To protect income tax values and ensure that returns on capital are actually subjected to tax, Congress should not align financial and tax accounting. Rather it should consider a return to the original income tax rule, which required taxpayers to use the cash method of accounting for tax purposes, subject to a strong capitalization requirement. If this proposal is deemed a bridge too far, Congress should tighten the tax accounting rules to ensure that disconnects between income and expense reporting and cash flow do not undermine the tax base. Moreover, it should amend Code § 446(b) to make clear that the IRS may challenge a taxpayer's accounting method whenever the accounting method in question significantly undermines the income tax base. Absent congressional action, courts should construe Code § 446(b) as broadly as possible.

Congress Should Consider a Return to Cash Accounting for Tax Purposes

To ensure that income is fully taxed, Congress should require taxpayers to use the cash method of accounting for tax purposes, subject to a strong capitalization rule, regardless of their financial accounting method. This was the rule in the original income tax.[101] Congress first permitted companies that used the accrual accounting method for financial purposes to do so for tax purposes in 1916.[102] Since then, it has required an increasing number of taxpayers to use the accrual method.[103] Congress has also enacted a number of provisions that deviate from what a pure income tax would require. For instance, Congress allows significant deductions on the purchase of assets.[104] It also permits taxpayers to exclude from income amounts contributed to 401(k) plans and traditional IRAs.[105] In both cases, permitting returns to be earned on pre-tax dollars yields consumption-tax treatment.

Given this history, one could conclude that Congress has embraced accrual accounting as another exception to income tax norms and would be loath to abandon it. However, Congress's decision to

100 *E.g.*, 26 U.S.C. § 461(h).

101 *See supra* note 3.

102 *See* Geier, *supra* note 64, at 71.

103 *E.g.*, 26 U.S.C.§ 448 (requiring most C corporations to use the accrual method of accounting).

104 *E.g.*, *id.* §§ 168(k), 179.

105 The traditional IRA violates the rule that investments should be made with after-tax dollars, while the Roth IRA violates the rule that returns on capital should be included in income. In both cases, this means that the return on IRA investments is excluded from tax.

enact Code § 461(h), which requires payment before most deductions, suggests otherwise. In fact, Congress's expansion of accrual accounting may reflect an effort to *avoid* the timing mismatches that undermine core income tax values.[106] The initial decision to allow accrual accounting appears to have been a concession to companies at a time when the definition of income for tax purposes was being developed[107] and the impact of accrual accounting was not fully understood. Companies that kept their books on an accrual basis were permitted to use that method for tax purposes, so that they did not need to create a second set of books.[108]

That Congress significantly expanded the use of accrual accounting in 1986, after the effects of accrual accounting were well known,[109] is far more difficult to explain. While some evidence suggests that Congress believed that accrual accounting reflected income for tax purposes better than cash accounting,[110] the move toward accrual accounting could also be seen as an effort to solve a problem occasioned by a deduction and income-inclusion mismatch *between* taxpayers.[111] Most expenses incurred by taxpayers lead to income for others. When taxpayers use different accounting methods, the deduction of an expense may precede the inclusion of income, significantly reducing the amount of taxes collected. For example, this might occur when an accrual method taxpayer incurs an obligation to make a payment to a cash method taxpayer.[112] As with a deduction taken before cash payments are made, amounts earned on the tax savings will be excluded from tax.[113] In other words, a mismatch between expense deduction and income inclusion on transfers between taxpayers can convert a nominal tax on income into a de facto consumption tax, just as accrual accounting can do the same for a single taxpayer. Requiring most C corporations to use accrual accounting ameliorates this problem.[114]

This argument is not meant to suggest that the cash method is free of problems. If receipts are lumped together in one year, taxpayers may end up in a higher tax bracket and pay more in taxes. Lumping deductions into a given year may also change a taxpayer's tax bracket. Companies that have no income over a two-year period, for instance receiving $100,000 in income in year one and spending $100,000 to earn it in year two, would be required to pay income tax and then seek a refund using the net operating loss provision.[115] Moreover, moving to the cash method will put significant pressure on the constructive-receipt and cash-equivalent doctrines, because

106 *See* Geier *supra*, note 64, at 100–01.

107 Henry Simons did not publish his seminal work, incorporating the insights of Robert Haig and George Schanz, until 1938. *See* Henry C. Simons, Personal Income Taxation: The Definition of Income as a Problem of Fiscal Policy 50 (1938); *see also* Robert Murray Haig, *The Concept of Income—Economic and Legal Aspects*, *in* The Federal Income Tax 1, 7 (Robert Murray Haig ed., 1921); Georg von Schanz, *Der Einkommensbegriff und die Einkommensteuergesetze*, 13 FinanzArchiv 1 (1896).

108 Given the advanced state of computing, requiring companies to restate their books on a cash basis would now impose a small burden.

109 For example, Code § 7872 governing below-market loans, the original issue discount (OID) rules, and various other sections imputing interest.

110 *See* H.R. Rep. No. 99-426, at 605 (1985).

111 *See id.*

112 *But see* 26 U.S.C. § 267(a)(2).

113 *See* Geier, *supra* note 64, at 152–58.

114 The same is true for the OID rules found in Code § 163(e), which require taxpayers to report OID using the accrual method, thus putting individuals receiving such amounts on the same accounting method as those who pay them.

115 26 U.S.C. § 172.

taxpayers will have significant incentives to push income into future years.[116] However, most firms would likely be willing or able to push income only into the immediately succeeding year because delaying income would require firms to forego cash. The timing benefit of doing so would be relatively minimal because it would entail only a one-year delay in the inclusion of the income.

The extent to which the cash method would create more problems than the accrual method is empirical and may differ from taxpayer to taxpayer. Moreover, not all financial accounting rules create timing problems that undermine income tax values. Accordingly, adopting cash method accounting for tax purposes is not a step Congress should take lightly. However, Congress should at the very least develop data to determine which accounting system best protects both taxpayers and the values underlying the income tax. Ultimately, Congress must decide whether a system that explicitly eschews accrual accounting is better than one that purports to embrace it and then weakens the embrace through case law and provisions such as Code § 461(h), which force taxpayers onto the cash method.

Congress and the Courts Should Tighten the Tax Accounting Rules

Assuming that Congress is not yet ready to abandon accrual accounting, it should still act to protect the income tax base. First, Congress should create rules that limit the ability of taxpayers to exploit timing differences to reduce their tax burdens, as it did when it enacted Code § 461(h). For instance, Congress should enact rules that require taxpayers to include prepaid income in gross income when received, unless it will be earned within a very short period. Second, as a backstop measure, Congress should make clear that Code § 446(b), which grants the IRS the power to challenge a taxpayer's accounting method when that method does not "clearly reflect income," permits the IRS to challenge a tax accounting method whenever timing effects threaten to undermine the goal of taxing returns on capital.

If, as most accountants believe, accrual accounting is the most accurate way to measure income, then the power granted under Code § 446(b) is an empty one, at least in regard to companies that use accrual accounting. It would be the rare case, indeed, where some other method of accounting yielded a more accurate measure of income. However, accrual accounting is considered accurate for financial accounting purposes because it ignores timing differences. In contrast, timing is everything in tax. Significant divergence between the reporting of income and the receipt of cash or between the deduction of expenses and the payment of cash can result in returns on capital escaping tax entirely despite being nominally taxed. Accordingly, the term "clearly reflect income" in Code § 446(b) should be understood to cover situations where timing issues convert a nominal income tax into a de facto consumption tax. Put differently, income is not clearly reflected for tax purposes where the accounting regime fails to impose a tax on both components of income.

To avoid any question regarding the proper interpretation of Code § 446(b), Congress should amend the language of that section. One option would be to add the words "in an income tax sense" after "clearly reflect income" to eliminate claims that accrual accounting is the most accurate way to measure and report income. Congress could authorize the Treasury to issue regulations fleshing out the added language. Alternatively, Congress could be more explicit in the statute, using language such as "yields a result consistent with consumption taxation." To protect accrual

---

116 For an explanation and examples of the doctrine of constructive receipt, see Treas. Reg. § 1.451-2. For the doctrine of cash equivalency, see Treas. Reg. § 1.446-1(c)(i), which indicates that, in addition to cash, items to be included in the calculation of gross income include receipts and disbursements of property or services.

accounting in the main, either the statute or regulations could include a threshold below which no challenge would be allowed. For instance, the IRS could be permitted to act only if timing effects caused more than a 15 percent reduction in taxes when compared to an income-tax baseline. Or the threshold could be based on a specific dollar amount, say $10,000.

Assuming Congress fails to act, the courts should construe the existing statute to permit the IRS to challenge a taxpayer's accounting method when timing issues distort the amount of tax owed in net-present-value terms. The phrase "clearly reflect income" appears in a taxing statute and, therefore, it is logical to construe "income" in a tax, as opposed to a financial accounting, sense. Moreover, if the phrase is to have any meaning, it must give the IRS some power to challenge accrual accounting results. The income tax was designed to reach returns on capital. Congress has clearly shown that it knows how to deviate from this goal.[117] In light of this history, courts should be loath to afford consumption-tax treatment absent express congressional approval. Nothing suggests that Congress made its decisions to permit or expand accrual accounting with this purpose in mind.

This is precisely what the U.S. Tax Court did in *Ford Motor Co. v. Commissioner*.[118] In that case, Ford incurred tort liabilities that it satisfied by purchasing annuities. For financial reporting purposes, it deducted the amounts paid for the annuities. However, for tax purposes, it sought to deduct the full value of the obligations it had incurred, as opposed to the amounts paid for the annuities. Using a time-value-of-money analysis, the court showed that permitting such a deduction would actually leave the taxpayer in a better position than if the accident had never happened. The court found that the IRS did not abuse its discretion in finding that Ford's accounting method did not clearly reflect its income, even if the claimed deductions satisfied the all-events test.

Despite the taxpayer's seemingly egregious position, one tax court judge dissented. Judge Gerber argued that Ford had met the all-events test and therefore was entitled to the deduction, regardless of the effect on the company's after-tax result. This case pre-dated Code § 461(h), and therefore payment was not required before a deduction was allowed. As Judge Gerber noted, a taxpayer who had not purchased annuities, thus incurring a current present value for future obligations would likely have been allowed to deduct the full amounts, creating inconsistent treatment and a huge tax incentive not to purchase annuities.

While the particular issue in *Ford Motor Co.* has been taken care of by Code § 461(h), other situations exist, especially on the income side, that raise the same questions. Judge Gerber's dissent supports the need for a statutory or regulatory clarification that elevates the impact on tax liability above compliance with technical accounting rules, thus providing guidance to both the courts and the IRS. Most cases are not nearly as clear as *Ford Motor Co.* in that the timing differences will lessen tax liability, not put taxpayers in a better position than they would have been in had they not incurred the liability. It is not at all clear when timing distortions rise to the level that income is not being clearly reflected.

Current jurisprudence focuses on whether a particular item of income or expenditure fits within the technical financial or tax accounting rules governing accrual. Fixing the tax accounting rules to prevent timing effects from undermining the income tax would be the best solution. Failing that, clarifying the statutory language in Code § 446(b) would give the IRS a potent tool that gets to the heart of the matter in a way that technical accounting rules cannot.

117 For example, traditional and Roth IRAs.

118 102 T.C. 87, 92–94 (1994).

Conclusion

A number of commentators have argued that many of the problems in the tax system could be resolved easily by requiring companies to report the same figures to the IRS as they do to investors. It has been argued that doing so would simplify tax and financial accounting obligations, broaden the tax base, and impose a check on some types of aggressive tax planning. In *Thor Power Tool*, the U.S. Supreme Court focused on the different purposes underlying financial and tax accounting and the effects these purposes had on the respective regimes as a reason to keep them separate. In particular, the Court noted that financial accounting is designed to provide information to managers and investors and is thus flexible, permits estimates, and should be conservative in nature. In contrast, tax accounting is designed to collect revenue and ensure that similarly situated taxpayers are treated similarly. As a result, it cannot abide the flexibility of financial accounting, does not allow estimates, and eschews a conservative approach to calculating income.

In this chapter, I have argued that a difference in purpose far more fundamental than that identified in *Thor Power Tool* warrants keeping financial and tax accounting separate. To give a complete picture of a business's financial health, financial accounting divorces the reporting of income and deductions from the actual flow of cash. As demonstrated above, this mismatch between income and expense reporting and cash flow can undermine the income tax goal of ensuring that *all* elements of income, including both consumption and returns on capital, are subjected to tax. The income tax can survive with flexibility, estimates, and even a conservative approach to income calculation. However, if alignment effectively eliminates the tax on returns on capital—undoing rules like Code § 461(h) that are specifically designed to prevent such a result—it will be an income tax in name only. Rather than align financial and tax accounting, Congress should push them further apart, either by requiring companies to use the cash method accounting for tax purposes or by making clear that the IRS may challenge taxpayers' methods of accounting when they undermine the core goal of the income tax to ensure that all elements of income are subjected to tax.

I do not argue that financial and tax accounting should deviate in all regards. Indeed, as Lily Kahng notes in Chapter 6, the two regimes should probably be closer in a number of areas, including the treatment of expenditures that create intellectual capital. It would be a good thing if the Code were used primarily to measure economic income and stripped of the numerous provisions designed to promote some other public policy, such as the exclusion of municipal bond interest in Code § 103. Ridding the Code of the timing rules that permit immediate deductions for capital purchases (e.g., Code §§ 179 and 168(k)) would also be a good idea.

Where Kahng and I differ is the justification for conformity, which necessarily informs our views on when the two regimes should differ. Kahng believes that the tax accounting rules should more closely hew to those found in financial accounting because the latter more accurately reflect economic income. However, measuring economic income is not the core goal of an income tax. Rather, it is imposing a real tax upon all elements of income. Any measurement system that fails to accomplish this goal undermines the very purpose of the income tax. Capitalization of expenditures used to create intellectual capital is appropriate not only because such a rule better reflects economic income but also because capitalization ensures that a real tax is imposed on returns on that investment. Over the past century, significant effort has been made to create a tax-specific income definition and to create a tax-specific accounting regime. Where fundamental tax principles and goals conflict with financial accounting rules, as is the case with accrual accounting, tax accounting should forge its own path, regardless of the claim that accrual accounting is the best measure of economic income.

PART IV
Taxation of Flow-Through Entities

Chapter 8
A People's Subchapter K

Andrea Monroe*

Introduction

Partnership tax is a system in search of balance. The story of subchapter K, which contains the rules governing the taxation of partnerships and their partners, is rife with tensions—theoretical and practical tensions that produce instability for the partners, practitioners, and government officials that must navigate this system annually.[1] From an intellectual vantage, subchapter K is animated by competing theories that are often difficult to reconcile. For instance, long-standing debates persist within the partnership tax community regarding the proper characterization of a partnership, with one theory treating a partnership as an aggregate of its owners and another treating a partnership as an entity separate and distinct from them.[2] A rich literature also explores the proper balance among subchapter K's values of equity, efficiency, flexibility, and simplicity.[3]

Alongside these intellectual tensions, practical tensions continue to surface in partnership tax. Subchapter K is faced with the daunting task of regulating a wide array of commercial arrangements in a constantly evolving business environment. Its uniform approach to taxing partnerships must offer a rational system for all entities falling along the partnership spectrum, from the simplest "mom and pop" operations to the most sophisticated ventures in the marketplace. At the same time, subchapter K must combat the partnership tax abuse that remains a perennial problem in the federal income tax system. When taken together, these practical and intellectual challenges shape everything in partnership tax from its rules to its theoretical trajectory. Indeed, these tensions lead to one simple truth about subchapter K: it is, was, and will always be a complicated system of taxation.

---

* Many thanks for comments on earlier drafts to Jane Baron, Bradley Borden, Craig Green, and Anthony Infanti. Thanks also to Jonathan Dunlap and Michael Zeitler for marvelous research assistance.

1 I.R.C. §§ 701–761.

2 *See, e.g.*, George K. Yin & David J. Shakow, Am. Law Inst., Federal Income Tax Project: Taxation of Private Business Enterprises: Reporters' Study 78 (1999) [hereinafter Am. Law Inst., 1999 Reporters' Study]; Bradley T. Borden, *Aggregate-Plus Theory of Partnership Taxation*, 43 Ga. L. Rev. 717 (2009); J. Paul Jackson et al., *A Proposed Revision of the Federal Income Tax Treatment of Partnerships and Partners—American Law Institute Draft*, 9 Tax L. Rev. 109 (1954) [hereinafter Jackson et al., *American Law Institute Draft of 1954*]; J. Paul Jackson et al., *The Internal Revenue Code of 1954: Partnerships*, 54 Colum. L. Rev. 1183 (1954).

3 *See, e.g.*, Am. Law Inst., 1999 Reporters' Study, *supra* note 2; Borden, *supra* note 2; Jeffrey L. Kwall, *Taxing Private Enterprises in the New Millennium*, 51 Tax Law. 229 (1998); Lawrence Lokken, *Taxation of Private Business Firms: Imagining a Future Without Subchapter K*, 4 Fla. Tax Rev. 249 (1999); Andrea R. Monroe, *Integrity in Taxation: Rethinking Partnership Tax*, 64 Ala. L. Rev. 289 (2012); Philip F. Postlewaite et al., *A Critique of the ALI's* Federal Income Tax Project—Subchapter K: Proposals on the Taxation of Partners, 75 Geo. L.J. 423 (1986); George K. Yin, *The Future Taxation of Private Business Firms*, 4 Fla. Tax Rev. 141 (1999).

Whether perfect harmony is possible—or even desirable—in subchapter K remains a subject of great debate and little resolution, yet the problems of partnership tax are in urgent need of attention. Subchapter K today is fractured, with the current law increasingly falling at the theoretical and practical extremes of the partnership world. At the same time, this discord coincides with a period of marked growth in the use of pass-through entities, which play an increasingly vital role in the federal income tax system. According to the most current tax return data, in 2011, partnerships held approximately $20.6 trillion in assets and generated approximately $581 billion in net income.[4] More broadly, the growing importance of partnerships is consistent with a larger trend in business taxation—more than half of the net business income reported in recent years has been attributable to partnerships and other noncorporate entities.[5]

This chapter focuses on two interrelated dimensions of subchapter K's discord—polarization and complexity—in the hope of providing greater perspective on the problems and the future of partnership tax. Subchapter K has always accommodated a diverse range of commercial enterprises, but there is a growing divide within the system, with more and more of these enterprises falling into one of two categories, which I will refer to as "everyday" partnerships and "elite" partnerships. In 2011, for example, approximately 3.25 million enterprises were treated as partnerships for federal income tax purposes.[6] The overwhelming majority of these partnerships, 76 percent, held less than $1 million in assets.[7] Yet these everyday partnerships held only 1.6 percent of total partnership assets and generated 12 percent of partnership net income.[8] At the other extreme, partnerships with $100 million or more in assets comprised a mere 0.6 percent of the partnership community. Nonetheless, these elite partnerships held approximately 74 percent of total partnership assets and generated 64 percent of all partnership net income.[9] There is thus a significant wealth gap within the partnership tax community, where a small number of elite partnerships hold the overwhelming majority of partnership wealth.

Alongside this practical polarity, elite partnerships have largely driven subchapter K's legal development. Subchapter K offers partnerships great flexibility in structuring their affairs, and elite partnerships have exploited this freedom, pursuing tax shelters that reduce their partners' aggregate federal income tax liability at the expense of the public fisc. When the taxing authorities become aware of these abuses, Congress or the U.S. Department of the Treasury typically responds with narrowly tailored provisions designed to prevent the identified abuse without unnecessarily collaring subchapter K's flexibility. These antiabuse provisions are typically quite elaborate, isolating particular transactions through a complex combination of technical language, computational tests, and multifactored analyses.

The cumulative effect is dysfunction—partnership tax today lacks the balance necessary to provide legal stability. This absence has caused a vicious cycle in subchapter K where complexity

4 *See* Ron DeCarlo et al., *Partnership Returns, 2011*, Stat. Income Bull., Fall 2013, at 84 fig.D.

5 *See* President's Econ. Recovery Advisory Bd., The Report on Tax Reform Options: Simplification, Compliance, and Corporate Taxation 74–75 (2010); Karen C. Burke, *Passthrough Entities: The Missing Element in Business Tax Reform*, 40 Pepp. L. Rev. 1329 (2013); Pamela F. Olson, *And Then Cnut Told Reagan ...*, 131 Tax Notes 993, 995 (2011).

6 DeCarlo et al., *supra* note 4, at 83 fig.C. In this chapter, the term "partnership" is used to refer to any entity, including a limited liability company, treated as a partnership for federal income tax purposes. Treas. Reg. §§ 301.7701-1, -2, -3.

7 *SOI Tax Stats—Partnership Data by Size of Total Assets*, IRS (Nov. 5, 2013), http://irs.gov/uac/SOI-Tax-Stats---Partnership-Data-by-Size-of-Total-Assets.

8 *Id.*

9 *Id.*

breeds additional complexity while frustrating the system's other values of equity, efficiency, and fairness: Elite partnerships engage in abusive transactions that manipulate subchapter K's efforts to blend flexibility and "technicality." Congress and Treasury respond with targeted "fixes" that are elaborate and complex. Elite partnerships, in turn, exploit these fixes, capitalizing on a new array of technical gaps and unanticipated interactions. And the cycle continues.[10] Despite best intentions, many of the government's remedial measures have proven counterproductive, introducing such complexity into subchapter K that the remedies themselves imply roadmaps to the next generation of abusive transactions.[11]

Complexity has thus become the hallmark of subchapter K, transforming the system into a thicket of provisions that stymie all but the most experienced partnership tax specialists.[12] Of equal importance, complexity has crowded out subchapter K's other values, diminishing the roles of equity, efficiency, and flexibility in partnership taxation. Tax abuse remains a perennial problem, and elite partnerships still find strategic opportunities within subchapter K's porous provisions. Likewise, the fight against partnership tax shelters has eroded the flexibility and efficiency of partnership tax, as increasing collars are placed on partnerships' historic freedom to structure their transactions in whatever manner they consider optimal. When considered in this light, partnership tax today suffers from a dangerous imbalance of values: it is neither equitable nor efficient; it is decreasingly flexible; and it is surely not simple. On the contrary, subchapter K is enormously complicated.

Even worse, the burden of this complexity falls disproportionately on everyday partnerships. Although subchapter K's antiabuse provisions were largely designed to target the abusive transactions of elite partnerships, these provisions apply equally to all partnerships. Everyday partnerships, whose activities share little in common with elite partnerships, are thus forced to negotiate this complicated system. And they are often required to do so without the assistance of partnership tax specialists, as such legal services may be cost prohibitive for many of these partnerships. This places everyday partnerships in a precarious position if they want to comply with the law but lack the resources necessary to understand and apply subchapter K's complicated provisions. Indeed, many of these partnerships have simply given up trying, instead following an

---

10 *See* Lawrence Lokken, *As the World of Partnership Taxation Turns*, 56 SMU L. Rev. 365, 367 (2003) ("The revolutionary accretion of detail in subchapter K is largely a response to aggressive uses of partnerships for tax avoidance, resembling a steady build-up in the arsenal of an army caught in an unwinnable guerilla war.").

11 *See, e.g.*, Margaret Milner Richardson, Comm'r, Internal Revenue Serv., Remarks at the ABA Tax Section Annual Meeting (Aug. 6, 1994) (transcript available at 94 TNT 157–67 (LexisNexis)) ("As all of you know from experience, precise, mechanical rules cannot possibly cover all conceivable situations. Moreover, such rules tend to be the oil fields into which the perennial loophole seekers punch holes looking for a gusher.").

12 *See* Foxman v. Comm'r, 41 T.C. 535, 551 n.9 (1964) ("The distressingly complex and confusing nature of the provisions of subchapter K present a formidable obstacle to the comprehension of these provisions without the expenditure of a disproportionate amount of time and effort even by one who is sophisticated in tax matters with many years of experience in the tax field."). Indeed, "generalist" tax practitioners increasingly struggle to navigate subchapter K. *See* Lokken, *supra* note 10, at 366 ("Even highly competent tax generalists may stumble badly on partnership issues not resolved by the basic pass-through idea of subchapter K."); Martin J. McMahon, Jr., *Reflections on the Regulations Process: "Do the Regulations Have to Be Complex" or "Is Hyperlexis the Manna of the Tax Bar?,"* 51 Tax Notes 1441, 1450 (1991) ("[R]egulations that are not too complex for a tax practitioner who specializes in the area with which the regulations deal often are too intricate to be understandable by the typical generalist who nevertheless must deal with those regulations in order to serve clients. We can't all be specialists, and generalists can't refer all their problems to specialists.").

"intuitive" approach to subchapter K where they do the best they can with available resources and hope their positions are close enough to avoid drawing the government's attention.[13] The result is deeply troubling—large numbers of everyday partnerships are effectively denied access to the substantive content of subchapter K.

This chapter explores the fractures in modern partnership tax, focusing on the theoretical and practical forces that have excluded everyday partnerships from participation in the law. It traces the evolution of this complicated system, with a particular focus on subchapter K's rules, their goals, and their design. This chapter next turns to the project of recalibrating partnership tax. Subchapter K currently operates at the extremes, with enormous complexity and a primary focus on elite partnerships. Yet this path is not sustainable—partnership tax must work for all partnerships if it is to work at all.

In this chapter, I offer a path forward, one grounded in a commitment to greater balance among subchapter K's values and between the partnerships falling within its jurisdiction. I begin with the premise that a more harmonious subchapter K is in fact possible. Accordingly, this chapter focuses on rebalancing subchapter K through incremental reforms that prioritize simplification and access for everyday partnerships. To this end, I propose a more holistic approach to subchapter K, where streamlined rules operate in service of stable, consistently ranked values. A simplified subchapter K, in turn, would require a more collaborative approach to fighting partnership tax abuse. Congress and Treasury would be forced to rely more heavily on tax provisions of general application, including statutory and judicial antiabuse doctrines like the economic substance doctrine, in policing sophisticated partnership transactions. Perfection may be impossible, but a recalibrated subchapter K would be a fairer, simpler, and more efficient system of taxation for all members of the partnership tax community. Grounding subchapter K in balance and accessibility would also serve a larger, more expressive function, signaling that the same law applies to all partnerships, whether rich, poor, sophisticated, or otherwise.

How Did We Get Here?

When Congress codified subchapter K in 1954, it took a distinctively laissez-faire approach to partnership tax, generally providing partnerships with the freedom to structure their affairs in whatever manner the partners considered commercially optimal. At the time, Congress did not believe that the revenue stakes in partnership tax were particularly high; hence, it viewed the government's role in subchapter K as that of a neutral referee among partners in what were largely intrapartnership matters.[14] Congress therefore did not prioritize equity in designing

13 Lokken, *supra* note 3, at 252 ("A large number of partnerships thus seem to be governed by what might be called an 'intuitive subchapter K.' Taxpayers and tax advisers who want to comply account for partnership transactions in ways that are consistent with their conceptions of the basic aims of subchapter K."); Lokken, *supra* note 10, at 367 ("[W]e already have a K lite, consisting of the present subchapter K stripped of all the rules and nuances that tax practitioners serving ordinary partnerships do not understand and simply ignore."); Yin, *supra* note 3, at 201 ("[I]t may well be that many small firms … already utilize a watered-down, intuitive version of subchapter K.").

14 *See* H.R. Rep. No. 83-1337, at 65 (1954); S. Rep. No. 83-1622, at 89 (1954). Contemporary commentators also shared this view. *See Forty Topics Pertaining to the General Revision of the Internal Revenue Code—Topic 29—Partnerships: Hearing Before the H. Comm. on Ways & Means*, 83d Cong. 1368, 1370 (1953) (statement of Mark H. Johnson, American Bar Association); *see also* Jackson et al., *American Law Institute Draft of 1954*, *supra* note 2, at 112 ("Most of the problems encountered in the partnership

subchapter K's rules, focusing instead on the development of simple and flexible rules.[15] In the few instances where Congress believed that partnership transactions raised revenue concerns, it enacted antiabuse rules.[16] Unlike the remainder of subchapter K, these antiabuse rules were quite complicated, sacrificing simplicity and flexibility in order to achieve a more equitable result.[17] In doing so, they highlighted the deep tensions within partnership tax: if Congress's estimation of the low revenue stakes associated with partnership transactions proved incorrect, subchapter K's initial design, with its focus on simplicity and flexibility, would prove unsustainable.[18]

In this chapter, I trace the intellectual tensions within subchapter K to the competing values—flexibility, simplicity, and equity—that animate partnership tax.[19] Bradley Borden offers an alternative perspective in Chapter 9, framing these tensions in terms of the conflicting theories of partnerships. To Borden, codifying subchapter K required Congress to find the right balance between the aggregate and entity theories of partnerships. As codified, subchapter K represents a hybrid of the two theories, with Congress grounding individual rules in whichever theory best promotes the system's underlying values.[20]

Although our foundations differ, Borden and I are not far apart on the intellectual drivers of partnership tax.[21] Indeed, one can think of the aggregate and entity theories as rough proxies for the system's values of flexibility, simplicity, and equity. In very general terms, the aggregate theory reflects the values of flexibility and equity in partnership tax. Likewise, the entity theory reflects the value of simplicity. Accordingly, Borden would maintain that subchapter K skewed toward the entity theory of partnerships at codification, highlighting a congressional desire for simplicity and a hands-off approach to equity in partnership tax. He would also assert that this balance would prove problematic if the revenue stakes in subchapter K were higher than Congress's original estimation. Considered in this light, Borden and I are largely focused on the same foundational tensions; we simply view them from different vantages.

---

area are concerned with the distribution of the burden of taxation among the members of the group. Since the Treasury from the standpoint of tax policy is not greatly concerned about this allocation, the issues are essentially not between Treasury and taxpayer-partner but between partner and partner. Consequently, tax technicians should be able to agree on the formulation of rules to govern the complex partnership relationship, and this formulation should not raise issues that pass beyond technical tax policy.").

15 *See* H.R. REP. NO. 83-1337, at 65; S. REP. NO. 83-1622, at 89.

16 I.R.C. §§ 731(a)(2), 735, 751(b).

17 Indeed, one of these rules—the Code § 751(b) disproportionate distribution rule—is often described as subchapter K's "least understood and most widely ignored rule." James S. Eustice, *Subchapter S Corporations and Partnerships: A Search for the Pass Through Paradigm (Some Preliminary Proposals)*, 39 TAX L. REV. 345, 383 (1984); *see also, e.g.*, William D. Andrews, *Inside Basis Adjustments and Hot Asset Exchanges in Partnership Distributions*, 47 TAX L. REV. 3, 52–55 (1991); Karen C. Burke, *Partnership Distributions: Options for Reform*, 3 FLA. TAX REV. 677, 713–17 (1998); Mark P. Gergen, *Reforming Subchapter K: Contributions and Distributions*, 47 TAX L. REV. 173, 200 (1991).

18 These tensions were apparent even before subchapter K's codification. Congress, the American Law Institute, and the American Bar Association all struggled to develop a rational and unified system of partnership taxation. *See generally* Mark P. Gergen, *The Story of Subchapter K: Mark H. Johnson's Quest, in* BUSINESS TAX STORIES 207 (Steven A. Bank & Kirk J. Stark eds., 2005).

19 Efficiency, subchapter K's fourth value, emerged as an important value in partnership tax, and the federal income tax more generally, in the decades following codification.

20 *See, e.g.*, 2 AM. LAW INST., FEDERAL INCOME TAX STATUTE: FEBRUARY 1954 DRAFT, at 354 (1954).

21 As will be discussed throughout this chapter and Chapter 9, Borden and I nonetheless disagree about the proper balance of these intellectual drivers within partnership tax.

By the 1970s, it became clear that Congress had in fact miscalculated the revenue stakes associated with partnership transactions. Subchapter K's flexible rules offered partnerships myriad opportunities to pursue tax shelters, and partnerships freely exploited those opportunities.[22] As a result, Congress could no longer afford to take such a permissive approach to partnership tax, simply policing the system's boundaries; the revenue cost of the resulting tax shelter activity was too high. The time had come for Congress to play a more affirmative role in subchapter K.

In order to combat abusive transactions, Congress began to place greater system-wide emphasis on equity in partnership tax, introducing a series of antiabuse rules into subchapter K. The goal of these second-generation rules was to rebalance subchapter K, preventing tax shelters without impairing the historic flexibility afforded to partnership transactions. From a drafting perspective, this was a Herculean task with little margin for error. If these antiabuse rules were underinclusive, then tax abuse would persist; however, if they were overinclusive, then the market for legitimate partnership transactions might suffer. Accordingly, this new generation of partnership provisions prioritized precision, employing narrowly tailored rules to attack particular tax shelters pursued by particular, largely elite, partnerships.

While the tailored design of these antiabuse rules was novel, Congress's approach to rulemaking was largely shaped by the past, especially its mistaken estimation of the revenue stakes in partnership tax. This miscalculation created a variety of obstacles for the government as it entered the fight against tax shelters. For example, by the time Congress decided to pursue partnership tax abuse more aggressively, it was already too late; the government had fallen far behind the tax shelter market. Likewise, the taxing authorities possessed neither the money nor the enforcement resources necessary to match the army of professionals marketing tax shelters. As a consequence, the government was perpetually trying to catch up, responding to the last tax shelter rather than developing a forward-looking strategy to prevent the next tax shelter. A piecemeal approach to rulemaking in subchapter K thus emerged, where gap filling took priority over the development of a comprehensive vision of partnership tax.

Taken together, this new approach to rulemaking and rule design transformed subchapter K, making complexity the new hallmark of partnership tax. Considering Congress's goal in fighting tax shelters—preventing abuse without affecting legitimate partnership transactions—this rise in complexity was perhaps inevitable. Antiabuse rules require a taxpayer to consider numerous factors in order to determine the proper tax consequences of a transaction. However, the nuance required to achieve equitable results introduces complexity into the law. Drawing a functional line between permissible tax planning and impermissible tax abuse in subchapter K has created precisely this type of problem, with the piecemeal adoption of elaborate antiabuse rules injecting enormous complexity into partnership tax.

---

22 I do not mean to suggest that all partnerships engage in tax shelter transactions; on the contrary, many partnerships do not, using subchapter K solely as a means to conduct legitimate commercial transactions. However, for those partnerships intent on pursuing abusive transactions, subchapter K offered ample opportunities to engage in tax sheltering. *See, e.g.*, Mark P. Gergen, *Reforming Subchapter K: Special Allocations*, 46 Tax L. Rev. 1, 1 (1990) ("The flexibility of subchapter K, one of its most celebrated features, has given partners license to shift income and loss among themselves and dispose of assets while deferring recognition of gain in ways that are not otherwise possible under the income tax." (footnote omitted)); Mark P. Gergen, *The End of the Revolution in Partnership Tax?*, 56 SMU L. Rev. 343, 348 (2003); Lokken, *supra* note 3, at 250 ("The flexibility of the original conduit model facilitated devices to shift income, deductions, and other tax attributes from partner to partner and from property to property in ways that Congress found unacceptable.").

Once again, Bradley Borden and I part company in explaining this shift in subchapter K's intellectual trajectory. To Borden, the problem with subchapter K, as initially codified, was its excessive reliance on the entity theory of partnerships, which increased the risk of inequity and inefficiency in partnership transactions. In order to correct these entity-based distortions, Congress turned to the aggregate theory of partnerships, enacting a number of "reparative" rules beginning in the 1970s. As Borden describes in Chapter 9, these reparative rules, by design, shifted subchapter K's balance toward the aggregate theory of partnerships and away from the entity theory. Accordingly, our approaches to this intellectual shift differ, with Borden's perspective grounded in theories of partnership and mine grounded in the values that animate the federal income tax.

Despite our different characterizations of subchapter K's intellectual shift, Borden and I agree on many of the basic facts surrounding this transformative time. For instance, we agree that the legal evolution of subchapter K is largely a response to partnership abuse. Absent tax shelters, Congress would not have felt as urgent a need to reform partnership tax. Put another way, the ability of partnerships to exploit subchapter K—however characterized—was a primary trigger of the reforms enacted during this period. Of equal importance, Borden and I also agree about the results. The goal was precision, or as Borden would describe it, accuracy—preventing abusive transactions without impeding legitimate transactions. Complexity, in turn, was an inevitable byproduct of this drive toward precision and accuracy in partnership tax. Indeed, regardless of one's perspective, we can all agree that the intellectual transformation of partnership tax led to great complexity in subchapter K and its rules.

To illustrate the scope of subchapter K's complexity problem, it might be useful to consider two examples. These examples focus on two critical aspects of subchapter K—allocations and distributions—that all partnerships must negotiate annually. Accordingly, they highlight the many challenges partnerships face as they try to comply with subchapter K's complicated provisions.

Partnership Allocations

The provisions governing partnership allocations are the lifeblood of subchapter K, implementing its distinctive pass-through function. Like much of subchapter K, these provisions offer partnerships great flexibility in dividing up their taxable income. A partnership has two primary options when allocating taxable income among its partners. Under the first option, a partnership computes its taxable income and allocates this aggregate amount among its partners based on a single ratio.[23] Under the second option, a partnership separately allocates some of the items that would otherwise be included in the computation of partnership taxable income.[24] In making these "special" allocations, subchapter K permits a partnership to use almost any ratio contractually agreed to by its partners, including ratios that are not proportionate to the partners' economic interests in the partnership.[25]

Congress feared that partnerships would use this freedom strategically, specially allocating taxable items in a manner that reduced the partners' aggregate tax liability at the expense of the public fisc.[26] Accordingly, the provisions governing partnership allocations have always aimed to

23 With a few exceptions, a partnership computes its taxable income in the same manner as any taxpayer, adding together its items of income and gain and subtracting its items of deduction and loss. I.R.C. § 703.

24 *Id.* § 704(a)–(b).

25 *Id.*

26 *See, e.g.*, Am. Law Inst., 1999 Reporters' Study, *supra* note 2, at 78 ("But flexible tax-sharing rules also may be used simply to minimize the collective tax liabilities of the partners, to the detriment of the Treasury and all other taxpayers. By allocating items to the partner who is in a position to utilize them most

specify a boundary beyond which special allocations would no longer be permissible. However, this project of distinguishing permissible from impermissible allocations has proven to be a formidable challenge. Under current law, a partnership's contractual allocation of a taxable item will be respected so long as the allocation reasonably tracks the partnership's allocation of the corresponding economic item and is not merely a device to shift income among partners in a tax-advantaged manner.[27] Congress expressed this notion in a safe harbor that requires a partnership's contractual allocations to have substantial economic effect; then it left the challenging work of implementing this safe harbor to Treasury.

A partnership allocation has substantial economic effect if the allocation has economic effect and that economic effect is substantial.[28] A partnership can satisfy the safe harbor's first requirement—economic effect—in one of three ways,[29] all of which require the partnership to master an intricate series of tax accounting rules that govern virtually every aspect of its life.[30] The economic effect requirement also introduces much technical terminology into subchapter K's general allocation provisions, including "capital accounts,"[31] "deficit restoration obligations,"[32] and "qualified income offsets."[33] Once a partnership satisfies the economic effect requirement, the partnership must next establish that the allocation complies with the safe harbor's second

---

favorably for tax purposes, the partners can put their respective tax advantages to best use and share in the resulting tax savings."); Gregg D. Polsky, *Deterring Tax-Driven Partnership Allocations*, 64 Tax Law. 97, 97 (2010) ("One could envision a purely elective regime that allows partnerships to allocate items in any manner they desire. But in that case partnerships would choose to allocate items in such a way as to minimize the partners' aggregate tax liability … .").

27 As originally codified, subchapter K permitted a partnership to allocate a taxable item according to the partners' contractual arrangement so long as a principal purpose of such allocation was not the avoidance or evasion of tax. I.R.C. § 704(b)(2) (1954). If the allocation violated this antiabuse standard, the underlying taxable item would be reallocated in a manner reflecting the partnership's general allocations of "bottom-line" income or loss. *Id.* § 704(b).

28 Treas. Reg. § 1.704-1(b)(2)(i). Allocations have economic effect if they are "consistent with the underlying economic arrangement of the partners." *Id.* § 1.704-1(b)(2)(ii)(a). Put another way, a partner that is allocated one dollar of partnership income must also receive the economic benefit of such dollar. In contrast, substantiality requires that there be a reasonable possibility that an allocation will meaningfully affect the dollar amounts to be received by a partner, independent of tax consequences. *Id.* § 1.704-1(b)(2)(iii)(a).

29 The first "basic" economic effect test requires a partnership to satisfy three requirements: (1) it must maintain capital accounts in accordance with the regulations; (2) it must make all liquidating distributions in accordance with its partners' positive capital account balances; and (3) each partner must agree to restore a deficit balance in her capital account if one exists at the time her partnership interest is liquidated. *Id.* § 1.704-1(b)(2)(ii)(b). Unlimited obligations to restore deficit capital account balances have proven problematic, particularly for partners with limited liability. Thus, Treasury provides relief for these partners in the form of a second "alternate" economic effect test. *Id.* § 1.704-1(b)(2)(ii)(d). The economic effect requirement contains an additional relief-based test for partnerships. *Id.* § 1.704-1(b)(2)(ii)(*i*). Under this "economic effect equivalence" test, an allocation will be deemed to have economic effect if, as of the end of the relevant taxable year, a liquidation of the partnership would produce the same economic results that would have occurred had the partnership complied with the basic economic effect test.

30 *Id.* § 1.704-1(b)(2)(iv). These accounting rules are referred to as the capital account maintenance requirements, and they govern almost every partnership transaction from formation to liquidation.

31 *Id.*

32 *Id.* § 1.704-1(b)(2)(ii)(b)(3). A deficit restoration obligation is a provision requiring a partner to restore a deficit in her capital account if one exists at the time her partnership interest is liquidated. *Id.*

33 *Id.* § 1.704-1(b)(2)(ii)(d)(3), (d)(6) (flush language). A qualified income offset requires that, if certain enumerated events occur under the alternate test for economic effect, a partnership must make

requirement—substantiality. To this end, a partnership must demonstrate that the allocation satisfies a series of tests, each combining mathematical rules, open-textured standards, and economic projections in an effort to establish that the allocation has the potential to meaningfully impact the partners' relative economic positions.[34]

If an allocation lacks substantial economic effect, then the partnership must reallocate the taxable item based on a similarly complicated default rule, which requires the partnership to reallocate the item based on the partner's interest in the partnership.[35] Under this default rule, a partnership must allocate a taxable item in the same manner as it allocates the corresponding economic benefit or burden.[36] In determining a partner's interest in the partnership, a partnership may consider any relevant facts or circumstances, and the proper economic allocation may vary on an item-by-item basis.[37] Although relatively straightforward in the simplest of partnerships, the partner's interest in the partnership becomes impossibly indeterminate the moment disproportionate economic arrangements are introduced into a partnership.[38] Accordingly, this default rule provides little relief from the technicality of the substantial economic effect safe harbor.

Congress's desire to provide partnerships with flexible allocation provisions, coupled with the line-drawing that such an approach requires, has burdened partnerships with great complexity. Under the substantial economic effect safe harbor, a partnership must apply multiple layers of intricate, mathematical rules to every allocation it makes every year.[39] Even worse, this complexity is often counterproductive, blurring the line between legitimate and abusive partnership allocations.[40] Thus, abusive allocations remain a significant problem in partnership tax.

---

disproportionate allocations to a partner with a capital account deficit so as to eliminate such deficit balance. *Id.* § 1.704-1(b)(2)(ii)(d)(6) (flush language).

34 The first substantiality test is the after-tax substantiality test, and it targets allocations that are too good to be true, harming no partner but causing a revenue loss to the government. *Id.* § 1.704-1(b)(2)(iii)(a). An allocation violates the after-tax substantiality test if (1) it improves at least one partner's after-tax consequences as compared to the tax consequences that would have occurred if the partnership agreement had not included such allocation in its partnership agreement, and (2) there is a strong likelihood that no partner's after-tax consequences will be substantially diminished as a result of such allocation. *Id.* The second and third substantiality tests—the shifting and transitory tests—are almost indistinguishable, differing primarily in their relevant time frames. *Id.* § 1.704-1(b)(2)(iii)(b), (c). An allocation violates these substantiality tests if there is a strong likelihood at the time such allocations become part of the partnership agreement that (1) the net adjustments to the partners' capital accounts will not differ substantially from those that would have occurred if the partnership agreement had not included such allocations, and (2) the allocations reduce the partners' aggregate federal income tax liability. *Id.*

35 I.R.C. § 704(b); Treas. Reg. § 1.704-1(b)(3).

36 *Id.* § 1.704-1(b)(3)(i).

37 *Id.*

38 *See, e.g.*, Bradley T. Borden, *The Allure and Illusion of Partners' Interests in a Partnership*, 79 U. Cin. L. Rev. 1077, 1106–07 (2011); Lawrence Lokken, *Partnership Allocations*, 41 Tax L. Rev. 547, 613–14 (1986); Yin, *supra* note 3, at 154.

39 *See* Am. Law Inst., 1999 Reporters' Study, *supra* note 2, at 81 ("The [704(b)] rules are lengthy and complex, and the burden on those taxpayers who attempt to comply with them is considerable … .").

40 *See, e.g.*, *id.* at 82 ("Unfortunately, the economic-effect requirement fails to achieve its intended purpose and does not preclude purely tax-motivated allocations."); Edward J. Buchholz, *Substantiality Under Section 704(c)—Some Forgotten Issues and Some Ancient Concepts Revisited*, 19 Va. Tax Rev. 165, 267–69 (1999); Thomas W. Henning, *Partnership Exit Strategies and the Failure of the Substantiality Test*, 63 Tax Law. 43, 44 (2009); Polsky, *supra* note 26, at 99.

Partnership Distributions

Distributions are one of the most ubiquitous transactions in partnership tax. Although there is great variety in partnership distributions—depending, for instance, on whether the distribution involves cash or property or whether it involves the liquidation of a partner's interest in a partnership—these transactions all involve the transfer of value from partnership to partner. And subchapter K subjects them all to a unitary set of rules.[41] In very general terms, partnership distributions are treated as "nonrecognition" events, giving rise to no immediate tax consequences. Neither the partnership nor the distributee partner recognizes any gain or loss on a distribution.[42] Instead, any gains are deferred for future recognition when the distributee partner sells the distributed property or her partnership interest.[43] In doing so, subchapter K's distribution system ensures that the aggregate amount of predistribution gain remains intact, preserved for recognition when a future taxable event occurs.[44]

These rules create opportunities for partnerships to structure distributions that achieve an improper financial advantage for their partners. In particular, the general rules governing partnership distributions are not sensitive to the identity of the taxpayer that will bear the tax burden associated with distributed property, thus creating an opportunity for strategic partnerships to shift income through property distributions. Consider, for example, the consequences of a simple distribution of appreciated property. After the partnership distributes the property, the distributee partner alone will bear the tax consequences of the property's subsequent sale. If the partnership had sold the property rather than distributing it, the partnership would have recognized the gain and allocated such gain among its partners. As a result, all of the partners would have borne their share of the

41 I.R.C. §§ 731–734. These provisions contain the "basic" rules governing partnership distributions. In addition, as will be discussed, subchapter K includes a series of antiabuse rules that apply to all distributions. *Id.* §§ 704(c)(1)(B), 707(a)(2)(B), 735, 737, 751(b).

42 *Id.* § 731(a) (nonrecognition for distributee partner), (b) (nonrecognition for partnership).

43 The mechanism subchapter K uses to achieve this deferral is basis. Retaining a continuous relationship between value and basis is necessary to ensure that any predistribution gain is taxed on a future sale. Thus, to the extent possible, a partner takes a basis in the distributed property equal to the partnership's basis in such property immediately before the distribution. *Id.* § 732(a), (b). Likewise, the distributee partner's basis in her partnership interest is reduced by the basis she takes in the distributed property and the amount of cash, if any, received in the distribution. *Id.* § 733.

For ease of reading, I only refer to appreciated property and the recognition of gains in this chapter. Even so, the following discussion applies equally to depreciated property and the recognition of losses. Unless otherwise provided, readers may therefore assume that all references to gains, predistribution gains, and appreciated property also encompass their loss equivalents.

44 *Id.* §§ 732, 733. In certain instances, distributions create mismatches between the partnership's basis in its property and the partners' bases in their partnership interests. *Id.* §§ 733, 734(a). When this occurs, the partnership can no longer reliably ensure that the aggregate amount of predistribution gain remains intact. Some predistribution gains may be duplicated, and others may be eliminated as a result of the distribution. In order to prevent these distortions, a partnership may elect to adjust the basis of its remaining property following a triggering distribution. *Id.* §§ 734(b), 754. Like many of the rules discussed in this chapter, however, these elective basis adjustment rules are terribly complicated and provide an incomplete solution to the problem. *See, e.g.*, Howard Abrams, *The Section 734(b) Basis Adjustment Needs Repair*, 57 TAX LAW. 343 (2004); Andrews, *supra* note 17.

distributed property's tax burden. The distribution thus changed the incidence of tax associated with the distributed property, shifting income from the nondistributee partners to the distributee partner.[45]

Likewise, subchapter K's basic distribution rules are not sensitive to the character of any gain resulting from the future sale of distributed property, thereby allowing partnerships to convert ordinary income into preferentially taxed capital gains. To illustrate, consider again a distribution of appreciated property. This time, however, let's assume that the distributed property was inventory, which the partnership sold to customers in the ordinary course of its business. When the distributee partner sells the inventory, she would determine the character of any gain recognized based on her use of the distributed inventory.[46] Accordingly, if the inventory were considered a capital asset in the distributee partner's hands, the resulting gain would be treated as a capital gain taxed at preferential rates.[47] Had the partnership instead sold the inventory, the character of any recognized gain would have been determined at the partnership level based on the partnership's use of the property.[48] In this instance, the partnership would have recognized an ordinary gain subject to tax at the higher ordinary income rates. Again, the potential for abuse is evident—partnerships can use distributions to manipulate tax rates, reducing the amount of partnership gain subject to ordinary income rates.

As previously discussed, Congress generally took a permissive approach to taxing partnerships in subchapter K's early years. There was, however, one exception: Congress was concerned about character-based transactions at the time of subchapter K's codification, and it therefore enacted a series of antiabuse provisions designed to prevent partnerships from using distributions to convert ordinary income into preferentially treated capital gains.[49] It was not until the 1980s that Congress revisited subchapter K's distribution regime, enacting another series of antiabuse rules as part of the larger fight against partnership tax shelters. Unlike their predecessors, this second generation of antiabuse rules targeted partnerships that used distributions to shift income among their partners or to avoid the recognition of gain altogether.[50]

Although each of these antiabuse rules is distinctive, they share a number of common design-related characteristics. Each antiabuse rule is narrowly tailored to combat a particular type of improper distribution without impeding the traditional flexibility of partnership distributions.[51]

45 It is important to note that this shift is temporary, reversing itself on the sale or liquidation of each partner's partnership interest. Nonetheless, this type of income shifting remains problematic because the offsetting allocations may not occur for many years, if at all. The longer it takes to reverse the income shift, the more the deferral effect begins to look like a permanent exemption from the federal income tax. William D. Andrews, *A Consumption-Type or Cash Flow Personal Income Tax*, 87 Harv. L. Rev. 1113, 1124 (1974).

46 I.R.C. § 1221(a). The character of any gain or loss recognized on the sale of property is generally determined based on the selling taxpayer's use of the property.

47 *Id.* § 1222(3).

48 *Id.* § 702(b).

49 *Id.* §§ 731(a)(2), 735, 751(b). When Congress codified subchapter K in 1954, individual income tax rates were as high as 91 percent, while the capital gains rate was only 25 percent. *Id.* §§ 1(a) (individual income tax rate), 1201(b) (capital gains rate) (1954).

50 *Id.* §§ 704(c)(1)(B), 707(a)(2)(B), 731(c), 737 (2014).

51 The oldest of subchapter K's distribution-based antiabuse rules—Code § 751(b)—targets distributions where a partner receives a disproportionate share of the partnership's ordinary assets in a distribution. Although originally enacted to prevent partnerships from using distributions as a device to convert the character of partnership gains, Code § 751(b) has become subchapter K's primary bulwark against abusive distributions. *See* Andrews, *supra* note 17, at 4.

In contrast, Congress designed the second-generation antiabuse rules to prevent partnerships from shifting income or avoiding gain recognition through coordinated contributions and distributions. For example, the

To this end, these rules almost invariably employ a recognition rule, requiring the distributee partner—and, in some instances, the nondistributee partners—to recognize gain at the time of distribution in order to achieve a more equitable result.[52] Taken together, these antiabuse rules have added a formidable dimension to partnership distributions, layering a series of individualized, technical recognition rules onto a distribution system that remains grounded in nonrecognition.[53]

Yet the most challenging aspect of subchapter K's distribution system is the system itself. The sheer number of distribution rules is overwhelming to many, if not most, partnerships. The result is

---

Code § 707(a)(2)(B) disguised sale rule provides that a contribution and distribution will be recast as a taxable disposition between the partner and the partnership if, when considered together, the two transactions are more properly characterized as a sale. *Id.* § 707(a)(2)(B); Treas. Reg. § 1.707-3(b). Likewise, the mixing bowl rules of Code §§ 704(b)(1)(C) and 737 are designed to curtail transactions where the partners use the partnership as a "mixing bowl" to achieve results that they could not achieve outside the partnership context. Code § 737 operates as a backstop to the Code § 707(a)(2)(B) disguised sale rule, preventing the avoidance of gain recognition on transactions that, in substance, constitute property dispositions. I.R.C. § 737(a). It thus applies to a partner receiving a distribution if such partner contributed property to the partnership in the seven-year period preceding the distribution. *Id.* § 737(a)–(b). Code § 704(c)(1)(B) functions differently; it is designed to address transactions that shift built-in gain attributable to contributed property from the contributing partner to another partner. To that end, if a partner contributes appreciated property to a partnership and, within the seven-year period following the contribution, the contributed property is distributed to another partner, Code § 704(c)(1)(B) requires the contributing partner to recognize the precontribution gain remaining in the distributed property. *Id.* § 704(c)(1)(B)(i).

52 These antiabuse rules also approach recognition differently. The Code § 751(b) disproportionate distribution rule and the Code § 707(a)(2)(B) disguised sale rule follow an exchange-based approach, recharacterizing the transaction as a taxable exchange between the partnership and the distributee partner. Under this approach, both the distributee and the nondistributee partners may recognize gain on the distribution. Alternatively, the Code §§ 704(c)(1)(B) and 737 mixing bowl rules rely on a sales-based approach to recognition where the tax consequences are determined based on the partnership's hypothetical sale of the distributed property. I.R.C. §§ 704(c)(1)(B)(i), 737(a). In this scenario, only the distributee partner is required to recognize gain; the nondistributee partners are not affected by the antiabuse rules.

53 The operational mechanics of these antiabuse rules also vary, with each rule using different statutory tools to combat a particular abuse. Code § 751(b), for instance, is grounded in technical rules that require a partnership to navigate seven steps and three imaginary transactions between the partnership and the distributee partner. William S. McKee et al., Federal Taxation of Partnerships and Partners ¶ 21.03 (4th ed. 2007). In contrast, the Code § 707(a)(2)(B) disguised sale rule follows a standards-based approach to determining whether a contribution and distribution should be treated as a taxable sale. Treas. Reg. § 1.707-3(b)(2). The Code § 737 mixing bowl rule follows a third approach, turning on specialized terminology, such as "net precontribution gain," to prevent income avoidance through a coordinated contribution and distribution. I.R.C. § 737(b). These varied mechanics, in turn, ripple through each antiabuse rule, often requiring customized basis adjustments and character rules at both the partner and partnership levels. For example, when a partner or partnership recognizes gain under any of these rules, the character of such gain must be determined. To that end, many of these rules include special provisions governing how character determinations are to be made. *Id.* §§ 704(c)(1)(B)(ii) (character determined by a hypothetical sale), 737(a) (character determined by reference to proportionate character of the net precontribution gain); Treas. Reg. § 1.751-1(b)(2)(iii), (3)(ii) (character determined by reference to the character of the property relinquished in the exchange). Similarly, these recognized gains often trigger basis adjustments; hence, each antiabuse rule must specify how the recognized gain affects the partnership's basis in its property and the partners' bases in their partnership interests. I.R.C. §§ 704(c)(1)(B)(iii) (basis adjustments to contributed property and contributing partner's outside basis), 737(c) (basis adjustments to contributed property and contributing partner's outside basis); Treas. Reg. § 1.751-1(b)(2), (3) (basis adjustments in connection with all three fictional Code § 751(b) transactions).

confusion; partnerships often do not know what the law of distributions is. A partnership likely knows that, as a general matter, distributions are treated as nonrecognition events; hence, the partnership would not expect a distribution to trigger gain recognition by any of its partners. Even so, the partnership may not know that this general nonrecognition rule is subject to at least four separate antiabuse rules, any of which could require the recognition of gain by its partners.[54] Likewise, the partnership may not appreciate that each antiabuse rule operates differently, requiring it to work through four distinct triggers and four separate computational analyses in order to determine the tax consequences of a single distribution. When considered in this light, it is no wonder that so many partnerships struggle to negotiate subchapter K's distribution system—it is a technical minefield, particularly for the large number of everyday partnerships for which specialized partnership tax advice is often cost prohibitive.

The Price of Fracture

Subchapter K today consists of hundreds of pages of statutory and regulatory provisions and thousands of pages of rulings, memoranda, and guidance—both formal and informal—that clarify the application of individual provisions in specific situations.[55] The sheer quantity of authority is overwhelming, adding enormous complexity to partnership tax. Yet this complexity signals a much deeper systemic fracture in subchapter K: its rules focus on the activities of elite partnerships, but these rules apply to all partnerships by their terms, including everyday partnerships. More generally, the needs and abuses of elite partnerships have driven the legal development of subchapter K, as Congress increasingly relies on technical rulemaking to combat tax shelters. However, the burden of this complexity falls disproportionately on everyday partnerships whose day-to-day activities share little in common with elite partnerships. Even worse, this complexity imposes great hardship on everyday partnerships because these partnerships are less likely to have the resources, financial and otherwise, necessary to navigate the complicated thicket of modern subchapter K.

As a consequence, many everyday partnerships are effectively denied access to the substantive content of partnership tax. Partnerships that cannot apply and understand subchapter K's complicated rules, in turn, cannot participate in the system.[56] As a result, many of these everyday partnerships and their partners often follow what some scholars refer to as an "intuitive

54 Even the IRS recognizes this inconsistency between the commercial expectations of many partners and the current state of subchapter K's distribution system: "Although the general rule aims to treat partnership distributions as nontaxable events, the exceptions can quickly overshadow the general rule." Internal Revenue Serv., Partnership-Audit Technique Guide, ch. 4 (2007).

55 The statutory provisions of subchapter K span 33 pages, and the regulatory provisions of subchapter K span another 286 pages. I.R.C. §§ 701–777; Treas. Reg. §§ 1.701-1 to 1.777-1. To illustrate, a simple search on Lexis for administrative guidance containing the term "partnership" at least five times returned more than 3,000 documents. Narrowing the search to items using the term "partnership" at least five times and the term "passthrough" returned 2,897 items. To conduct this search on November 1, 2013, I went to www.lexis.com and clicked the "Area of Law—By Topic: Taxation" hyperlink. Then, I clicked the "Find Federal Administrative Materials" hyperlink followed by the "Agency Decisions" hyperlink and the "IRS Bulletins, Letter Rulings & Memoranda Decisions, Combined" hyperlink. I then searched for "partnership" at least five times and "passthrough."

56 Lokken, *supra* note 3, at 252 ("Americans have traditionally prided themselves as being a society of laws. Laws that cannot feasibly be understood and obeyed are the equivalent of no law at all.").

subchapter K."[57] Under this intuitive approach, everyday partners no longer strive for technical compliance with subchapter K's myriad rules. Instead, these partners take positions based on their general understanding of partnership tax and hope their positions are "compliant enough" to avoid the attention of the IRS.[58]

Of equal importance, complexity facilitates the noncompliance of elite partnerships that pursue abusive transactions. Complexity is surely not the only source of the modern tax shelter problem, but it plays an important role. As previously discussed, subchapter K's complicated rules offer partnerships many opportunities for strategic behavior.[59] But complexity also plays a more insidious role in tax shelters, functioning as a shield for the abusive activities of elite partnerships. Complexity hides the voluntary noncompliance of these elite partnerships in a larger mass of partnership noncompliance. In doing so, it decreases the risk that the IRS will discover such abusive transactions.

From the perspective of everyday partners, partnership tax must seem quite lawless, missing the statutory and regulatory markers that typically guide partners through the compliance process. In fact, it must seem as though our country has a dual tax system: one for the wealthy and well-advised and another for everyone else.[60] When considered in this light, complexity poses a much deeper challenge to subchapter K—it erodes the notion of legitimacy that nurtures respect for the law within the partnership tax community.

Public legitimacy is immensely important in a system like subchapter K that depends on the voluntary compliance of partners. In very general terms, a voluntary compliance system is one where each taxpayer is responsible for calculating and reporting her own tax liability in the first instance. The vast majority of taxpayers are not subject to audit; hence, they operate largely on an honor code basis with little risk of government intervention.[61] This is especially true in partnership tax where scant enforcement resources have driven down audit rates.[62]

Fostering a sense of stability and fairness in partnership tax is thus a vital feature of a functional subchapter K. Comprehensible and coherent partnership rules allow partners to participate in the system and "see" how it works. Equitable rules signal a commitment to fairness, subjecting all partnerships to the same rules without regard to wealth, geography, or sophistication levels. In doing so, these rules nurture a sense of legitimacy in partnership tax, thus strengthening the ties that foster fidelity to subchapter K and to the law more broadly.

---

57 *See supra* note 13 and accompanying text.

58 Partners are not the only stakeholders forced to rely on intuition when navigating subchapter K. The IRS also struggles with subchapter K's complexity. Enforcement resources dedicated to subchapter K are low; thus, IRS personnel face formidable challenges in the enforcement setting. *See infra* notes 61–62. Efficient administration requires that IRS personnel master the rules of partnership tax. Yet these individuals, like partners, lack the time and resources necessary to develop such mastery.

59 *See supra* notes 10–11 and accompanying text.

60 *See* U.S. Dep't of the Treasury, The Problem of Corporate Tax Shelters: Discussion, Analysis and Legislative Proposals 3 (1999); Sheldon I. Banoff, *The Use and Misuse of Anti-Abuse Rules*, 48 Tax Law. 827, 828–30 (1995); Edward J. McCaffery, *The Holy Grail of Tax Simplification*, 1990 Wis. L. Rev. 1267, 1281.

61 In 2013, the IRS examined 0.96 percent of all individual income tax returns filed for the 2012 taxable year. Internal Revenue Serv., Fiscal Year 2013 Enforcement and Service Results, at 2 (2013).

62 *See id.* at 5. In 2013, the Service examined 0.42 percent of all partnership returns. *Id.* Since 2004, the IRS has examined an average of 0.38 percent of all partnership returns annually. *Id.* In addition, with few exceptions, the percentage of partnership returns examined each year since 2004 has been lower than the percentage examined of any other type of income tax return. *Id.*

The opposite scenario is also possible. Complexity and instability can create the perception that partnership tax is unfair. Partners that cannot access subchapter K's rules often experience alienation and disillusionment.[63] As a consequence, these partners may consider the system corrupt, bestowing tax benefits on the wealthy and well-advised while excluding them from such rewards. This perception, in turn, increases the likelihood that partners will pursue tax shelters because "everyone else is doing it." And a pattern then emerges, with tax abuse triggering government responses, government responses leading to additional legal complexity and tax abuse, and partners increasingly losing confidence in subchapter K's public legitimacy.

Partnership tax is in fact experiencing this type of negative scenario today. Although there is little empirical evidence regarding partner compliance, anecdotal evidence suggests that partner compliance is failing at both extremes of the partnership spectrum.[64] As previously noted, everyday partnerships have few viable options in navigating subchapter K's complicated rules. Likewise, abuse remains a persistent problem among elite partnerships. Noncompliance, in turn, reinforces the perception that subchapter K is unfair and unprincipled, thereby eroding morale among partners. The result is a breakdown in subchapter K's public legitimacy—a breakdown that highlights the deep fractures in partnership tax.[65]

In Chapter 9, Bradley Borden objects to my characterization of the plight of everyday partnerships, suggesting that I overstate the problems created by subchapter K's complexity. In particular, Borden does not consider the intuitive approach to partnership tax problematic. To Borden, subchapter K's complexity is largely a byproduct of the fight against tax shelters. This complexity is thus designed to prevent the abusive activities of elite partnerships; it is not designed to disrupt the legitimate activities of everyday partnerships. Put another way, subchapter K's complicated antiabuse rules should not apply to the commercial transactions of everyday partnerships.[66] As a result, these everyday partnerships should be able to approximate the right

---

63 *See* U.S. Dep't of the Treasury, *supra* note 60, at 3.

64 *See* Am. Law Inst., 1999 Reporters' Study, *supra* note 2, at 105; Lokken, *supra* note 10, at 367; Lokken, *supra* note 3, at 252.

65 Voluntary compliance also serves an expressive function, allowing partnerships to participate in one of our most foundational democratic rituals. The federal income tax is one of the most visible contact points between individuals and the federal government; thus, compliance lies at a decisive juncture in the relationship between citizen and state, offering the government an important opportunity to make an impression on a large number of taxpayers. *See* Arthur E. Sutherland, Jr., *A New Society and an Old Calling*, 23 Cornell L.Q. 545 (1938).

> The pyramidal administration of justice, with an awe-inspiring appellate court at the apex, nevertheless exists for the great mass of individuals at the base; and no matter what form of tribunal is considered, if it is administering a complex regulatory system, the individual members of the public can not make effective use of it without skilled assistance. That assistance may take many forms: tax agents, "adjusters," trust officers, conscientious magistrates, social workers, or trained advocates and counsellors; but unless the public finds that fair treatment from the government is readily available it is resentful and suspicious.

Id. at 549.

66 Indeed, the Treasury has taken this position, repeatedly asserting that many of these antiabuse provisions are intended solely to combat the activities of sheltering partnerships and, hence, they should not interfere with the legitimate activities of nonsheltering partnerships. *See, e.g.*, Subchapter K Anti-Abuse Rule, 59 Fed. Reg. 25,581, 25,582 (proposed May 17, 1994) (to be codified at 26 C.F.R. pt. 1) ("The proposed regulation is not intended to interfere with bona fide joint business arrangements involving partnerships."). While these statements may be correct, a careful everyday partnership must nonetheless consider such

results without incurring the financial and emotional costs of navigating these complicated antiabuse rules, which are directed at the small number of elite partnerships that pursue tax shelters.[67]

I disagree. Even if one were to conclude that an intuitive approach to subchapter K produces accurate results for everyday partnerships, an intuitive subchapter K remains problematic from a legitimacy perspective and, more broadly, from a rule-of-law perspective.[68] Any system of partnership tax that excludes large numbers of partners—partners that want to comply with the law—from the possibility of compliance is problematic. From an excluded partner's perspective, an intuitive subchapter K is distressingly unstable. This partner would have little sense of what she did correctly or incorrectly in any given year; instead, the partner would simply be asked to trust the IRS—if she is not pursuing tax shelters, subchapter K's complexities will not affect her.

Yet this places everyday partners in a particularly vulnerable position. Consider, for instance, an everyday partner engaged in a legitimate commercial enterprise. Because this partner is not engaged in tax sheltering, she trusts the government's statement regarding subchapter K's antiabuse rules and follows an intuitive approach to subchapter K when computing her tax liability. The IRS then decides to audit this partner, asserting that she misapplied one of subchapter K's complicated rules and imposing penalties and interest for the resulting understatement. This scenario, perhaps even the fear of this scenario, would surely arouse feelings of anger and frustration in our everyday partner—she followed the government's advice, but that advice did not insulate her from an IRS audit. Indeed, it is precisely this sense of vulnerability that erodes the perception that partnership tax is fair and principled.

More generally, an intuitive approach to subchapter K sends a troubling signal to everyday partners, tacitly approving of a system that denies many of them access to the law. It communicates to everyday partners that it is not important that they comprehend the rules of partnership tax; it is only important that elite partners and their advisors understand the law. Put another way, an intuitive approach to subchapter K creates the perception that there is a positive relationship in partnership tax between access to the law and wealth, thereby jeopardizing the public legitimacy of subchapter K and the federal income tax system more broadly.

What Is to Be Done?

The time has come to rethink subchapter K, its priorities, and its rules. The goal should be access—all partnerships should be able to understand and apply subchapter K's basic rules without the expenditure of excessive resources. From a theoretical perspective, partnership tax should operate as a coherent whole, speaking with a single voice to all partnerships. To this end, Congress should replace subchapter K's scattershot collection of rules with a comprehensive system directed at those partnerships interested in complying with the law rather than those partnerships intent on exploiting it. Consistent rules written for everyday partnerships would

---

provisions in determining its federal income tax consequences. Accordingly, everyday partnerships, although not the target of these antiabuse provisions, are still adversely affected by their complexity.

67 *See* Emily Cauble, *Making Partnerships Work for Mom and Pop and Everyone Else*, 2 COLUM. J. TAX L. 247, 286 n.122 (2011); Philip F. Postlewaite, *I Come to Bury Subchapter K, Not to Praise It*, 54 TAX LAW. 451, 473 (2001).

68 Ultimately, the accuracy of an intuitive approach to subchapter K is an empirical question. The necessary empirical work, however, has yet to be done; therefore, this chapter proceeds provisionally using reasonable working assumptions.

provide a much-needed foundation for subchapter K, tying the system together and grounding its future development in cohesive principles.

From a practical perspective, accessibility would require Congress to simplify subchapter K. A first step would involve streamlining the number of provisions that govern partnership transactions. Congress should therefore eliminate many of the targeted antiabuse rules that currently attempt to draw a line between legitimate tax planning and abusive tax sheltering. As previously discussed, these rules are often counterproductive, failing to prevent elite partnerships from engaging in abusive transactions but frustrating everyday partnerships in their efforts to comply with subchapter K. A second step would emphasize rule design, improving accessibility through a more holistic approach to rulemaking. Simply put, Congress should focus its efforts on the development of a comprehensive and coordinated system of taxing partnerships. In particular, subchapter K's general operating rules should be less technical, with straightforward requirements and transparent results that, to the extent possible, cohere with the commercial expectations of everyday partnerships. Similarly, the use of specialized terminology, multifactored analyses, and computational tests in these provisions should be minimized.

Even so, accessibility is not a panacea. Partnership tax will never be simple, and it is possible that a reformed subchapter K would contain some complicated rules. However, this potential complexity should be tolerated to the extent that subchapter K's reformulated rules replace the existing thicket of rules, exceptions to rules, and exceptions to exceptions to rules with a coherent system of taxation. More generally, subchapter K would be better served by a system-wide commitment to accessibility and simplification, even if this pursuit requires individual instances of complicated rules. Unlike the current law, the contours of any particular rule would be secondary; instead, the primary goal of a reformed subchapter K would be to improve the functionality of partnership tax through a systemic focus on accessibility and harmonization.

Although this chapter takes a broad perspective in reimagining subchapter K, two examples might be useful. These examples return to the two critical aspects of partnership tax previously discussed—distributions and partnership allocations. In doing so, the examples highlight the different tradeoffs required to design a more stable system of taxing partnerships and their partners.

Partnership Distributions

As previously discussed, subchapter K's current distribution system is enormously complicated, involving a general nonrecognition rule, numerous recognition-based antiabuse rules, and a supporting cast of implementing rules that govern the basis and character consequences of a particular distribution. When this system is pulled apart, however, the source of its dysfunction becomes apparent—the nonrecognition premise at its core. Absent nonrecognition, subchapter K would not require an arsenal of equitable rules designed to ensure that predistribution gains are properly preserved and taxed to the appropriate partner at the appropriate tax rate. Deferral would instead end at the time of distribution, thereby eliminating the opportunity to convert character, shift income, or avoid gain altogether through an improper distribution. Indeed, subchapter K would look very different if distributions were no longer grounded in nonrecognition.

In very general terms, nonrecognition is appropriate when a taxpayer's investment in property is continuing, albeit perhaps in a modified form. Nonrecognition is not appropriate when a taxpayer terminates her investment in property. In these instances, the termination is an economically transformative event that fundamentally alters the nature of the taxpayer's investment. From this vantage, a recognition rule is more appropriate, capturing the substantive impact of the underlying transaction and aligning its tax treatment with commercial reality. A recognition rule is thus best viewed as a means of implementing the foundational notion that the tax consequences of a transaction should match its corresponding economic consequences.

A reformed subchapter K might thus rely on a general recognition rule for partnership distributions. Under this approach, property distributions would be treated as fully taxable events, requiring a partnership to recognize any gain in the distributed property.[69] The partnership, in turn, would allocate this gain among all of its partners based on their predistribution contractual arrangement. Similarly, liquidating distributions—distributions that involve the complete or partial termination of a partner's interest in a partnership—would be treated as fully taxable events to the distributee partner.[70] The distributee partner would be treated as if she relinquished her interest in each of the partnership's retained properties and, in exchange, received the distributed property. The tax consequences to the distributee partner would be determined accordingly, with the partner recognizing gain on the disposition of the property relinquished in the liquidating distribution.[71]

Grounding distributions in a recognition rule would align subchapter K's distribution system with a foundational notion that runs through the entire federal income tax—if a taxpayer terminates her investment in property, the transaction is generally treated as a taxable event. This is a notion that is familiar to all taxpayers, reflecting the same basic principles that govern the sale of a car or the liquidation of a corporate investment. When considered in this light, applying the same rule to distributions that terminate a partnership's or a partner's investment in property would offer a baseline that resonates with partners. Additionally, this approach to distributions would streamline subchapter K, allowing Congress to dismantle many of the complicated fixes that are necessary to police the current law's nonrecognition rule.[72] Of equal importance, this recognition-based approach would cut off deferral at a more appropriate time, thus putting an end to most

69 When a partnership distributes property, the partnership terminates its investment in the distributed property. Treating property distributions as taxable events is thus appropriate. Additionally, it would align the partnership-level treatment of property distributions with the treatment of corporate distributions. I.R.C. §§ 311(b), 336(a), 1371(a). Under these rules, a corporation recognizes gain on the distribution of appreciated property in all instances. *Id.* § 311(b). Losses, however, are only recognized in connection with the complete liquidation of a corporation. *Id.* § 336(a).

70 As a general matter, distributions that alter the distributee partner's share of the partnership's predistribution gains would be treated as liquidating distributions. These distributions are economically transformative events for the partnership and the distributee partner; thus, a recognition rule is an appropriate. If, on the contrary, a distribution has no effect on the distributee partner's interest in the partnership, then it would be treated as an operating distribution. Operating distributions would continue to be treated as nonrecognition transactions, generally giving rise to no immediate tax consequences.

71 This approach is referred to as "full fragmentation." Under full fragmentation, the partnership would be disregarded, and the distributee partner would be treated as if she disposed of her interest in each of the partnership's properties. In order to compute the gains recognized by the distributee partner, the partnership would be treated as if it sold all of its properties immediately before the liquidating distribution for fair market value. To the extent the distributee partner would have recognized any gains on the partnership's hypothetical sale, full fragmentation would require her to recognize these gains at the time of distribution. The distributee partner would then take a basis in the distributed property equal to its fair market value, and the partnership would adjust the inside basis of its remaining properties accordingly.

72 Most importantly, Congress could repeal the antiabuse rules that currently police the borders of subchapter K's distribution regime (i.e., Code §§ 704(c)(1)(B), 707(a)(2)(B), 737, and 751(b)) along with all of the basis, character, and supporting rules necessary to make the regime work. Although this approach to taxing distributions may produce new challenges for subchapter K, grounding partnership distributions in a general recognition rule would improve the functionality of partnership tax as a whole, making subchapter K and its distribution system more accessible to everyday partnerships.

of the abusive distributions that have plagued subchapter K. Taken together, the transition to a recognition rule would promote stability in partnership tax, with a reformed distribution system guided by a single, coherent rule that is comprehensible to all partners.[73]

Partnership Allocations

Unlike distributions, partnership allocations lack a corollary in the federal income tax. Accordingly, it is not possible to ground subchapter K's allocation system in rules that parallel those that partners face in other commercial contexts. On the contrary, partnership allocations, and the rules governing these arrangements, are unique to subchapter K. Even in a reformed subchapter K, it is therefore likely that the rules governing partnership allocations will remain relatively complicated.

Nonetheless, there is significant room for improvement. Despite the current law's technicality, there is a common thread running through subchapter K's allocation regime, one that runs through all of the federal income tax—the tax consequences of a transaction should match the corresponding economic consequences. The problem is that this basic notion is buried underneath an incomprehensible default rule and an impossibly complicated safe harbor provision.[74] Accordingly, reforms designed to streamline the technicality of partnership allocations through the use of less specialized terminology and accounting-based rules might offer a promising path forward. In doing so, these reforms would refocus partners' attention on the driving force behind

73 Some scholars, including Bradley Borden, suggest that this approach to distributions would create distortions within subchapter K. To these scholars, a recognition rule might adversely affect business arrangements, discouraging both partnership formation and dissolution. This suggestion, however, is factually uncertain. Most of the scholarly work regarding nonrecognition in partnership tax has taken place in the contribution context, as opposed to the distribution context. *See, e.g.*, Karen C. Burke, *Disguised Sales Between Partners and Partnerships: Section 707 and the Forthcoming Regulations*, 63 Ind. L.J. 489, 522–29 (1988); Laura E. Cunningham & Noël B. Cunningham, *Simplifying Subchapter K: The Deferred Sales Method*, 51 SMU L. Rev. 1 (1997); David R. Keyser, *A Theory of Nonrecognition Under an Income Tax: The Case of Partnership Formation*, 5 Am. J. Tax Pol'y 269, 279–85 (1986); Andrea R. Monroe, *Saving Subchapter K: Substance, Shattered Ceilings, and the Problem of Contributed Property*, 74 Brook. L. Rev. 1381 (2009); John P. Steines, *Partnership Allocations of Built-In Gain or Loss*, 45 Tax L. Rev. 615, 653–55 (1990). Whatever one's view of the merits of nonrecognition in the contribution context, the policy rationales supporting nonrecognition in distributions are far less strong. *See* Curtis J. Berger, *W(h)ither Partnership Tax?*, 47 Tax L. Rev. 105, 154–55 (1991); Burke, *supra*, at 534; Lokken, *supra* note 3, at 270; Andrea R. Monroe, *Taxing Reality: Rethinking Partnership Distributions*, 47 Loy. L.A. L. Rev. (forthcoming); Postlewaite et al., *supra* note 3, at 596–98; Yin, *supra* note 3, at 226. Distributions are often driven by personal considerations or commercial imperatives; hence, tax planning often plays a secondary role in these transactions. Likewise, many of the current law's antiabuse rules already subject distributions to recognition. Indeed, many distributions today are "not nonrecognition events" although treated as such by partnerships. Yin, *supra* note 3, at 226. To the extent this comes as a surprise to partnerships, it is yet another sign of subchapter K's inaccessibility.

Even so, a recognition-based approach to distributions would likely accelerate taxation by some partners. Yet this is appropriate. Nonrecognition is not justified, even in subchapter K, when a taxpayer's investment in property is terminated. When considered in this light, a recognition rule appears to correct the historic distortions embedded in subchapter K, aligning its distribution regime with more universal tax principles. In doing so, this approach would reduce the administrative costs of navigating subchapter K's distribution rules. Indeed, the administrative savings of a streamlined system of partnership distributions would surely mitigate a portion of the additional tax costs triggered by a recognition rule.

74 Treas. Reg. § 1.704-1(b)(2) (substantial economic effect safe harbor), (3) (partner's interest in the partnership default rule).

subchapter K's approach to allocations: matching the tax and economic treatment of a transaction. That is, they would highlight the aspect of partnership allocations that resonates with all partners, thereby improving the accessibility of the rules that are subchapter K's lifeblood.[75]

More generally, the continued complexity of partnership allocations would not diminish the appeal of a more holistic approach to subchapter K. So long as partnership tax as a whole is accessible to the larger partnership tax community, individual instances of heightened complexity would be tolerated. In the case of partnership allocations, this tradeoff appears particularly apt. Partnership allocations are at the core of subchapter K, affecting every transaction entered into by every partnership, every year. Developing a functional allocation system is thus vital to subchapter K, even if its rules are more complicated than other aspects of partnership tax. Indeed, this is precisely the type of tradeoff that a reformed subchapter K should make—heightened complexity in a small number of individual instances in exchange for enhanced accessibility throughout the entire partnership tax system.

The Future of Elite Partnerships

Even if one supports reforming subchapter K, one might nonetheless question the shift to simpler, more obtuse partnership rules. Blunt rules risk being overinclusive or underinclusive, either of which would increase the risk that future partnership transactions would be mischaracterized. Mischaracterizations, in turn, would create opportunities for partnerships to engage in tax sheltering and, consistent with historic practice, elite partnerships can be expected to exploit these opportunities for the benefit of their partners.[76] Accordingly, one might wonder whether simplifying subchapter K might prove counterproductive if partnerships were to take advantage of these potential mischaracterizations through tax sheltering.

---

75 Whether a more foundational overhaul of partnership allocations is necessary remains an open question. The current law, like much of subchapter K, is deeply flawed, but alternative approaches to partnership allocations also present challenges. Some scholars have proposed that Congress eliminate special allocations. *See, e.g.*, Mark P. Gergen, *Reforming Subchapter K: Special Allocations*, 46 Tax L. Rev. 1, 40–41 (1990); David Hasen, *Partnership Special Allocations Revisited*, 13 Fla. Tax Rev. 349, 383–87 (2012); Darryll K. Jones, *Toward Equity and Efficiency in Partnership Allocations*, 25 Va. Tax Rev. 1047, 1093 (2006). *But see, e.g.*, Lokken, *supra* note 3, at 265–69; Andrea R. Monroe, *Too Big to Fail: The Problem of Partnership Allocations*, 30 Va. Tax Rev. 465, 512–17 (2011).

Another potential, albeit controversial, approach is target allocations. *See, e.g.*, N.Y. State Bar Ass'n Tax Section, Report on Partnership Target Allocations, *reprinted in* 2010 TNT 185–15 (LexisNexis); William G. Cavanagh, *Targeted Allocations Hit the Spot*, 129 Tax Notes 89 (2010). Target allocations focus on a partnership's cash distribution provisions rather than its allocation provisions and their capital-account-based analyses. In order to allocate taxable income, a partnership using target allocations determines the aggregate distributions each partner would receive at the end of the year if the partnership were to liquidate. The partnership then allocates its taxable income such that each partner's year-end capital account balance equals the amount she would have received on the partnership's hypothetical liquidation. In this way, a partnership using target allocations "backs into" its annual allocations of taxable income.

76 Mischaracterizations are particularly salient in the federal income tax because they risk transforming an uncommon transaction into a common tax shelter. *See* David A. Weisbach, *Formalism in the Tax Law*, 66 U. Chi. L. Rev. 860, 886 (1999).

Before proceeding, it is important to note that tax shelters are an ongoing problem in partnership tax. Despite myriad antiabuse rules, partnerships continue to pursue transactions that exploit the current law's piecemeal approach to tax shelters. There is thus little downside to reimagining partnership tax from an alternative perspective. In fact, there is reason to believe that a streamlined subchapter K would be less susceptible to abuse.

Even so, simplifying subchapter K would require a different approach to combating partnership tax shelters. In particular, it would force the government to rely more heavily on generally applicable tax provisions (i.e., provisions outside of subchapter K) to address abusive partnership transactions.[77] These "external" tax provisions—including the economic substance doctrine,[78] enhanced penalty provisions,[79] and disclosure rules[80]—were all useful in fighting the most recent round of partnership tax shelters.[81] In many instances, these provisions proved more effective than subchapter K's "internal" array of targeted antiabuse rules. Considered in this light, relying more heavily on external tax provisions to address future partnership tax shelters would make sense. The Treasury should direct its scarce enforcement resources toward tools that have shown promise in the fight against tax shelters, whether or not such tools are located in a section of the Code that begins with the number "700."

At the same time, a simpler subchapter K would improve compliance among everyday partnerships. Improved compliance, in turn, would enhance the IRS's ability to enforce the law, allowing it to direct a larger portion of its resources toward the fight against abusive transactions. Likewise, the tax sheltering activities of elite partnerships would be more transparent, having lost the "shield" previously offered by subchapter K's technicality and the resulting involuntary noncompliance of everyday partnerships. Together, these shifts in the enforcement landscape would allow the IRS to more aggressively target tax shelters, thereby making it more difficult and more expensive for elite partnerships to pursue abusive transactions.

---

77 *See id.* at 876 (defending the use of antiabuse rules because they "attempt to allow the tax law to use simple rules without all of the associated costs" (footnotes omitted)).

78 *See, e.g.*, Klamath Strategic Inv. Fund *ex rel.* St. Croix Ventures v. United States, 568 F.3d 537 (5th Cir. 2009); Coltec Indus., Inc. v. United States, 454 F.3d 1340 (Fed. Cir. 2006); ACM P'ship v. Comm'r, 157 F.3d 231 (3d Cir. 1998). In 2010, the economic substance doctrine was codified. Healthcare and Education Reconciliation Act of 2010, Pub. L. No. 111-152, § 1409(a), 124 Stat. 1029 (codified at I.R.C. § 7701(o)). Under this provision, a transaction will only be treated as having economic substance if (1) the transaction changes the taxpayer's economic position in a meaningful way apart from its federal income tax consequences; and (2) the taxpayer has a substantial purpose for entering into such transaction apart from its federal income tax consequences. I.R.C. § 7701(o)(1).

79 I.R.C. §§ 6662, 6664. In connection with the codification of the economic substance doctrine, these penalty provisions were also amended, subjecting economic substance violations to a strict liability penalty. *Id.* §§ 6662(b)(6) (applying the accuracy-related penalty to underpayments attributable to the disallowance of a claimed tax benefit arising from a transaction lacking economic substance), 6664(c)(2) (disallowing the reasonable cause exception for underpayments attributable to a transaction lacking economic substance).

80 *Id.* §§ 6111, 6112.

81 *See* Pamela F. Olson, *Now that You've Caught the Bus, What Are You Going to Do with It? Observations from the Frontlines, the Sidelines, and Between the Lines, So to Speak*, 60 Tax Law. 567, 567 (2007); *see also* Jeremiah Coder, *Korb Reflects on Long Tenure as Chief Counsel*, 122 Tax Notes 20 (2009) (recounting the view of Donald Korb, outgoing IRS Chief Counsel, that Treasury has turned the corner on corporate tax shelters).

More generally, greater reliance on tax provisions of general application would serve an expressive function, better reflecting the reality of modern partnerships. The activities of elite partnerships are often unpredictable, and their transactions are increasingly individualized. The partnership rules that target their improper activities have proven deeply problematic for the large number of everyday partnerships that are not engaged in tax shelters but are nevertheless forced to bear the complexity of subchapter K's formidable antiabuse regime. In this increasingly polarized world of contemporary partnerships, it may simply no longer be possible—if it ever was possible—to design functional rules that prevent the abusive transactions of elite partnerships and simultaneously promote the legitimate commercial interests of everyday partnerships.

Yet a greater dependence on provisions external to subchapter K would mark a significant shift in the fight against partnership tax abuse. Bradley Borden, for instance, objects to this approach because he believes that it would effectively bifurcate subchapter K into two regimes—one for everyday partnerships and another for elite partnerships. To Borden, this bifurcated system would compromise the accuracy and efficiency of subchapter K in pursuit of simplification, which he considers a questionable goal. Borden believes that subchapter K is complicated because partnerships, by their nature, are complicated arrangements. Complicated rules are thus necessary in order to accurately and efficiently account for partnership transactions.[82] Likewise, Borden suggests that these complicated rules do not impose an undue hardship on everyday partnerships because these partnerships are not pursuing tax shelters; hence, they are unlikely to run afoul of these rules. As a result, Borden discounts the harm suffered by the many everyday partnerships that are denied access to large swaths of subchapter K.

I disagree with Borden's initial premise. My approach to partnership tax does not bifurcate subchapter K; subchapter K is already bifurcated. The current law divides partnerships into two categories: elite partnerships that are sufficiently wealthy or well-advised to access subchapter K and everyday partnerships that are forced to follow an intuitive approach to subchapter K. Indeed, bifurcation along some lines is inevitable in a system as diverse as partnership tax, with such a heterogeneous array of enterprises, sophistication levels, and sizes.

If, contrary to Borden's assertion, one begins with the premise that bifurcation is unavoidable, then the real question regarding the tax treatment of twenty-first century partnerships emerges—how does Congress design a functional subchapter K capable of accommodating this diversity while simultaneously promoting the values of equity, simplicity, and efficiency? As previously discussed, accessibility and legitimacy are vital to this project. Partners that cannot comprehend the law cannot comply with the law. Marginalized, noncompliant partners, in turn, are likely to lose respect for subchapter K, thus increasing the potential for tax abuse and decreasing the equity and efficiency of the law.

Borden, however, believes that there are real costs associated with this type of reform, namely the risk that a streamlined subchapter K would be less efficient. I believe there are even greater costs associated with the current law, the most distressing of which are those related to legitimacy and the rule of law. A subchapter K where everyday partnerships are denied access to the substantive content of the law is not a sustainable system of partnership taxation. And this is the case whether or not an intuitive subchapter K would arrive at approximately the same results. The underlying

82 For instance, Borden would argue that the complexity of partnership allocations is both important and inevitable, reflecting the economic factors that shape the partners' commercial arrangement. To him, subchapter K's allocation rules perform a critical function—promoting resource integration while minimizing agency costs. In doing so, these rules enhance the accuracy and efficiency of subchapter K, albeit at the cost of greater complexity.

fracture is simply too dangerous, signaling that it is more important that the wealthy and well-advised comprehend subchapter K's rules than the rest of the partnership tax community.

It is thus time to reform partnership tax. It is time to design a system of taxation that allows all partnerships—everyday and elite—to participate in subchapter K. A reimagined subchapter K accessible to all partnerships would represent an important and much-needed step toward functionality and fairness in partnership tax. Indeed, it would signal to all partnerships a congressional commitment to legitimacy in the taxation of twenty-first century partnerships and their partners.

Chapter 9
Economic Justification for Flow-Through Tax Complexity

Bradley T. Borden*

Introduction

Complexity is often associated with the flow-through tax treatment of partnerships.[1] The complexity of partnership flow-through taxation raises the fundamental question of whether such complexity is necessary or desirable. In Chapter 8, Andrea Monroe draws upon knowledge of contemporary large partnerships that take advantage of the partnership tax rules to unfairly reduce their tax burdens. From that perspective, coupled with a philosophical framework that relies upon fairness, she sees complexity as providing a means to an undesirable end for scheming sophisticated taxpayers. This chapter, on the other hand, focuses on the nature and origin of arrangements taxed as partnerships. It draws upon the history of ancient partnerships and economic concepts that help define the boundaries of firms and the motivations for forming arrangements and allocating profits and losses to help put resources to their highest and best uses. Such arrangements can be quite complex, and the proper taxation of such entities requires complex rules. The two chapters' different temporal and theoretical starting points provide different perspectives and lead to somewhat different conclusions about the need for flow-through taxation and the structure it should take.

Arrangements that appear to be simple because of the finances at stake or the perceived lack of sophistication of the members of the arrangement can raise very complex tax issues and require a tax regime that addresses the associated complexity. This chapter applies economic principles to help describe the source of some of the complexity that such arrangements can raise and then uses those principles to help explain why the flow-through regime for taxing partnerships must be an integral part of a fully functioning income tax system in the United States. The chapter begins by recounting economic aspects of partnerships through the lens of simple partnerships that have been in existence for centuries. That discussion reveals the source of complexity in this area and the natural attraction of such entities. The chapter then discusses how partnership tax has attempted to account for the complex nature of partnerships and provide a regime that does not unduly interfere with the economic arrangements of partners. That discussion recognizes, however, that the administration of tax law requires several rules that must recognize partnerships as entities separate from their owners and impose entity-type rules. Finally, the chapter considers why the perspective presented in this chapter leads to analyses and conclusions that differ from those presented by Monroe in Chapter 8 and then ends with brief concluding thoughts.

---

* Thanks to Anthony Infanti and Andrea Monroe for comments on earlier drafts of this chapter. This chapter draws on materials originally published in Bradley T. Borden, *Aggregate-Plus Theory of Partnership Taxation*, 43 Ga. L. Rev. 717 (2009), and Bradley T. Borden, *Residual-Risk Model for Classifying Business Arrangements*, 37 Fla. St. U. L. Rev. 245 (2010).

1 In this chapter, the term "partnership" is used to refer to any entity, including a limited liability company, treated as a partnership for federal income tax purposes. Treas. Reg. §§ 301.7701-1, -2, -3.

Economic Aspects of Partnerships

Economic theory mandates flow-through taxation for partnerships and limited liability companies. Even everyday partnerships and limited liability companies can create complexities that demand a sophisticated tax regime to accompany them. Since the dawn of business, people have integrated property and services to help maximize profits.[2] They recognize, however, that integration creates agency costs that demand complex economic arrangements. Thus, modern economic theory helps explain why parties integrate resources in this age-old fashion and why they allocate economic items.[3] Economic theory also helps explain why tax law should apply aggregate-plus taxation to partnerships by attempting to treat partnerships as aggregates of their owners and only adding entity-type rules when necessary to meet administrative needs. The aggregate starting point with added entity-type rules is the essence of aggregate-plus taxation.[4]

Economic Reasons for Resource Integration

Property and services (i.e., capital and labor) are the basic resources of business arrangements. The owners of resources determine the extent to which they will make them available to other parties and the price at which they will make them available. The residual right of control (i.e., the right to control all aspects of property that have not been given away by contract[5]) determines who owns and controls a particular resource. Even a seemingly simple business arrangement illustrates how both property and services have residual rights of control.[6] Assume Land Baroness owns arable property, and Old McDonald is a highly reputed farmer. If Baroness hires McDonald to manage the farm for one year, at the end of that one-year contract, Baroness would still have complete control of the future use of the property, and McDonald would have complete control of his services.

As the holder of the residual right of control of a piece of property, a property owner determines the extent to which a service provider may perform services with respect to the property.[7] Simple examples of the types of partnerships used since ancient times illustrate the economic aspects of partnerships. For example, Baroness determines the extent to which McDonald will manage the property. She may determine that McDonald's greatest expertise is in preparing ground and planting and hire him just for that purpose. She could hire another person to cultivate and harvest

---

2 For a more in-depth retelling of the historical development of partnerships see Bradley T. Borden, *Aggregate-Plus Theory of Partnership Taxation*, 43 GA. L. REV. 717, 723–43 (2009) (citing Henry Hansmann et al., *Law and the Rise of the Firm*, 119 HARV. L. REV. 1333 (2006); A. Ladru Jensen, *Is a Partnership Under the Uniform Partnership Act an Aggregate or an Entity?*, 16 VAND. L. REV. 377 (1963); Henry Fr. Lutz, *Babylonian Partnership*, 4 J. ECON. & BUS. HIST. 552 (1932); William Mitchell, *Early Forms of Partnership*, *in* 3 SELECT ESSAYS IN ANGLO-AMERICAN LEGAL HISTORY 183 (1909)).

3 Recent scholarship has also discovered that modern economic theory nicely explains various aspects of ancient business arrangements and their development. *See generally*, *e.g.*, Hansmann et al., *supra* note 2 (applying economic theory to explain why corporate law developed legal aspects such as entity shielding).

4 *See* Borden, *supra* note 2.

5 Sanford J. Grossman & Oliver D. Hart, *The Costs and Benefits of Ownership: A Theory of Vertical and Lateral Integration*, 94 J. POL. ECON. 691, 695 (1986).

6 Grossman and Hart use the example of a printer and publisher to illustrate the residual right of control in property. *Id.* at 695. Courts grant specific performance only if a money damages remedy is inadequate, so if other printers are available to complete the print job, money damages would probably be the publisher's sole remedy. *See* Anthony T. Kronman, *Specific Performance*, 45 U. CHI. L. REV. 351, 355 (1978).

7 *See* Oliver Hart & John Moore, *Property Rights and the Nature of the Firm*, 98 J. POL. ECON. 1119, 1121 (1990).

the crop. Baroness determines the discretion McDonald may exercise in carrying out the details of the job. Nonetheless, hiring McDonald to manage the property and giving him discretion does not transfer a residual right of control over the property.

As the holder of the residual right of control of his services, McDonald should be able to contract away the economic product of those services.[8] For example, McDonald may agree to provide services only with respect to Baroness's property, and Baroness could sue for breach of contract if McDonald fails to perform the services. If Baroness were successful in her cause of action, she could receive damages and a possible injunction that would prohibit McDonald from performing the services elsewhere.[9] Thus, Baroness can contract to receive the economic equivalent of the services. In that regard, McDonald can sell the economic value of his services. After performing the contracted services or paying the damages, McDonald would control the full economic value of his services not contracted away. Thus, McDonald retains the residual right of control of his services.

Arrangements in which property owners and service providers retain the residual rights of control of their respective resources do not pose significant economic or tax challenges. If Baroness holds the residual right of control of just the land, her income would come from the land. If McDonald holds the residual right of control of just the services, his income will be compensation for those services.[10] Instead of hiring McDonald, Baroness could grant him use of the property and charge the service provider a fee for using the property. Such an arrangement is a lease, just as granting use of capital for a fee is a loan. Consequently, any payment the property owner receives from the service provider with respect to the property should be rent or interest regardless of the method used to determine the payment amount.[11] Arrangements that keep the residual right to control property and services separate provide for convenient accounting of income from the property and services. The parties are able to trace the product of the property and services to the owner of the respective resources and characterize the product accordingly.

Economic theory suggests, however, that the separation of property ownership and services ownership may give rise to costly opportunistic behavior and suggests why parties formed partnerships in ancient times.[12] For example, assume Baroness and McDonald agree that McDonald will plant, cultivate, and harvest the corn crop for 10 percent of the harvested crop. The demand for good managers grows because more managers are moving to the city to take jobs as futures traders.

---

8 The U.S. Constitution prohibits one party from compelling another to perform services. *See* U.S. CONST. amend. XIII, § 1. This is consistent with John Locke's understanding of the product of labor as property. Nonetheless, a party should be able to contract away the economic product of those services. *See* JOHN LOCKE, TWO TREATISES OF GOVERNMENT § 27 (1690).

9 Courts are not likely to grant an injunction, however, if money damages are adequate. *See* E. ALLAN FARNSWORTH, CONTRACTS § 12.5 (2d ed. 1990). A court would be more likely to grant an injunction "if the employee's services are unique or extraordinary, either because of special skill that the employee possesses … or because of special knowledge that the employee has acquired of the employer's business." *Id.*

10 The method used to compute the amount paid to the service provider will not affect the nature of the relationship between the property owner and service provider or the character of the payments to the service provider. *See* Grossman & Hart, *supra* note 5, at 694 ("A firm may pay another firm or person by the piece or a fixed amount (salary), irrespective of the ownership of the machines.").

11 *See, e.g.*, Harlan E. Moore Charitable Trust v. United States, 9 F.3d 623, 625–27 (7th Cir. 1993); Arthur Venneri Co. v. United States, 340 F.2d 337, 342 (Ct. Cl. 1965); Place v. Comm'r, 17 T.C. 199, 204–06 (1951).

12 *See* Benjamin Klein et al., *Vertical Integration, Appropriable Rents, and the Competitive Contracting Process*, 21 J.L. & ECON. 297, 298–302 (1978) (illustrating how parties may appropriate quasi rents if parties keep asset ownership separate).

Property owners who have not entered into contracts agree to hire qualified managers and pay them as much as 15 percent of their crop. The change in market conditions creates a specialized quasi rent that McDonald may seek to appropriate.[13] The appropriable portion of the quasi rent is roughly the difference between the 15 percent other property owners have to pay to hire a manager and the 10 percent Baroness agreed to pay.[14] McDonald may demand a change in contract terms and justify the change because his family would otherwise refuse to remain in the rural setting. Baroness would have to pay significantly more to replace McDonald, so she may agree to increase his share of crops to retain his services.

The market could also shift, creating appropriable quasi rents for Baroness. For example, following the execution of the contract, a flood could destroy a significant amount of crops on property other than Baroness's. The destruction could put numerous other farm managers out of work, increasing the supply of managers. The destroyed crops could also increase the value of any crops that ultimately make it to the market. Such factors present Baroness an appropriable quasi rent. She could obtain the same services McDonald agreed to provide for a fraction of the price. Because crop prices have increased, McDonald could receive the same expected value of crops even though he receives less than 10 percent. To appropriate that specialized quasi rent, Baroness could assert that she would not pay him 10 percent of the yield. Because McDonald knows he could receive his same original expected value with a lower percent of the yield and the market is not favorable for managers he would likely accept a lower percentage to retain his position.

Baroness and McDonald undoubtedly have many alternatives that they could consider to reduce the appropriation of specialized quasi rent by anticipating future contingencies and providing for them in their contract. Identifying and enforcing all future contingencies is, however, difficult, if not impossible, and can be very costly. They may instead attempt to rely upon market forces to help enforce their contract. For example, one of the parties may offer a future premium that will exceed the appropriable specialized quasi rents to be obtained through opportunistic behavior. The cost of a contract should include all future contingencies and premiums and be positively related to the level of appropriable specialized quasi rents. Thus, parties use contractual and market mechanisms to control appropriable specialized quasi rents only when such rents are relatively low. Otherwise, they would consider alternatives for reducing such rents.

If appropriable specialized quasi rents are high, parties can integrate their resources to help reduce opportunistic behavior. For example, if appropriable specialized quasi rents in agriculture were high, McDonald could consider acquiring Baroness's property, or Baroness could consider developing farming skills equal to McDonald's. One party's acquisition of another party's resource is one way in which the parties could integrate the resources. That type of integration defeats the benefits of specialization. Consequently, parties with specialized skills may prefer to integrate their resources through reciprocal transfers of the residual rights of control in the resources by forming partnerships. Such a co-ownership arrangement would help prevent both parties from engaging in opportunistic behavior and would form a partnership under the current definition.[15] It would also

---

13 Entering into a contract for a fixed period of time is a form of investment that exposes each party to the other party's potential opportunistic behavior. *See id* at 298.

14 *See* D. Bruce Johnsen, *The Quasi-Rent Structure of Corporate Enterprise: A Transaction Cost Theory*, 44 Emory L.J. 1277, 1281 (1995) (recognizing the definition of quasi rents is "the payment to an asset above that which is necessary to keep it in its present use").

15 *See* Unif. P'ship Act § 101(6), 6 U.L.A. 61 (2001). The idea that co-ownership of property and services creates a partnership rejects the claim that integration is no different from a long-term contract. *See generally* Friedrich Kessler & Richard H. Stern, *Competition, Contract, and Vertical Integration*, 69 Yale L.J. 1 (1959) (discussing long-term contracts as a form of integration). Economists assume that opportunistic

allow the parties to retain their respective specializations to a significant extent. Thus, integration through partnership formation would have been as attractive anciently as it is today, because it helps reduce appropriable specialized quasi rents and allows the parties to retain their specialties.

Agency Costs in Integrated Arrangements

Integration has definite economic benefits, but it also may give rise to agency costs. As a consequence, parties who integrate resources must consider how they will minimize agency costs. Agency costs are those costs incurred when parties with different personal preferences form an arrangement.[16] Agency costs may arise between Baroness and McDonald if they integrate their resources. After transferring a portion of the residual right to the property to McDonald, Baroness shares any decline in the property's value with McDonald, so her focus could shift more to short-term production and away from the long-term arability of the property. A decrease in the long-term arability would adversely affect McDonald's newly acquired interest in the property, so the Baroness's short-term perspective is an agency cost. McDonald on the other hand may work with less vigor, realizing that he will not only share in the short-term production but also any increase in the value of the property. In partnerships and quasi partnerships, the parties allocate the economic items of the arrangement to help reduce agency costs.[17] Such allocations help determine parties' economic rights to partnership assets and should inform the construction of a theory of partnership taxation.

Combining their respective resources through resource integration gives each partner an interest in the property and services contributed to the arrangement.[18] As a result, economic items allocated to any member of the arrangement will derive from every source that member co-owns. Thus, the law cannot merely look to the contributed resource to determine the source of a partner's allocated items. Furthermore, the output of integrated resources should be greater than the sum of the output of the resources operating individually. Thus, parties to an integrated arrangement must allocate that excess among themselves. These aspects of integration give partnership taxation its uniqueness. Tax law must recognize the parties' economic arrangement and that, in many situations, the arrangement makes tracing economic items from a source to the contributor of a specific resource extremely difficult, if not impossible. To recognize the economic arrangement, tax law must understand why parties use allocations and why they are important in defining the tax attributes of a partnership.

To help reduce agency costs, Baroness and McDonald may agree to allocate annual production 60 percent to McDonald to help ensure that he puts full effort into managing operations, with the remaining 40 percent allocated to Baroness. They may also agree to allocate 60 percent of the

behavior can only occur without integration. *See* Klein et al., *supra* note 12, at 302. To the extent a long-term contract eliminates opportunistic behavior, the contract would integrate resources. Thus, economic theory would disregard the form of the arrangement and consider the parties' rights under the governing documents.

16 Michael C. Jensen & William H. Meckling, *Theory of the Firm: Managerial Behavior, Agency Costs and Ownership Structure*, 3 J. Fin. Econ. 305, 308 (1976).

17 *See* Larry E. Ribstein, *The Rise of the Uncorporation* (Ill. Law and Econ. Research Papers Series, Research Paper No. LE09-024, 2009), *available* at http://papers.ssrn.com/pape.tar?abstract_id=1463684 (describing how partnership and quasi-partnership allocation rules allow investors and other partners to align the interests of managers with their own, especially in large or publicly traded integrated business arrangements).

18 *See, e.g.*, Unif. P'ship Act, *supra* note 15, § 101(6) (including in the definition of partnership the requirement that parties co-own property).

increase in property value to Baroness to ensure that she uses her skill as a property owner to help maintain the property's long-term value, with the remaining 40 percent allocated to McDonald. The economic reasons for allocating different types of income among the partners in different ratios are unlimited. Tax law should focus on the arrangement's economic qualities and provide a tax system that takes account of those economic realities.

An example of a simple accounting firm further demonstrates the economic aspects of partnerships. A successful accounting firm requires business development and technical expertise. Assume Denise is a successful accountant with significant business development skills. Unfortunately, her business development activity limits the time she is able to devote to her clients' work. Her annual income is therefore limited to $150,000. Ed, on the other hand, is an outstanding technical accountant, but he develops business poorly, so he has significant downtime. Consequently, Ed makes only $95,000 per year.

If Denise and Ed were to combine their specialized skills, they could each enjoy larger annual revenue. They could consider combining their services without integrating them. To do so, one of the parties would have to hire the other. That, of course, would create appropriable specialized quasi rents.[19] To avoid the problems associated with quasi rents, they could integrate their resources by forming a partnership and use allocations to help discourage shirking. After integrating their resources, the parties may be able to generate $300,000 of annual income if both accountants work full time. Their combined efforts therefore could generate $55,000 more than the sum of their individual efforts.[20] The parties could not, however, determine the extent to which either party's efforts generate that additional income. After forming the partnership, Ed has enough work to stay busy full time and clients are happy with his work and bring the firm return business. Denise is able to attract more clients because they know that they will obtain Ed's expert services, if needed. Thus, the additional income does not derive from a single source, but from a combination of the sources. The parties cannot, therefore, accurately allocate income based upon the parties' relative contributions.

Denise and Ed will likely decide to allocate the income to reduce agency costs. For example, they may decide to give Denise a larger share of income from first-time work she generates and give Ed a larger share of income from repeat clients. Such an allocation formula should help motivate Denise to continue to aggressively develop new business. It should also motivate Ed to care for existing clients and provide them service they will wish to receive in the future. Consequently, the allocations should help increase overall firm performance. Such allocation formulae may not, however, reflect the partners' estimate of the extent to which the relative contributions of the separate services contribute to the production of income. Because the allocation formulae increase the overall profitability for all partners, however, the allocation is consistent with the economic theory for forming partnerships and allocating profits to affect performance. Nonetheless, because each partner would receive the allocated income on liquidation, the allocations accurately represent a portion of the partners' interests in the partnership. Tax law must recognize this aspect of partnerships.

Other arrangements also use profit apportionment to affect behavior and face the same tracing problems. Private equity funds, for example, often grant the managing partners a profits interest in

19 For example, if Denise were to hire Ed and bring in a significant amount of repeat clients, Ed could threaten to terminate his relationship with Denise to expropriate more compensation. If the clients would follow Ed, Denise would have to meet Ed's demands or risk losing a share of the future income from those clients.

20 Individually, Denise could generate $150,000 and Ed $95,000 of annual income for a total of $245,000. That amount is $45,000 less than the $300,000 they can generate together.

the fund. The performance of the managers attracts or repels potential investors. Seeing managers' success, investors will contribute to the fund. Investors wish to receive the highest possible return on their investment. To help ensure that happens, the investors grant a significant profits interest to the managers. Thus, the managers' and investors' interests align. Both groups increase their returns when the managers' services and the investors' capital produce at maximum capacity. Each group benefits from the other group's contributions, but tracing difficulties prevent the parties from knowing the exact source of profits received from the venture. All profits will include income from capital and income from services. Tax law must recognize the economic aspects of allocations and the inability to precisely identify the source of allocated economic items, regardless of business form.

Modern law provides resource owners several alternative business forms to use to integrate resources. Parties may choose from various partnership and quasi partnership forms in structuring arrangements. Quasi partnerships evolved to provide certain legal attributes to business participants to help facilitate economic activity. Nonetheless, quasi partnerships provide their members the same opportunities partnerships provide for reducing agency costs by allocating economic items. Therefore, partnerships and quasi partnerships are similar from an economic perspective that is important to tax law. Legal theory's focus on whether a business arrangement is an entity separate from its members or an aggregate of its members becomes irrelevant. Therefore, this chapter recommends that any arrangement that allocates economic items to reduce agency costs in the same manner partnerships allocate economic items should be subject to aggregate-plus taxation.

Examining arrangements that integrate resources reveals that the members of such arrangements cannot trace the arrangement's output directly to a specific contributed resource. Thus, partners cannot allocate rewards based exclusively on the proportionate contributions of each partner and a particular contribution's effect on output. Partners may, however, apportion items to discourage shirking, to align interests, and to increase the partnership's productivity. Allocated items reflect the partners' respective economic rights to partnership assets. Partnership law is less concerned with the allocation of economic items and can therefore generally treat partnerships as entities separate from their owners. However, the analysis of partnership tax allocations presented below suggests that tax allocation rules should account for the economic factors of a partnership and should require tax items to follow the economic items partners apportion to each other. After establishing the primacy of allocating tax items according to the allocation of economic items, the discussion demonstrates how such a mandate should also affect other provisions of partnership tax law. In short, this chapter suggests that tax law should not necessarily follow state law's view of partnerships.

Economic Principles and the Aggregate-Plus Theory

Economic theory contributes to the aggregate-plus theory of partnership taxation. Economic theory suggests that individuals form partnerships to increase productivity and reduce rent-seeking behavior. The integration of resources can produce output that is greater than the sum of the separate outputs of the respective resources, but integration also creates agency costs. Partners therefore allocate economic items, including the increased output, to help reduce agency costs. Additionally, allocation is important because partners cannot accurately determine whether partnership profit derives from contributed property or contributed services. Thus, all amounts of allocated partnership profit likely include profits from each source. If partnership tax law does not recognize such use of allocations, it will stymie economic behavior. A person will be less inclined to allocate income to a partner if the person will be liable for tax on such income. Without the benefit of the allocation tool to reduce agency costs, people will be less inclined to form partnerships. Furthermore, partnership tax law must recognize partnerships as an integration of resources. That recognition requires that partnership profit must retain its character as it flows through to the partners pursuant to the apportionment agreement. Only aggregate taxation can serve all of the economic demands of partnerships. Nonetheless, other demands suggest that partnership tax law must incorporate some entity provisions.

Aggregate-Plus Taxation

The study of the law of partnerships and the economic nature of partnerships lays the groundwork for considering the aggregate-plus theory of partnership taxation. The discussion to follow proposes that partnership tax law should first apply the aggregate concept and resist entity components, largely for efficiency and accuracy purposes. Partnership tax law should adopt entity components only when needed to simplify tax administration. Entity components should not, however, interfere with the efficiency and accuracy obtained through aggregate taxation. If lawmakers begin with the entity concept when enacting partnership tax laws, the result will often be inefficient rules that inaccurately assign tax liability and provide opportunity for abuse. In such situations, lawmakers will be forced to create reparative aggregate provisions to address the deficiencies the entity concept created. The discussion below illustrates how past entity-oriented partnership tax lawmaking has required such measures. It also illustrates how the aggregate-plus theory can guide future lawmaking.

Overview of Aggregate-Plus Taxation

The historical perspective of partnerships indicates that humans have a tendency to combine resources in the pursuit of profit. To avoid causing economic inefficiency, partnership tax rules, to the extent administratively possible, should not discourage or interfere with the human tendency to combine resources for business purposes.[21] Rational business people would not combine resources unless they expected the combination to produce more output than the sum of the output of the separate resources. If tax law discouraged the combination of businesses, the potential business partners would lose the benefit of joining together and the government would gain no revenue. In formulating standards for applying either the aggregate concept or entity concept to partnership taxation, the law should recognize the human tendency to combine resources for the purpose of conducting business and should not interfere with that tendency. The aggregate concept provides the means for doing that.

Tax law avoids interfering with the combination of business resources by allowing tax-free partnership formations.[22] Under either the aggregate or entity concept, the formation of a partnership could be tax free. Thus, neither concept guides lawmaking at this point. Formation is, however, only but one part of the life of a partnership. The tax treatment of the partnership following formation could affect the parties' decision to combine resources in a partnership. The economic study of partnerships reveals that partners apportion partnership income and loss to achieve economic goals,

21 Commentators have cited this as the basis for allowing tax-free formation of business entities. *See, e.g.*, J. Paul Jackson et al., *The Internal Revenue Code of 1954: Partnerships*, 54 Colum. L. Rev. 1183, 1204 (1954) ("This policy of non-recognition of gain (and, of course, loss) is based primarily on a desire not to discourage the formation of partnerships and is continued by Section 721 of the new law.").

22 *See* I.R.C. § 721(a).

such as reducing agency costs. Entity taxation could not effectively address the apportionment of economic items. Entity taxation treats the entity as controlling its income. Thus, any distributions to the members of the entity would be transfers between two different persons (i.e., the entity and the member), and tax law must recognize those transfers. Thus, under the entity concept, capital gain could become compensation to the member for tax purposes.[23] That may discourage people from joining together. Aggregate taxation, on the other hand, treats the members as controlling the arrangement's income. Because the members control the arrangement's income, aggregate taxation does not recognize distributions from the arrangement to its members. Thus, aggregate taxation can recognize the apportionment of economic items as the members' respective shares of those items. So the character of capital gain flows through to a member under aggregate taxation. Aggregate taxation is efficient because it reflects the economic arrangement of the partners; thus, it should not discourage partnership formation.

The entity concept's inability to recognize the apportionment of economic items places the allocation of tax items at the center of the aggregate-plus theory of partnership taxation. Other aspects of partnership taxation could be addressed with the entity concept,[24] but the economic nature of partnerships requires the aggregate concept to appropriately treat apportioned economic items. All aggregate provisions help ensure that apportioned items are taxed correctly to the partners. Aggregate taxation also helps reduce tax liability burden shifting.[25] For example, aggregate taxation prevents the allocation of precontribution gain or loss to partners other than the contributing partner. With the aggregate concept as the fundamental theory of partnership taxation, the entity concept should serve the sole function of easing administrative complexity. When Congress overextends the use of the entity concept, it must create reparative aggregate rules to remove inefficiencies and inaccuracies the entity concept creates. In fact, a significant percentage of the aggregate provisions in subchapter K are reparative provisions.[26] The following discussion reveals problems that overextended entity provisions can create and how Congress addresses such problems with reparative aggregate provisions.

The Perils of Overextending Entity Provisions

Congress has added several entity provisions to partnership taxation to help with tax administration, but some of the entity provisions extend beyond the administrative function and cause other

23 This is the result that would obtain under subchapter S of the Code because subchapter S requires allocations to be in accordance with shareholders' interests in the corporation. *See id.* § 1362(a). As discussed above, however, partners apportion items for various economic reasons, and the recharacterization may not reflect the partners' arrangement.

24 For example, rules governing computation of partnership income and the partnership's taxable year should follow the entity concept.

25 *See* Bradley T. Borden, *Partnership Tax Allocations and the Internalization of Tax-Item Allocations*, 59 S.C. L. Rev. 297, 340–46 (2008) (arguing that allocations, an inherently aggregate concept, that do not follow the partners' economic arrangement create tax-item transactions that tax law otherwise prohibits). Commentators writing at the time Congress enacted subchapter K recommended the aggregate approach in many situations with an election to apply the entity approach. *See* Jackson et al., *supra* note 21, at 129, 142 (recommending an aggregate approach for both formation of a partnership and disposition of a partnership interest and an election to apply entity concepts).

26 *See* Borden, *supra* note 2, app. B (revealing that 7 of the 17 aggregate provisions are reparative provisions enacted to address problems the entity concept created).

problems.[27] When Congress takes reparative steps to alleviate those problems, the law switches from aggregate-plus taxation to entity-minus taxation with respect to such provisions. The partnership-interest-basis (so-called outside-basis) rules illustrate problems that entity provisions can cause and how Congress uses reparative aggregate provisions to address those problems. The partnership-interest-basis rules treat partners as holding interests in the partnership and the partnership as holding partnership property, so the rules are entity provisions.[28] Those rules recognize partners' transfers of interests in the partnership, as opposed to recognizing their transfers of interests in the partnership's property.[29] Upon partnership formation, the rules treat partners as transferring property to the partnership in exchange for partnership interests. The partners take a basis in the partnership interest equal to the basis of the contributed property plus the amount of money contributed.[30] The partnership takes a basis in the contributed property equal to the basis the contributing partner had in the property.[31] The partnership-interest-basis rules also adopt the entity concept for dispositions of partnership interests.[32] Thus, these rules treat partners as disposing of interests in the partnership, not interests in the partnership's property. The rationale for the partnership-interest-basis rules appears to be administrative convenience.[33]

If Congress had based the partnership formation rules on the aggregate concept, then the law would treat the formation of a partnership as a series of transfers of undivided property interests among partners and the subsequent contributions of those interests to the partnership.[34] Under the aggregate concept, a disposition of a partner's interest would be a disposition of the partner's interest in all of the assets of the partnership.[35] The entity approach appears simpler because it does not require the deemed transfer of undivided interests at the time of formation or the look-through accounting on the disposition of a partnership interest. The entity concept, however, creates other more troubling concerns.

In the case of partnership formation and the disposition of partnership interests, the cost of simplicity manifested itself in opportunities that the partnership-interest-basis rules provided for abuse and the potential they created for misallocation of tax items.[36] The combination of the policy supporting tax-free partnership formation with the entity concept required that partners take a basis in their partnership interests equal to the sum of contributed cash and the basis of contributed

---

27 *See* Jackson et al., *supra* note 21, at 1204 (describing the entity concept, as adopted in Code § 722).

28 I.R.C. §§ 705(a), 722.

29 *Id.* § 741.

30 *Id.* § 722.

31 *Id.* § 723.

32 *Id.* § 741.

33 *See* Jackson et al., *supra* note 21, at 125 ("The entity approach, at least up to the point of liquidation or other disposition of the partnership interest, has the advantage of simplicity.").

34 *Id.* at 119.

35 *Id.* at 141.

36 *See* Borden, *supra* note 25, at 340–46 (discussing how (1) the current partnership allocation rules create opportunities for tax-item transactions and (2) the failure to allocate tax items in accordance with the economic arrangement of a partnership may create inadvertent tax-item transactions); Jackson et al., *supra* note 21, at 121 (observing that the contributing partner should bear the tax incurred on the entire precontribution gain when the partnership sells contributed property); *id.* at 125 ("This simple entity approach, however, means that a partner who contributes cash or high basis properties is, to a degree, penalized on account of the low-basis of properties contributed by another.").

property.[37] It also required the partnership to take a basis in contributed property equal to the basis the contributor had in the property.[38] Taxpayers learned quickly that they could use these rules to change the character of income and loss. They also learned that they could use the rules to shift the incidence of taxation.

To illustrate the potential for abuse, consider a dealer in real property. A dealer in real property holds property as inventory, and gain recognized on the disposition of inventory is taxed at ordinary income rates.[39] To avoid being taxed at ordinary income rates on the sale of inventory, a dealer may consider contributing the property to a partnership. The partnership would take the dealer's basis in the property and could hold it as a capital asset and obtain long-term capital gains on the disposition of the property that are taxed at preferential rates.[40] Thus, the entity concept combined with the partnership-interest-basis rules provided the opportunity for taxpayers to change the character of income or loss by contributing property to a partnership.

Congress used aggregate concepts to repair the problems the entity-oriented rules created. For example, Congress recognized that taxpayers could convert the character of gain or loss by contributing property to a partnership. To reduce the potential for abuse, Congress enacted reparative aggregate provisions that prohibit changing the character of built-in gain or loss to the contributing partner for a number of years following the contribution to the partnership.[41] Congress enacted that reparative aggregate provision in 1984.[42]

The partnership-interest-basis rules also create the potential for inappropriate allocations of partnership items that shift the incidence of taxation. Property contributed to a partnership by a partner will likely have built-in gain or built-in loss, representing the difference between the property's basis and its fair market value on the date of contribution.[43] Built-in gain and built-in loss reflect economic changes that occurred with respect to property before it was contributed to the partnership. For example, if a contributing partner purchased raw land for $50,000 and contributed it to a partnership when it was worth $100,000, the property would have a $50,000 built-in gain.[44] That built-in gain represents the amount the property appreciated while the contributing partner held it. That amount also represents $50,000 of income to the contributing partner,[45] an amount of

37 I.R.C. §§ 721, 722; Jackson et al., *supra* note 21, at 1204.

38 I.R.C. § 723; Jackson et al., *supra* note 21, at 1204.

39 *See* Biedenharn Realty Co., Inc. v. United States, 526 F.2d 409 (5th Cir. 1976) (holding that efforts to develop, frequency of sales, and other factors demonstrated that taxpayer held property for resale and gain on sale was ordinary income; stating that "the real estate capital gain-ordinary income issue [is] 'old, familiar, recurring, vexing, and ofttimes elusive'").

40 I.R.C. §§ 1(h)(1), 702(b).

41 *Id.* § 724.

42 Deficit Restoration Act of 1984, Pub. L. No. 98-369, § 74(a), 98 Stat. 494, 592.

43 Treas. Reg. § 1.704-3(a)(3)(ii). Contributed property will generally have built-in gain or built-in loss because property tends to fluctuate in value, whereas basis remains constant with respect to property that does not qualify for cost recovery (and cost recovery may not reflect fluctuations in the property's value).

44 The built-in gain would equal the difference between the $100,000 fair market value at the time of contribution and the partner's $50,000 basis in the land, representing gain that the contributing partner would have recognized had the partner sold the property instead of contributing it to the partnership. I.R.C. § 1001(a).

45 *See* Henry C. Simons, Personal Income Taxation: The Definition of Income as a Problem of Fiscal Policy 50 (1938) ("Personal income may be defined as the algebraic sum of (1) the market value of rights

income the partner would have recognized upon contribution but for the tax-free-formation rules.[46] Because such income accrues while the contributing partner holds the property, the contributing partner should pay tax on that income.[47]

Under the partnership-interest-basis rules the partnership takes the contributing partner's basis in the property, so the built-in gain carries over to the partnership. To ensure the contributing partner pays tax on the built-in gain, the partnership should allocate the built-in gain to the contributing partner when the partnership recognizes the gain. The 1954 Code allowed partnerships to disregard built-in gain or loss or to elect to allocate tax items to account for the built-in gain or loss.[48] The first option reflects the entity concept. The entity concept would suggest that the partnership should allocate the gain based upon ownership in the entity.[49] Such allocations produce an undesirable tax result because they would likely allocate a portion of built-in gain or loss to noncontributing partners. For example, if an equal partnership of two partners receives from one partner contributed property that has a $50,000 built-in gain, equal allocations will result in a split of that gain between the partners when the partnership recognizes it. With such an allocation, the noncontributing partner would pay tax on half of the built-in gain. That represents a shift of the tax burden from the contributing partner to the noncontributing partner.[50] Such an allocation not only shifts the incidence of taxation, it also may discourage partnership formation because the noncontributing partner may be hesitant to join a partnership that will require the assumption of the tax burden associated with the contributing partner's precontribution gain—or at a minimum require complicated negotiations to address the sharing of that tax burden.[51]

The potential misallocation of built-in gain and loss further illustrates the primacy of the allocation rules in partnership taxation. To avoid discouraging partnership formation, tax law must allow tax-free partnership formation. In the case of contributed property, the law could discourage

---

exercised in consumption and (2) the change in the value of the store of property rights between the beginning and end of the period in question.").

46 *See* I.R.C. § 1001(c) (providing that taxpayers must recognize gain or loss on the sale or exchange of property, unless provided otherwise—Code § 721 provides otherwise in the case of contributions to partnerships).

47 *See* Helvering v. Horst, 311 U.S. 112, 114, 119–20 (1940) (holding that the owner of property must pay tax on income from the property); Jackson et al., *supra* note 21, at 121.

48 I.R.C. § 704(c)(1), (2) (1954).

49 Students of corporate tax will recognize that subchapter S requires shareholders of S corporations to take into account their pro rata share of corporate income. *Id.* § 1366(a) (2014). This simple allocation rule makes sense in the subchapter S context because the one-class-of-stock rule, *id.* § 1361(b)(1)(D), prohibits the allocation of economic items in a manner that varies from the shareholder's pro rata interest in the corporation. The subchapter S allocation rules fail, however, to account for built-in gain or loss in property contributed to the corporation in a tax-free contribution. Thus, the rigid, simple subchapter S allocation rules do not accurately tax the person who realized income or loss on contributed property. A recent amendment to the Code sought to remove that flaw from the corporate tax with respect to certain built-in losses. *Id.* § 362(e). The flaw remains with respect to built-in gains.

50 *See* Borden, *supra* note 25, at 343–44 (describing how allocations based on capital accounts may shift tax burden).

51 The partners may be able to include the tax burden shift in their negotiations by, for example, ensuring that the noncontributing partner receives sufficiently disproportionate distributions from the partnership to offset the tax burden arising from the allocation of built-in gain. Such disproportionate distributions may create taxable income to the noncontributing partner as the amount of the distribution could exceed the partner's basis in the partnership. The law taxing distributions in excess of basis has been a part of statutory partnership tax law since 1954. *See* I.R.C. § 731(a)(1) (1954).

partnership formation if the allocation rules did not properly account for built-in gain or loss. The entity concept does not recognize these important nuances of partnerships. Starting from an entity concept, the law must adjust for its shortcomings with reparative aggregate provisions. To reduce the potential of allocating built-in gain or loss to a noncontributing partner, in 1984 Congress required partnerships to make allocations in a manner that took into consideration any built-in gain or loss.[52] The application of that rule has generated a complicated set of regulations[53] that undoubtedly require sophisticated accounting software to implement in the case of large, multiasset partnerships. Nonetheless, the rule is efficient and accurate.

Finally, the entity-oriented partnership-interest-basis rules could provide favorable tax results to the transferor of a partnership interest. For example, assume a partnership holds inventory, which would generate ordinary income if the partnership were to sell it. The gain from the sale of inventory would flow through to the partners as ordinary income.[54] The entity concept provides partners the opportunity to convert the gain from the sale of partnership inventory into capital gain. The entity concept treats the partner as owning a partnership interest, not an interest in partnership property. An interest in a partnership is arguably a capital asset,[55] so the sale of the partnership interest should generate capital gain. But the value of the partnership interest should include the unrealized ordinary gain in the partnership's inventory. Thus, by selling an interest in the partnership, the partner could convert the unrealized ordinary gain in the inventory into capital gain taxed at preferential rates.[56] Recognizing that partners could convert ordinary income into capital gain by selling partnership interests instead of partnership assets, Congress enacted aggregate rules that looked through the partnership interest so as to tax the partner on his or her share of the ordinary gain in the inventory.[57] Those rules were part of the original subchapter K, indicating that Congress foresaw the potential for abuse.[58] Thus, upon enactment of the entity rules, Congress already recognized the need to address problems that the entity concept would raise in the partnership tax context.

In addition to the reparative aggregate rules just discussed, Congress has enacted several other reparative aggregate rules to address problems arising from treating partnerships as entities for property-ownership purposes.[59] The reparative aggregate provisions carve so many holes in the original entity rules that the entity framework has become a veritable slice of Swiss cheese. In fact, it is difficult to tell whether the framework is more entity cheese or more aggregate hole at

52 *Id.* § 704(c) (2014). Congress enacted the original version in 1984. *See* Deficit Restoration Act of 1984, Pub. L. No. 98-369, § 71(a), 98 Stat. 494, 589.

53 Treas. Reg. § 1.704-3. For an in-depth discussion of the rules, see Laura Cunningham, *Use and Abuse of Section 704(c)*, 3 FLA. TAX. REV. 93 (1996).

54 I.R.C. § 702(b).

55 The 1954 law adopted this view, *see id.* § 741 (1954), and the current law retains it. *See id.* § 741 (2014).

56 *See* Jackson et al., *supra* note 21, at 144–45 (recognizing that gain realized on the sale of a partnership interest is "on account of the appreciation or depreciation in the value of the partnership's assets").

57 I.R.C. § 751(a) (1954). The same law survives in the current subchapter K. *Id.* § 751(a) (2014).

58 *See* Jackson et al., *supra* note 21, at 145 (discussing, prior to the enactment of subchapter K, the difference between the results obtained alternatively using the entity or aggregate concepts).

59 *E.g.*, I.R.C. §§ 731(c) (addressing the abusive distribution of marketable securities), 734 (providing elective rules for adjusting the basis of partnership property to reflect gain recognized by a partner on a distribution from the partnership), 737 (prohibiting mixing-bowl transactions), 743 (providing elective rules for adjusting the basis of partnership property upon the disposition of a partnership interest to reflect the proportional basis of the acquiring partner), 751(b) (providing rules for determining the character of gain recognized by a partner on the distribution of partnership assets).

this time. The simplicity promised by the entity rules is thus largely replaced by the more accurate and efficient aggregate rules. In fact, instead of simplifying things, the entity rules may have complicated matters.

After the enactment of the reparative aggregate provisions, the partnership-interest-basis rules retain the entity concept with respect to capital assets and nondepreciable assets acquired by the partnership.[60] The aggregate concept applies to all property contributed by a partner to the partnership and to all property that would produce ordinary income if sold by the partnership. The classes of assets to which the aggregate provisions apply (namely, depreciable property and contributed property) generate the most complex accounting issues. Thus, the entity concept, which is supposed to simplify tax administration, is left largely to govern only the assets which create the least complex administrative demands. In the end, the entity concept has limited utility and may be the source of unneeded complexity.

Congress could have avoided some of the problems with the current system by retaining the original aggregate focus and adding entity provisions as needed, instead of shifting to entity-oriented rules and adding aggregate concepts. It would have added to the entity rules only as warranted by tax administration. The end result might have been similar to that obtained under the current entity-minus basis rules, which began with the entity concept and added reparative aggregate rules as needed to ensure an economically efficient and appropriately allocative set of rules. The difference between an entity-minus approach and an aggregate-plus approach, each of which obtain the same end result, is the tax treatment between the inception of the original rule and the addition of the final reparative provisions that equalize the two rules.[61] Thus, in comparing an entity-minus end result to a similar aggregate-plus end result, the focus should be on the interim period between the inception of the rule and the point of equalization.

Under entity-minus taxation, simplicity reigns during the interim, at the expense of efficiency and accuracy. Under aggregate-plus taxation, simplicity is lost to some extent during the interim, but the rules are efficient and accurately allocate partnership income and loss. The simplicity sacrificed under aggregate-plus taxation is a small price to pay during the interim because the aggregate concept promotes economic efficiency and allocates partnership tax items accurately. Furthermore, end results may vary. An aggregate starting point may allow lawmakers to create aggregate rules that are simpler than reparative aggregate rules. Thus, the end result of aggregate-plus rules may be simpler than the end result of entity-minus rules. This analysis of existing law provides an example of the strength of the aggregate-plus theory of partnership taxation. It also helps explain the source of complexity in the current flow-through regime and provides a basis for analyzing proposals for changing the current system.

---

60 The aggregate concept of Code § 751 applies to all inventory and unrealized receivables. The definition of unrealized receivables is broad enough to include a wide variety of property, including contractual rights to receive payments for goods and services; gains from certain properties under Code §§ 617(f)(2), 992, 1248, 1252, and 1253; and recapture of cost-recovery deductions under Code §§ 1245, 1250, 1251(e)(1), and 1254. *Id.* § 751(c). Income from such property is ordinary income.

61 Professor Ali Khan would refer to the interim as ΔT, beginning upon the enactment of the original rules and ending when the rules equalize. *See* L. Ali Khan, *Temporality of Law*, 40 McGeorge L. Rev. 55, 57–58 (2009).

Perils of a Bifurcated Regime

The focus on the origins of partnerships and the economic theory for allocating economic items in this chapter differs from the perspective Andrea Monroe adopts in Chapter 8, which appears to view subchapter K as the tool of mischievous taxpayers and their clever advisors. Of course, subchapter K does get used in that manner, but dismantling it to create a bifurcated regime is not the solution. The different conclusions are not surprising because the chapters adopt fairly divergent views of complexity based upon the authors' different perspectives. This chapter asserts that complex tax law is necessary to govern partnership arrangements, which by their very nature, can be quite complex. Monroe, on the other hand, views complexity as a tool for sophisticated taxpayers to use to reduce tax liability. These differing perspectives lead to different conclusions. Monroe's focus on the exploitation of complexity appears to stem from her contemporary view of partnership behavior, while the economic view that favors complexity derives from a historic perspective of partnerships and the economic activity of such arrangements. Those differences in temporal perspective undoubtedly influence the views presented in both chapters.

The analyses in both chapters recognize that partnership tax is a complicated body of law, but they reach that conclusion from different points of reference and with different end results. Monroe sees subchapter K deriving its complexity from laws that Congress has enacted to combat the abuses of subchapter K. The economic theory adopted in this chapter attributes the complexity of partnership taxation to the very complex nature of the arrangements that are subject to subchapter K. The economic view of partnerships recognizes complexity in arrangements that are seemingly quite simple. Consequently, the economic perspective acknowledges the need for a complex body of law to govern arrangements that may be small from a financial perspective but complex based upon the profit-and-loss sharing that partners use to influence partner behavior or recognize certain contributions. In fact, if an arrangement is simple enough, it would qualify for tax treatment under subchapter S. Thus, the tax system already provides a simple flow-through tax regime for simple arrangements. Bifurcating subchapter K will not provide the simplicity that Monroe seeks.

Monroe focuses on two aspects of partnership flow-through taxation to argue that it is too complicated and should be reformed to provide simpler rules for everyday partnerships. First, she focuses on the rules governing allocations of partnership tax items. No one will quibble with Monroe over the complexity of the rules governing substantial economic effect of tax allocations. Those rules are undoubtedly complex, but partners only have to deal with the complexity if they use the allocation rules to unfairly reduce tax liabilities. If an allocation is not abusive, the IRS would not challenge it. For instance, if parties in the examples above were to allocate tax items to track the economic arrangement, there is no reason why the IRS would challenge those allocations. The members of the arrangement would not have to do an analysis to determine whether the allocations had substantial economic effect because the allocations reflected the parties' economic arrangement. Tax law allows partners to allocate tax items in accordance with their interests in the tax partnership.[62]

In fact, the allocation provisions in the statute provide that an allocation must have substantial economic effect only if it is not in accordance with the partners' interests in the partnership.[63] That

62 I.R.C. § 704(a), (b). For an in-depth discussion and analysis of allocations in accordance with partners' interests in a partnership and the difficulty of defining partners' interests in a partnership, see Bradley T. Borden, *The Allure and Illusion of Partners' Interests in a Partnership*, 79 U. Cin. L. Rev. 1077 (2011).

63 *Id.*

leniency allows members of partnerships to completely ignore the substantial-economic-effect rules and allocate tax items in accordance with their economic arrangement. If the members of an everyday partnership do not attempt to manipulate tax allocations to obtain favorable tax treatment, they should have nothing to worry about when the IRS challenges their allocations—even if they completely ignore the substantial-economic-effect rules. The complex aspects of the rules govern and prevent tax allocations that are specifically designed for tax-avoidance or tax-evasion purposes. Congress could simplify the tax rules by repealing the requirement that allocations have substantial economic effect, and the IRS could still challenge abusive tax allocations. In fact, before Congress enacted the substantial-economic-effect requirement, the IRS successfully challenged abusive tax allocations.[64]

Second, Monroe claims that the rules governing distributions from partnerships are too complicated and should be replaced with rules that generally tax distributions. A primary objection to this proposal is the adverse effect it would have on business arrangements. It would not only discourage the formation of partnerships, but it would also discourage the subsequent dissolution of partnerships even if the resources had a higher and better use in a different context. For instance, to continue the earlier example, if Baroness and McDonald know that they will be taxed on any distribution of property from the partnership that they wish to form, they may be less likely to form the partnership. In fact, in making their decision to form the partnership, they will have to weigh the potential tax costs of dissolution (or other distributions) against the economic costs of not forming the partnership. Once they form the partnership, a tax on distributions will affect their decision to dissolve the partnership or make distributions. If the tax cost of such distributions exceeds the cost of continuing the partnership, they will continue the partnership.

Remaining in partnership form to avoid the tax cost of dissolution may adversely affect Baroness, McDonald, and the broader economy. For example, if McDonald is at a point in his career where he is ready to dial down his participation in the partnership, his services may cease to make maximum use of the land. Nonetheless, the parties realize that they are better off with McDonald's reduced performance than they would be if they dissolved the partnership, paid the tax, and had Baroness form a new partnership with a different manager. Because they stay in the partnership simply to avoid taxes, McDonald must perform services that he otherwise would not perform and Baroness misses out on the opportunity of maximizing the property's productivity with a new partner. The broader economy also suffers because the property is not put to its most productive use. Consequently, a tax on distributions creates economic inefficiency, making such a tax very unattractive.

As with the allocation rules, the distribution rules do not provide an undue hardship on everyday partnerships, and such partnerships generally do not look to the tax rules for tax-avoidance or tax-evasion opportunities. For example, if Baroness and McDonald decide to liquidate their partnership, the primary asset for distribution will be the land. A distribution of the land generally will not be tax abusive, and the rules governing such a distribution are not overly complicated. If they decide to liquidate at a time when the partnership also holds a crop that would generate ordinary income, they may perhaps manipulate the distribution to obtain an overall tax reduction by distributing the crop to the member with the lower marginal tax rate on ordinary income. The current distribution rules prevent that abuse by taxing the distribution. The complexity of the rules only becomes manifest, however, if partners engage in abusive or manipulative tactics, which signifies sophistication that warrants complex rules. Thus, Baroness and McDonald in effect become subject to the complex distribution rules only if they attempt to make a distribution that creates an abusive tax situation.

64 *E.g.*, Orrisch v. Comm'r, 55 T.C. 395 (1970).

Nonetheless, even if the parties lack abusive intent, Monroe's proposal would appear to require the partnership to recognize gain and allocate it to Baroness and McDonald.

Finally, Monroe's proposals would most likely require more entity-oriented rules (i.e., simple allocation rules would disregard economic allocations, and gain recognition on distributions would treat partnerships as entities separate from their members). After adopting such entity-oriented rules, Congress would have to make other reparative aggregate rules to help alleviate the problems that the entity rules create, as it has done with other entity-oriented rules. As shown above with the discussion of the basis rules, the entity-minus approach to flow-through taxation does not lead to greater simplicity and efficiency when it applies to complex arrangements.[65] Instead of applying entity-minus theories to fix partnership taxation, any efforts to fix the current system should begin with the aggregate perspective and add entity provisions only as necessary to ensure accurate administration of the tax laws. The discussion of the economic aspects of partnerships and other arrangements illustrates that they are complex and that they require a sophisticated tax regime. Aggregate-plus taxation is best suited to address the special attributes of such arrangements.

Conclusion

Economic theory supports the aggregate-plus nature of the current flow-through partnership tax regime. The regime is complex, but it matches the complex nature of tax partnerships. Most tax partnerships can exist and apply the current tax regime without getting too caught up in the most complex aspects of the partnership tax rules. Consequently, the partnership tax rules do not call for radical simplification measures. The simplest business arrangements can benefit from the simple subchapter S tax regime for small corporations. All other noncorporate arrangements should be subject to the partnership tax flow-through regime.

This conclusion is somewhat at odds with the conclusion that Monroe reaches, which is not surprising because the two conclusions represent differing perspectives of flow-through taxation. The economic perspective outlined in this chapter recognizes the complex nature of partnerships and the need for a complex body of law that addresses the complexity inherent in partnerships. Monroe, on the other hand, recognizes complexity as a tool that sophisticated taxpayers use to gain an unfair tax advantage and avoid paying taxes that similarly situated taxpayers must pay. From her perspective, the law must change to help curb the exploitation of the partnership tax rules for such purposes, and she believes that simplification could help reduce some of the abuse and provide relief to less sophisticated taxpayers who operate businesses in partnership form.

Fortunately, tax law already provides a simpler tax regime for the most basic business structures, and the complex aspects of the current aggregate-plus system for the most part do not affect simple, nonabusive partnerships. As scholars, commentators, practitioners, regulators, courts, and others continue to study this area of law and the evolving business environment to which it applies, undoubtedly change will occur. Such efforts should attempt to curb abuse while continuing to recognize the unique and complex nature of many partnerships that appear to have existed since time immemorial.

65 Nonetheless, entity-minus taxation has proven effective for simple arrangements, such as those with a single class of stock to which subchapter S applies.

PART V
Taxation of Corporations

Chapter 10
Should Corporations Be Taxpayers?

Yariv Brauner*

Introduction

Corporate income taxes are today virtually universal. Yet, they are also—and seem to have always been—controversial, difficult to justify, and newsworthy. Recently, the largest multinational enterprises (MNEs) have caught headlines, being accused of paying "too little tax" and engaging in objectionable corporate tax planning.[1] This media exposure brought together the rarely unified world powers to launch a cooperative attack on such practices.[2] Yet, despite the constantly contemporary nature of corporate taxes, they continue to be an enigma, enflaming a policy debate that is based on slogans more than knowledge. The perception of the debate is quite simplistic: conservatives and business interests oppose the corporate tax because of its costs, while liberals insist on its qualities in terms of redistribution. In this chapter, I argue that rational analysis should lead to a reversal of these roles. In particular, I argue that she who supports redistribution should wish for the tax's abolition. The path to this conclusion is winding, so I will begin with the basics.

Relying on the legal construct of separate corporate personality (itself a universally accepted legal fiction or metaphor), countries generally view corporations as taxpayers essentially independent of their shareholders and other stakeholders, who may (separately) be taxpayers themselves. Countries impose income taxes on these corporate taxpayers under rules that are similar in principle, yet different in detail, from the rules applicable to, for example, flesh and blood taxpayers. Some of the differences between the individual and corporate income taxes stem from the different personhood properties of corporations and individuals (e.g., the residence rules[3]) while other differences are perhaps policy driven because they have nothing to do with such properties (e.g., the rate schedule).

---

* I thank Anthony Infanti, the editor of this book and the author of the paired contribution to this volume, and Caitlin Foster, for their insightful comments. All mistakes or inaccuracies are mine. Some of the ideas presented in this article were first presented in Yariv Brauner, *The Non-Sense Tax: A Reply to New Corporate Income Tax Advocacy*, 2008 MICH. ST. L. REV. 591 (2008).

1 *See, e.g.*, Charles Duhigg & David Kocieniewski, *How Apple Sidesteps Billions in Taxes*, N.Y. TIMES, Apr. 28, 2012, at A1. Bloomberg has maintained a now well-known website for articles of the kind. *The Great Corporate Tax Dodge*, BLOOMBERG, http://topics.bloomberg.com/the-great-corporate-tax-dodge (last visited Jan. 29, 2014).

2 *See, e.g.*, G20 Leaders Declaration ¶ 48 (June 18–19, 2012), *available at* http://www.consilium.europa.eu/uedocs/cms_Data/docs/pressdata/en/ec/131069.pdf. In response, the OECD launched the so-called BEPS project. *See* ORG. FOR ECON. COOPERATION & DEV., ACTION PLAN ON BASE EROSION AND PROFIT SHIFTING (2013); ORG. FOR ECON. COOPERATION & DEV., ADDRESSING BASE EROSION AND PROFIT SHIFTING (2013).

3 That is, flesh-and-blood persons are most often considered residents in countries where they are mostly physically present, born, or maintain relationships that are of the type that is unique to their being flesh-and-blood. In contrast, with corporations being "legal" persons, corporate residence relies primarily on legal relations.

Corporate taxes constantly struggle with the duality that inheres in dealing with taxpayers that are legal persons but not natural persons. In the same manner that business organizations laws require antiabuse norms that at times shatter the fiction and "pierce the corporate veil," tax laws employ antiabuse norms with similar goals and means. Tax norms are necessarily more voluminous and complex because taxes impose direct economic burdens while business organizations laws are designed to regulate the behavior of market participants to facilitate the efficacy of the market itself. The economic burdens imposed by tax laws are exclusively borne by natural persons and never by the fictional persons that we call corporations. These burdens and their consequential effects and incentives for natural persons are difficult to model and predict (or even to simply quantify).[4] Naturally, countries imposing corporate income taxes find these burdens, effects, and incentives difficult, and perhaps impossible, to control or fine-tune.[5] Consequently, corporate income taxes are complex and are still hotly debated despite their copious analysis over many years.

This chapter aims to capture the essence of the long-standing debate over the desirability of the corporate tax. It focuses on U.S. law and circumstances, yet it often indulges in conclusions or insights that may be more universal. Beyond the biased and incomprehensive (yet, as complete as possible) review of the debate, the chapter makes the point that the corporate tax has no rational rationale while being very costly and, therefore, that it should, and could, be repealed. To clarify, the chapter advocates a repeal of the independent corporate tax. It would retain a taxing norm at the corporate level, yet one that would be a mere—and never more than a mere—collection mechanism in the service of the individual income tax (akin to a withholding tax).

In the context of this volume, this chapter plays the role of the traditional analysis of the corporate tax, despite its somewhat nontraditional critique of the tax. In Chapter 11, Anthony Infanti engages in an interesting critical analysis of the debate over the tax, drawing attention to the legal similarities of corporations and families on one hand, and to the dissimilarities in the tax policy discourse of the two institutions, on the other hand, eventually claiming that the perspective of the traditional debate presented by this chapter is misguided, focusing on the desirability of reform rather than on identifying the instances where the corporate tax could be desirable and where it could not. Infanti's main concern, however, unlike this chapter's, is not with the outcome of the corporate tax debate itself, but rather its place in the more general discourse about American society's power structure, and more specifically the so-called public–private divide. I have little disagreement with Infanti over his critique of the current disservice of tax law to American society, and I share his concerns about the too-minor role of redistribution and true fairness, rather than nominal inequality, in the design of our legal system. Nevertheless, I disagree, first, with his conclusion regarding the corporate tax because I argue that the tax can never be used in a desirable manner and, therefore, it is futile to reframe the debate to explore instances where it could be so used. Second, my analysis of the history and background of the tax and my analysis of tax policy making, especially in the United States, lead me to conclude that a desirable use of a separate corporate tax is politically so unlikely that even if it were theoretically possible, the outcome would likely be undesirable if fairness and equality are one's concerns. Finally, I point to some fundamental differences between corporations and families that lead me to question the strength

4 *See infra* text accompanying notes 22–40.

5 *See* David A. Weisbach, *The Irreducible Complexity of Firm-Level Income Taxes: Theory and Doctrine in the Corporate Tax*, 60 TAX L. REV. 215 (2007) (arguing that the corporate tax has an irreducible core of complexity, stemming from the ability to hold and sell an asset in two ways: directly or through the stock of a subsidiary. Both methods of selling must be taxed, but coordinating the tax at each level—stock and assets—leads to complexity and line drawing. Weisbach further argues that reform proposals that include firm-level taxes will not be able to eliminate this core of complexity.).

of the parallel drawn in Chapter 11. At the end of the day, the difference between Infanti and me is not normative, but rather one of approach and of politics. I operate "within the system," and in that sense I represent the traditional approach of designing a technical solution to tax policy challenges and policies. My technical solution is to eliminate the separate corporate income tax rather than somehow reformat or repurpose it to achieve more desirable outcomes. This approach is based on a political belief that it is futile to expect that our tax politics could realistically effect such repurposing. I politically prefer to design a principled legal regime based on transparence. Such a regime should limit undesirable political outcomes, which, I believe, is the best one can hope for in the current circumstances.

The chapter proceeds, next, with the essential background for the traditional analysis of the corporate tax.

The Debate

The core corporate tax discourse revolves around three analytically separate yet not independent questions: (1) Why do we tax corporations? (2) How should we tax corporations? (3) And is it politically feasible to reform our rather universally homogenous corporate tax systems?

Why Tax Corporations?

The rationale for taxing corporations is surprisingly unclear.[6] There may however be technical, policy, or political reasons for wanting to tax corporations. The technical argument is straightforward: corporations enjoy legal personhood and consequent benefits and, therefore, should bear the (nominal) burdens of such separate personhood, including taxation. This argument is weak, and at this time it is not a serious factor in the sophisticated corporate income tax discourse.

The policy argument includes various elements and versions, yet its core relates to the view of corporations as real entities that are different and in that manner separate from their stakeholders. According to this view, one cannot simply view corporations as aggregations of their shareholders (or stakeholders) because such a view would skew the economic position of corporations in the market. This argument is criticized as either false (i.e., corporations should not be viewed as real entities because they generate no independent value (rents) as such) or useless in better regulating (from a tax policy perspective) corporations in the market.

Finally, the political argument, simplified, is that corporations create opportunities to the better-off in our societies and taxing them would contribute to better redistribution of wealth, which is

6 The following quotes of prominent scholars of the subject, including scholars that do not typically count themselves as opponents of the corporate tax, demonstrate this point: "Economists are sometimes accused of agreeing on almost nothing … . An important policy question on which many economists appear to agree, however, is that there is not much to be said in favour of taxing corporations." Richard M. Bird, *Why Tax Corporations?*, 56 Bull. for Int'l Fiscal Documentation 194, 194 (2002). "There are decent rationales for each piece of the corporate tax … . The overall system, however, would be extremely hard to defend if one were starting from a blank slate. Only political and administrative constraints on changing it properly in midstream could make retention of the current system seem desirable." Daniel N. Shaviro, Decoding the U.S. Corporate Tax 23 (2009). Even the most persuasive of recent corporate tax proponents, Reuven Avi-Yonah, admits that prior attempts to defend the existence of the corporate tax are unconvincing. *See* Reuven S. Avi-Yonah, *Corporations, Society, and the State: A Defense of the Corporate Tax*, 90 Va. L. Rev. 1193, 1200 (2004).

desirable and a goal of our income tax systems. The response to this argument may be political disagreement or disbelief in the efficacy of corporate tax systems as redistribution devices.[7]

How to Tax Corporations?

Next, assuming that one supports corporate taxation, the question of how to implement it arises. This depends on the rationale and goal for taxing corporations. Design is important even when the rationale for taxing corporations is in doubt because it is possible to reject separate taxation of corporations yet accept using them as collection agents; for example, designing a tax at the corporate level that would be fully credited against the individual income tax.

Is It Politically Feasible to Tax Corporations?

Finally, the political feasibility of reforming corporate taxation is also important, because the political rationale for taxing corporations, even if economically doubtful, is quite powerful and universal. Therefore, attempts to tax corporations more rationally may be received with suspicion by the public as actions undesirably influenced by lobbying for the interests of corporations and their wealthy shareholders and stakeholders. At the same time, corporate shareholders and stakeholders, being more sophisticated economically, use widespread political beliefs about taxing corporations to keep the corporate income tax in place—but in a form that has minimal impact on their profits, which redounds to their benefit. A second major feasibility issue relates to the possibility of taxing corporations on a look-through basis, which is often dismissed as impossible. Whether this is true or not depends on both one's politics and technical analysis.

I next turn to providing some historical background, both of the rise of the corporation in modern societies and of income taxes, in order to put the discourse outlined above in perspective before elaborating on it further.

Origins[8]

Corporations may be traced back to as early as the Roman Empire. Roman law permitted certain entities existence in perpetuity, which was the primary reason for originally having them. They had various rights and obligations independent from their human representatives. In general, these early corporations were related to the church (indeed, the Catholic Church itself was one), municipalities, etc. Their legal status was created by charter, usually from an emperor.

Many view the origins of the modern corporation in the various colonial corporations that facilitated international trade for the European powers of the time, beginning with the Dutch East India Company and "perfected" by the British East India Company, which clearly had commercial

---

7 There is an additional argument in favor of taxing corporations simply because it is administratively convenient (e.g., because they have deep pockets). Bird, *supra* note 6, at 199–201. This seemingly administrative argument, however, is always paired with a political justification of the kind mentioned above and hence is not viewed here as an independent argument in support of a separate corporate tax.

8 A comprehensive and rigid study of the history of corporations and income taxes is, of course, beyond the scope of this chapter. This section provides a brief summary solely of background points relevant to the discussion in succeeding sections of this chapter. For a more comprehensive introduction to the topic, see generally, for example, STEVEN A. BANK, FROM SWORD TO SHIELD: THE TRANSFORMATION OF THE CORPORATE INCOME TAX, 1861 TO PRESENT (2010), and Ron Harris, *The Institutional Dynamics of Early Modern Eurasian Trade: The* Commenda *and the Corporation*, 71 J. ECON. BEHAVIOR & ORG. 606 (2009).

profits as their primary goal.[9] In the eighteenth century, English law even began to see treatises on the law of corporations. Toward the nineteenth century, corporations grew further in the direction of aiming to make private profits and having commercial rather than public purposes.

In the United States, corporations were explicitly given independent rights as well as freedom from the tight public purpose regulations of years past.[10] States began enacting laws to attract incorporated business, beginning with New Jersey and Delaware—competition that has lasted to the present. An 1886 U.S. Supreme Court decision, *Santa Clara County v. Southern Pacific Railroad Co.*, solidified this progression when it held that a corporation was a "natural person" under the U.S. Constitution and was thus entitled to the protections afforded in the Bill of Rights.[11] These processes initiated the evolution of the modern corporation toward the end of the nineteenth century in the United States. Corporations could now be large enterprises with complex structures and diffuse ownership that has increasingly been disassociated from their actual control. The trend toward legal personification of corporations has continued, and corporations may now be held criminally liable and even claim civil rights. Corporate law has also evolved to deal with the challenges that the new, modern corporation poses to society, such as facilitation of market operation, protection of investors in general, and regulation of the various agency problems arising from the separation of ownership and control.

Income taxes gained in popularity at the same time that the modern corporation was evolving. A general income tax is a very recent invention. Prior to the twentieth century there were just a few examples of taxes measured by income, with the first traditionally attributed to William Pitt the Younger in the very last year of the eighteenth century.[12] Yet, until the twentieth century, income taxes had been very limited in scope and instituted exclusively for war-financing purposes. This included the United States' Civil War income tax first enacted in 1861. In 1894, Congress enacted the first peace-time income tax, but it was ruled unconstitutional,[13] which eventually led to the Sixteenth Amendment and the enactment of the individual income tax in 1913. Since then, almost all of the world's countries have adopted income taxes of one form or another. Income taxes became the primary source of revenue in most countries during the twentieth century; yet, with the advent of globalization, they have become more difficult to enforce and in many countries have been losing importance—primarily to consumption taxes.

The U.S. corporate income tax was enacted in 1909—prior to the current individual income tax—but that happened solely due to particular political and historic circumstances, rather than for any policy or other intellectual reasons. The standard study of the U.S. corporate income tax has reached somewhat of a general consensus about the origins of the tax. It was enacted as a political compromise among the supporters of an income tax, who failed to institute one at the beginning of the twentieth century due to constitutional constraints (and would not succeed until the passage

9 *See generally, e.g.*, NICK ROBINS, THE CORPORATION THAT CHANGED THE WORLD: HOW THE EAST INDIA COMPANY SHAPED THE MODERN MULTINATIONAL (2006).

10 Which was the reason why many large businesses had originally chosen not to incorporate. The legal sea change was solidified in the U.S. Supreme Court decision in *Trustees of Dartmouth College v. Woodward*, 17 U.S. 518 (1819). This decision shattered the last franchise or charter elements of corporate law. In the United Kingdom, it took a few more years—until the Joint Stock Companies Act of 1844 and Limited Liability Act of 1855. Corporations can now simply register as such rather than apply to the authorities for a discretionary charter.

11 118 U.S. 394 (1886).

12 There are indications of short-lived prior examples in the Eastern United States and even in the United Kingdom itself.

13 Pollock v. Farmers' Loan & Trust Co., 157 U.S. 429, *aff'd on reh'g*, 158 U.S. 601 (1895).

of the Sixteenth Amendment and the Revenue Act of 1913) and large corporate interests who were particularly opposed to the taxation of undistributed earnings.[14] Thus, the corporate income tax was enacted as a surtax measured by corporate earnings. It is accepted that at least on the side of the executive branch the so-called real-entity view of the corporation and the hope to control corporate power accumulation were central to the original political decision to enact the tax in 1909. Note, however, that the origins of corporate taxation in the United States date further back—to the nineteenth century, when the "real entity" of corporations was inconsequential.[15]

The stated justifications for enactment of the corporate income tax included:[16] (1) a benefits theory, viewing the tax as one that is imposed on the distinct privilege of doing business in the special corporate form (limiting the liability of shareholders); (2) administrative convenience—the ease of collection at the "source" of income and from a "person" that is able (at that time) to pay the tax; and (3) the federal government's desire to regulate corporations.[17] An important aspect of this desire was the understanding that corporate tax returns would be public.[18] Nonetheless, this crucial element in the compromise was violated—except for a short period, corporate tax returns have not been made public in the United States. The compromise was further violated when this temporary proxy tax was not abolished upon the enactment of the individual income tax in 1913. Again, corporate interests worried about the regulatory power that might be given to the federal government if undistributed earnings were subject to income tax and the executive branch focused on keeping a façade of regulatory monitoring of corporations, even if not very effective in practice.[19] This formula—established by an ill-studied, very time- and situation-specific political compromise—still serves as the backbone of the U.S. income tax system, despite tremendous changes in circumstance. Needless to say, such historical analysis cannot assist in present-day normative research of the corporate income tax.[20]

The next section proceeds with the economic background for the discourse, focusing on the most critical, yet also enigmatic, question of who bears the burden of the corporate tax.

---

14 *See, e.g.*, BANK, *supra* note 8; Avi-Yonah, *supra* note 6, at 1212–31.

15 *See* Steven A. Bank, *Entity Theory as Myth in the US Corporate Excise Tax of 1909*, *in* 2 STUDIES IN THE HISTORY OF TAX LAW 393 (John Tiley ed., 2007).

16 *See* Avi-Yonah, *supra* note 6, at 1218–20.

17 *Id.*; *see also* Marjorie E. Kornhauser, *Corporate Regulation and the Origins of the Corporate Income Tax*, 66 IND. L.J. 53 (1990).

18 This idea was in line with Theodore Roosevelt's focus on increasing the power of the federal government vis-à-vis large corporations. *See* Avi-Yonah, *supra* note 6, at 1215–16.

19 It is quite clear that the original compromise had not included "double taxation" of corporate profits. This feature, in violation of the original compromise, materialized due to industry's resistance to transparent taxation of corporate profits. *See, e.g.*, Steven A. Bank, *Is Double Taxation a Scapegoat for Declining Dividends*, 56 TAX L. REV. 463 (2003); *see also* SHAVIRO, *supra* note 6, at 20.

20 *See* Yariv Brauner, *The Non-Sense Tax: A Reply to New Corporate Income Tax Advocacy*, 2008 MICH. ST. L. REV. 591 (2008). The historic analysis does, however, teach us that even at its origins the tax had not been enacted after rigorous analysis or on satisfactory policy grounds. Interestingly, this picture is not much different in other jurisdictions—even the United Kingdom, whose corporate tax nominally preceded that of the United States. Yet, careful study demonstrates that the United Kingdom's modern, real corporate tax only followed closely that of the United States. *See* John Avery Jones, *Defining and Taxing Companies 1799 to 1965*, *in* 5 STUDIES IN THE HISTORY OF TAX LAW 1, 35–36 (John Tiley ed., 2012).

The Incidence of the Corporate Income Tax

Who bears the burden of the corporate tax? This is obviously the most fundamental question in the whole debate. If we could simply or even not so simply answer this question then most of the debate would be about implementation. Alas, we cannot answer this question. The answer is inherently complex and rich in variations to the extent that it is not useful to seek a singular answer.[21] We must, however, understand the complexity of the question to comprehend the composite of consequences that the tax imposes on our society.

The debate among economists over the incidence of the corporate tax is more than a half-century old.[22] The duality of real and fictional existence of corporations necessitates much of the complexity. First, the nominal incidence (i.e., who actually pays the tax to the government) provides no useful guidance in determining the real incidence of the tax. Second, attribution in proportion to ownership stakes is difficult and raises the same complexity issues that the real incidence question raises.[23] Finally, we get to the actual incidence analysis, where there are many candidates for bearing this burden: shareholders, other stakeholders, employees, consumers, and really everybody who comes into contact with the corporation. Timing matters and the incoherence of the corporate tax itself further complicate the analysis.[24]

The original, and most famous, work on corporate tax incidence was done by Arnold Harberger, who concluded that the tax "was borne fully by owners of capital, economy-wide."[25] In simple terms, this means that the corporate tax distorts the allocation of capital between the corporate and noncorporate sectors and that it is not as helpful in progressivity terms because, in general, owners of capital are less affluent than corporate shareholders.[26] Moreover, this conclusion does not reject the possibility that labor suffers some of the burden in certain circumstances.

Later dynamic analyses criticized Harberger's model, which captured solely the long run, while in the transitional periods (short- and midterms) the effects of the tax may be very different in terms of redistribution.[27] Hedging tax risks may further distort the picture—and likely in favor of the better-off in society. These dynamic analyses overcame some of the more problematic limitations of Harberger's model, including the international effects. The key issues here include: the degree of mobility of capital between countries, the elasticity of substitution between countries (e.g.,

---

21 *See, e.g.*, Alan J. Auerbach, *Who Bears the Corporate Tax? A Review of What We Know*, *in* 20 Tax Policy and the Economy 1, 33 (James A. Poterba ed., 2006) ("[O]ne-dimensional incidence analysis—distributing the corporate tax burden over a representative cross-section of the population—can be relatively uninformative about who bears the corporate tax burden, because it misses the element of timing."); John Whalley, *The Incidence of the Corporate Tax Revisited* 10, 13 (Technical Comm. on Bus. Taxation, Working Paper No. 1997-7, 1997) (concluding that the complex web of various effects makes a general analysis "not well-posed" or "misfocused"), *available at* http://www.fin.gc.ca/taxstudy/wp97-7e.pdf.

22 Auerbach, *supra* note 21, at 8–10. For additional information about the chronology of the debate, see Diane Rogers, Cong. Budget Office, *The Incidence of the Corporate Income Tax* (1996), *available at* http://www.cbo.gov/ftpdocs/3xx/doc304/corptax.pdf.

23 Auerbach, *supra* note 21, at 5–8. We should acknowledge that the better-off do own more corporate stock than the less affluent.

24 *Id.* at 33–34.

25 *Id.* at 8; *see* Arnold C. Harberger, *The Incidence of the Corporation Income Tax*, 70 J. Pol. Econ. 215 (1962).

26 *See* Auerbach, *supra* note 21, at 9. Nonetheless, Auerbach adds that because capital owners are generally more affluent than workers or consumers, the corporate tax may contribute something to the overall progressivity of the tax system.

27 *Id.* at 10–13.

substitutability of products manufactured in one country for products manufactured in another), and the relative sizes of the relevant countries.[28] Results of these dynamic analyses ranged from showing the burden falling completely on global capital[29] to a shifting of the burden to countries' nonmobile factors (e.g., labor).[30] The country size aspects are particularly interesting, although they significantly complicate the analysis, because it is possible that a large country will "export" the corporate tax burden to other countries and may even benefit overall from the tax.[31]

Alan Auerbach summarizes the literature as cautioning against simple assignment of the economic burden of the corporate income tax to all capital at once, even if it is true in the long term.[32] He also cautions against an attempt to describe the effects of the tax in terms of a simple breakdown of households by wealth or income, for instance.[33] He asserts that simply assigning the burden to certain groups in our society at certain times may not be very informative.[34] Recognizing that certain components of the tax have different incidences, Auerbach concludes that it is more meaningful to analyze corporate tax changes rather than the corporate income tax in its entirety.[35] In terms of time perspective, little work has been done on the lifetime incidence of the corporate tax in contrast to annual or other shorter perspectives, but existing scholarship indicates that the tax is less distributionally desirable from the long-term perspective.[36]

Little work has been done on the role of consumption in the analysis. Consumers deviate in their responses, both in total consumption and in specific choice changes, making real-world behavior different from what Harberger's model assumes. At least one notable study in this context exposed the importance of consumption to the analysis.[37] This study also acknowledged the hybrid properties of the corporate income tax—being partly a tax on cash flow, a feature normally ignored—which led them to conclude that the tax is less progressive than has been assumed.[38]

In conclusion, there is not enough empirical evidence on the corporate tax burden on people in America today, and the empirical evidence that does exist points in the direction that (at least some) of the burden is shouldered by labor, and, to a different extent, by consumers. This part of

---

28 *Id.* at 33–37.

29 Jane G. Gravelle, *Corporate Tax Incidence in an Open Economy*, 86 Nat'l Tax Ass'n Proc. 173 (1994). A more recent paper by the same author revisits the issue and particularly tests the issue of exportation of the burden, concluding that most of the burden is borne by domestic capital (similar to Harberger's conclusions) and, when it is not, the burden is mostly exported (i.e., little, if any, of the burden is borne by domestic labor). Jane G. Gravelle & Kent Smetters, *Who Bears the Burden of the Corporate Tax in the Open Economy?* (NBER Working Paper No. 8280, 2001), *available at* http://ssrn.com/abstract=268889.

30 John H. Mutti & Harry Grubert, *The Taxation of Capital Income in an Open Economy: The Importance of Resident-Nonresident Tax Treatment*, 27 J. Pub. Econ. 291 (1985).

31 *See* Rogers, *supra* note 22, at 19–20 (citing several studies).

32 Auerbach, *supra* note 21, at 13.

33 *Id.*

34 *Id.* This is because different points in time present arbitrary snapshots that are difficult to interpret in terms of what is desirable and what is not. They may result in very different distributions, and only the changes over time can really tell us what is happening in terms of fairness (based on redistribution as it occurs over time).

35 *Id.* at 33–34.

36 Don Fullerton & Diane Lim Rogers, Who Bears the Lifetime Tax Burden? (1993); *see* Rogers, *supra* note 22, at 20–21.

37 Rogers, *supra* note 22, at 25–26 (citing Gerald E. Auten & Laura T.J. Kalambokidis, Office of Tax Analysis, U.S. Dep't of Treasury, The Effect on the Distribution of the Tax Burden of Replacing the Corporate Income Tax with a Consumption Tax (1995)).

38 *See id.*

the controversy is the most heated and most politicized, but this is for a reason. If workers and consumers bear a good portion of the burden, then the tax may be redistributing from the less well-off to the better-off. International analysis further inflames this debate because it may suggest that more of the burden is shifted to immobile factors, yet also perhaps to nonvoting factors. The international model is very complex and its variables constantly change—economies open and the substitutability of products change as globalization thrives.[39] In addition, the tax is not a tax on pure profits of corporations and there is no basis, therefore, to conclude that those who benefit from corporate profits suffer from the imposition of this tax. Beyond the lack of data, and perhaps further study, the complexity of corporate behavior and globalization effects makes it essentially impossible to control the fairness of the corporate tax, even if we had agreement over its goals.

With this in mind, the next section proceeds with a more detailed review of the most common justifications for the corporate tax.

Traditional Arguments in Support of the Corporate Income Tax

This section reviews, and criticizes, the traditional arguments in support of retention of the corporate tax, beginning with the technical arguments.

The Technical Arguments

The basic version of the technical argument is that corporations are separate legal persons and, therefore, should not only enjoy the benefits of such status but also bear its burdens—or even pay the "price" for such benefits in the form of taxation. The problem with this assertion is that corporations do not actually bear the burden of the tax; people do. Thus, it is people rather than corporations that both enjoy the benefits of incorporation and potentially suffer the tax on corporations. The benefactors and the sufferers, however, may not be the same people, and as we have already learned, it is not possible to ascertain who is affected by the corporate tax and how much. The simplistic articulation of this argument may have been appropriate in times when corporations acquired their status from a charter discretionally granted by the ruler, but it simply does not fit modern reality. Also, the corporate tax base and rates are very different from those applying to individuals, which belies any argument about parity between corporations and natural persons.

Moreover, corporate taxes worldwide are not designed based on the logic of this argument. Corporations are taxed on their "income" rather than on the benefits that they or the people affected by them enjoy as a result of the entity's legal status. Therefore, a simple benefit theory of the corporate tax would never lead to the unified taxation of corporate income. As already mentioned above, a benefit theory looking to corporate stakeholders also cannot justify the corporate tax. The argument that corporations earn rents (i.e., profits beyond what the investment would earn without the corporate status and other legal attributes) and that the corporate tax is the only way to capture these rents is clearly false, because, again, the benefit of earning these rents is enjoyed by people, not pieces of paper, to which society has decided to grant a legal status. Any benefit argument must, therefore, turn on the appropriate manner of taxing the individuals who ultimately benefit from incorporation and not on taxing the corporations themselves, because corporations cannot benefit or suffer from anything.

---

39 *See* Auerbach, *supra* note 21, at 33–37.

Finally, a more sophisticated version of the technical argument may be that corporations are "real" entities enjoying the protection and benefits of the country and its legal regime and, hence, should be taxed separately from their stakeholders and shareholders. The real entity theory of corporations also has some historical basis and, more importantly, proven implications in other areas of regulatory law. Yet, it is not sufficient to argue that corporations are real and separate for business law or securities or environmental regulation purposes to justify their taxation as such. The purpose of tax law is to collect revenue and perhaps facilitate other social policies of governments.[40] Therefore, to justify corporate taxation a relevant policy should be clearly identified and its impact evaluated—costs and benefits—against the specific relevant tax policy goal identified. There is only one argument that seriously attempts to go through this intellectual necessity. This is the more sophisticated version of the technical argument, as argued by Reuven Avi-Yonah, that the goal of the corporate tax has always been to regulate large corporations.[41]

According to Avi-Yonah, corporations as such acquire immense powers. Their real entity qualities permit and facilitate this power acquisition, so the corporate tax is appropriately applied to them and not to their various stakeholders. Although these corporate powers are identified with corporate management, it would not do to tax the individuals comprising management directly, because they do not have these powers as individuals but only as part of the real, separate organism (i.e., entity) that we call a "corporation." I responded to this argument by noting that the corporate tax is by no means designed to meaningfully curb these powers, and even Avi-Yonah did not argue that it could do so effectively by itself. The corporate tax is simply too small to act as a curb, even if these powers manifested themselves only in terms of cash available to the corporation.[42] Moreover, there are other regulatory devices that deal with corporate power more directly, so the debate should shift to their perfection rather than the use of crude and indirect mechanisms such as the corporate tax.[43] I added to this that the original purpose of the corporate tax—that is, to regulate large corporations—may equally be achieved with a zero percent tax because it is the information gathered by, and control exerted through, taxation that matter and not the actual revenue.[44]

The real entity theory could reignite a benefit theory of taxing corporations. On this basis, one could argue that, as a separate entity, the corporation enjoys certain benefits that it would not enjoy in any other form because it is a whole that is more than just the sum of its parts. Yet, this argument would fare no better than the other benefit arguments addressed above because it does not explain why the corporation—rather than its stakeholders—should be taxed, when these special benefits, materializing as rents, are eventually taxed in the hands of stakeholders. In response, it could be argued that these stakeholders (e.g., shareholders) are not necessarily the beneficiaries of the rents and thus the corporation should be taxed. Yet, again, whoever enjoys these benefits is not necessarily (and likely is not) the person who bears the real burden of the corporate income tax.

---

40 This idea itself is a rather controversial political matter, and a deep exploration of the idea that tax law can or should be used to facilitate social policy is beyond the scope of this chapter. Nonetheless, in practice, there is no doubt that tax law serves many purposes beyond simple revenue collection, so I simply accept this idea for purposes of the instant discussion.

41 *See* Avi-Yonah, *supra* note 6.

42 *See* Brauner, *supra* note 20.

43 *Id.*

44 *Id.*

The Policy Arguments

The technical arguments discussed in the previous section often tie into or mask policy arguments. For instance, some arguments are based on the universal ability-to-pay principle and thus purport to be driven by policy or fairness concerns. These arguments assume that the better-off in society disproportionately benefit from the special legal status of corporations. Implicit in these arguments is the further assumption that the better-off enjoy tax benefits (e.g., the ability to manipulate the timing of income by postponing the disposition of stock) that allow them to defer taxation of (and, therefore, compound) the benefits of the special legal status of corporations. This imbalance is righted through the taxation of corporations, which is viewed as adhering to the ability-to-pay principle and striving for a more just or more truly progressive tax system. However, this argument is again based on a false perception of the incidence of the corporate tax. It ignores the fact that some of the incidence may fall on labor, consumers, or foreigners. It further ignores the fact that workers hold a very large proportion of corporate ownership, whether directly or indirectly (e.g., through mutual funds).

A related, administrative or policy argument in support of the corporate tax is that other countries tax corporations and we should do so, too.[45] This argument is equally indefensible. What this argument says is really that we should tax foreigners investing in our country through corporations. There has been a lengthy debate over this issue in the context of integrating the corporate and individual income taxes, but there is no need for a separate corporate tax for this purpose. It is the foreign investors that one actually wishes to tax—not the corporations—so the focus should be on how to tax those investors in the most desirable manner. There are many options here, some of which depend on the ability to coordinate taxation with the investors' countries of residence. Nevertheless, there is a more direct solution of the kind recommended in this chapter; namely, to use an entity-level withholding tax rather than a stand-alone corporate tax. It may require relief of double taxation for some investors, but that is not a true hurdle because tax treaties and domestic law do that anyway with regard to noncorporate investments.

Another quasi-administrative argument is that the corporate tax is necessary to ensure compliance with the individual income tax. There are several versions of this argument, from a claim that absent a corporate tax individuals could incorporate and avoid full taxation to the use of corporations to obscure ownership and other relationship patterns. These arguments cannot support retention of our corporate tax because the effect of the tax is the opposite of that which is assumed by these arguments. In other words, the corporate tax obscures the relationship between the income and the individuals who eventually bear the burden of the tax or who may enjoy the benefits of incorporation, whoever they are. Eliminating the corporate tax would necessarily result in increased transparency. Moreover, experienced tax professionals know—and, independently, the recent BEPS initiative proves—that there is much tax avoidance at the corporate level;[46] so, the corporate tax would be a poor device to fight avoidance of the individual income tax. Finally, the basic concern about incorporation of individuals would necessarily be better relieved under a tax scheme where corporations would be subject to a transparency-enhancing withholding tax as advocated in this chapter rather than the current independent corporate tax.

45 *E.g.*, Bird, *supra* note 6, at 200–01.

46 *See supra* note 2 and accompanying text.

The Political Arguments

The freshest and perhaps most appealing argument in support of the corporate income tax is that it restrains the power of corporate management.[47] This is primarily a political argument, although there is a policy flavor to it as well, as explored (and rejected) above. The argument is appealing because it is consistent with the basic, popular intuition that it is not fair that large corporations do not pay enough tax and that corporate management is unjustly enriched at the expense of the public anyway. This argument is smart because it avoids the critique of the corporate tax as a poor revenue collection and redistribution mechanism, including, at first glance, the debate over the incidence of the corporate tax. Finally, it is built on steady historical grounds, as this was a primary motivation for the enactment of the tax in the first place.[48]

Making this argument, Avi-Yonah primarily targets corporate management and its accumulation of power. According to Avi-Yonah, such accumulation of power is undesirable for several reasons. It concentrates political power in the hands of management without democratic protection.[49] It also gives management economic power over employees[50] and market power over consumers.[51] Moreover, power in any of these spheres can convert to power in other spheres. Avi-Yonah argues that taxation may be one of the only ways to curb such power. I have already responded[52] by noting, among other things, the notorious influence of politics on tax policy, which calls into question the utility of taxation in this context. Further, I noted that it is unclear whether taxation can curb management's economic and market power, given that this power does not directly arise from the income or wealth of the corporation. I added that it may be the case that the corporate tax itself adds to the market power of management over consumers because of how it obscures corporate actions.[53] Finally, I noted that there are other, potentially more powerful devices to curb management powers, including corporate governance, consumer regulation, and antitrust law.

I further explained that the corporate tax does not tax (or even purport to tax) the accumulation of power by corporate management. It is a very bad and rough proxy for this purpose. Even if one makes the heroic assumption that the corporate tax reduces the power of management by reducing the income of the corporation, one would find it difficult to demonstrate that this reduction in power is meaningful, let alone significant. One definitely could not demonstrate that the significant costs associated with the corporate tax are justified by its desirable consequences. Consequently, even if valid, this argument cannot explain the corporate tax we have.

Another argument mentioned above that may be viewed as political is the argument that it is desirable, and perhaps efficient, to tax foreigners (who do not vote), which renders the incidence of the corporate tax—falling, as it does, on all capital and not just domestic shareholders—advantageous. A different version of this argument is that the corporate tax is perhaps the only way for us to tax

47 For the most explicit and most comprehensive version of this argument, see Avi-Yonah, *supra* note 6. *See also* Shaviro, *supra* note 6, at 11–12.

48 Avi-Yonah, *supra* note 6, at 1219–20.

49 *Id.* at 1237. Lobbying is the obvious example of this type of power.

50 *Id.*

51 *Id.* at 1238.

52 *See* Brauner, *supra* note 20.

53 Most ubiquitously, shareholders asking questions of management are answered that decisions were taken for "tax reasons" that only few can adequately understand. For example, certain merger and acquisition transactions are promoted by management as "tax-free" reorganizations, masking the more important consequences of such transactions that on average result in losses to these same shareholders, often to the benefit of management.

foreigners investing in corporations that do business in the United States, making the tax desirable on both benefits and administrative (i.e., "just because we can …") grounds.[54] The difficulty with this argument is that it applies to all countries. Indeed, some of the burden of our corporate tax falls on nonvoters, but then some of the burden of foreign corporate taxes falls on U.S. taxpayers. It is unclear whether the United States is a "winner" on balance, and it would be difficult to predict the balance changes as countries respond to that effect.

The next section sketches the traditional objections to the corporate tax. It focuses on the costs of the tax and its distortive nature rather than providing responses to the justifications for the corporate tax that have already been discussed above.

Traditional Arguments Against the Corporate Income Tax

History is perhaps the most powerful opponent of the corporate tax. As demonstrated above, and more comprehensively elsewhere, it was not until well into the twentieth century that corporate taxes became independent of the individual income tax. This is ironic because this independence occurred due to historical events, mistakes, or political compromises that had nothing to do with the so-called justifications for the corporate tax and have nothing to do with the reality in which we live today.

Nonetheless, path dependence (or perhaps the political interest of the powerful corporate sector) has directed the discourse into the unfortunate territory of proving the negative. The traditional opposition to the corporate tax has developed around examining the tax's costs even though its benefits have never been demonstrated. The primary costs discussed in the scholarship are the efficiency costs of the tax due to its distortive nature and the compliance and enforcement costs of the tax.[55]

The straightforward inefficiency created by the corporate tax is that it distorts the allocation of investment between the corporate and noncorporate sectors. One can make an investment directly or indirectly through a corporation or an unincorporated entity. At the end of the day, it is the same economic investment, but if the investment is made through an incorporated entity the investor suffers an additional layer of taxation—the corporate tax—that creates a disincentive to invest through corporations. This position is simple and easy to understand, but the law has added to it a multitude of layers of complexity that create additional incentives and disincentives to invest (or not to invest) through corporations. For example, tax law provides significant disincentives to the use of branches (e.g., the branch profits tax) while providing other incentives to invest through corporations (e.g., special allowances, reorganization opportunities, and the opportunity to indefinitely defer taxation of the shareholders without a loss of accounting value). This tangle of incentives and disincentives obviously results in significant planning, compliance, and enforcement losses; we all understand that the best, brightest, and highest-charging tax planners all focus on exactly this tangle of incentives and disincentives. Yet, beyond such costs, the tax clearly shifts

---

54 *See, e.g.*, Bird, *supra* note 6, at 196.

55 Much of the discussion of these costs took place in the context of reform aimed at integration of the corporate and individual income taxes, which resulted from a successful diverting maneuver that preferred a debate about integration to a debate about the more fundamental question of whether we should have a corporate tax at all. Politicians thus became interested in integration and, in turn, that became the focus of scholarship. Nevertheless, the costs discussed in the context of that debate remain relevant to this discussion. For the classical original exposure of the issue, see Charles E. McLure, Jr., Must Corporate Income Be Taxed Twice? (1979).

investment from and to the corporate sector that would not end up where it does absent the tax, resulting in efficiency losses.

A tangential distortion that may be viewed as part of the same problem is the effect of the corporate tax on the decision to incorporate. Assuming that business law is rational in the benefits it bestows upon entities in general and corporations in particular, the corporate tax may distort the effect of business law if it alters behavior. Thus, the corporate tax may cause too few or too many incorporations, resulting in efficiency losses. The question of choice of entity is beyond the scope of this chapter because it has too many "moving parts" and scholars seem unable to agree on the basic assumptions required for a fruitful debate on this matter. Two conclusions may, however, be reached: (1) the corporate tax distorts the incorporation decision; and (2) the question of choice of entity and its social benefits or costs requires further theoretical study before we can have a discussion of the magnitude or even the direction of such distortion.[56]

The second classical inefficiency created by the corporate tax is its distortion of the financing of investment. The basic argument is that corporations rely too much on debt rather than equity because corporations can deduct interest but not dividends when computing tax. This distortion may also affect the dividend payout policies of corporations. Some commentators have also observed that the corporate tax is undesirable from a national policy standpoint because it may hurt capital accumulation and consequently economic growth.

The third general distortion introduced by the corporate tax is its effect on particular investment decisions (at the margin). The effective tax rate applicable to income from investments depends on the detailed rules that may increase or decrease the effective tax rate in comparison to the effective tax rate that would apply if the investment were made otherwise. Uncertainty that is often more prevalent in the corporate tax context may also influence investment decisions.

The complexity of the effects of the corporate tax often masks the more straightforward or direct costs of the tax. The corporate tax is not a critical revenue source for almost any countries. Corporate tax revenue in most of the strong economies, where an overwhelming portion of large corporations reside and pay taxes, have been declining and plateaued around 5 percent of total revenue around the turn of the millennium. In some countries, including the United States, this percentage has increased slightly, but is still less than 10 percent, in recent years for a variety of reasons, including the economic decline in most traditional Western powers. At the same time, there is no question that the most sophisticated and expensive tax planning focuses solely on corporate tax planning exactly for these largest of taxpayers. Consequently, tax authorities must expend their best resources to respond with equally sophisticated and expensive enforcement. Once the inherent complexity of corporations, their ability to reorganize and divide, their ability to change seat, etc. are added together, it is not difficult to understand that the corporate tax is considerably more expensive than, for example, the individual income tax. These significant costs are never taken into account in the debate over the corporate tax.

56 In a working paper, I have explored the state of choice-of-entity law and concluded that it has not developed based on rigorous study or any sound theoretical basis, but rather has evolved through historical happenstance and arbitrary interest-group pressure. Yariv Brauner, *Whither Choice of Entity?* (2013), *available at* http://ssrn.com/abstract=2318825.

Diversions: Rate Reduction and Integration

Quite a lot of the corporate tax discourse over the years has been devoted to implementation problems, thus taking for granted the unsubstantiated desirability of the tax or the claim that it would be politically impossible to repeal it. The two most common and significant reform proposals have been the calls for rate reductions and for integration of the tax on corporate earnings (i.e., the corporate income tax) with the tax on corporate distributions (i.e., the dividend tax or the individual income tax as imposed on dividends).

Rate-reduction advocacy shares many of the characteristics of the politics of the corporate tax discourse. If indeed the tax is primarily a smokescreen that serves corporate managers and other corporate functionaries to maintain the opacity of their actions, rent-seeking behavior, and power accumulation, as I argue, then rate reduction can get them the best of all worlds. It simply reduces the "price" that they pay—and we know that the price is quite low and declining—as the reduced tax rate has less of an impact on their profits and available cash. Also, a reduced corporate tax rate requires less involvement with costly tax planning. Yet, the tax remains almost as effective as an opacity buffer. It is not as effective a buffer because lower taxes may increase the political pressure of those who oppose corporations paying "too little" in taxes; however, this pressure may be kept in check and fluctuates with the general political climate and circumstances. Nonetheless, beyond this potential political disadvantage, rate reduction enjoys important political advantages. It appeals to politicians who buy the argument that it is possible to raise more revenue with rate reductions,[57] and it appeals to those who believe that rate reductions result in growth and, hence, job creation. But, most importantly, rate reduction retains the corporate tax itself, which is the most important thing for those who believe in its progressive nature.

Overall, rate-reduction advocacy is an undesirable diversion. In some circumstances, rate reduction is not undesirable in comparison to higher rates because it potentially eliminates some of the distortion created by the corporate tax. For instance, lower rates reduce the benefits of some undesirable "special treatments" within the corporate tax. As mentioned above, rate reduction may also increase awareness of the undesirable tax status of corporations, albeit often inaccurately.[58] Yet, the potential advantages of rate reduction are dwarfed by the damage that it does by diverting the discourse from the real question and the fundamental debate over the desirability of the corporate tax as a whole. The end result of this diversion is always some sort of an alleged compromise, where the corporate sector achieves its most important goal—namely, the retention of opacity, often accompanied by some effective rate reduction—and the so-called protectors of the public claim to have achieved some concessions in the form of a smaller rate reduction than was originally sought. Ironically, we are still far from getting back to even the original compromise that required publicity of corporate tax returns.

Integration advocacy is an even bigger distraction. Its bottom line is desirable; in fact, it is practically not much different from proposals to eliminate the corporate tax such as those made here. Integration eliminates the so-called double taxation of corporate earnings and aspires to eliminate the distortions created by the taxation of corporations. Full imputation, which used to be the most obvious (and perhaps even most common) method of integration, does, indeed, meet that

57 This argument is most often associated with the so-called "Laffer Curve." *See* Arthur Laffer, *The Laffer Curve: Past, Present, and Future*, Heritage Found. (June 1, 2004), http://www.heritage.org/research/reports/2004/06/the-laffer-curve-past-present-and-future.

58 Because the public more often than not focuses on how little tax is paid by corporations, and not on the undesirable effects of the corporate tax regime as a whole.

end. Under full imputation, the corporate tax serves as a credit in the hands of shareholders against their individual income tax liability.

The problem is that once the discourse is diverted away from the question of whether we should tax corporations independently and toward integration, the debate is universally and immediately overshadowed by implementation concerns. The question then becomes not what is the most desirable tax regime but what is the most desirable integration regime. That instantaneously leads some sort of partial (rather than full) imputation to become the front runner, usually for one or more pragmatic reasons. The logical leap over the more fundamental question regarding the desirability of the corporate tax is completely ignored, and policy quickly becomes overwhelmed by administrative concerns. Many countries that swore by the policy merits of integration fell into this trap and for a variety of reasons switched to partial integration that is akin to any other corporate tax regime in terms of the undesirable effects described above.[59] Other countries insisted on keeping the benefits of imputation and essentially maintained full imputation regimes, with success.[60] For these reasons, although I agree that full imputation is desirable, I prefer to emphasize that the important points are to insist on transparency and on accounting for the tax burden solely at the shareholder level by eliminating an independent corporate tax.

The next section addresses perhaps the most formidable hurdle; namely, the often self-fulfilling prophecy that it is politically infeasible to abolish the corporate tax.

Feasibility of Abolition

The most powerful argument made for the retention of the corporate tax, notwithstanding all of the arguments made above, is that it is not politically feasible to abolish the corporate tax and, therefore, the focus should be on reform rather than on the fundamental question of whether to have a corporate tax at all.[61] This argument is intimately related to the political argument in support of the corporate tax because it simultaneously feeds on that political appeal while feeding the diversion of scholarship and policy making away from the fundamental question. It is powerful because it is self-fulfilling. It is quite clear that there is some truth to it; yet, the real question is whether the political resistance to repeal of the tax can stand on a defensible ground. I argue that this is not the case.

In this chapter, I have demonstrated that there is no policy ground for the preservation of the corporate tax. In order to avoid falling into the trap of the integration debate, which is one of the primary undesirable diversions discussed above (although I do support integration standing alone), I here propose an alternative. It is to convert the current corporate tax into a withholding mechanism in support of the individual income tax. Shareholders in public corporations would be taxed on a mark-to-market basis (i.e., on the price difference of their stock between the beginning of the relevant fiscal year and its end).[62] Shareholders in other corporations, most of which pay little corporate tax anyway, would be taxed similarly to all other unincorporated business, generally by

59 Notably, most of the European countries switched due to European Union law constraints. *See generally* Walter Hellerstein et al., *Constitutional Restraints on Corporate Tax Integration*, 62 Tax L. Rev. 1 (2008).

60 For example, Australia.

61 *See, e.g.*, Shaviro, *supra* note 6, at 178–79.

62 This system is essentially the one suggested by Michael Knoll and Joseph Dodge. Joseph M. Dodge, *A Combined Mark-to-Market and Pass-Through Corporate-Shareholder Integration Proposal*, 50 Tax L. Rev. 265 (1995); Michael S. Knoll, *An Accretion Corporate Income Tax*, 49 Stan. L. Rev. 1 (1996).

attribution of all relevant income tax attributes of the corporate business to the shareholders.[63] In both cases, the corporations who control the best and the most information will bear the primary responsibility for the collection of the taxes and their remittance to the government, much like they do in the case of payroll taxes.

On Corporations and Families

In Chapter 11, Anthony Infanti criticizes the scope of the corporate tax debate. He establishes the legal similarities of corporations and families as social constructs viewed as generating value beyond the sum of their parts. Then, he raises a question about the dissimilarities in the tax policy discourse regarding the two institutions—or, more accurately, about the perception of this discourse—as the corporate tax discourse focuses on stripping its special treatment while the family tax discourse focuses on whom to include in the network of special tax treatment granted to families. Yet, Infanti's true agenda is the public–private divide in American society and his critique of the power structure of our society.

Although I share Infanti's critique, I would have interpreted the parallel in perhaps the opposite way. I share Infanti's complaint about joint returns and would argue that this chapter's analysis of the corporate tax is conceptually parallel to his own past work that calls for elimination of joint returns and taxation of all people at the individual level only.[64] The principle is quite straightforward: promote a transparent and fair tax policy, which is always obviously measured at the individual level. This is because only individuals are actually affected by tax policy, because it seems to be the most obviously legitimate level of assessment of policies, and because it is the least subject to manipulation through planning or legal (rather than real) construction.

Infanti's critical analysis provides the discourse with an interesting perspective. To me, it simply fortifies the conviction that simplicity and transparency may be the only way to maximize legitimacy of our tax system. I should mention that I do not agree that the comparison of corporations and families may be taken further than in contemplation of the normative principles of tax policy-making analysis. Substantively, I am uncomfortable drawing too close a parallel between these two institutions. Corporations are purely legal constructs, and the various rights and obligations associated with them may be quite simply defined and observed among their stakeholders, regardless of their complex structures. Families are primarily social institutions that obviously preceded even the earliest roots of the income tax. Regardless of what one thinks about families, one must admit the power that they capture in the minds of much of the populace and thus the importance of legally recognizing them in one way or another and the legitimacy benefits of doing so, in the eyes of both society and the law. Unlike corporations, it would be substantially more difficult to clearly define and trace the various separate rights and obligations associated with families among the family members. I believe that it is possible and desirable to do so, but acknowledge the qualitative difficulty when compared with doing so for corporations. Finally, corporations are in existence with the purpose of producing profits, and they have been promoted solely for efficiency and wealth-promotion goals. Families have many diverse goals, regardless of one's view of them, and their recognition by the law goes much beyond wealth maximization.

---

63 This does not mean that partnership taxation is perfectly designed in the United States, but the basic premises are clear and transparent. The need to reform them is beside the point made in this chapter.

64 *See* Anthony C. Infanti, *Decentralizing Family: An Inclusive Proposal for Individual Tax Filing in the United States*, 2010 Utah L. Rev. 605.

Finally, Infanti claims that the perspective of the traditional debate presented by this chapter is misguided, focusing on the desirability of reform rather than on identifying the instances where the corporate tax could be desirable and where it could not. I disagree in the specific case of the corporate tax, because I argue that the tax can never be used in a desirable manner, and therefore it is futile to reframe the debate to explore instances where it could be so. The disagreement between Infanti and me is not based on different norms or substantive political tastes; it stems from different approaches to legal reform and perhaps different levels of trust in our political system, which we both criticize. My "traditional" approach prefers a technically sound design of the tax system using the existing pieces in a more desirable manner. It advocates eliminating one of these pieces (i.e., the corporate tax), yet not introducing new pieces or repurposing existing pieces in the way Infanti alludes to. Infanti's critical approach focuses on the goals and generally wishes to reshape the current system to meet them. I do not believe it is possible, primarily because, based on past experience and evaluation, I do not trust our tax politics to be capable of doing that. Even if it were capable of such dramatic evolution then there are reforms better than repurposing the corporate tax to achieve the goals both Infanti and I deem desirable. I nevertheless believe that in the current political circumstances the best one can do is to limit intervention of populist politics in tax law design. The best way to do that is to ensure transparency—for example, by eliminating the separate corporate tax—and consequently enhance public understanding and hence legitimacy of the regime.

Conclusion

In this chapter, I have reviewed the traditional debate over the desirability of the corporate income tax and demonstrated that no sound policy rationale supports preservation of the tax. This conclusion is not revolutionary; however, political circumstances have secured the tax's universality. As discussed above, the most reflexive proponents of the corporate tax, who are supposedly driven by fairness and concerns about redistribution, are misguided in their support of the tax and should in fact oppose it. They should oppose the tax because the tax mainly serves as a smokescreen that permits corporate management to accumulate power at the expense of all other stakeholders. Yet, at a more fundamental level, I have called for a realistic assessment of the effects of tax policy devices on the relevant constituency—flesh-and-blood persons. The inability to simply evaluate the effects of the corporate tax on individuals militates in favor of its repeal because it is a tax policy instrument that cannot be effectively controlled by policy makers. If not repealed, the corporate tax should be converted into a corporate-level withholding mechanism for the individual income tax.

Chapter 11
Of Families and Corporations: Erasing the Public–Private Divide in Tax Reform Debates

Anthony C. Infanti*

"Corporations are people, my friend."[1] On the campaign trail in Iowa, Mitt Romney defended his position not to raise taxes on "people" by responding with this quick retort to a heckler who had urged him to increase the corporate tax burden instead. Romney was, of course, correct in asserting that corporations comprise groups of people—including directors, shareholders, officers, managers, employees, and other stakeholders. In reply, however, some members of the audience shouted back that corporations are not people.[2] Interestingly, these audience members were also correct because, when groups of people come together under the guise of the corporate form, they create something more than just an assemblage of individuals. That is, the corporation is both a part of, and apart from, the groups of people it comprises.

But to read the stacks of law review articles devoted to discussing and debating the repeal/integration of the corporate income tax, you might think that corporations are the only groups of people who, by working together, create something that is more than just the sum of its parts. There is, however, a more ubiquitous form under which groups of people come together to work toward a common end and, in the process, create something that is more than just the sum of its parts—the family. The federal tax laws take special account of both of these entities. In some cases, this may mean the conferral of special tax advantages; in other cases, it may mean the imposition of special tax disadvantages.

Although the corporation and the family both fall in the same general category, the terms of academic debates about their tax treatment differ markedly. While tax academics endlessly discuss and debate the most effective means for eliminating the differential treatment of investments made in corporate form, there is no debate about eliminating the differential treatment of the family under the federal tax laws. Put differently, the debate about corporate tax repeal/integration is about leveling down; that is, the debate focuses on minimizing the tax burden on corporate investment by having the tax treatment of corporations more closely track that of fiscally transparent entities. To the contrary, the debate about reforming the taxation of the family is about leveling out or even up—that is, the debate focuses either on fine-tuning the existing special treatment of the family or opening the way for a more diverse array of families to qualify for this special treatment.

* Thanks to the participants at the 2014 Law and Society Annual Meeting for their comments on an earlier draft of this chapter.

1 Ashley Parker, *"Corporations Are People," Romney Tells Iowa Hecklers Angry over His Tax Policy*, N.Y. Times, Aug. 12, 2011, at A16.

2 *Id.*

The dichotomy in the academic debates regarding these similar entities is but another illustration of the public–private divide that surfaces in so many places within the tax laws.[3] In these debates, the public/business sector that is the subject of the corporate income tax is privileged in its treatment as compared to the private/family sector that is the subject of the personal income tax. In this chapter, I deconstruct this hierarchy and question why there is not more debate about leveling up the tax treatment of fiscally transparent entities to bring it in line with the tax treatment of corporations in the same way that commentators have proposed leveling up the tax treatment of the family to make it more inclusive.

Taxing "Associations"

Both corporations and families are sociolegal constructions.[4] As constructions, the federal tax laws sometimes choose to ignore them, at other times treat them as artificial entities, and at yet other times endow them with real meaning for tax purposes. Unsurprisingly, dramatically different tax treatments attach to the differing approaches to dealing with these sociolegal constructions. Yet, there are strong parallels between the multiplicity of tax treatments that apply to corporations and families—parallels that call into question the extant public–private/business–family hierarchy in tax reform debates.

Corporations

When individuals come together to engage in business, the business entity is classified for federal tax purposes either as a corporation, a partnership, or a disregarded entity.[5] An entity that is formed as a corporation under state or federal law must be classified as a corporation for federal tax purposes.[6] For most other business entities, classification as a corporation for federal tax purposes is purely elective.[7]

3 Mary Louise Fellows, *Rocking the Tax Code: A Case Study of Employment-Related Child-Care Expenditures*, 10 Yale J.L. & Feminism 307, 357 (1998) ("The public/private distinction is mirrored in the tax law's business/personal distinction."); Nancy C. Staudt, *Taxing Housework*, 84 Geo. L.J. 1571, 1571 (1996) ("Many features of the Federal Income Tax Code reflect the assumption that our society is composed of heterosexual married couples, with men occupying the 'public' sphere and women occupying the 'private' domestic sphere.").

4 *See* Martha A. Fineman, The Autonomy Myth: A Theory of Dependency 57 (2004) ("The significance of the family as a societal construct is revealed by its position as a primary terrain for the cultural wars in which our society is increasingly mired."); Tracy E. Higgins & Rachel P. Fink, *Gender and Nation-Building: Family Law as Legal Architecture*, 60 Me. L. Rev. 375, 385–86 (2008) ("[A]lthough often understood as natural or pre-political, the family is a legal construct, not a preexisting entity which the law regulates in some respects and fails to regulate in others."); Joseph E. Stiglitz, *Regulating Multinational Corporations: Towards Principles of Cross-Border Legal Frameworks in a Globalized World Balancing Rights with Responsibilities*, 23 Am. U. Int'l L. Rev. 451, 468 (2008) ("I approach these issues from the perspective of an economist, an economist that sees institutions like 'corporations' and 'property rights' as social constructions, to be evaluated on how well they serve broader public interests.").

5 Treas. Reg. § 301.7701-3(a).

6 *Id.* § 301.7701-2(b)(1), (3). Certain listed foreign business entities also must be classified as corporations for federal tax purposes. *Id.* § 301.7701-2(b)(8). Banks, insurance companies, certain governmental entities, and any entity that is specifically taxable as a corporation (e.g., a publicly traded partnership) must also be classified as corporations for federal tax purposes. *Id.* § 301.7701-2(b)(4)–(7); *see* I.R.C. § 7704.

7 Treas. Reg. §§ 301.7701-2(b)(2), -3(a).

Yet, not all entities classified as corporations for federal tax purposes fall into the category of "C corporations"—that is, those actually subject to the corporate income tax.[8] For instance, a small business corporation that meets certain requirements regarding the nature and number of its shareholders, its place of incorporation, and its ownership structure may elect to be treated as an "S corporation" for federal tax purposes.[9] A corporation making this election is not itself a taxpayer. Instead, like a partnership, the S corporation passes its income, deductions, credits, and other items through to its shareholders, who report their shares of these items on their own tax returns.[10]

Sometimes the separate entity status of corporations is disregarded. Thus, certain domestic corporations are treated as paying foreign taxes that are actually imposed on, and paid by, their foreign subsidiaries.[11] In addition, certain domestic shareholders (both corporate and noncorporate) are treated as incurring the income of controlled foreign corporations, whether it is distributed or not.[12] And this is without even taking account of the fact that business entities that are "virtually indistinguishable from … corporation[s]"[13] can now elect to be disregarded for federal tax purposes if they have a single shareholder.[14] A disregarded entity is not generally recognized for federal tax purposes; that is, "its activities are treated in the same manner as a sole proprietorship, branch, or division of the owner."[15] In the argot of tax professionals, disregarded entities are commonly labeled "tax nothings."[16]

These are three quite distinct approaches to dealing with the taxation of corporations. At times, the federal tax laws treat the corporation as a distinct unit separate from the groups of people it comprises (i.e., C corporations). At other times, the federal tax laws treat the corporation as an aggregate of its shareholders (i.e., S corporations). At yet other times, the corporation is ignored and treated as if it did not exist at all (e.g., controlled foreign corporations and disregarded entities). These distinct approaches are accompanied by similarly distinct tax consequences. The U.S. "classical"[17] system of corporate taxation imposes tax on the income of C corporations both in the hands of the corporation when it is earned[18] and again in the hands of shareholders when it is distributed.[19] This treatment differs markedly from that of S corporations and disregarded entities, whose income is taxed just once.[20] As described below, commentators have sharply criticized the distortions created by imposing a nominally heavier tax burden on corporations than on other business entities.

8 I.R.C. §§ 11, 1361(a)(2), 1363.

9 *Id.* § 1361.

10 *Id.* §§ 1363, 1366.

11 *Id.* § 902.

12 *Id.* §§ 951–965.

13 Simplification of Entity Classification Rules, 61 Fed. Reg. 21,989, 21,990 (proposed May 13, 1996) (to be codified at 26 C.F.R. pt. 301).

14 Treas. Reg. § 301.7701-2(a). Those with multiple shareholders can choose between being taxed as a corporation or a partnership for federal tax purposes. *Id.*

15 *Id. But see id.* § 301.7701-2(c)(2)(iv)(B); Temp. Treas. Reg. § 301.7701-2T(c)(2)(iv)(A) (together treating otherwise disregarded entities as corporations for employment tax purposes).

16 *E.g.*, David S. Miller, *The Tax Nothing*, 74 Tax Notes 619 (1997).

17 U.S. Dep't of Treasury, Report on Integration of the Individual and Corporate Tax Systems: Taxing Business Income Once, at vii (1992).

18 I.R.C. § 11.

19 *Id.* § 61(a)(7).

20 *See supra* notes 9–10 and accompanying text.

Families as Entities

A similar pattern can be detected in the taxation of the family. At times, the family is treated as a distinct unit for federal tax purposes. In particular, the married couple is treated as a single economic unit for federal tax purposes.[21] When the couple files a joint return (as most do),[22] the federal tax laws do not see two streams of income and two sets of deductions; rather, the federal tax laws see the couple's income only in "an aggregate amount[,] and the deductions allowed and the taxable income are likewise computed on an aggregate basis."[23] In fact, the couple can file a joint return even if one of the spouses has no income or deductions and would not otherwise be required to file a tax return at all.[24] When the couple has minor children with unearned income, the unit expands to include the children's unearned income and associated deductions—either by taxing the children at the parents' rates or, under certain circumstances, by the parents' electing to include the children's unearned income on their own return.[25]

There are, of course, additional ways in which the married couple is treated as a single unit for federal tax purposes. For instance, despite requiring individual return filing,[26] the federal gift and estate taxes both treat married couples as a unit by refraining from taxing transfers of property until the property leaves the marital unit.[27] The gift tax also allows married couples to split gifts to third parties between them for reporting purposes.[28] Furthermore, through the medium of the deduction for medical expenses, the federal income tax actually goes so far as to corporealize the family by treating it as a separate and distinct body.[29]

Like C corporations, married couples experience different tax consequences as a result of being treated as a taxable unit. As mentioned above, the separate taxation of corporations allegedly causes investments to be taxed more heavily when made in corporate form than when made in noncorporate form (or even through a corporation making an S election).[30] Others point out, however, that the combination of our classical system of corporate taxation and a graduated rate schedule has actually created opportunities for well-advised, wealthy shareholders of privately held C corporations to shelter their income from taxation—achieving *better* tax results than could be

---

21 S. Rep. No. 97-144, at 127 (1981). Following the decision in *United States v. Windsor*, 133 S. Ct. 2675 (2013), the marriages of at least some same-sex couples will now be recognized for federal tax purposes. Nevertheless, some same-sex couples in evasive marriages as well as those in civil unions and domestic partnerships still may not have their relationships recognized for federal tax purposes. Anthony C. Infanti, *The Moonscape of Tax Equality:* Windsor *and Beyond*, 108 Nw. U. L. Rev. Colloquy 110 (2013); *see* Rev. Rul. 2013-17, 2013-38 I.R.B. 201. Moreover, even those same-sex couples whose marriages are recognized for federal tax purposes may find that their relationships are not treated fully equally. Infanti, *supra*.

22 *See* I.R.S. Pub. No. 1304, Individual Income Tax Returns 2010, at 39–40 tbl.1.2 (2012) (indicating that, for taxable year 2010, the number of married filing jointly returns was 53,526,090 while the number of married filing separately returns was 2,532,292).

23 Treas. Reg. § 1.6013-4(b).

24 I.R.C. §§ 6012, 6013(a).

25 *Id.* § 1(g).

26 *Id.* §§ 6018, 6019.

27 *Id.* §§ 2056, 2523.

28 *Id.* § 2513.

29 *See generally* Anthony C. Infanti, *Dismembering Families*, *in* Challenging Gender Inequality in Tax Policy Making: Comparative Perspectives 159 (Kim Brooks et al. eds., 2011).

30 Jeffrey L. Kwall, *The Uncertain Case Against the Double Taxation of Corporate Income*, 68 N.C. L. Rev. 613, 623 (1990).

achieved if the entity were treated as fiscally transparent for federal tax purposes.[31] Similarly, joint filing can produce tax advantages or disadvantages depending upon the individual circumstances of the married couple.

Some married couples suffer a tax detriment as a result of joint filing. These couples—generally speaking, those with relatively equal individual incomes—pay a so-called marriage penalty; that is, they pay more tax than they would have paid had they not married.[32] Since 2000, there has been movement toward reducing the marriage penalty.[33] Nevertheless, so long as the married couple remains a taxable unit and the income tax adheres to a progressive rate schedule, some form of tax penalty based on marital status—whether a marriage penalty or a singles penalty—will persist because any reduction in the marriage penalty will come at the expense of unmarried taxpayers, who will pay correspondingly more tax.[34]

Even though some married couples pay a penalty as a result of joint filing, other married couples—generally, those with a large disparity in individual incomes—actually receive a marriage bonus.[35] For example, a married couple in which one spouse works in the paid labor force and the other works in the home caring for the family pays less tax than the spouse working for a wage would have paid had they not married. This marriage bonus is compounded by the concomitant exclusion of the value of the stay-at-home spouse's services from the income tax base.[36]

The married couple is treated as a single unit for purposes aside from filing and applying the rate schedule, again producing advantages or disadvantages that vary from married couple to married couple. For example, provisions in the income, estate, and gift taxes allow spouses (and, in some cases, former spouses) to transfer property to each other without the payment of tax.[37] However, a natural corollary of avoiding income tax on any appreciation in transferred property is the denial of a deduction for the loss associated with any depreciation in the property.[38] For income tax purposes, these rules apply regardless of whether the couple files their tax return together or separately (separate returns are mandatory for gift and estate tax purposes).[39]

Families as Aggregates

When moving beyond the "core" of the married couple and their minor children, the extended family is not seen as a separate, cohesive unit, but as a group of individuals acting together in

---

31 *See generally* John W. Lee, *A Populist Perspective of the Business Tax Entities Universe: "Hey the Stars Might Lie but the Numbers Never Do,"* 78 Tex. L. Rev. 885 (2000).

32 Boris I. Bittker & Lawrence Lokken, Federal Taxation of Income, Estates and Gifts ¶ 111.3.2(1) (2013).

33 Economic Growth and Tax Relief Reconciliation Act of 2001, Pub. L. No. 107-16, §§ 301–303, 115 Stat. 38, 53–57 [hereinafter EGTRRA 2001]; *see* Jobs and Growth Tax Relief Reconciliation Act of 2003, Pub. L. No. 108-27, §§ 102–103, 117 Stat. 752, 754 (accelerating the tax relief provided in EGTRRA 2001); Tax Relief, Unemployment Insurance Reauthorization, and Job Creation Act of 2010, Pub. L. No. 111-312, § 101, 124 Stat. 3296, 3298 (extending the EGTRRA 2001 tax relief); American Taxpayer Relief Act of 2012, Pub. L. No. 112-240, § 101(a), 126 Stat. 2313, 2315–16 (making the EGTRRA 2001 tax relief permanent).

34 Bittker & Lokken, *supra* note 32, ¶ 111.3.5; Lawrence Zelenak, *Marriage and the Income Tax*, 67 S. Cal. L. Rev. 339, 339, 342 (1994).

35 Bittker & Lokken, *supra* note 32, ¶ 111.3.2.

36 *See* Dorothy A. Brown, *The Marriage Bonus/Penalty in Black and White*, 65 U. Cin. L. Rev. 787, 794 (1997).

37 I.R.C. §§ 1041, 2043(b)(2), 2056, 2516, 2523.

38 *Id.* § 1041(a).

39 *Id.*; Temp. Treas. Reg. § 1.1041-1T(a), Q&A-2, ex. 2; *see supra* note 26 and accompanying text.

their common interest. That is, they are treated more like fiscally transparent S corporations or partnerships than like C corporations for federal tax purposes.

For federal tax purposes, the extended family generally begins with the married couple and their children and then expands to varying degrees beyond this core.[40] For instance, only one of the two primary attribution rules in the Code includes among the taxpayer's family her brothers and sisters, grandparents and more distant ascendants, and great grandchildren and more distant descendants.[41] Neither of these attribution rules includes aunts, uncles, nieces, nephews, cousins, stepparents, or stepchildren among a taxpayer's family.[42] By embracing both the core and (to varying degrees) extended families, these rules parallel the partnership tax rules in their blending of entity and aggregate views of the family.[43]

And, as is the case with partnerships, extended families are afforded a great deal of flexibility in arranging their affairs. One of the hallmarks of the partnership tax regime is how it "permit[s] taxpayers to conduct joint business (including investment) activities through a *flexible* economic arrangement without incurring an entity-level tax."[44] Accordingly, the partnership tax rules generally respect the allocation of items of income, deduction, and credit set by the partners, so long as the partners bear the economic consequences of those allocations.[45] Like partners in a partnership, extended family members are generally afforded a great deal of flexibility in arranging their affairs. Absent a specific rule, intrafamily transactions are treated the same as transactions between unrelated persons—no matter how close the personal or emotional ties might actually be between the parties to the transaction.[46]

When the federal tax laws take extended family into account, they generally do so for one of two purposes: either (1) to prevent abuse of the tax laws; or (2) to remove tax impediments to intrafamily transactions. This is similar to the tax treatment of partnerships, as the Code contains both rules designed to prevent partners from taking undue advantage of the partnership tax regime and rules designed to facilitate partners' access to, and use of, that regime. For example, an entire constellation of rules in subchapter K aims to prevent partners from using the partnership form to convert ordinary income into capital gain.[47] In contrast, other provisions permit partners to contribute property to a partnership without the recognition of gain or loss and to receive distributions of property from the partnership (other than cash or cash equivalents) without recognition of gain or loss.[48] This tax-free treatment eases entry into and exit from partnership form, as contributions and distributions would otherwise be taxable events.[49] (Notably, the cognate

---

40 *See generally* Bridget J. Crawford, *The Profits and Penalties of Kinship: Conflicting Meanings of Family in Estate Tax Law*, 3 PITT. TAX REV. 1 (2005).

41 *Compare* I.R.C. § 267(c)(4), *with id.* § 318(a)(1); *see* Treas. Reg. § 1.267(c)-1(a)(4).

42 *Cf.* I.R.C. §§ 267(c)(4), 318(a)(1).

43 WILLIAM S. MCKEE ET AL., FEDERAL TAXATION OF PARTNERSHIPS AND PARTNERS ¶ 1.02 (2012).

44 Treas. Reg. § 1.701-2(a) (emphasis added).

45 *Id.* § 1.704-1(b)(2)(ii)(a), (iii)(a).

46 *See* Graves Bros. Co. v. Comm'r, 17 T.C. 1499, 1507 (1952) ("[T]he respondent … urges that because of the close blood and personal relationship between the two families, the stock interests of the families should be combined for the purpose of deciding this issue. This is not permissible under the statute.").

47 *E.g.*, I.R.C. §§ 707(b)(2), 724, 735(a), 751. For a lively debate about subchapter K, see chapters 8 and 9 of this volume.

48 *E.g.*, I.R.C. §§ 721, 731.

49 *Cf. id.* § 1001 (generally providing that the sale or other disposition of property is both a realization and a recognition event); Cottage Sav. Ass'n v. Comm'r, 499 U.S. 554, 560–67 (1991) (broadly defining a "disposition" for purposes of § 1001).

provisions applicable to C corporations and their shareholders do not provide as easy entry into or exit from the corporate form.[50])

With regard to family, tax rules are often crafted to prevent family members from obtaining undue tax advantages through manipulation of Code provisions that are premised on the notion that taxpayers are purely self-interested. Thus, there are many attribution rules in the Code that recognize that family members will act together in their common interest to achieve tax savings in ways that they would not with unrelated individuals.[51] These attribution rules will often treat one family member as owning the property of other family members or essentially ignore the transfer of property from one family member to another in order to prevent family members from acting together to obtain undue tax advantages.[52]

Other tax rules are designed to prevent families from being harmed when they diffuse wealth or property ownership among family members and run afoul of tax provisions that are premised on the same notion that taxpayers are entirely self-interested. For instance, access to the S corporation tax regime is limited to "closely held" companies. To avoid disadvantaging families who widely disseminate stock ownership in a company among family, a special attribution rule treats an extremely broad group of family members as a single shareholder for purposes of applying this limitation.[53] This broad attribution rule ensures that families can obtain the benefits of this tax regime notwithstanding a decision to widely diffuse ownership of property within the family.

Disregarded Families

Some families are not taken into account at all for federal tax purposes. In other words, they are treated much like the foreign corporations whose separate entity status is sometimes conveniently disregarded or the disregarded entities that are a creature of the "check-the-box" entity-classification regulations. Particularly with regard to so-called tax nothings, conventional wisdom seems to hold that being ignored or disregarded is a wonderful thing.

In keeping with the general theme of simplification that permeated the check-the-box regulations, the IRS decided to permit entities with a single owner to be disregarded for federal tax purposes.[54] Taxpayers and their advisors, however, viewed the advent of disregarded entities as a planning boon. One practitioner described how "the legitimacy of tax nothings permitted significant self-help efficiency and simplification by enabling taxpayers to avoid consolidated returns, S corporations, and title-holding companies, reduce state and foreign tax liabilities, enhance loss and foreign tax credit utilization, maintain active trade or business status, and improve asset

50 *See* I.R.C. §§ 301 (generally making distributions of property by a corporation taxable events for shareholders); 311(b) (taxing corporations on the distribution of appreciated property to shareholders); 351 (affording nonrecognition treatment upon a contribution of property to a corporation only if the contribution is made by one or more persons possessing at least 80 percent control of the corporation immediately after the exchange).

51 For an enumeration of these many attribution rules, see Anthony C. Infanti, *Inequitable Administration: Documenting Family for Tax Purposes*, 22 Colum. J. Gender & L. 329, 378–411 (2011).

52 *E.g.*, I.R.C. §§ 108(e)(4), 302(c), 1031(f).

53 *E.g.*, *id.* § 1361(c)(1).

54 Simplification of Entity Classification Rules, 61 Fed. Reg. 21,989, 21,990 (proposed May 13, 1996) (to be codified at 26 C.F.R. pt. 301).

securitization structures."[55] This same practitioner then noted that "[t]ax nothings also presented a powerful international tax planning tool."[56]

But where taxpayers and their advisors saw a neatly wrapped gift box from the federal government, the IRS realized that beneath the wrapping they had actually made a gift of a Pandora's box filled with tax problems that would bedevil the agency for years to come. Congress and the IRS quickly began to take steps to rein in perceived abuses.[57] Not all of those efforts have been successful,[58] but the problems for the IRS and the need to issue guidance to prevent abuse both continue.[59]

Similarly, conventional wisdom seems to hold that those whose familial relationships are ignored for federal tax purposes are better off for it—after all, they avoid the storied tax disadvantages associated with familial relationships (e.g., the marriage penalty and antiabuse rules that turn on marital status). The most obvious example of a familial relationship that is ignored for federal tax purposes is the relationship of an unmarried couple. Prior to the U.S. Supreme Court's invalidation of section three of the federal Defense of Marriage Act in *United States v. Windsor*,[60] all same-sex relationships fell into this category. In the wake of the *Windsor* decision, interesting (and, for same-sex couples, potentially quite vexing and burdensome) questions have arisen regarding which same-sex couples will continue to fall into the category of "unmarried" and which will have their relationships recognized (and to what extent) for federal tax purposes.[61]

Feeding into (or echoing) the conventional wisdom, some commentators have focused overwhelmingly (and, in my opinion, troublingly[62]) on the ability of unmarried same-sex couples not only to avoid the tax disadvantages associated with marriage but also to actively reap unwarranted advantages from the tax system.[63] In popular discourse, this conventional wisdom has been fueled by a widely cited Congressional Budget Office report "estimating that, if the federal government and all fifty states were to recognize same-sex marriage, there would be a small, positive impact on

55 Daniel S. Miller, *The Strange Materialization of the Tax Nothing*, 87 Tax Notes 685, 686 (2000). For other descriptions of the tax planning that is possible using disregarded entities, see Alice G. Abreu, *Domestic Tax Planning with Disregarded Entities: Paradise Found* 25–54 (2009), *available at* 2009 ABATAX-CLE 0924019 (Westlaw); Richard Wild & Michael Hirschfeld, *Check-the-Box Knows No Boundaries (At Least, for the Moment)—2002 Update*, at *134–49, *155–65 (2002), *available at* SH036 ALI-ABA 123 (Westlaw).

56 Miller, *supra* note 55, at 686.

57 *Id.* at 686–87.

58 *E.g.*, Changes in Entity Classification: Special Rule for Certain Foreign Eligible Entities, 64 Fed. Reg. 66,591 (proposed Nov. 29, 1999) (to be codified at 26 C.F.R. pt. 301) (permitting the IRS to treat a foreign disregarded entity as a corporation in the event of an "extraordinary transaction"), *withdrawn by* I.R.S. Notice 2003-46, 2003-2 C.B. 53 (responding to comments that the regulations were overbroad, but indicating that the IRS would continue to use other tools at its disposal to attack abuses of the check-the-box regulations); *see generally* Lee A. Sheppard, *Putting Checks on the Check-the-Box Rules*, 85 Tax Notes 1353 (1999).

59 *E.g.*, Treas. Reg. § 1.752-2(k) (proscribing potential planning opportunities with regard to the sharing of partnership liabilities); *see generally* Lee A. Sheppard, *A Look at Obama's International Proposals*, 123 Tax Notes 651 (2009).

60 1 U.S.C. § 7 (2013), *invalidated by* United States v. Windsor, 133 S. Ct. 2675 (2013).

61 *See generally* Infanti, *supra* note 21.

62 *See* Anthony C. Infanti, *Bringing Sexual Orientation and Gender Identity into the Tax Classroom*, 59 J. Legal Educ. 3, 15–16 (2009).

63 *E.g.*, Anthony Rickey, *Loving Couples, Split Interests: Tax Planning in the Fight to Recognize Same-Sex Marriage*, 23 Berkeley J. Gender L. & Just. 145 (2008); Theodore P. Seto, *The Unintended Tax Advantages of Gay Marriage*, 65 Wash. & Lee L. Rev. 1529 (2008).

federal tax revenues"—even though this study admits to being based on incomplete information and may be based on questionable assumptions.[64]

Just as the IRS quickly realized that the gift of the check-the-box regulations would bedevil them for years to come, some commentators looked past the conventional wisdom regarding the advantages associated with ignoring same-sex couples' relationships for federal tax purposes. These commentators painted a much more complex picture that underscored the inability of same-sex couples (then and now) to reap the tax advantages associated with marriage as well as the intolerable burdens and stigma imposed by the uncertainty surrounding how they should be treated for federal tax purposes.[65] These commentators also focused on the privileging of marriage in the tax laws and how it operated (and still operates) to exclude so many "others" from consideration in the formation of tax policy.[66]

Tax Reform Debates

As described in the previous section of this chapter, there are strong parallels in the taxation of familial and business entities. Both types of entities are sociolegal constructions that are taxed in a variety of different (but, at the same time, very similar) ways—from being treated as a separate entity, to being treated as an aggregation of individuals, to being disregarded altogether. Against this background, we can now consider the debates regarding the reform of corporate and familial taxation. Interestingly, rather than containing similar parallels, these two reform debates sharply contrast with each other.

Corporate Tax Reform

Commentators have sharply criticized the distortions created by imposing a nominally heavier tax burden on taxable corporations than on fiscally transparent business entities (i.e., partnerships and disregarded entities). Whether these critiques take aim at repealing the corporate-level or the shareholder-level tax associated with investments made through C corporations, they all generally aim at—or, at the very least, leave the door wide open to—integration of these two taxes. The main subject of debate for tax academics is not whether to impose a "double" tax on corporate investments but whether it is better to eliminate the corporate-level or the shareholder-level tax. It is the rare academic who defends imposing tax at both the corporate and shareholder levels.[67]

The arguments in favor of integrating the corporate and individual income taxes are so well accepted that integration "has long had the enthusiastic backing of academic observers, professional

---

64 Infanti, *supra* note 62, at 27; *see* CONG. BUDGET OFFICE, THE POTENTIAL BUDGETARY IMPACT OF RECOGNIZING SAME-SEX MARRIAGES 2, 3 (2004).

65 *E.g.*, Patricia A. Cain, *Heterosexual Privilege and the Internal Revenue Code*, 34 U.S.F. L. REV. 465 (2000); Patricia A. Cain, *Taxation of Domestic Partner Benefits: The Hidden Costs*, 45 U.S.F. L. REV. 481 (2010); Anthony C. Infanti, *The Internal Revenue Code as Sodomy Statute*, 44 SANTA CLARA L. REV. 763 (2004); Anthony C. Infanti, *LGBT Families, Tax Nothings*, 17 J. GENDER RACE & JUST. 35 (2014).

66 *See generally, e.g.*, Anthony C. Infanti, *Decentralizing Family: An Inclusive Proposal for Individual Tax Filing in the United States*, 2010 UTAH L. REV. 605; Infanti, *supra* note 21; Nancy J. Knauer, *Heteronormativity and Federal Tax Policy*, 101 W. VA. L. REV. 129 (1998).

67 *E.g.*, Terrence R. Chorvat, *Apologia for the Double Taxation of Corporate Income*, 38 WAKE FOREST L. REV. 239 (2003); Kwall, *supra* note 30; Herwig J. Schlunk, *I Come Not to Praise the Corporate Income Tax, but to Save It*, 56 TAX L. REV. 329 (2003).

groups, various Treasury Department reports, and several presidential administrations."[68] Indeed, in response to a general mandate in the Tax Reform Act of 1986 to study reform of the corporate income tax, the U.S. Department of the Treasury chose to undertake "a comprehensive study of the issues presented by integration of the corporate and individual income tax."[69] Interestingly, the text of this study ran more than 150 pages (with more than 100 additional pages of appendices, notes, etc.); yet, only about 14 pages (much of which is taken up with tables and figures) were devoted to actually making the case for integrating the corporate and individual income taxes.[70] In those few pages, Treasury argued in favor of reducing the tax burden on corporate investments as a means of increasing economic efficiency. Reducing the corporate tax burden, it argued, would reduce distortions in the choice between (1) noncorporate versus corporate form for business entities (the corporate income tax creates a bias in favor of noncorporate form); (2) financing corporations with debt versus equity (the deductibility of interest payments creates a bias in favor of debt financing of corporations); and (3) retaining or distributing corporate earnings (the taxation of dividends at both the corporate and shareholder levels creates a bias in favor of retaining earnings).[71]

Several months later, Treasury recommended that these taxes be integrated by adopting a dividend exclusion system coupled with optional dividend reinvestment plans to reduce the incentive to distribute (rather than retain) earnings.[72] This approach to integration would eliminate the shareholder-level tax on corporate investments. Others advocated replacing the corporate income tax with a corporate-level tax on the changes in market value of publicly traded entities on the theory that they comprise the lion's share of taxpaying C corporations, providing another option for implementing integration by eliminating the shareholder-level tax.[73] Yet others proposed the elimination of the corporate tax in favor of the enactment of a shareholder-level, mark-to-market regime for publicly traded stock.[74]

These latter proposals are in keeping with other calls for integration through the elimination of the corporate income tax.[75] In Chapter 10, Yariv Brauner issues just such a call. By way of background, Brauner summarizes the policy rationales articulated in support of the corporate tax, traces the history of the corporation, summarizes research on the incidence of the corporate tax, and dissects the arguments that have traditionally been made in support of the corporate tax.

---

68 Jennifer Arlen & Deborah M. Weiss, *A Political Theory of Corporate Taxation*, 105 Yale L.J. 325, 330 (1995).

69 Letter from Kenneth W. Gideon, Assistant Sec'y (Tax Policy), U.S. Dep't of Treasury, to Dan Rostenkowski, Chair, Comm. on Ways & Means, U.S. House of Representatives (Jan. 1992), *in* U.S. Dep't of Treasury, *supra* note 17, at ii.

70 U.S. Dep't of Treasury, *supra* note 17, at 1–14.

71 *Id.* at 3; *see id.* at 3–11 (explaining these three types of distortion).

72 U.S. Dep't of Treasury, A Recommendation for Integration of the Individual and Corporate Tax Systems 2 (1992).

73 *E.g.*, Joseph Bankman, *A Market-Value Based Corporate Income Tax*, 68 Tax Notes 1347 (1995); Michael S. Knoll, *An Accretion Corporate Income Tax*, 49 Stan. L. Rev. 1 (1996).

74 *E.g.*, Joseph M. Dodge, *A Combined Mark-to-Market and Pass-Through Corporate-Shareholder Integration Proposal*, 50 Tax L. Rev. 265 (1995); *see* David A. Weisbach, *A Partial Mark-to-Market Tax System*, 53 Tax L. Rev. 95, 115–21, 129–31 (1999) (explicating the benefits of accompanying a shift to a mark-to-market tax regime for publicly traded property with integration of the corporate- and shareholder-level income taxes).

75 Reuven S. Avi-Yonah, *Corporations, Society, and the State: A Defense of the Corporate Tax*, 90 Va. L. Rev. 1193, 1197 (2004); Yariv Brauner, *The Non-sense Tax: A Reply to New Corporate Income Tax Advocacy*, 2008 Mich. St. L. Rev. 591; Anthony P. Polito, *Advancing to Corporate Tax Integration: A Laissez-Faire Approach*, 55 S.C. L. Rev. 1 (2003).

Ultimately, Brauner makes a move one might expect more from a critical tax scholar and argues that conservatives should support (rather than oppose) and liberals should oppose (rather than support) the corporate tax. Brauner argues that liberals should advocate repeal of the corporate tax (and its replacement by a mere withholding mechanism for the individual income tax) because it would lead to greater redistribution of income.

Despite the rising tide in favor of repeal or integration of the corporate income tax, the tax persists. Commentators have advanced a variety of explanations for the tax's tenacity. The most widely accepted explanation is the divergence of interests between shareholders (who would prefer integration of the taxes) and corporate managers (who do not).[76] Michael Doran argues, however, that it is not the differing interests between these two groups but the complex patchwork of differing interests among shareholders, among managers, and among interested third parties that stymies attempts at integrating these taxes.[77] In contrast, Reuven Avi-Yonah and others ascribe the longevity of the tax to the political popularity of the tax; that is, because "ordinary Americans have a viscerally negative reaction to the notion that large, profitable corporations should pay no tax while they bear the income tax burden."[78]

Notwithstanding these overtly political explanations for the continued existence of the tax, respected commentators have taken up the cause of making policy arguments in favor of imposing tax on corporations—but not necessarily of maintaining our current system of "double" taxation. Notably, Reuven Avi-Yonah has surveyed the existing defenses of the corporate tax and the conceptualizations of the corporation that underpin them—namely, the alternating views of the corporation as an artificial creation of the state, as a mere aggregation of its individual shareholders, or as a real entity separate from its owners and controlled by its managers.[79] After surveying these defenses of the corporate income tax, Avi-Yonah pronounced them unconvincing.[80]

In their place, Avi-Yonah defends the corporate income tax on the ground that corporations are "real" entities controlled by their managers and, as such, the corporate income tax is justifiable as "a means to control the excessive accumulation of power in the hands of corporate management."[81] In this regard, Avi-Yonah maintains that the corporate income tax can serve both a limiting and a regulatory function.[82] It limits the power of management by reducing the amount of the corporation's wealth, which is the "foundation of managerial power."[83] Because, absent a confiscatory tax, the corporation's wealth can still continue to grow, the corporate income tax rate can be used to influence how management uses corporate resources by increasing (or threatening to increase) the tax rate on disfavored activities or by lowering the tax rate on favored activities.[84] Though

76 Michael Doran, *Managers, Shareholders, and the Corporate Double Tax*, 95 Va. L. Rev. 517, 522 (2009); *see generally* Arlen & Weiss, *supra* note 68.

77 *See generally* Doran, *supra* note 76.

78 Avi-Yonah, *supra* note 75, at 1211; *see* Arlen & Weiss, *supra* note 68, at 331 & n.21.

79 *See* Avi-Yonah, *supra* note 75, at 1197–1212 (surveying the current defenses of the corporate tax); Reuven S. Avi-Yonah, *The Cyclical Transformations of the Corporate Form: A Historical Perspective on Corporate Social Responsibility*, 30 Del. J. Corp. L. 767, 772–813 (2005) (describing the different conceptualizations of the corporation).

80 Avi-Yonah, *supra* note 75, at 1210.

81 *Id.* at 1244.

82 *Id.* at 1246.

83 *Id.* at 1247.

84 *Id.* at 1248–49.

he defends the corporate income tax, Avi-Yonah leaves the door wide open to the possibility of integrating the corporate and individual income taxes.[85]

Writing from a Canadian perspective, Richard Bird has made the weak case for imposing tax on corporations.[86] Bird sets forth a farrago of different arguments that, in his view, can be cobbled together in support of taxing corporations. He groups these arguments under three different headings. First, Bird articulates reasons why it may be desirable to tax corporations; for example, to exact compensation for the negative impacts of their activities, to tax pure profits, or to export taxation to nonvoters.[87] Next, Bird articulates reasons why it may be necessary to tax corporations; for example, to backstop the individual income tax or because departing too far from the international norm of imposing a corporate income tax may jeopardize investment, tax revenue, or the creditability of the country's taxes elsewhere.[88] Finally, Bird articulates reasons why it may be convenient to tax corporations; for example, because corporations are an administratively convenient tax collection device, taxes on corporations are politically popular, or to influence corporations' economic behavior.[89] Like Avi-Yonah, Bird leaves wide open the question of whether the corporate and individual income taxes should be integrated.[90]

Reforming Taxation of the Family

One of the key areas of debate in the taxation of the family is whether to repeal joint filing by married couples—the aspect of family taxation that, as described above, is most akin to the treatment of C corporations as separate taxable entities for federal tax purposes. Many commentators—myself included—have advocated repeal of joint filing and its replacement with an individual filing system. But, in contrast to the corporate tax reform debate, contributors on both sides of the debate over joint filing aim not to roll back the special treatment of the married couple, but to maintain it, tweak it, or even expand it.

Those who oppose joint filing and favor separate filing have articulated many and varied reasons in support of their position. Some have called into question the assumption upon which joint filing is based; namely, that married couples—and only married couples—pool their income.[91] Others point out that joint filing is inconsistent with the choice to impose an income (rather than a consumption) tax. Tax liability under an income tax generally turns on the control of income; however, by treating the married couple as a unit, joint filing has tax liability turn on the shared consumption of income (regardless of which spouse controls that income).[92] In a similar vein, yet

85 *Id.* at 1254.

86 Richard M. Bird, *Why Tax Corporations?*, 56 Bull. for Int'l Fiscal Documentation 194 (2002).

87 *Id.* at 195–98.

88 *Id.* at 198–99.

89 *Id.* at 199–201.

90 *Id.* at 199 n.36.

91 *See generally* Marjorie E. Kornhauser, *Love, Money, and the IRS: Family, Income-Sharing, and the Joint Income Tax Return*, 45 Hastings L.J. 63 (1997); *see also* Pamela B. Gann, *Abandoning Marital Status as a Factor in Allocating Income Tax Burdens*, 59 Tex. L. Rev. 1, 31 (1980); Jeannette Anderson Winn & Marshall Winn, *Till Death Do We Split: Married Couples and Single Persons Under the Individual Income Tax*, 34 S.C. L. Rev. 829, 851 (1983); Laura Ann Davis, Note, *A Feminist Justification for the Adoption of an Individual Filing System*, 62 S. Cal. L. Rev. 197, 216–17 (1988).

92 Kornhauser, *supra* note 91, at 109; Zelenak, *supra* note 34, at 354–58.

others have noted the many problems and inequities associated with the joint and several liability for tax obligations that is associated with joint filing.[93]

Probably the most trenchant critique of joint filing focuses on the disincentive effects on secondary earners entering the paid labor market.[94] As I have explained elsewhere, "[t]his disincentive results because the aggregation of the couple's income causes the secondary earner's wages effectively to be taxed beginning at the primary earner's marginal tax rate, depriving her of the benefit of the zero bracket amount and the lower initial brackets in the tax rate schedule (which have already been applied to, and exhausted by, the primary earner's income)."[95] The obverse of the tax disincentive to working in the market is a tax incentive to perform unpaid work in the home. In the literature, the group of secondary earners who are encouraged to work in the home is generally thought of as being composed of women; however, Dorothy Brown has shown that a closer analysis—one that considers not only gender but also race and class—reveals that women in some groups are actually a couple's primary or equal earner.[96]

Commentators have put forth a range of additional arguments against joint filing. A sampling includes: the achievement of a marriage-neutral income tax that would alleviate the stigmatization of single people,[97] the elimination of the administrative burden created by the numerous rules for determining whether a taxpayer is married for tax purposes,[98] and the creation of "a salutary incentive for husbands to transfer property to their wives to achieve a measure of income splitting, which under the current joint filing system can be achieved without the actual sharing of property."[99] There have also been attacks on other aspects of the treatment of the married couple as a taxable unit, including feminist arguments against the so-called QTIP provisions in the estate tax.[100]

Despite the wide-ranging nature of these critiques, there is a common thread that runs through them. The general aim of these critiques is to better tailor the special tax treatment of the family to economic reality and tax policy norms, while simultaneously addressing gender equality issues that have long plagued the institution of marriage. Thus, although these proposals may advocate the repeal of joint filing, they do *not* advocate wholesale elimination of the special treatment of the family from the tax laws.[101] Indeed, most commentators do not even consider "the appropriate design for an individual filing system. In the few cases where commentators have explored how one might implement an individual filing system, they have focused their attention almost exclusively

93 *See generally* Amy C. Christian, *Joint and Several Liability and the Joint Return: Its Implications for Women*, 66 U. Cin. L. Rev. 535 (1998); Lily Kahng, *Innocent Spouses: A Critique of the New Tax Laws Governing Joint and Several Liability*, 49 Vill. L. Rev. 261 (2004).

94 *E.g.*, Grace Blumberg, *Sexism in the Code: A Comparative Study of Income Taxation of Working Wives and Mothers*, 21 Buff. L. Rev. 49, 88–95 (1971); Amy C. Christian, *The Joint Return Rate Structure: Identifying and Addressing the Gendered Nature of the Tax Law*, 13 J.L. & Pol. 241, 287–303 (1997); Edward J. McCaffery, *Taxation and the Family: A Fresh Look at Behavioral Gender Biases in the Code*, 40 UCLA L. Rev. 983, 989–96, 1014–29 (1993).

95 Infanti, *supra* note 66, at 616.

96 Dorothy A. Brown, *Race, Class, and Gender Essentialism in Tax Literature: The Joint Return*, 54 Wash. & Lee L. Rev. 1469, 1488–1507 (1997).

97 *See generally* Lily Kahng, *One Is the Loneliest Number: The Single Taxpayer in a Joint Return World*, 61 Hastings L.J. 651 (2010).

98 *See generally* Toni Robinson & Mary Moers Wenig, *Marry in Haste, Repent at Tax Time: Marital Status as a Tax Determinant*, 8 Va. Tax Rev. 773 (1989).

99 Infanti, *supra* note 66, at 618.

100 *See generally* Wendy C. Gerzog, *The Marital Deduction QTIP Provisions: Illogical and Degrading to Women*, 5 UCLA Women's L.J. 301 (1995).

101 *See, e.g.*, *supra* notes 26–29 and accompanying text.

on whether—and, if so, how—that system should continue to accommodate financial transactions between … spouses."[102] My own work in this area, which has taken up the challenge of fashioning an individual filing regime, does *not* seek to eliminate the special treatment of the family in the tax laws. To the contrary, it attempts to widen the scope of that special treatment by allowing taxpayers to choose for themselves who will be counted as "family" for tax purposes.[103]

Others have actively defended the joint filing regime as the best means of preserving the special tax treatment of the core of the family. One commentator has argued that joint filing is necessary to staunch rampant tax avoidance by married couples—a phenomenon that existed prior to the adoption of joint filing in 1948 and that might resurface under any new individual filing regime.[104] This same commentator further asserted that "there remains something unique about the married couple that warrants unique tax treatment. That unique something about marriage that makes tax avoidance more likely also makes the couple the best measure of the collective's ability to pay taxes."[105] Another commentator has not only embraced joint filing but would expand the taxable unit to fully include married couples' children.[106] In addition, many of those who have been concerned with the inequitable treatment of same-sex couples under the federal tax laws have likewise embraced the joint filing regime and advocated its extension (in one form or another) to same-sex couples.[107]

Public–Private Divide

As the previous sections of this chapter have demonstrated, there are striking parallels between the taxation of the corporation and the family, and there are lively debates about how to reform the taxation of both of these sociolegal constructions. But the parallels end there, as the two reform debates take widely divergent courses. In this section, we will explore, interrogate, and work to erase the public–private divide between these tax reform debates.

The Public Side of the Divide

As described above, the strong consensus in the corporate tax debate is to level down. In other words, faced with a legal landscape in which corporations are subject to "double" taxation and partnerships and disregarded entities are subject to only a single layer of taxation, commentators generally argue that we should eliminate one of the two layers of tax on corporate investments. Commentators differ on how to reach this result (e.g., whether to retain or repeal the corporate income tax), but they generally agree that we should equalize the tax burden on these different forms of capital investment by reducing the burden on corporate investment.

102 Infanti, *supra* note 66, at 621–22 (footnotes omitted).

103 *See generally id.*

104 *See generally* Stephanie Hunter McMahon, *To Have and to Hold: What Does Love (of Money) Have to Do with Joint Tax Filing?*, 11 Nev. L.J. 718 (2011).

105 *Id.* at 721–22.

106 *See generally* Stephanie Hoffer, *Adopting the Family Taxable Unit*, 76 U. Cin. L. Rev. 55 (2007).

107 *E.g.*, Patricia A. Cain, *Taxing Families Fairly*, 48 Santa Clara L. Rev. 805, 851–55 (2008); Shari Motro, *A New "I Do": Towards a Marriage-Neutral Income Tax*, 91 Iowa L. Rev. 1509, 1543–52 (2006); Keeva Terry, *Separate and Still Unequal? Taxing California Registered Domestic Partners*, 39 U. Tol. L. Rev. 633, 649–52 (2008).

However, equalizing the tax burden on different forms of capital investment does not necessarily mean minimizing or erasing that burden. When the check-the-box regulations were proposed, the preamble to the regulations explained: "One consequence of the increased flexibility under local law in forming a partnership or other unincorporated business organization is that taxpayers generally can achieve partnership tax classification for a nonpublicly traded organization that, in all meaningful respects, is virtually indistinguishable from a corporation."[108] But if these new entities are "virtually indistinguishable" from corporations, why not classify them as corporations rather than as partnerships or disregarded entities? This question squarely raises the alternative of leveling up—that is, of equalizing the tax burden on the different forms of capital investment by imposing an entity level tax on *all* of them—instead of bowing to the conventional wisdom of reducing the tax burden on corporations to match that of partnerships and disregarded entities.

The Private Side of the Divide

In contrast, as discussed above in the context of proposals to abolish joint filing, the strong consensus in the family tax debate is to level out or level up. This is surprising given how "advantaged" the conventional wisdom portrays those whose personal relationships are disregarded for federal tax purposes (e.g., the same-sex couples who long escaped both the marriage penalty and the antiabuse rules that turn on marital status). Given how naturally the corporate tax debate leans toward leveling down, one might thus have expected to encounter the same inclination toward leveling down in the family tax debate.

Yet, those who advocate the elimination of joint filing do not do so to reduce the tax burden on married couples to equalize it with that of singles or those in disregarded relationships.[109] They advocate the separate reporting of items of income, deduction, and credit by spouses, but leave untouched the many other ways in which the tax laws treat the married couple as a taxable unit. Put differently, these commentators do not advocate removing the special account taken of married couples from the tax laws; rather, they propose adjusting it in a way that levels out that special treatment so that it better comports with tax policy norms and economic reality while addressing gender equality issues associated with marriage. In addition, many of those who have embraced joint filing advocate its expansion to cover other family forms (particularly, nontraditional families headed by same-sex couples). These commentators thus advocate leveling up the treatment of same-sex couples, whose relationships have historically been disregarded for federal tax purposes, by including them in the same category as married different-sex couples.

Erasing the Divide

Juxtaposing these two tax reform debates—one that strongly tends toward leveling down and another that strongly tends toward leveling out or up—naturally raises the question of why there is such a stark difference in approaches to reforming the taxation of such similar entities. It is certainly not because of a difference in analytical approach. After all, commentators in both debates approach reform from conventional tax policy perspectives, framing their discussions in terms of

108 Simplification of Entity Classification Rules, 61 Fed. Reg. 21,989, 21,990 (proposed May 13, 1996) (to be codified at 26 C.F.R. pt. 301).

109 In fact, joint filing provides a tax benefit to some married couples as compared with individual filing. *See supra* notes 35–36 and accompanying text.

tax equity, efficiency, or administratibility.[110] Perhaps the explanation lies in the public–private divide. Despite its general salience in the tax laws,[111] this divide has held little meaning up to this point in the analysis because of the strong similarities between the entities on opposing sides of the divide.

In the popular imagination, however, notions of the corporation and the family are of widely divergent levels of concreteness. How concrete each of these sociolegal constructions is varies inversely with their location along the public–private divide. In other words, the family, which is located on the private side of the divide, is far more concrete in the popular imagination than the corporation, which is located on the public side of the divide. This inversion is not unusual. As I have explained elsewhere, those in more public, legally recognized relationships have been afforded a privileged zone of privacy under the federal tax laws in the arrangement of their financial affairs, while those in more private, legally closeted relationships have been open to searching public scrutiny of their financial affairs by the IRS.[112]

Families can take different forms, some more "traditional" than others. And some feel more connection with the family that they have chosen for themselves than they do with their blood or adoptive relatives. But none of this detracts either from the conventional understanding of who composes one's family (i.e., those related by marriage, blood, or adoption) or from a particular individual's perception of who comes within the circle of her own family.[113] The inability to synthesize a single, all-encompassing definition of family does not signal a lack of concrete understanding of what the family is, but rather highlights the difficulty associated with reconciling the increasing diversity of individual understandings of who counts as family.[114] In light of this multiplicity of concrete starting points and the general importance of family in our lives, it is easy to understand why family relationships are taken into account for tax purposes and why the tax reform debate revolves around how encompassing the family circle ought to be.

The corporation, on the other hand, is far more amorphous. Douglas Litowitz has explored the social and cultural meaning of the corporation—and its infinite malleability—through the lens of religion and mythology.[115] Litowitz explains that corporate law acts as a mediator, bridging views of the corporation as "an economic set of relations as well as a social actor. We need the engine of large corporations for our nation to prosper … . Yet, we are appalled when these corporations engage in antisocial behavior in search of profits."[116] To defuse the tension between these inconsistent aspects

110 *E.g.*, Dodge, *supra* note 74, at 294–303; Kornhauser, *supra* note 91, at 105–11; Kwall, *supra* note 30, at 627–32, 641–44.

111 *See supra* note 3 and accompanying text.

112 Infanti, *supra* note 62, at 24–25.

113 Leslie A. Baxter et al., *Lay Conceptions of "Family": A Replication and Extension*, 9 J. Fam. Comm. 170, 187 (2009) (indicating that "the general pattern of findings suggests constancy in how 'family' is conceptualized" by laypersons).

114 *See id.* at 171–73 (discussing different conceptualizations of family among family communication scholars); *id.* at 187 (pointing to findings in their study that suggest some shifts in lay conceptualizations of family may be underway). *Compare* Kathleen M. Galvin, *Diversity's Impact on Defining the Family*, *in* The Family Communication Sourcebook 3 (Lynn H. Turner & Richard West eds., 2006) (recognizing the increasing diversity of families and its impact on defining the family), *with* Kory Floyd et al., *Defining the Family Through Relationships*, *in* The Family Communication Sourcebook, *supra*, at 21 (cautioning family communication scholars against generally embracing an inclusive definition of family that corresponds to individual conceptualizations of family because it risks conceptual obfuscation and does not acknowledge the importance of narrower sociolegal and biogenetic definitions).

115 Douglas Litowitz, *The Corporation as God*, 30 J. Corp. L. 501 (2005).

116 *Id.* at 507–08.

of the corporation, corporate law creates "a vague, hollow, catch-all entity of mythical proportions that subsumes these contradictory demands for profit and justice."[117] Litowitz goes on to explain:

> As an empty signifier, the corporation is all things to all people: it is a frugal profit-maximizer yet it doles out princely salaries to managers; it is "publicly-held" yet has no enforceable obligations to the community; it is a democracy yet it holds uncontested elections; its "transparency" is based on public filings yet its filings are indecipherable; it is a taxpaying citizen yet it can move overseas to avoid taxation; it is a person with Constitutional rights yet it cannot vote; it is subject to criminal law yet cannot be put into prison.[118]

Consistent with Litowitz's description, the corporation is all things to all people in the tax context. Reuven Avi-Yonah has recounted at length the historical alternation between the aggregate, artificial entity, and real entity theories of the corporation.[119] As the corporation has transformed through the centuries, "every time there was a shift in the role of the corporation, all three theories were brought forward in cyclical fashion."[120]

This merry-go-round of alternative conceptualizations of the corporation serves a role of mediation and legitimation in the leveling down of the taxation of the corporation. Endless debates over whether the corporation is most appropriately viewed as a real entity, an artificial entity, or an aggregate of its shareholders do little more than provide smoke and mirrors that hide efforts to reduce the tax burden on capital investments. Contributors to these debates engage in a constant tug of war over whether the corporate tax ought to burden (wealthy) shareholders (under the aggregate and artificial entity views) or restrain (wealthy) corporate managers (under the real entity view). They cannot seem to make up their minds about which of these two privileged groups should be burdened, making it easy to cover efforts not to burden either of them and to instead quietly shift the tax burden to lower- and middle-income taxpayers. All the while, "corporate law ratifies, enables, and sanctifies a corporate system of property holdings which leads to vast inequalities of power and shocking concentrations of capital in a few hands."[121]

Yet, corporations and families are both artificial, sociolegal constructions that are built around the coming together of individuals. When individuals come together, they have the potential to create something that is far more than just the sum of its parts. In the case of the family, the tax laws see and embrace the multidimensional relationships that can arise when individuals come together—that is, the tax laws simultaneously see the family as a set of individuals, as a group of persons acting together toward common goals, and as a separate entity of its own. As a result, the tax laws contain varying (and somewhat arbitrary) legal rules demarcating the boundary between the individual and the family, and tax policy debates revolve around how to most appropriately establish the contours of the family.[122] At the same time, the tax laws recognize that families are groups of individuals who come together for common benefit, providing tax benefits that facilitate the formation and operation of families.[123] In addition, the tax laws recognize that families are more than just a group of individuals and that, acting together, families can advance their

117 *Id.* at 508.
118 *Id.* at 508.
119 Avi-Yonah, *supra* note 79, at 772–813.
120 *Id.* at 771.
121 Litowitz, *supra* note 115, at 508.
122 *See, e.g.*, *supra* note 107 and accompanying text.
123 *E.g.*, I.R.C. §§ 21, 129, 213.

economic interests in ways that unrelated individuals cannot.[124] The family can potentially amass great wealth that can be passed from one generation to the next in perpetuity, consolidating their power and creating a dynasty.[125] The tax laws simultaneously see and embrace all of these different dimensions of the family. The debate over reforming the taxation of the family in no way revolves around choosing one—and only one—"authentic" view of the family.

In the current corporate tax reform debate, the same variety of dimensions of the corporation are seen; however, contributors to that debate feel the need to choose one dimension over all others as the most appropriate lens through which to view the corporation. Taking a page from our approach to the family, we need to ignore the smoke and mirrors and acknowledge that the corporation, as an empty signifier, is likewise all things simultaneously. It is not just an aggregate of its shareholders, an artificial creation of the state, *or* a real entity; instead, it is *all* of these things.

Once we finish erasing the public–private divide in this way, we will be free to carry the parallels in the tax treatment of families and corporations into the debates over reforming the taxation of these two sociolegal constructions. This will allow us to more easily treat corporations the same way that we treat families and to make distinctions between different levels of association or relationship for tax purposes. In other words, it will become easier to justify treating investments in corporate (or similar) form sometimes better and sometimes worse than noncorporate investments. It might also help us to see that to repeal or integrate the corporate income tax would be to inappropriately disregard the fact that the corporate whole can be greater than the sum of its parts.

Conclusion

In this chapter, I have argued that, rather than reifying the public–private divide in tax reform debates, we should erase that divide. We should acknowledge that there might be justifiable reasons for taxing corporations (and similar entities) differently from entities that represent a far looser connection among their constituent parts, just as we aim to draw distinctions between more tightly and less tightly knit family members. This is both a similar and a very different view from that taken by Yariv Brauner in Chapter 10 of this volume. And, drawing on the subtitle of this volume, it is a view that is produced by looking at the issue from a different perspective.

In Chapter 10, Brauner makes a nominally critical move by turning the world as we know it upside down. He argues that the traditional roles taken on by conservatives in opposition to the corporate tax and by liberals in support of that tax should actually be reversed. Brauner argues that the corporate tax does little more than act as a smokescreen for protecting power and that repealing the corporate tax would advance redistributionist goals. Yet, in between this critical move and his conclusion, Brauner engages in conventional argumentation that accepts the tax policy debate on its own terms.

Brauner paints a picture of the corporate tax as a subterfuge by employing conventional tax policy analysis—he considers the history of the corporation, the development of the corporate tax, and the incidence of the corporate tax. Against this background, Brauner weighs the different arguments made in support of the corporate tax and ultimately rejects them. In other words, he considers basically the same facts, arguments, and evidence as other scholars contributing to the

124 *See supra* notes 51–52 and accompanying text.

125 Indeed, one of the principal justifications for the estate and gift taxes is to break up such dynastic concentrations of wealth. *See* James R. Repetti, *The Case for the Estate and Gift Tax*, 86 Tax Notes 1493, 1497–1500 (2000).

debate over corporate tax reform, but simply takes a different view of the result dictated by those facts, arguments, and evidence than some others do.

Both Brauner and I agree that a subterfuge is being deployed to protect the power and prerogatives of a privileged few. But we see different subterfuges and we see them in different ways. For Brauner, the subterfuge is the corporate tax itself. He sees the corporate tax as a device conveniently used to appease those calling for corporations to pay their fair share of taxes while every effort is made to minimize (if not virtually eliminate) the actual impact of the tax on corporations. For me, the subterfuge is not really (or, at least, only) the corporate tax but the incessant (and incessantly shifting and unstable) debate over its reform.

Our methods for detecting these subterfuges also differ. Brauner comes at the debate over corporate tax reform from the "inside," engaging the debate on its own terms and within its own narrow focus. However, by coming at the corporate tax reform debate from the "outside," I prefer neither to engage with the facts and evidence generally considered by scholars contributing to this debate nor to engage with the debate in the generally accepted fashion. Instead, I aim to take a broader view that considers how this debate fits into other power structures in American society (i.e., the public–private divide) and to explore how those power structures influence the course of that debate (i.e., resulting in a general consensus to level down rather than level up, as in the analogous debate over reforming the taxation of the family).

Ultimately, however, I have less of a stake in the final outcome of the corporate tax reform debate than Brauner does. My goal, as is often the case, is not to advocate a specific policy prescription or solution but to influence the course of the debate. It should therefore come as little wonder that I have embraced the traditionally nontraditional (and oft-criticized by "mainstream" tax scholars) lack of a definitive policy prescription at the end of my chapter, focusing my energies instead on examining and revealing hidden imbalances of power. Perspective does seem to matter in the debate over corporate tax reform. Thus, even though we share a concern about the distribution of the tax burden, Brauner and I diverge significantly in our approaches to addressing this and other concerns in this context.

PART VI
Transfer Taxation

Chapter 12
Norms and Transfer Taxes

Joseph M. Dodge

Introduction

In this chapter, I attempt to sort out various norms as they apply to the taxation of gratuitous transfers. The norms themselves are taken as "given." That is, no attempt is made to justify or critique the norms in question. Rather, the task is to disentangle the norms and to ascertain their implications for the taxation of gratuitous transfers beyond the level of knee-jerk assertion and cliché. The norms in question will be brought to bear on the issue of whether gratuitous transfers should be taxed, and, if so, by what means. This chapter is not about wealth transfer tax doctrine or estate tax reform, although these topics are mentioned insofar as they impact on the choice of wealth transfer tax system.

My position is that norms are plural, and often lead in different directions. This chapter does not posit a "unified field theory" governed by an all-encompassing metanorm (such as welfarism or property rights), nor is it an advocacy piece premised on a single norm or political goal. I view norms in a way similar to the way they are seen by a sociologist or anthropologist. An individual's prioritization of norms would be based on emotion, perceived self-interest, ideological commitment, sense of fairness, group identity, or political affiliation. Additionally, norms may be invoked by an individual sincerely or cynically; that is, as a way of concealing a non-norm-based agenda, because norms are considered more high-minded and/or neutral than motives based on naked self-interest. Nevertheless, norms exist and are, these days, routinely invoked in academic and political discourse. In fact, it is bad form in legal academia to feign neutral disinterestedness by failing to spell out the norms one relies on.

With regard to taxation, I discern four categories of norms, two of which are internal to tax and two of which are external to tax but implicate society generally. The two internal-to-tax norm categories relate to (1) practicality, or perhaps administrative efficiency (i.e., whether the tax can perform its assigned tasks); and (2) tax fairness (i.e., whether the tax is fairly apportioned among the relevant population). Because taxation converts private wealth to public wealth, the two relevant external-to-tax norm categories bear on (1) the maximization of social wealth (i.e., economic efficiency); and (2) a notion of a good society in terms of the distribution of social wealth (often, but unhelpfully, referred to as "equity"). These norm categories are not picked at random, but are obtained by crosscutting the internal/external distinction with that of "means versus ends": "practicality" and "economic efficiency" are "instrumental" norms concerned with means of achieving goals, whereas "tax fairness" and "good society" refer to ends or the goals themselves.

Applying plural norms to the problem at hand could produce contrary recommendations, in which case one would weigh or prioritize norms according to one's personal values or tastes. In this instance, however, the norms more or less align in a way that justifies a transferee-oriented tax on wealth transfers, whether it be an accessions tax or the inclusion of gratuitous receipts in the income tax base.

Internal-to-Tax Norms

Internal-to-tax norms pertain to the institution of taxation, as opposed to society at large. The noninstrumental internal-to-tax norm is "tax fairness." The instrumental, practical internal-to-tax norm is more related to tax system design, doctrine, and enforcement—considerations that will be touched upon in discussing the various means of taxing wealth transfers.

Tax fairness deals with the issue of apportioning the tax burden among the population being taxed.[1] The task of apportionment requires a principle of apportionment. Apportionment could, in the abstract, be according to a principle of per capita equality, but, because taxation requires the sacrifice by individuals of cash, the consensus is that some economic attribute of individuals (such as income, consumption, or wealth) is the appropriate metric for apportionment, which in turn defines the tax base. The core concept of the tax base can then be spun out into its details, including that of the treatment of gratuitous transfers and receipts.

Under any principle of apportionment, it is axiomatic that persons who measure the same on the economic metric should be taxed equally. This principle, known as "horizontal equity," is (therefore) derivative of the apportionment principle. In contrast, the issue of how differently situated (i.e., rich versus poor) taxpayers should be taxed—the issue of "vertical equity"—cannot be resolved by any internal-to-tax-norm, but instead must be resolved according to external-to-tax norms, which cluster in the domains of economics and social justice theory. Because the use of the term "equity" (unmodified) is confusing and the term "vertical equity" is imprecise, it is an unhelpful term that should be dropped from the tax lexicon.

Concepts of Income

Income taxes appear to be a universal feature of the tax systems of nonpoor countries that do not rely on tourism. Income can be defined in terms of the economy as a whole or, instead, as an attribute of individual taxpayers.

A National-Income Income Tax

National income is the sum of the (market) value or prices obtained for (final) goods and services produced by nationals of a given country. Per capita national income is a commonly used measure of the relative economic strength of countries. As far as taxation is concerned, national income can be taxed to the individuals and entities that earn it, but it is axiomatic that such income can only be taxed once in the economy. Thus, corporate income taxes are allowed, but if a corporation is taxed on its profits, then dividends and capital gains would not be taxed to shareholders. Similarly, interest and royalties could be taxed by inclusion in the income of recipients or by disallowance of any deduction to the payors. Therefore, a tax on national income is indifferent to the issue of income attribution, which then might be dealt with simply on the basis of administrative convenience. Because no principle exists for apportioning national income among the population, such a tax posits no internal fairness criterion.[2]

What is important for present purposes is that pure transfers of wealth, including gratuitous transfers, are not a component of national income, but instead represent a transfer of previously

1 *See* Henry H. Simons, Personal Income Taxation 3, 41 (1938).

2 Ironically, the leading advocacy piece for this approach is Alvin C. Warren, *Would a Consumption Tax Be Fairer than an Income Tax?*, 89 Yale L.J. 1081 (1980).

acquired income. Therefore, gratuitous transfers would not be taxed as such.[3] In the case of transfers of earned but unrealized income, presumably the gratuitous transferee would be taxed on such income when realized by her.

Two external-to-tax norms underlie the national-income approach to taxation. One norm is a purported justification for taxation in a liberal (i.e., individualistic) society, in which taxation is looked upon with suspicion. The claim is that government, by providing legal, security, and physical infrastructure, is a "partner" to the private sector in the production of economic output. This claim is an elaboration of the "benefit" principle of taxation; namely, that taxation is justified (or tolerated) because of the benefits government provides.

The benefit principle can be critiqued and cabined on various grounds. First, it is appealing only to those who crave a deontological (i.e., nonconsequentialist) justification for taxation as an institution. In contrast, consequentialists would justify taxation on the grounds that the overall (i.e., welfare) benefits of government exceed the inconveniences of taxation. Second, the benefit principle cannot explain or justify taxation for purposes of redistribution. Third, the benefit principle is at odds with libertarian theory by treating the government as an independent actor rather than an agent of the citizenry. Fourth, the benefit principle is unworkable, because the indirect benefits received by taxpayers cannot be measured and cannot be assumed to be either uniform or proportionate to any index (e.g., income, consumption, or well-being). Finally, as a purported justification for taxation and government, the benefit principle does not necessarily dictate a tax on national income (or any other type of tax). Once government (even a very limited government) is legitimized, the design of the tax system that would support such a government is an open question.[4]

The second external-to-tax norm is that of economic efficiency, which in this context yields the axiom that a given item of income should only be taxed once in the economy, because productive activity that is subject to double taxation is disfavored relative to productive activity that is taxed only once.[5] This axiom, insofar as it appears to disfavor double taxation of gratuitous transfers, is discussed in due course.

Value-Added Tax

Another type of tax that can be characterized as a tax on national income is the value-added tax (VAT), which is a tax on the gross receipts from a transaction reduced, in effect, by the monetary cost (if any) of producing those gross receipts (e.g., labor and capital costs).[6] Mechanically, the VAT on the producer is, in principle, added to the selling price (i.e., it is paid by the purchaser to the seller) and then remitted by the seller to the government. Thus, the tax "on" the producer is (at least nominally) passed on to the purchaser. The VAT is designed so that the tax on the full value

---

3 *See id.* at 1088; Norman H. Lane, *A Theory of the Tax Base: The Exchange Model*, 3 Am. J. Tax Pol'y 1, 31, 43–44 (1984).

4 A lengthier version of this exposition and critique of the benefit principle is found in Joseph M. Dodge, *Theories of Tax Justice: Ruminations on the Benefit, Partnership, and Ability-to-Pay Theories of Tax Justice*, 58 Tax L. Rev. 399 (2005).

5 This axiom, cleverly advanced as a fairness principle, is a recurring theme in Robert E. Hall & Alvin Rabushka, The Flat Tax 40 (2d ed. 1995).

6 The notion and implementation of a VAT is explained at *Value Added Tax*, Wikipedia (Aug. 1, 2014), http://en.wikipedia.org/wiki/Value_added_tax. Although the notion of the VAT would seem to encompass wages, it appears that most countries view wage earning as outside of the scope of a VAT—perhaps because wages are taxed separately under an income tax. However, self-employed professionals might be subject to VAT in some countries.

added to a particular item is ultimately paid by the final consumer upon purchase of the item, as with a retail sales tax (but without the "cascading tax" problem associated with retail sales taxes). At the individual level, the VAT (as well as the retail sales tax) is a tax on spending on personal consumption, without regard to the source of funds.

As applied to gratuitous transfers, a value-added tax is paid by an individual only on the purchase of a final good for consumption. Suppose *T* earns wages of $10 million over her lifetime, and spends $6 million on current consumption, bequeathing $4 million to *L*. *T* will pay VAT on the $6 million spent on consumption, but the $4 million *T* bequeaths to *L* will not have generated VAT to *T*, nor will *L* pay VAT on the $4 million when received. Instead, *L* will pay VAT only on so much of the $4 million bequest (plus the income thereon) as *L* spends on consumption. This result is consistent with the axiom that a given item of national income be taxed only once as it passes through the economy. But note that here (in contrast to the current personal income tax) the tax, if any, with respect to a gratuitous transfer is paid by the transferee when spent on consumption and not by the transferor when acquired or transferred.

Obviously, a norm underlying the VAT is that consumption spending is a better tax base (at the individual level) than income or wealth, mainly because it is the more economically efficient system. However, the characterization of the VAT as a tax on consumption (as opposed to the accumulation or obtaining of wealth) assumes that the burden of the tax is not borne at all by producers. This assumption is unlikely: because taxes on consumers reduce aggregate demand, producers bear the burden of the tax to the extent market prices of consumer items are reduced. Both the VAT and the retail sales tax are "indirect" taxes (in the sense used by economists), meaning that the full burden of the tax is not necessarily borne by the nominal payor. Since the tax burden on various consumer items cannot be assumed to be uniformly allocated between producers and consumers, indirect taxes cannot satisfy any reasonable fairness criterion. That is, consumers having the same aggregate consumption (over any time period) will not bear equal taxes.

Since the VAT is essentially a tax on national income, it is not really important who bears the ultimate burden of the tax. Nevertheless, the VAT gives the appearance of fairness, in that individuals incurring equal personal consumption would *pay* equal tax. Whether consumption spending is really the preferred fairness norm is a matter taken up below.[7]

Additionally, because the VAT is a tax on transactions—as opposed to the aggregate personal consumption of an individual over the taxable year—the VAT cannot be accompanied by a progressive rate structure. Attempts to render it progressive through exemptions (e.g., for food) or through rebates for the poor are crude, create economic inefficiencies, and/or impose additional administrative burdens. Moreover, any such indirect progressivity only operates at the bottom; no progressivity can exist at the top—the traditional domain of wealth transfer taxes—except by way of a surtax on luxuries.

Personal Income Taxes

A *personal* income tax (as opposed to *national* income tax), as advocated by the American economist Henry Simons in his seminal 1938 book *Personal Income Taxation*, is explicitly based on the notion that tax fairness—that is, how the tax burden should be apportioned among the population—can only be determined by reference to the relative economic attributes of the various individuals subject to the taxing jurisdiction.[8] Simons further stipulated that the economic

7 *See infra* text following note 37.

8 *See* SIMONS, *supra* note 1, at 31, 47–51 (also rejecting national income as the norm).

attributes of persons to be taken into account should be based on objective phenomena (as opposed to subjective satisfaction or utility).[9]

The very notion of "fairness" is typically said to be imprecise and not worthy of academic analysis.[10] It is true that the everyday conception of tax fairness is typically limited to a kind of standardless, equal-treatment notion (as in, "If you get a tax break, then I should get one too," or as manifested in the political appeal of flat tax rates). Nevertheless, the Simons project was precisely to fashion an objective conception of tax fairness, harnessed to top-down redistribution, and not to promote economic neutrality.[11] Of course, academic conceptions of tax fairness do not necessarily take hold in the political arena. Thus, the distinction between national (i.e., economic) income and personal income may not be readily grasped by the layperson, who may well view "income" as a "thing," "out there"—as opposed to being a personal attribute.

The discussion of a personal income tax continues below, first with respect to accretion and realization income taxes and then with respect to the consumed-income tax (commonly called a "cash-flow consumption tax").

Accretion and Realization Income Taxes

The classic formulation of the accretion income tax is that a person's income is the algebraic sum of (1) net accessions to wealth; and (2) personal consumption.[12] Under a realization income tax, income is the algebraic sum of (1) net *realized* accessions to wealth; and (2) personal consumption. The term "realization" generally means that income items are not taken into income until reduced to cash (or its equivalent) by way of a sale, exchange, or other asset disposition.[13] In contrast, an accretion income tax takes items into account when (1) rights to receive (or obligations to pay) future cash or nonmonetary wealth are acquired or incurred; and (2) values of existing rights and obligations change from year to year. Costs of producing income are deductible, but other costs (i.e., personal consumption) are not deductible from the tax base of either the accretion or

9 *See id.* at 42, 50.

10 *See* Stephen Utz, Tax Policy: An Introduction and Survey of the Principal Debates 41–45 (1993) (claiming that "ability to pay" is vague); David A. Weisbach, *Line Drawing, Doctrine, and Efficiency in the Tax Law*, 84 Cornell L. Rev. 1627–28, 1646–50 (1999) (stating that tax-base issues should be resolved by reference to efficiency and distributional issues by reference to rates).

11 *See* Simons, *supra* note 1, at 2, 15–20, 31. Later commentators have seized on the accretion version of the income tax, discussed in the text immediately below, as having a principal virtue of promoting economic efficiency. *See* Calvin H. Johnson, *Soft Money Investing Under the Income Tax*, 1989 U. Ill. L. Rev. 1019 (investments should always be after tax, a condition that requires accretion taxation); David J. Shakow, *Taxation Without Realization: A Proposal for Accrual Taxation*, 134 U. Pa. L. Rev. 1111 (1986) (proposal for comprehensive accretion tax); Reed Shuldiner, *A General Approach to the Taxation of Financial Instruments*, 71 Tex. L. Rev. 243 (1992) (income tax should be moved toward accretion income tax).

12 *See* Simons, *supra* note 1, at 51.

13 *See* Marjorie E. Kornhauser, *The Story of* Macomber*: The Continuing Legacy of Realization*, *in* Tax Stories 93 (Paul L. Caron ed., 2d ed. 2009); Deborah H. Schenk, *A Positive Account of the Realization Rule*, 57 Tax L. Rev. 355 (2004); Daniel N. Shaviro, *An Efficiency Analysis of Realization and Recognition Rules Under the Federal Income Tax*, 48 Tax L. Rev. 1 (1992) (observing economic efficiency aspects of existing realization rules); Edward A. Zelinski, *For Realization: Income Taxation, Sectoral Accretionism, and the Virtue of Attainable Virtues*, 19 Cardozo L. Rev. 861 (1998).

realization income tax.[14] Gifts are not deductible, and, because a taxpayer's existence ceases at death,[15] no possibility exists of deducting bequests.

Given that an accretion income tax would require the annual valuation of all assets and liabilities of a taxpayer, it is not surprising that all personal income taxes in the world are realization income taxes. The realization principle derives from at least three norms. The first is the substantive tax fairness norm that the tax burden should be apportioned among the population in accordance with the respective abilities to pay of individuals during the taxable period. Because taxes are almost universally payable only in cash, personal ability to pay is equated with the receipt and payment of cash or items that (to preclude easy tax avoidance) are deemed to be the equivalent of cash.[16] Second, the realization principle is based on a public–private distinction: reckoning items only when acquired or disposed of in market-based transactions or transactions that entail interaction with other members of society. (Thus, purely private matters, such as consuming self-grown crops, do not count.[17]) Third, the realization principle is practical, because it refers to economic outcomes (rather than estimates and projections), and, as with business accounting, generally avoids valuation issues. It might also be mentioned that this "outcome" orientation respects the economic choices of individuals and takes into account matters beyond the taxpayer's control for which she should not be deemed responsible.

To state the obvious, the ability-to-pay principle—conceived objectively in terms of material resources under the control of an individual—is tailored to distributive justice theories that allow (or require) the redistribution by government of individual material resources.[18] Objective ability-to-pay defines the baseline capacity for redistribution from a tax subject, whereas welfare (a subjective phenomenon) cannot be redistributed.[19] Nevertheless, objective ability-to-pay exists, as an internal-to-tax substantive fairness norm, independently of a redistributive agenda.[20]

As Simons and others (including myself) have noted,[21] the idea of a *personal* income tax mandates that gratuitous transfers be included in the income tax base of the transferee and not deducted by the transferor. Under a realization income tax, in-kind accessions to wealth of a transferee might not be taxed until realized, which would entail assigning a zero basis to the excluded item. Gratuitous receipts represent ability to pay of the transferee. The point can be

14 *See* I.R.C §§ 162(a), 165(c), 167(a), 262.

15 *See id.* § 443(e)(2); Treas. Reg. §§ 1.451-1(b), 1.691(b)-1(a).

16 For example, in-kind compensation is generally treated as the deemed equivalent of cash. *See* I.R.C. §§ 61(a)(1), 83.

17 *See* Morris v. Comm'r, 9 B.T.A. 1273 (1928), *acq.*, VII-2 C.B. 28 (consumption of self-grown crops).

18 *See* Simons, *supra* note 1, at 31. Although Simons purported to reject an "ability" or "faculty" principle, he was actually rejecting utilitarian (i.e., subjective) versions of these concepts.

19 *See id.* at 15.

20 Although a person only interested in external-to-tax norms would view substantive tax fairness as being irrelevant, both philosophers and laypeople view internal-to-institution norms as being important. *See* John Rawls, A Theory of Justice 93 (1971). The tension between internal and external norms plays out in other areas of law. For example, internal fairness norms in criminal law and tort law are retribution and restorative justice, respectively, and external-to-institution norms are deterrence (in both instances), rehabilitation (criminal law), and internalization of externalities (tort law).

21 *See* 3 Report of the Royal Commission on Taxation 477–507 (1966); Simons, *supra* note 1, at 57–58; Joseph M. Dodge, *Beyond Estate and Gift Tax Reform: Including Gifts and Bequests in Income*, 91 Harv. L. Rev. 1177 (1978); Charles O. Galvin, *Taxing Gains at Death: A Further Comment*, 46 Vand. L. Rev. 1525, 1528–29 (1993); Marjorie E. Kornhauser, *The Constitutional Meaning of Income and the Income Taxation of Gifts*, 25 Conn. L. Rev. 1 (1992); John K. McNulty, *A Transfer Tax Alternative: Inclusion Under the Income Tax*, 4 Tax Notes 24 (1976).

illustrated by imagining a society consisting of three individuals (*A*, *B*, and *C*): In year 1, *A* earns wages of $100,000; *B* earns wages of $200,000; and *C*, being a student, earns no wages. In year 1, the tax burden is properly assigned one-third to *A* and two-thirds to *B*, with *C* obtaining a free ride. Fast forward to year 30, when *A* earns $100,000; *B*, having retired, earns nothing and dies, leaving a bequest of $100,000 to *C* (possibly out of the year 1 earnings); and *C*, being a beachcomber, earns nothing on her own. The tax burden for year 30 should be assigned one-half to *A*, nothing to *B*, and one-half to *C*; that is, in proportion to the personal income (i.e., increase in realized wealth) of *A*, *B*, and *C* in year 30. If *B*'s gratuitous transfer in year 30 had been a gift (instead of a bequest), the result would be the same: *B*'s ability to pay in year 30 would not have been reduced by the gift, because *B* could have used those funds to pay the tax instead of devoting them to personal use.

Doug and Jeff Kahn have argued that *C* should not be taxed, because a gratuitous transfer is a form of consumption by *B*.[22] This argument is correct, in my view, not only as to why gratuitous transfers should not be deductible but also as to why *support* is (and should be) viewed as nonincome to its beneficiary. In a support scenario, the provider not only obtained the funds but also expended them for his own ends (i.e., to satisfy his legal obligation or to fulfill the dictates of love, affection, and familial expectations). Support refers to mostly in-kind consumption benefits (lodging, meals, use of tangible personal property, plus small cash amounts that are implicitly earmarked for donee consumption). The recipient of a support payment has not obtained personal income because the recipient has not, as a general matter, obtained wealth that he or she (in principle) controls. This analysis highlights the fact that personal income is about a person's accessions to wealth, not a person's consumption (broadly conceived). Consumption is merely a principle of nondeductibility. The basic principle of income attribution is that income is taxed to the earner, not the enjoyer.[23] In the support scenario, the fact that the recipient is the consumer is immaterial. Support is, however, to be distinguished from a true wealth transfer, which the recipient *does* control.[24] A gratuitous accession to wealth is, therefore, personal income (leaving aside the issue of realization).

Treating gratuitous receipts of wealth differently from the receipt of support would somewhat complicate the income tax, because the distinction between the two would have to be elaborated upon and factual issues would have to be resolved. However, the same distinction occurs under the U.S. federal gift tax, where the distinction has been dealt with through per se rules and the gift tax annual exclusion.

It appears that no country currently has an income tax in which gratuitous receipts are included in income.[25] Perhaps the principal reason for this state of affairs is that during the period when the idea of an income tax was developed (roughly 1810–1920), gratuitous receipts were considered "principal" and not "income." This distinction derived from trust accounting law, the purpose being to assign entitlements to income and remainder beneficiaries, respectively.[26] In business accounting, this distinction ("income" translating into "earnings and profits") marked off the territories of creditors and holders of equity. A parallel strand of business accounting doctrine was

22 Douglas A. Kahn & Jeffrey H. Kahn, *Gifts, Gafts, and Gefts—The Income Tax Definition and Treatment of Private and Charitable Gifts and a Principled Policy Justification for the Exclusion of Gifts from Income*, 78 Notre Dame L. Rev. 441, 466–67 (2002–2003).

23 *See, e.g.*, Lucas v. Earl, 281 U.S. 111 (1930).

24 The distinction between support and gifts is problematical, especially in the case of small cash transfers. In the gift tax, the distinction is dealt with (not very satisfactorily) by the annual exclusion. I.R.C. § 2503(b).

25 Gratuitous receipts are excluded from the U.S. federal income tax under Code §§ 101(a) and 102(a). An exception lies for annuities and survivor benefits under retirement plans. *See id.* § 691(a), (d).

26 *See* Kornhauser, *supra* note 21.

that "irregular receipts" were not income. Finally, a general cultural norm was the importance of the preservation of "capital."

None of these notions is relevant to the design of a personal income tax. Rules affecting the allocation of private entitlements should not affect the tax base,[27] and, besides, trust and corporate law have their own rules as to the allocation of taxes between principal and income. Even in trust law (at least in the United States), the traditional distinction between principal and income has been rendered obsolete by modern portfolio theory.[28] Irregular receipts increase personal ability to pay as much as regular receipts. Indeed, because irregular receipts are not factored into personal budgets, irregular receipts (i.e., "windfalls") arguably can be characterized as especially ripe fruit for the tax collector. Gratuitous receipts are not "capital" but rather "income" as that term is conceptualized under a *personal* income tax. In the absence of a statutory exclusion, it is likely that gratuitous receipts would be income under U.S. federal tax law.[29] (For more on the intersection of financial and trust accounting with tax accounting, see Chapter 7 of this volume.)

Whether a one-time tax on a transfer of capital in the economic sense truly "impairs capital," and (if so) whether impairing capital is an absolute no-no, are issues discussed in a later section of this chapter.

Aggregate Personal Consumption

A consumed-income tax (CIT)—more commonly called a "cash-flow consumption tax"—posits a tax base constituted annually, subject to a progressive rate schedule, that is comprised of the sum of total cash receipts (including borrowed money and sales proceeds without basis offset) and in-kind receipts of personal consumption property (but not of business and investment property) minus total business and investment outlays (without regard to possible capitalization).[30] Conceptually, the CIT tax base can be described as consumption receipts plus cash receipts available for consumption minus nonconsumption outlays.

How are gratuitous transfers and receipts to be dealt with under a CIT? This issue is lightly discussed in the literature.[31] This state of affairs could be interpreted as assuming that no special rules attend gratuitous transfers and receipts. Thus, a gift or bequest of cash would be included in income by the transferee.[32] (However, the transferee could obtain an offsetting deduction by

27 *See* Marjorie E. Kornhauser, *The Origins of Capital Gains Taxation: What's Law Got to Do with It?*, 39 Sw. L.J. 869, 894 (1985).

28 *See* Revised Unif. Principal and Income Act § 104, 7A U.L.A. pt. III, at 434 (2006) (allowing equitable adjustments between income and principal; additionally, many states allow conversion of an "income" trust to a unitrust (i.e., a trust that pays out a fixed percentage of corpus annually)).

29 *See* Comm'r v. Glenshaw Glass Co., 348 U.S. 426 (1955) (cash windfalls held to be income because of being an "accession to wealth").

30 The CIT is explained in William Andrews, *A Consumption-Type or Cash Flow Personal Income Tax*, 87 Harv. L. Rev. 1113 (1974).

31 *See* U.S. Dep't of Treasury, Tax Reform for Fairness, Simplicity, and Growth 33 (1984) (one-paragraph discussion under the heading "The Dilemma of Gifts and Bequests").

32 In Michael J. Graetz, *Implementing a Cash-Flow Consumption Tax*, 92 Harv. L. Rev. 1575, 1624–25 (1979), the author states that single taxation within the family dictates that the donor should obtain a deduction for gifts of cash that have already been taxed to the donor. This result appears to be dubious on grounds apart from the "single-tax" premise. First, a deduction for bequests is impossible (and bequests are far more weighty than gifts). Second, the tax is a *cash-flow* consumption tax, meaning that cash is includible unless it is invested—and a gift is not an investment. Stated more broadly, the consumption tax is really about the taxation of investments, as opposed to actual consumption.

spending the cash for business or investment purposes.) As for a gift or bequest of business or investment property, the transferor would have obtained deductions for obtaining, improving, and maintaining the property, and the transferee would have no income upon receiving the property, although later conversion to cash or personal use would result in income. In short, business or investment property would avoid CIT from one generation to the next, so long as it were held for investment or used in business.

Gifts or bequests of personal-use property would presumably be income to the transferee (without deduction by the transferor). However, CIT proponents have shied away from textbook treatment of personal-use property,[33] partly because of uncertainty over the "when" and "how much" of consumption[34] and partly because mortgage-financed purchases of such property would (on account of the borrowing) yield current income,[35] which would possibly render a pure CIT politically unacceptable. The consumer-credit issue could be fixed by excluding consumer purchase-money debt while disallowing deductions for principal and interest. As to gratuitous transfers of personal-use property, proponents of the CIT (or the political system) might balk at inclusion in income of such property when received, especially if the transferor has already been taxed on the same property (by disallowing a deduction for its cost).

It can be argued that even gratuitous transfers of business and investment property should be taxed under a CIT. The argument begins with the observation that the rationale for a CIT is to prevent what is commonly referred to as the "double taxation" of future consumption that occurs under the income tax. This phenomenon is described as follows: First, the purpose of investing is to defer consumption into the future; second, by disallowing a deduction for an expenditure of investment capital, the future returns from the investment, reduced to present value, are taxed *ex ante*; third, the net return on the investment is taxed when realized. Under a CIT, in contrast, only the investment yield actually spent on consumption is taxed, *ex post*. Thus, the CIT is allegedly "fair" as between current consumers and those who save for future consumption. Taking this rationale for the CIT at face value, it can be argued that the CIT (as opposed to a VAT or a retail sales tax) is a "personal" consumption tax (as opposed to a tax on aggregate national consumption), and that the making of a gratuitous transfer is a form of consumption (i.e., end use) by the transferor. Another way of stating the matter is that the deduction for investment is conditioned on the investor herself being taxed on the future consumption funded by the investment. If the gratuitous transfer is not viewed as future consumption of the transferor, it violates the bargain implicit in the rationale for the consumption tax—or, in income tax doctrinal jargon, an event has occurred that is inconsistent with the premise upon which the initial deduction was based.[36] But instead of undoing the original deduction (which could be barred by the statute of limitations), the practical remedy is income inclusion at the time of the gratuitous transfer. Another version of the argument is that the purpose of investment is to fund either future consumption or future gratuitous transfers *of an individual*,

33 *See id.* at 1615–22 (discussing personal-use assets under a consumption tax; however, gratuitous transfers of such assets are not discussed).

34 The consumption of a personal-use asset could be described by any of (1) its cost; (2) imputed income yield; or (3) a depreciation formula. Furthermore, such an asset (especially if a collectible) could be treated as an "investment."

35 The normal consumption tax treatment of borrowing is to include the loan proceeds in the tax base and to deduct both principal and interest payments.

36 In the income tax, an event inconsistent with an earlier deduction may give rise to current income. *See* I.R.C. § 111; Hillsboro Nat'l Bank v. Comm'r, 460 U.S. 370 (1983).

which are both end uses of economic resources by individuals. The deduction for investment is the trade-off for future taxation of the consumption *or* of gratuitous transfers.[37]

The weakness (or irrelevance) of these arguments is that the fairness argument for the CIT is really a smokescreen. No plausible tax fairness norm holds that two taxpayers with differing consumption patterns over time should be taxed the same in present-value terms because the present value of their consumption (or consumption plus gratuitous transfer) patterns are equal. As noted earlier, government (with the consent of the governed) demands periodic budget cycles funded by periodic taxes. A government liberally funded by a one-time endowment would be unconstrained. Present-value analysis is an analytic tool that describes investments. It is not itself a norm.

That leaves the Hobbesian argument that consumption is the proper subject of taxation because consumption takes away from social wealth while investment adds to it.[38] This appears to be an economic, or perhaps programmatic, argument rather than a fairness argument. In any event, the argument is as weak as the mercantilist economic system that constitutes its premise, and confuses economics with pseudoecology. Economic activity (and wealth creation) is driven by demand (which is mostly demand for consumption items produced by others). Investment is socially worthwhile only insofar as it satisfies demand. Consumption is not a form of material waste, nor is it antisocial, except where nonrenewable resources are involved.[39]

The one and only normative argument for a CIT is that it would eliminate an alleged tax preference for consumption over savings and investment, with the (claimed) likely result that GDP would grow at a faster rate than under an income tax.[40] (An evaluation of this claim is beyond the scope of this chapter.[41]) Stripped down to the economic rationale to exempt business and investments from tax until reduced to personal consumption, it follows that gratuitous transfers and receipts of business and investment property would not be taxed under a CIT.

It is claimed that the CIT, as a personal tax base keyed to a person's aggregate consumption, is a suitable vehicle for redistribution, because progressive rates are possible.[42] Although the CIT is preferable to a VAT (or retail sales tax) in this regard, the CIT tax base omits business and investment spending, which is disproportionately high among the upper classes, so that the personal CIT tax base of the wealthy would, in general, be much smaller than their ability-to-pay (or personal income tax) base. Progressivity would need to be very steep to attain meaningful top-down redistribution.

---

37 *See* Joseph M. Dodge, *Taxing Gratuitous Transfers Under a Consumption Tax*, 51 Tax L. Rev. 529, 573–85 (1996).

38 This argument is used to justify the "flat tax," a hybrid wage tax/VAT type of consumption tax. *See* Hall & Rabushka, *supra* note 5, at 40.

39 *See* Anne L. Alstott, *The Uneasy Case Against Income and Wealth Transfer Taxation: A Response to Professor McCaffery*, 51 Tax L. Rev. 363, 368–82 (1996) (critiquing the view that savings is a liberal value).

40 *See, e.g.*, Joseph Bankman & David A. Weisbach, *The Superiority of an Ideal Consumption Tax over an Ideal Income Tax*, 58 Stan. L. Rev. 1413 (2006). It is also claimed that a consumption tax is not inherently regressive, because the rate schedule can be tweaked to render it as progressive as an income tax with a broader base and less progressive rates. *Id.* at 1428–30. However, I discern no political constituency for a highly progressive consumption tax.

41 In my opinion, the notion that a consumption tax is neutral between present and future consumption is strictly mathematical and unrealistic from the behavioral angle, especially if the saver is never taxed on gratuitous transfers, because people generally attach a high discount rate to future outcomes. In the present, a consumption tax provides a strong incentive to save (and no incentive to make direct productive investments).

42 *See* Edward J. McCaffery & James R. Hines, Jr., *The Last Best Hope for Progressivity and Tax*, 83 S. Cal. L. Rev. 1031 (2010).

The existing U.S. "income" tax is full of CIT features; namely, provisions that allow expensing of capital expenditures and exemption (or partial exemption) of certain investment income.[43] Nevertheless, even Republican administrations have balked at advancing a CIT.[44] The chief political obstacle is that a CIT would heavily tax retired persons of modest resources, who must liquidate savings and investment. Also, inclusion of borrowing would negatively impact students and homeowners. Additionally, transition to a CIT would allow a windfall to existing investors, who would continue to exclude economic returns by way of basis offsets, while obtaining a full deduction for new investment. Finally, capitalists may be content with the existing system insofar as the combination of CIT features on the investment side with the income tax treatment of borrowing can produce negative tax.

Taxes on Wealth

Three types of wealth taxes are considered here in terms of internal-to-tax norms: (1) a one-time tax on the acquisition of material endowment; (2) a periodic wealth tax; and (3) a tax on wealth transfers.

Endowment Tax

The idea of an endowment tax is to tax the acquisition of economic endowment but to allow economic outcomes to avoid tax. The endowment tax idea might appeal to hard-core libertarians insofar as private individuals would be entitled to 100 percent of the economic outcomes that they obtain. Logically, gratuitous transfers received would be the principal form of endowment subject to tax upon receipt.[45]

The endowment tax concept is, in a sense, a tax on economic potential.[46] Historically, taxation has always been keyed to economic outcomes, reflecting a deep norm that legal consequences should attend behavioral results and consequences, and not thoughts or predictions. An endowment tax is also impractical—and has never been adopted—because the notion of economic endowment: (1) includes human capital (wage-earning capacity), the acquisition of which is hard to ascertain and measure; (2) implies significant taxes at birth and as education is acquired; and (3) possibly requires huge deductions as human capital is lost. Ironically, application of the endowment tax idea to nonmaterial endowment (i.e., human capital) seems profoundly antilibertarian, because it would force persons to work against their will, as the only way to pay a tax on human capital is to obtain wages commensurate with wage-earning capacity.[47]

---

43 *See, e.g.*, I.R.C. §§ 72(e)(5)(C), 83(e)(2), 103, 174, 179, 219.

44 *See* U.S. Dep't of Treasury, *supra* note 31, at 30–36 (a Reagan administration study that, after considering the CIT and other consumption taxes, opted to recommend a proposal for a reformed income tax).

45 However, the libertarian position, which initially might find an endowment tax appealing, also generally adheres to the view that gifts and bequests are essential property rights. *See generally* Jennifer Bird-Pollan, *Death, Taxes, and Property (Rights): Nozick, Libertarianism, and the Estate Tax*, 66 Maine L. Rev. 1 (2013) (arguing that libertarianism is compatible with a wealth transfer tax).

46 *See, e.g.*, Kirk J. Stark, *Enslaving the Beachcomber: Some Thoughts on the Liberty Objections to Endowment Taxation*, 18 Can. J.L. & Jurisprudence 47 (2005).

47 *See* Linda Sugin, *A Philosophical Objection to the Optimal Tax Model*, 64 Tax L. Rev. 229 (2011); Ilan Benshalom & Kendra Stead, *Values and (Market) Valuations: A Critique of the Endowment Tax Consensus*, 104 Nw. U. L. Rev. 1511 (2010).

Periodic Wealth Tax

A periodic wealth tax is a tax, usually imposed annually, on (ideally) the aggregate value of property owned by a person, possibly at progressive rates. At the federal level, a wealth (or property) tax is considered to be off the table, because the U.S. Constitution requires "direct taxes" (construed by the courts to include capitation and property taxes) to be apportioned among the states according to population.[48] Thus, although all states have taxes on real property, only a smattering of states have meaningful taxes on tangible property (usually related to business) or intangible property (usually investment securities), and no state has a progressive tax on cumulative wealth.[49]

A *comprehensive* national wealth tax would not only be unconstitutional but would also be impractical, because taxes on tangible personal property (and nonregistered intangible property) are easily evaded, and attempted enforcement would entail the invasion of privacy. Accurate valuation has always been a problem for taxes on various kinds of property, especially real property, where individualized valuations are not feasible and assessments often inequitable. Property taxes on residences breed political revolts in periods of high appreciation, as unrealized gains are considered to be "paper" and "unreal" because nonliquid.

It might seem that a wealth tax (as opposed to an income tax) is the appropriate baseline for ability to pay. However, taxes entail an annual cash contribution to the annual appropriations of government. Periodic (i.e., annual) budget cycles are an essential feature of a government that is responsible to the governed. Just as government budgets encapsulate a flow, so should the tax base be described in terms of a flow. *Personal* wealth itself is the net result of a flow over time, and that flow is already subject to income tax.

An annual wealth tax subjects the same wealth to tax over and over again to the same person. Consequently, the tax would strongly discourage the accumulation of wealth unless the tax rate were well below the net income yield (actual or imputed) for the property. Wealth taxes have been condemned as violating liberal values (in the political theory sense) as well as undermining economic efficiency.[50] Indeed, actual wealth and property tax rates appear to average about 1 percent on value.[51] A low-rate wealth tax amounts to a tax on a hypothetical rate of return. In the case of personal-use tangible property, no cash return exists. Taxes on hypothetical returns violate a fairness notion that taxes should be keyed to actual economic outcomes.

A comprehensive wealth tax can be used as a redistributive tool, because wealth is highly concentrated.[52] But a tax only on tangible (especially real) property would not be very efficacious

48 *See* Joseph M. Dodge, *What Federal Taxes Are Subject to the Rule of Apportionment Under the Constitution?*, 11 U. Pa. J. Const. L. 839 (2009) (rejecting theories that would deny that a federal property or wealth tax would be unconstitutional). The apportionment requirement would have the perverse effect of imposing higher tax rates on persons in poorer states.

49 *See* Joyce Errecart et al., *States Moving away from Taxes on Tangible Personal Property*, Tax Found. (Oct. 4, 2012), http://taxfoundation.org/article/states-moving-away-taxes-tangible-personal-property.

50 *See* Eric Rakowski, *Can Wealth Taxes Be Justified?*, 53 Tax L. Rev. 263 (1998).

51 *See* Gilbert Paul Verbit, *France Tries a Wealth Tax*, 12 U. Pa. J. Int'l Bus. L. 181, 188 (1991) (highest wealth tax rate in France is 1.5 percent); Tonya Moreno, *Best and Worst States for Property Taxes*, About.com, http://taxes.about.com/od/statetaxes/a/property-taxes-best-and-worst-states.htm (last visited Aug. 12, 2014) (New Jersey has highest tax rate, 1.89 percent).

52 *See* G. William Donhoff, *Wealth, Income, and Power,* Who Rules America? (Feb. 2013), http://www2.ucsc.edu/whorulesamerica/power/wealth.html (for 2010, the top 1 percent in the United States held, by value, 35 percent of net worth and 42 percent of financial assets, and the top 5 percent held 63 percent of

in this regard, as real property constitutes a decreasing percentage of wealth at high income levels.[53] Taxes are only provisionally redistributive, of course. The redistribution story is complete only after considering the effects of government spending.

Wealth Transfer Taxes

Wealth transfer taxes—one of the most venerable forms of taxation with antecedents in ancient Egypt and imperial Rome—have been a permanent fixture in the Anglo-American world since at least the Norman conquest, initially as a fee exacted by the sovereign (i.e., the owner of all land) on his feoffees for the privilege of inheritance. In the United States, inheritance taxes were imposed by the states in the nineteenth century and by the federal government to help finance, respectively, the undeclared naval war with France (the 1797–1802 stamp tax on wills, letters of administration, estate inventories, and certain estate distributions), the Civil War (1862–1870), and the Spanish-American War (1898–1902). These taxes all had low rates by contemporary standards. The current U.S. estate tax was launched in 1916 a few months prior to the United States's entry into World War I, but, as a Progressive Era tax, it was not intended as only a temporary war-finance tax[54] and has lasted until the present (except for decedents dying in 2010). The estate tax throughout its history has been characterized by fairly high rates (typically exceeding the highest income tax rates) coupled with significant exemptions that rendered the tax applicable to only the highest wealth strata.[55]

Wealth transfer taxes are a relatively easy mechanism for obtaining revenue, because probate is public and third parties (e.g., executors, trustees, brokers, and insurance companies) can be enlisted in enforcement efforts. However, the revenue obtainable is modest, as wealth is transferred no more frequently than once a generation, and often less frequently than that. Additionally, the federal wealth transfer taxes have always been characterized by substantial exemptions, so that only those with substantial wealth pay any tax.[56]

The discussion of wealth transfer taxes continues below, first with respect to inheritance taxes, then with respect to estate taxes, and finally with respect to accessions taxes.

Inheritance Taxes

An inheritance tax is a tax on the receipt of bequests and inheritances. Inheritance taxes not only fail to tax inter vivos gifts but they often also fail to reach inter vivos transfers of a testamentary nature (i.e., nonprobate transfers such as joint tenancies, life insurance, survivor benefits under

---

net worth and 72 percent of financial assets). For a global/historical view of wealth concentration, see Thomas Piketty, Capital in the Twenty-First Century (2014).

53 *See* Edward N. Wolff, *Who Are the Rich? A Demographic Profile of High-Income and High-Wealth Americans*, *in* Does Atlas Shrug? 74, 91 (Joel B. Slemrod ed., 2000).

54 Some have, however, argued that these taxes were little more than revenue-raising expedients during wartime. *See* Louis Eisenstein, *The Rise and Decline of the Estate Tax*, 11 Tax L. Rev. 223 (1956).

55 For an expanded version of this brief history, see Darien B. Jacobson et al., *The Estate Tax: Ninety Years and Counting*, Stat. Income Bull., Summer 2007, at 118.

56 *See* Michael D. Steinberger, Presentation Regarding Federal Estate Tax Disadvantages for Same-Sex Couples, fig.1 (Dec. 17, 2009), *available at* http://www.taxpolicycenter.org/events/upload/Steinberger_Handout.pdf (percentage of decedents paying any tax varied from 2.25 percent to 0.5 percent in the period between 1982 and 2009). Starting in 2011, the exemption level is $5 million per decedent, indexed for inflation after 2010. I.R.C. § 2010(c)(3).

retirement plans and IRAs, and revocable trusts). However, this particular shortcoming could be cured under an ideal inheritance tax. In addition, the fact that the tax is separately imposed on the estate transfers of a particular decedent creates some incentive for splitting marital estates, because each spouse obtains a full set of exemptions and lower marginal rate brackets.

The principal distinguishing feature of an inheritance tax is that of different rate and exemption schedules for various classes of legatees (i.e., spouse, descendants, ancestors, collaterals, and nonrelatives), with decreasing exemptions (and increasing rates) as the relationship becomes more remote. Of course, the details can vary greatly among taxing jurisdictions. In any event, this structure creates an incentive for dispersal of a testator's wealth, especially if each beneficiary (within a class) is entitled to a separate exemption.

With the exception of spouses (who are favored under all wealth transfer taxes[57]) and possibly orphaned minor children of the decedent (for whom the decedent owed a duty of support), it is not clear that a convincing case can be made for the distinctions among classes of legatees and heirs. The fact of higher rates and lower exemptions for remote relatives or nonrelatives appears to operate as a kind of back-handed partial escheat. However, escheat is a state institution, irrelevant to the federal government. (In fact, only a few states still maintain inheritance taxes.[58]) In any event, at the state level, partial escheat by a tax that discriminates among classes of legatees is inconsistent with the principle of freedom of testation, not to mention state escheat laws themselves.[59] Instrumentally speaking, the class discrimination is likely to distort estate plans, and create incentives to adopt adult individuals as "children." The class distinctions do not necessarily correlate with affection, dependency, or sense of entitlement—even assuming that these fact issues could be sorted out or are relevant to taxation. Finally, class discrimination is irrelevant to the ability-to-pay norm, as well as to revenue raising.

If the tax is charged against each transfer, estate administration is rendered more difficult, as each legacy (net of the tax thereon) must be separately determined, and adjustments to estate transfer amounts after the return date would necessitate amended tax returns.

Estate Tax

An estate tax is a tax on the aggregate death-time transfers of a decedent. An estate tax can be (and currently is) combined with a gift tax. The current integrated estate/gift tax is a pay-as-you-go tax on the cumulative lifetime and death-time gratuitous transfers of an individual.[60] The tax is currently structured so that the "first" $5 million (as indexed for inflation) of taxable transfers[61] by a donor/decedent is not subject to tax at all, with any excess over that amount being taxed at a flat

57 In the federal estate tax, an unlimited deduction for qualifying transfers to surviving spouses has existed since 1981 and, as discussed in Chapter 13 of this volume, beginning in 2011, a decedent spouse's unused exemption may pass to the surviving spouse. I.R.C. §§ 2001(c)(2)(B), (c)(4); 2056; 2523.

58 As of 2013, the states are Indiana, Iowa, Kentucky, Maryland, New Jersey, Nebraska, Pennsylvania, and Tennessee.

59 For a parallel critique of inheritance taxes, see Wendy C. Gerzog, *What's Wrong with a Federal Inheritance Tax?*, 49 Real Prop. Tr. & Est. L.J. (forthcoming).

60 *See* I.R.C. § 2001(b) (cumulative tax base is taxable estate plus adjusted taxable gifts).

61 Taxable transfers are gross transfers (net of certain gift exclusions) less the deductions for the decedent's debts, state death taxes, administration expenses (not deducted for income tax purposes), funeral expenses, qualified transfers to the spouse, and qualified transfers to charity. I.R.C. §§ 2053–2057; 2503(b), (e).

rate of 40 percent.[62] (A federal generation-skipping-transfer tax is also in place,[63] but it will not be discussed here.[64])

An estate tax is perhaps the most compatible with freedom of testation because, apart from the marital and charitable deductions, no favoritism is shown among various classes of beneficiaries. Indeed, the decedent can allocate the burden of the tax to one or more legatees, whereas under an inheritance or accessions tax the legatee bears the burden of the tax on what he or she receives.[65] At the same time, the estate tax allows for highly concentrated wealth to be passed on to a single member of the next generation, thereby preserving the concentration. Although testators in the United States tend to follow a cultural norm of equal distribution among children and others,[66] this may not apply to closely held businesses and family farms, where the testator may prefer centralized or unified ownership and control.

An estate tax is relatively hard to evade, because the wealth included in the estate constitutes a hotchpot that generates, at a single moment, a single tax that can be apportioned among estate-included transfers according to the decedent's directions as supplemented by applicable estate tax apportionment rules.[67] The estate's personal representative, having access to relevant information, files one return and pays the tax due out of estate-included assets.[68] The gift tax is paid by the donor.[69] Donees and beneficiaries of the estate are involved in the process only where the tax is not paid through the normal process.[70]

A structural flaw in the estate and gift taxes (and existing inheritance taxes) is that assets and deductible transfers must be valued at the date of death or completed gift transfer,[71] which allows for strategies aimed at undervaluing taxable assets and overvaluing deductible transfers by taking advantage of actuarial tables, converting liquid assets into nonliquid assets, restricting the sale or liquidation of assets, and fractionalizing interests.[72] Coping with these valuation strategies burdens the administration of the tax, and such strategies are economically inefficient by restraining alienation, destroying value, and diverting assets from their highest and best use.

---

62 *Id.* §§ 2001(b), 2010(c)(3). The baseline year for the cost-of-living adjustment is 2010.

63 *Id.* §§ 2601–2663.

64 This tax is a separate tax—apart from the estate/gift tax—that attempts to impose tax on generational shifts in enjoyment that avoid estate/gift tax. The current tax has been counterproductive because it actually encourages dynastic trusts. *See* Lawrence W. Waggoner, *Effectively Curbing the GST Exemption for Perpetual Trusts*, 135 Tax Notes 1267 (2012).

65 A "hybrid" inheritance/estate tax is one where the tax is computed as under an inheritance tax but the tax can be allocated by the testator as the testator pleases.

66 *See* Paul L. Menchik, *Unequal Estate Division: Is It Altruism, Reverse Bequests, or Simply Noise?*, *in* Modelling the Accumulation and Distribution of Wealth 105 (Dennis Kessler & Andre Masson eds., 1988).

67 *See* Unif. Estate Tax Apportionment Act, 8A U.L.A. 229 (Supp. 2013).

68 I.R.C. § 2002.

69 *Id.* § 2502(c).

70 *See id.* § 6324 (liens and transferee liability for estate and gift tax).

71 *See id.* §§ 2031 (date of death), 2032 (alternate valuation date), 2512(a) (date of gift).

72 The classic expose of estate planning techniques is George Cooper, *A Voluntary Tax? New Perspectives on Sophisticated Estate Tax Avoidance*, 77 Colum. L. Rev. 161 (1977). *See also* Joseph M. Dodge, *Redoing the Federal Estate and Gift Taxes Along Easy-to-Value Lines*, 43 Tax L. Rev. 241 (1988) (explaining how actuarial tables can be abused); James R. Repetti, *Minority Discounts: The Alchemy in Estate and Gift Taxation*, 50 Tax L. Rev. 415 (1995).

Accessions Tax

An accessions tax, favored by many academics,[73] entails a personal tax base on an individual's aggregate lifetime gratuitous accessions that is subject to a progressive rate schedule with a lifetime exemption amount. The accessions tax can be thought of as a kind of mirror image of a combined estate and gift tax. An accessions tax is sometimes referred to as an inheritance tax because it is a tax "on" a gratuitous recipient, but this usage is confusing—first, because the accessions tax reaches all gratuitous receipts (not just probate transfers), and second, because the accessions tax, being keyed to a transferee's accession history, is computed and personally paid by the transferee (as opposed to an inheritance tax, which is paid by the executor).

It can be argued that an accessions tax would be harder to enforce than an estate/gift tax because all gratuitous transferees would be required to report gratuitous receipts. But the accessions tax would be no harder to enforce than an income tax, except for modest inter vivos gifts (a problem for any system of wealth transfer taxation), because reporting and withholding obligations can be imposed on third parties, such as executors, trustees, banks, brokers, insurance companies, and donors. The accessions tax could even be an "additional tax" on the individual income tax return.

An accessions tax is not, in principle, constrained by having to value assets and tax-favored transfers at the time of gift or on the transferor's death. Instead, the taxable event and time of valuation can be deferred until the transfer is realized in cash or its equivalent.[74] For example, a remainder interest in fee simple would be taxed and valued when it comes into possession. The taxable accession with respect to a trust interest could be deferred to the time distributions are received, as opposed to when the trust interest is acquired, thereby avoiding reliance on actuarial tables. *Ex ante* qualification rules, such as currently exist for the marital and charitable deductions, would be pointless. Instead, the cash receipt of a charity or of one spouse from another would simply be excluded. The lapse of transferor-imposed restrictions on property (including the recombination of minority interests into controlling interests) would itself be viewed as an accession. (In an estate/gift tax, delayed realization would be difficult as the transferor would no longer exist, and the tax would have to be borne entirely by the assets involved in the delayed transfer.) In short, the accessions tax is capable of solving most of the doctrinal problems attendant upon estate and inheritance taxes.

The design choices made in constructing an accessions tax could well influence transfers in a way that is different from under the current system. The effects of the present system on interspousal transfers is highlighted in Chapter 13 of this volume, in which Bridget Crawford and Wendy Gerzog examine the recently enacted feature of the estate tax known as "portability" that allows a deceased spouse's unused exemption amount to pass to the surviving spouse.[75] Enactment of portability was intended to allow the first decedent spouse to leave his or her entire net estate

---

73 *See generally* AM. LAW INST., FEDERAL ESTATE AND GIFT TAXATION, RECOMMENDATIONS AND REPORTERS' STUDIES: STUDY OF ACCESSIONS TAX SYSTEM (1969); William D. Andrews, *The Accessions Tax Proposal*, 22 TAX L. REV. 589 (1967) (describing the American Law Institute's accessions tax project); Lily L. Batchelder, *What Should Society Expect from Its Heirs: The Case for a Comprehensive Inheritance Tax*, 63 TAX L. REV. 1 (2009); Joseph M. Dodge, *Replacing the Estate Tax with a Re-imagined Accessions Tax*, 60 HASTINGS L.J. 997 (2009); Edward C. Halbach, Jr., *An Accessions Tax*, 23 REAL PROP. PROB. & TR. J. 211 (1988); Harry A. Rudick, *A Proposal for an Accessions Tax*, 1 TAX L. REV. 25 (1925).

74 *See supra* note 73; Sergio Pareja, *Taxation Without Liquidation: Rethinking "Ability to Pay,"* 2008 WIS. L. REV. 841.

75 The term "exemption amount" as used here is officially known as the "applicable exclusion amount," which is the maximum gift/estate tax base that will produce a zero tax after application of the taxpayer's

in a form that qualifies for the marital deduction, thereby foregoing use of the exemption amount, which then passes to the surviving spouse if the deceased spouse's executor so elects on an estate tax return.[76] This result appears to make sense, as the absence of portability under prior law drove married couples into tax-driven bifurcated estate plans involving marital trusts and bypass trusts.[77] However, a postportability, single-trust estate plan can be carried out with the first decedent spouse making a transfer in trust that only gives the surviving spouse an income interest for life (i.e., a QTIP trust) that nevertheless qualifies for the marital deduction.[78]

In Chapter 13, Crawford and Gerzog also show how portability discourages the wealthier spouse from making inter vivos gifts to the poorer spouse to hedge against the possibility that the poorer spouse might die first and waste her exemption amount. However, the poorer spouse's gross estate could be augmented by the wealthier spouse making an inter vivos QTIP trust.[79] I might add that, if the poorer spouse dies first, portability encourages her to leave her entire estate to the wealthier surviving spouse, although this also can be done with a QTIP trust.[80]

Thus, as far as the ultimate control of wealth by women is concerned (on average, women have less wealth than men), the real culprit is the QTIP trust. As a generalization, in a QTIP scenario the true beneficiaries of the current estate tax marital deduction are third parties (rather than the surviving spouses). Crawford and Gerzog point out that the current portability regime is excessively generous in giving the surviving spouse the deceased spouse's entire unused exemption amount, rather than the maximum exemption amount that could have been used by her estate. This outcome gives an advantage to married couples (really, the legatees of married couples) not available to unmarried couples.[81]

Portability privileges marriage, but so does the marital deduction itself—not to mention the nontax incidents of marital status. Under the estate and gift taxes, the original impetus for the

---

unified transfer-tax credit. Thus, the credit has the effect of exempting the exemption amount (of the tax base) from tax. I.R.C. § 2010(c)(2)(B), (4).

76 *See id.* § 2020(c)(5)(A).

77 A bypass trust is a trust designed to avoid inclusion in the surviving spouse's gross estate while not qualifying for the marital deduction, thereby being taxable to the transferor but avoiding tax on account of the transferor's exemption amount.

78 *See* I.R.C. §§ 2056(b)(7), 2523(f).

79 A QTIP trust is ultimately included in the transfer-tax base of the transferee spouse. *Id.* §§ 2044, 2519.

80 Assume that the exemption amount is $5 million and that the net wealth of husband is $7 million and that of wife is $3 million. Suppose wife dies first and leaves everything to husband in a form that qualifies for the marital deduction, so that husband's net estate is now $10 million. Portability, in this scenario, provides an incentive for the poorer spouse to leave marital deduction estate transfers to the wealthier spouse! Under current law, wife's entire unused exemption amount of $5 million passes to husband, who now has an exemption amount of $10 million. However, the maximum exemption amount that wife could have used was $3 million (against a maximum possible taxable estate of $3 million). If portability only extended to that $3 million, husband would only end up with an exemption amount of $8 million, and, in that scenario, husband would have a tax incentive to augment wife's net estate during life by $2 million. Under current law, that end can be accomplished with an inter vivos QTIP trust, providing wife with only an income interest for life, raising yet other issues.

81 Assume that the exemption amount is $5 million, and that the net wealth of husband is $5 million and that of wife is $2 million. Suppose wife dies first, and leaves everything to husband in a form that qualifies for the marital deduction. Although husband's net estate is initially $7 million, it could grow to $10 million, and all of it could be passed free of tax to third parties. If husband and wife were not married, the maximum they could pass tax free to third parties would be $7 million.

marital deduction in 1948 was to achieve parity between married couples in common-law states with those in community-property states. If the community-property (more broadly, partnership) concept of marriage is taken as the ideal, then it would follow that tax-free estate equalization would be allowed because it occurs automatically (and tax-free) in a community-property state. Such a result is perhaps easier to obtain under an estate tax than under an accessions tax or income-inclusion approach.[82] Of course, the partnership model can itself be critiqued from various angles. In any event, the estate and gift taxes abandoned the partnership model in 1981 with simultaneous enactment of the unlimited marital deduction and the allowance of the QTIP trust as a qualifying form of marital-deduction transfer. It is hard to say what model of marriage is embodied in the present transfer tax system, which only implicates wealthy couples in any event, except possibly the retro notion that the wealthier spouse should be allowed to maintain dead-hand control over "his" property, subject only to a dower-type interest in the surviving spouse.[83]

In contrast, under an accessions tax the off-the-bottom exemption amounts reside in the transferees, and no advantage is obtained by having married (or multiple) transferors. At the same time, the system would encourage gratuitous transfers from third parties to be made to both the "normal" (i.e., related) transferee but also to such transferee's spouse, or perhaps just to whichever of them has received the least amount of accessions. Such an influence would counter the existing culture of not providing for spouses of descendants and other loved ones.

The accessions tax literature has so far assumed that accessions by a person from such person's spouse would be excluded in full, separately from the exemption amount otherwise available to each spouse. Qualification for the marital exclusion (if any) would not be governed by rules imposed *ex ante* pertaining to the form of the transfer. Instead, qualification for any marital exclusion would be conditioned on the *ex post* fact of actual receipt in cash (or in fee ownership of property). In other words, the marital exclusion would actually benefit the transferee spouse, rather than (as with the current system) third parties.

Crawford and Gerzog appear to be skeptics on the issue of whether marriage should be associated with wealth transfer tax benefits (or detriments). However, unless the federal wealth transfer tax system were to override community-property laws and treat property transfers on divorce as taxable transfers[84]—an impossible task politically—it can be safely assumed that such benefits will persist. In any event, elsewhere Crawford and Gerzog appear to favor marital tax benefits insofar as those benefits would encourage wealth transfers from the richer spouse to the poorer spouse (which, statistically, entails a net transfer from men to women). One might wonder why we care about this issue with respect to the top one percentile of the population wealth-wise (i.e., the group potentially influenced by the federal wealth transfer taxes), especially considering that the institution of marriage itself mandates interspousal transfers by way of support and property claims on divorce and death or by way of the community-property system in effect for over 30 percent of the U.S. population. A wealth transfer tax system premised on large exemption amounts can only play a marginal role with respect to women's property rights and economic opportunities. If a redistributive (perhaps welfarist) model of marriage is to be encouraged through wealth transfer taxes, then the exemption equivalent amount ($5.25 million per individual in 2013) needs to be

82 At the death of the first spouse, the amount needed to equalize estates can be calculated. Under transferee-oriented taxes, taxable receipts can occur long after the death of the first decedent.

83 *See* Wendy C. Gerzog, *The Marital Deduction QTIP Provisions: Illogical and Degrading to Women*, 5 UCLA Women's L.J. 301 (1995); Joseph M. Dodge, *A Feminist Perspective on the QTIP Trust and the Unlimited Marital Deduction*, 76 N.C. L. Rev. 1729 (1998).

84 The acquisition (or division) of community property does not entail a gift or bequest, and divorce-related transfers are not considered gifts. *See, e.g.*, I.R.C. § 2516.

drastically lowered. In that case, the wealth transfer tax could pursue a redistributive norm among couples of moderate to considerable means.

Internal-to-Tax Norms and Wealth Transfer Taxes

A problem with wealth transfer taxes—at least those with high rates—has been their political acceptability. It has been stated that the historical evidence supports the proposition that the political acceptance of high-rate wealth transfer taxes requires confining them to the top 2 percent (or less) of estates.[85] Possibly, an income-inclusion approach (with only a spousal exclusion and the usual income tax rates) would obtain political acceptance by reason of recharacterizing gratuitous receipts as a common kind of ordinary income (like wages or lottery winnings), but that is only speculation. It is true, nevertheless, that the main internal-to-tax rationale of the estate tax has been the same as that for the income tax; namely, that of ability to pay. In the gestation period of the federal estate tax (i.e., the late nineteenth and early twentieth centuries),[86] the institution of inheritance, especially as it perpetuated wealthy dynasties, came into question at a time when the wealthy were also grossly undertaxed, as the federal government (not to mention the states) relied more on import duties and/or other consumption excise taxes. Newly emergent intangible wealth could be reached by an estate or inheritance tax (in contrast to state taxes on real property). In short, the estate tax was viewed as a component of the larger tax system by which the very wealthy would eventually be made to pay their fair share.[87]

The ability-to-pay rationale may be useful politically, but from an academic perspective it is untidy as applied to wealth transfer taxes. For starters, a wealth transfer tax is not (like the income tax) a broad-based tax that can encompass a taxpayer's entire ability to pay, and it is not capable of financing government. The personal income tax itself captures ability to pay, at least in principle, and thus a wealth transfer tax is superfluous from this point of view, at least to the extent that it is imposed on income previously taxed to the decedent (or donor). It is true that the income tax has gaps in the form of exempt income (viewing net capital gains as partially exempt income), income that is effectively exempt by way of CIT provisions, and (especially) the permanent exclusion of unrealized appreciation at death.[88] However, these gaps can be dealt with by reforming the income tax.[89] Certainly, the integrated gift/estate tax does not specifically plug these gaps. As noted earlier, the estate tax has always been characterized by substantial exemptions.[90] Thus, the U.S. tax system in the aggregate permanently exempts a good deal of income from any tax, while subjecting some income to double taxation.

---

85 *See* David G. Duff, *The Abolition of Wealth Transfer Taxes: Lessons from Canada, Australia, and New Zealand*, 3 Pitt. Tax Rev. 72, 115 (2005); Joseph J. Thorndike, *Are You Rich Enough to Soak?*, 128 Tax Notes 705 (2010).

86 The modern estate tax was enacted in 1916, but it was preceded by the 1898–1902 inheritance tax (enacted to help finance the Spanish-American War), not to mention the 1894 income tax (held to be unconstitutional) that included gratuitous receipts in income.

87 *See* Barry Johnson & Martha Britton Eller, *Federal Taxation of Inheritance and Wealth Transfers*, *in* Inheritance and Wealth in America 61, 66–73 (Robert K. Miller, Jr. & Stephen J. McNamee eds., 1998); Joseph J. Thorndike, *A Century of Soaking the Rich*, 112 Tax Notes 293 (2006).

88 Code § 1014 gives the successor an income tax basis equal to the asset's fair market value at death.

89 Commentators are virtually unanimous in their condemnation of § 1014. *See, e.g.*, Joseph M. Dodge, *Why a Deemed-Realization Rule for Gratuitous Transfers Is Superior to Carryover Basis and Avoids Most of the Problems of the Present Estate and Gift Tax*, 54 Tax L. Rev. 421 (2001) (and authorities cited therein).

90 *See supra* note 56.

Another problem—at least with the estate tax—is discerning "whose" ability to pay is being targeted. From the perspective of the decedent, his or her entire wealth represents ability to pay, given that a dead person has no needs (except for costs of interment) or desires. The nature of the estate tax has allowed it in recent years to be characterized as a "death tax" or even as a penalty on economic success and entrepreneurship—characterizations that divert attention from the nature and purposes of the tax, in turn rendering the tax politically vulnerable.[91] Of course, dead people are not really taxpayers, and the estate tax is (disregarding economic effects) actually borne by the decedent's successors and not by the decedent (who is dead). But, because the burden of the tax is under the decedent's control and is paid before distributions to beneficiaries are made, the tax does not appear to be on the transferees and may well reduce net legacies in a way that is wildly disproportionate to the amount of stated gross legacies. Thus, to the extent that the estate tax is perceived as a tax on the ability to pay of an estate transferee, it would be seen as an unfair and irrational tax.

At least an accessions tax is expressly a tax on what is gratuitously received by a transferee, payable by that transferee. Moreover, what is gratuitously received by the transferee cannot, generally speaking, be said to have been earned by the transferee. Thus, an accessions tax is the wealth transfer tax that is most closely aligned with the ability-to-pay rationale.

However, the accessions tax has its own problems conforming to an ability-to-pay ideal. First, ability to pay is generally determined annually, whereas an accessions tax is a tax on cumulative lifetime gratuitous receipts. As previously noted in the discussion of a consumption tax, a lifetime perspective is not an appropriate frame for tax fairness, because taxes fund government in annual budget cycles. Perhaps the cumulative lifetime tax base feature is simply an ad hoc way of making a progressive rate structure hard to avoid by spreading gratuitous receipts over many years (e.g., if the tax were an annual tax with a significant annual exemption amount). But such a tactic would be of little avail under an income-inclusion approach that would offer no (or an insignificant) exemption for gratuitous receipts.

Second, perhaps the most problematic feature of the U.S. accessions tax proposals that have been made—and the one that most clearly distinguishes these proposals from an income-inclusion approach—is that of a significant lifetime exemption amount, typically in the neighborhood of the prevailing exclusion amount of the integrated estate and gift taxes. This feature cannot be justified from an ability-to-pay perspective. The likely explanation for why the accessions tax proposals posit a very large exemption is that the accessions tax has been offered as a replacement for the integrated estate and gift taxes, with the thought that the accessions tax would have no chance of being enacted without mimicking the salient features of the estate and gift taxes.

Third, an accessions tax base bears no relationship to a transferee's aggregate annual income (or possibly aggregate wealth), which is the correct measure of ability to pay.

Fourth, no objective metric exists for the exemption amount, which, therefore, appears to be simply the outcome of a political compromise (or perhaps calculation).[92] One might attempt to construct an exemption amount on the basis of an amount needed to construct an annuity stream that generates some level of income for persons receiving an accession.[93] However, the lump-

---

91 *See* Michael J. Graetz & Ian Shapiro, Death by a Thousand Cuts: The Fight over Taxing Inherited Wealth 41–42 (2005).

92 Similarly, no serious attempt has been made to justify the various exemption amounts under the estate tax that have been enacted in the United States since 1976, which have risen at a rate that significantly exceeds the rate of inflation.

93 For example, an annuity of $200,000 for a person age 65 could be funded by a lump sum of $2.3 million (at a 4 percent discount rate).

sum amount would increase as the age of the recipient decreases.[94] No one has proposed an exemption keyed to a recipient's life expectancy (or, for that matter, family support obligations), and any rule to that effect would distort behavior by creating a strong incentive to make gratuitous transfers to youngsters. Additionally, a decreasing lifetime exemption with increasing age would be unworkable. Yet another problem is that of deciding what annuity amount should wholly avoid any tax whatsoever. In the income tax, exemption amounts are close to poverty levels—an appropriate amount under the ability-to-pay notion—whereas proposed exemption levels under the accessions tax would fund an annuity far in excess of the poverty level. Moreover, the accessions tax would add an exemption on top of the income tax exemptions, thereby favoring individuals receiving gratuitous accessions over wage earners and investors. Finally, a high exemption keyed, for example, to a "comfortable" standard of living (say, an annuity of $100,000 per year, or some larger amount) would appear to discourage market labor.

The poor fit of wealth transfer taxes with internal-to-tax norms has perhaps led to a shift in focus to the possible role of taxes on gratuitous transfers to curb growing income and wealth inequality,[95] and this shift leads us to consider external-to-tax norms.

External-to-Tax Norms

External-to-tax norms revolve around theories of distributive justice (including welfare maximization) and economic efficiency.

Redistribution

Deontological and consequentialist (i.e., welfarist) theories alike take positions on the extent to which social income and wealth inequality can be condemned, tolerated, or celebrated. This chapter does not discuss or evaluate one or more of these theories, but instead assumes that some top-down redistribution by government is to be desired and asks what tax measures, particularly those relating to gratuitous transfers, are best suited to this end. (The economic effects of such taxes are considered below.)

It has been claimed that the estate taxes have been a failure in curbing excessive concentrations of wealth.[96] However, the fact of increasing wealth concentration is not itself proof that wealth transfer taxes are ineffective in this regard, because without a wealth transfer tax wealth could be even more concentrated than at present. Indeed, a more plausible hypothesis is that increasing concentrations of wealth starting in the early 1980s[97] are at least partly the result of the emasculation of the wealth transfer taxes that began with the Economic Recovery Tax Act of 1981.[98]

94 The same annuity as described in the preceding note would require $4.33 million for a person age 20.

95 *See supra* note 52.

96 *See* Joel C. Dobris, *A Brief for the Abolition of All Transfer Taxes*, 35 SYRACUSE L. REV. 1215, 1219 (1984); Gilbert P. Verbit, *Do Estate and Gift Taxes Affect Wealth Distribution?*, 117 TR. & EST. 598 (pt. I), 674 (pt. II) (1978).

97 The postwar increase in income inequalities began about 1980–1982. *See* Thomas Pikkety & Emmannuel Saez, *Income Inequality in the United States, 1913–1998*, 118 Q.J. ECON. 1, 7–11 (2003).

98 The Economic Recovery Tax Act of 1981 (ERTA), Pub. L. No. 97-34, 95 Stat. 172, made protaxpayer changes in the federal wealth transfer taxes, including removing the limit on the marital deduction, reducing the highest marginal rates (from 70 percent to 50 percent), increasing the gift tax annual exclusion, and providing for increases in the exemption amount that significantly exceeded the inflation rate. Subsequently,

Another position might be that, assuming wealth concentrations are undesirable, nontax (and nongovernmental) mechanisms (e.g., regression to the mean by lazy or incompetent heirs, dispersal of wealth to numerous beneficiaries,[99] and excessive wealth in trust earning a low rate of return) act as self-correctives. (Moreover, the point that excessive wealth equates with excessive political power can be countered by the argument that this is a separate problem that might be better dealt with by nontax means.) This deconcentration position is plausible, at least in the statistical sense, but it nevertheless appears that a significant percentage of the wealthiest individuals have obtained their wealth primarily by (and through) gratuitous transfer.[100] This point sharpens the focus on identifying the problem and the (tax) solutions that can be envisioned to solve it.

Little political support would exist for the proposition that certain individuals acquire too much wealth by exercising their human capital, investing wisely, or a combination of both (e.g., entrepreneurship). Besides, if this were the problem, then the appropriate tax "cure" would be to increase *income* tax rates at the very high end while closing income tax loopholes. (A federal annual wealth tax is not only assumed to be unconstitutional, but also would carry a very low rate.) But it appears to be politically impossible to raise the highest marginal income tax rate to even 40 percent.[101] In contrast, taxes on wealth transfers (including treating gratuitous accessions as income) can only come into play after wealth is accumulated in a person's hands, and any such tax can be effectively deferred until the death of the person accumulating the wealth and that person's spouse.

Thus, from a redistributionist perspective, the problem is best defined as curbing excessive concentrations of wealth *acquired by gratuitous transfer*, characterized as being "unearned" by the recipient.[102] In this respect, an accessions tax would be superior to an income-inclusion approach, because an accessions tax can be designed to have high rates combined with a substantial exemption so that it is tailored precisely to curb excessive acquisitions of unearned wealth acquired by gratuitous transfer.[103] These features are also politically convenient because even the upper middle class (which includes most legal academics) would avoid the tax—with the rallying cry, "Tax them, not us!"

---

the only move to close transfer-tax loopholes occurred with the enactment of Code §§ 2701–2704, effective starting in 1992, but these have been largely ineffective due to the allowance of GRATs (grantor retained annuity trusts) and FLPs (family limited partnerships that are holding companies for liquid assets that secure discounts for lack of marketability, minority interests, and restrictions on liquidation). The Economic Growth and Tax Relief Reconciliation Act of 2001 (EGTRRA), Pub. L. No. 107-16, 115 Stat. 38, again increased the exemption levels (while somewhat lowering rates), and even resulted in repeal of the estate tax for decedents dying in 2010.

99 Equality of distribution to children (rather than primogeniture or unequal distribution) is overwhelmingly the dominant bequest pattern in the United States. *See* Menchik, *supra* note 66.

100 Studies showing that inherited wealth constitutes a significant portion of wealth accumulations include: John A. Britain, Inheritance and the Inequality of Material Wealth (1978); C. Ronald Chester, Inheritance, Wealth, and Society (1982); Laurence J. Kotlikoff & Lawrence H. Summers, *The Role of Intergenerational Transfers in Aggregate Capital Accumulation*, 89 J. Pol. Econ. 706 (1981); Edward N. Wolff, *Changing Inequality of Wealth*, 82 Am. Econ. Rev. 552 (1992). Curiously, however, estimates of the portion of wealth attributable to inheritance range widely from 20 percent to 80 percent. *See* Paul L. Menchik & Nancy Jianakoplos, *Economics of Inheritance*, *in* Inheritance & Wealth in America, *supra* note 87, at 45.

101 The highest nominal rate since 1981 has been 39.6 percent.

102 *See* Mark L. Ascher, *Curtailing Inherited Wealth*, 89 Mich. L. Rev. 69 (1990); David G. Duff, *Taxing Inherited Wealth: A Philosophical Argument*, 6 Can. J.L. & Jurisprudence 3 (1993).

103 *See* Henry J. Aaron & Alicia H. Munnell, *Reassessing the Role for Wealth Transfer Taxes*, 45 Nat'l Tax J. 119 (1992).

A final issue with the redistributive agenda is that taxation by itself can only accomplish so much. Unless the tax is confiscatory above a certain level, a decedent can still pass vast wealth to a legatee. A 90 percent tax on a $10 billion bequest still leaves $1 billion in a legatee's hands. A tax with high rates at the top would be characterized as a soak-the-rich scheme deployed in a mean-spirited class war, although this claim is less convincing in the case of an accessions tax because the legatee is not already rich. In any event, soaking the rich by taxation is undermined if government programs favor the rich. More subtly, the redistributive agenda is undermined when the federal government itself is held in low repute or perceived (correctly, in my view) as giving low priority to the social safety net. Accordingly, consideration should be given to earmarking wealth transfer tax revenues to programs aimed at the poor and less fortunate. The danger inherent in an earmarking approach is that Congress would simply reduce general appropriations aimed at the poor. The best counter to this danger is to use the earmarked funds for a wholly new and nonduplicative program, such as the one proposed by Bruce Ackerman and Anne Alstott that would establish an initial wealth endowment for all.[104]

Economic Efficiency

Four types of economics arguments are deployed against wealth transfer taxes: (1) they destroy capital; (2) they reduce productive effort and investment; (3) they distort gratuitous transfers; and (4) they entail excessive transaction costs relative to the slight amount of revenue gained. Because I have dealt with these issues in a previous article,[105] the discussion here will be relatively brief.

Do Wealth Transfer Taxes Destroy Capital?

In debates about whether wealth transfer taxes destroy capital, the term "capital" presumably means investment in business or income-producing property (here collectively referred to as "investment"), rather than "income previously subject to tax" as it does when used in an income tax context. The charge is thus that wealth transfer taxes reduce national investment.

Any tax is payable in cash, and the cash paid to the government reduces the taxpayer's economic resources relative to what they would have been in the absence of tax. However, the fact that the tax is on "wealth" does not mean that wealth is destroyed, because the tax is paid in cash and taxpayers can obtain cash by reducing either consumption or investment. This point holds for all taxes. Furthermore, even assuming that a wealth transfer tax reduces private capital, so would any other tax. To frame the matter in a meaningful way, the claim must be that wealth transfer taxes are worse than other taxes in terms of reducing national investment (relative to consumption). It would be hard to empirically test the hypothesis that wealth transfer taxes are worse for national investment than, for instance, income taxes, because other factors (including government programs) impact national investment. In any event, I have not seen any study that shows that a country that has repealed its wealth transfer tax (e.g., Canada, Australia, or Italy), but perhaps has not reduced total tax revenues, has experienced a higher level of economic growth as a result of such repeal.

The destruction-of-capital charge contains two assumptions and a value judgment. The first assumption is that investment (including personal savings), as opposed to consumption, is what drives the economy. However, both theory and history suggest that consumer demand is what

104 *See* Bruce A. Ackerman & Anne Alstott, The Stakeholder Society (1999).

105 *See* Dodge, *supra* note 37.

drives the economy[106] and that excessive saving by individuals (including debt repayment) slows it. The best that can be said is that individual investment is sometimes to be desired, but this point only raises the question of whether tax design has a significant effect on the supply of savings and investment. The second assumption is that a reduction in social capital attributable to taxes is irretrievably lost. However, government can (and does) subsidize both physical and human capital. Thus, if a wealth transfer tax were worse than other taxes, government could compensate for the excess burden and the tax might still be worthwhile if it effectively achieved a goal such as redistribution.[107] The value judgment is that *Americans* should be encouraged to save—even if capital is in plentiful supply in the United States.[108] Although capital inflows into the United States can have economic effects, the effects are not necessarily harmful.[109] Indeed, global economic policy favors the free movement of capital, and U.S. tax policy gives preferential treatment to the importation of capital.[110] Thus, the argument appears at its core to be political (i.e., nationalistic).

The destruction-of-capital argument only makes theoretical sense as a hypothesis when it is reduced to the charge that a wealth transfer tax forces the liquidation of family enterprises (at least those that are businesses rather than investment holding companies).[111] (The argument that jobs are lost as a result of any such liquidation would be hard to prove, because both the tax and the proceeds of liquidation could be spent in a way that results in no net job loss.) The extent to which enterprise liquidation actually occurs is hotly contested between academics and politicians.[112] A liquidation would often not be necessary, as the taxable estate of a wealthy person could well include sufficient nonbusiness assets (e.g., cash, term life insurance, homes used for personal use, collectibles, and other marketable investments) to pay the tax. Additionally, the Code contains provisions mitigating the impact of (and deferring the payment of) estate taxes on closely held

---

106 *See, e.g.*, Daniel J. Boyer & Susan M. Russell, *Is It Time for a Consumption Tax?*, 48 Nat'l Tax J. 363, 365–67 (1995).

107 *See* Kotlicoff & Summers, *supra* note 100, at 727–29 (finding that confiscatory wealth taxation would not reduce national capital stock).

108 The "savings glut hypothesis" is that global savings exceed global investment (presumably because there is insufficient global demand to sustain high levels of investment). The hypothesis—which is controversial—has been advanced by former Chairman of the Federal Reserve Ben Bernanke as an explanation for (1) U.S. capital account imbalances; (2) the slow recovery from the recession of 2008; and (3) low interest rates. *See* Ben S. Bernanke, Governor, Fed. Reserve Bd., Remarks at the Sandridge Lecture at the Virginia Association of Economists (Apr. 14, 2005); *Global Saving Glut*, Wikipedia (July 8, 2014), http://en.wikipedia.org/wiki/Global_saving_glut.

109 A description of such effects is found in Soyoung Kim & Doo Yong Yang, *Managing Capital Flows: The Case of the Republic of Korea* 11–18 (Asian Dev. Bank Inst., Discussion Paper No. 88, 2008), *available at* http://www.adbi.org/files/dp88.managing.capital.flows.korea.pdf.

110 *See* I.R.C. §§ 871(h), 881(c) (foreign persons exempt from tax on U.S. source portfolio investment income).

111 *See* C. Lowell Harriss, *Estate Taxes and the Family-Owned Business*, 38 Calif. L. Rev. 117 (1950). Capital in the form of assets that can readily be sold is not implicated by the "destruction-of-capital" argument because these assets will be sold to willing buyers. Nonfamily but closely held interests in enterprises can (and often are) sold to nonfamily coentrepreneurs.

112 Politicians loudly sing this refrain. However, the reality appears to be somewhat different. *See* Cong. Budget Office, Effects of the Estate Tax on Farms and Small Business 12 (2005) (finding that only 5 percent of estates filing estate tax returns had to liquidate a farm or business); Chye-Ching Huang & Nathaniel Frentz, *Myths and Realities About the Estate Tax* (Aug. 29, 2013), http://www.cbpp.org/cms/?fa=view&id=2655 (finding minuscule effect). Of course, the slight effect is largely attributable to large exemptions and liquidity-facilitative features of the estate tax itself.

business interests,[113] and both an income-inclusion approach and accessions-tax approach could be even more accommodating in this regard by deferring realization until sale. Even liquidation would normally entail a sale rather than a destruction or abandonment of assets. Most small enterprises passed on to family members fail in any event,[114] whereas a sale of the enterprise at the founder's death moves the assets into the hands of their highest and best users. Thus, for the economy as a whole, forced liquidations caused by a wealth transfer tax are likely to preserve enterprise capital. Moreover, the capital that is lost at the death of an entrepreneur is human capital, and no government policy, much less the tax law, can preserve or revive it.

Do Wealth Transfer Taxes Distort Economic Activity?

Whether a wealth transfer tax distorts an individual's choice among savings, consumption, and working implicates an underlying policy norm that economic distortions reduce individual welfare. The distortion (if any) would be caused by the fact that the wealth transfer tax is a "second tax" on previously taxed invested income, which operates (via the "substitution effect") as an incentive to consume current and accumulated income rather than attempt to acquire wealth to pass on to future generations. The issue is often framed as whether wealth accumulation is primarily a "life cycle" phenomenon (i.e., to finance retirement income and/or to save for a rainy day) or is instead primarily motivated to fund the making of bequests. The standard theory is that life-cycle economic activity is uninfluenced by the prospect of a future wealth transfer tax because bequests are "accidental," whereas bequest-motivated savings are sensitive to wealth transfer taxes (i.e., the testator would avoid income-producing activity that would incur the second tax).[115]

In my opinion, the matter is not quite correctly framed. The dichotomy is better described as between self-centered[116] and other-centered economic activity. Self-centered activity is to provide for the individual's own economic needs; that is, to prepare for retirement or emergencies (i.e., future consumption), to amass wealth for its own sake (i.e., miserliness), to obtain power over others, or to obtain the esteem or gratitude of others. Other-centered economic activity may be driven by altruism, family reciprocity, or conformity to social expectations.[117] Accepted theory holds that self-centered activity is not responsive to wealth transfer taxes, because such taxes are imposed after the individual's death and are borne by those who are secondary on the individual's priority list. Accepted theory also holds that other-centered (i.e., bequest-motivated) activity should be responsive to a tax that would reduce after-tax bequests. However, I believe that theory errs in assuming that the behavioral response would be to forego labor income or savings (or to consume existing savings) to reduce the future tax, because the whole point of other-directed economic behavior is to benefit others at the expense of oneself. If the desire is conceived of as an after-tax "target" amount, the taxpayer would be expected to increase before-tax bequests.

113 *See* I.R.C. §§ 303, 2032A, 6161, 6166.

114 *See* Danny Miller et al., *Lost in Time: Intergenerational Succession, Change, and Failure in Family Business*, 18 J. Bus. Venturing 513 (2003).

115 *See* Douglas Holtz-Eakin, *The Uneasy Empirical Case for Abolishing the Estate Tax*, 51 Tax L. Rev. 495, 507–11 (1996).

116 "Self-centered" includes "couple-centered," because qualified gift and estate transfers to one's spouse avoid transfer tax. *See* I.R.C. §§ 2056(a), 2523(a).

117 Economists sometimes refer to "reciprocity." However, except for spouses, reciprocity among generations (i.e., children caring for aging parents) is not a conspicuous aspect of American culture. A more relevant hypothesis is that children expect inheritances to supplement (or provide) a retirement nest egg for themselves. Also, the expectation of bequests tends to bind families together.

Although this may be viewed as a distortion of some sort, it would be considered a socially benign one. Alternatively, the distortion would be minimal if the individual conceived of her wealth-transfer obligations in before-tax terms, which is a plausible supposition if it happens that people generally are not influenced by taxes paid by others.[118] Regardless, the trade-off among savings, consumption, and labor supply should be far more influenced by the income tax, which operates in the present, than by a wealth transfer tax.

Turning to empirical research, virtually all of it is concerned with sorting out life-cycle versus bequest motives.[119] Evidence that bequest motives exist includes (1) the relatively low rate of voluntary annuitization; (2) the trend toward defined-contribution retirement plans and away from defined-benefit retirement plans; and (3) the persistent demand for life insurance.[120] A counter indicator is the large amount spent on medical and nursing care, especially near life's end. However, this literature is pointless if it turns out that even bequest-motivated individuals are unresponsive to transfer taxes. What scant evidence exists suggests that individuals are just not very responsive to wealth transfer taxes as far as consumption, savings, and work are concerned.[121]

What the economics literature largely ignores is the possible effect of wealth transfer taxes on legatees. The so-called Carnegie effect refers to the plausible hypothesis—supported by empirical research—that people who are well-off by gratuitous receipt are less likely to work or save than those with little or no such endowment.[122] Accordingly, it would follow that a high wealth transfer tax on gratuitous accessions would increase productive activity.

Do Wealth Transfer Taxes Distort Gratuitous Transfers?

It would be impossible to deny that the present wealth transfer tax system egregiously distorts gratuitious transfers. In the absence of this tax, it is unlikely that we would have multiple-trust estate plans, GRATs, private annuities, *Crummey* powers, "five and five" powers of withdrawal, holding companies for publicly traded assets, irrevocable insurance trusts, and restrictions on liquidity. Other common features of contemporary estate planning (e.g., QTIP trusts, split-interest charitable trusts, and multigenerational dynasty trusts) would also be less common.[123] In the aggregate, these features tend to impose restrictions and constraints on gratuitous transferees that

118 Transfers to charity avoid estate and gift tax by reason of being deductible. *See* I.R.C. §§ 2055(a), 2522(a).

119 *See* B. Douglas Bernheim, *How Strong Are Bequest Motives? Evidence Based on the Demand for Life Insurance and Annuities*, 99 J. Pol. Econ. 899, 924 (1991); B. Douglas Bernheim et al., *The Strategic Bequest Motive*, 93 J. Pol. Econ. 1045 (1985); Donald Cox, *Motives for Private Income Transfers*, 95 J. Pol. Econ. 508 (1987); Michael D. Hurd, *Savings of the Elderly and Desired Bequests*, 77 Am. Econ. Rev. 298 (1987). *See generally*, Martin Browning & Annamaria Lusardi, *Household Saving: Micro Theories and Macro Facts*, 34 J. Econ. Lit. 1797 (1996) (survey of literature on various possible savings motives).

120 The aggregate quantity of bequests is not itself a good indicator of bequest motive, because of the phenomenon of the "accidental bequest," referring to bequests resulting from overestimation of one's future retirement and health needs.

121 As to empirical evidence, the reduction in estate taxes starting in 1976 apparently did not cause an increase in private savings or investment. *See* Joel Slemrod, *Do Taxes Matter? Lessons from the 1980s*, 82 Am. Econ. Rev. 250 (1992).

122 *See* Jeffrey R. Brown et al., *The Effect of Inheritance Receipt on Retirement*, 92 Rev. Econ. & Stat. 425 (2010) (similar results for retirement saving); Douglas Holtz-Eakin et al., *The Carnegie Conjecture: Some Empirical Evidence*, 108 Q.J. Econ. 413 (1993) (finding that large inheritances significantly depress the labor supply).

123 *See* Cooper, *supra* note 72.

amount to restraints on alienation. Additionally, the tax creates a demand for insurance products (to provide estate liquidity) that would otherwise not exist.

However, bad tax design should not be considered the norm. Virtually all of these distortions (including excess insurance) would disappear under a "realization" accessions tax or an income-inclusion approach, because only cash or property (but not trust interests) actually received would be included in the tax base, and lapsing restrictions on value would be counted as gratuitous receipts.[124] Of course, the realization feature—which essentially solves the liquidity problem—would allow deferral of receipt (and taxation) through the use of long-term trusts, but the value (if any) of deferral in this context cannot be predicted in advance.[125]

Is a Wealth Transfer Tax Worth the Effort?

It is alleged that the revenue yield from the existing wealth transfer tax system barely (if at all) exceeds its costs, including private planning and compliance costs,[126] but this claim seems greatly exaggerated,[127] especially as the percentage of estates subject to tax has declined.[128] In any event, the tax could easily be designed to extract a lot more revenue, especially under an income-inclusion approach lacking a separate lifetime exemption.[129] Moreover, raising revenue is not the only purpose of wealth taxes; reducing excessive concentrations of (inherited) wealth is another. Incidentally, private costs related to the estate/gift tax entail redistribution from the very wealthy to the moderately wealthy.

It can also be claimed that the tax might have collateral effects on the transferor, such as creating incentives for marrying (or staying married), expatriation outside of the United States, concealing wealth, or encouraging gifts and bequests to charity. However, wealth transfer taxes are certainly no more susceptible to evasion than income taxes, and encouraging marital and charitable transfers is usually cited as a "private redistribution" positive collateral effect of a wealth transfer tax.[130]

124 *See* Dodge, *supra* note 73.

125 Deferral of realization is advantageous only under certain conditions (e.g., where the amount included in the tax base grows at a slower rate than the increase, if any, in exemption levels).

126 The most cited source for this claim is a statement in a 1992 article by Aaron & Munnell, *supra* note 103, at 138, but the statement was only that administrative and compliance costs constituted a "sizeable fraction" of the revenue yield. However, the article treated the entire income of the estate planning bar as estate/gift tax compliance costs.

127 *See* Joel Friedman & Ruth Carlitz, *Cost of Estate Tax Compliance Does Not Approach the Total Level of Estate Tax Revenue*, CTR. ON BUDGET & POLICY PRIORITIES (June 9, 2006), http://www.cbpp.org/cms/?fa=view&id=389 (citing Charles Davenport & Jay A. Soled, *Enlivening the Death-Tax Death-Talk*, 84 TAX NOTES 591 (1999) (estimating costs at only 7 percent of revenues)).

128 The 2008 estate tax exemption of $2 million was estimated to result in tax being paid by 0.76 percent of decedents' estates. Raising the exemption to $3.5 million in 2009 was estimated to reduce the percentage of taxed estates by almost half (to 0.39 percent), while decreasing revenue yield by only 20 percent (from $27.1 billion to $21.8 billion). STAFF OF J. COMM. ON TAXATION, 110TH CONG., HISTORY, PRESENT LAW, AND ANALYSIS OF THE FEDERAL WEALTH TRANSFER TAX SYSTEM 29 (Comm. Print 2007).

129 If total bequests (other than to spouses or charity) in a year total $200 billion, a tax thereon at an average rate of 25 percent would produce a tax yield of $50 billion, a figure far in excess of the current estate tax yield.

130 *See, e.g.*, Jon M. Bakija & William G. Gale, *Effects of Estate Tax Reform on Charitable Giving*, 6 TAX POL'Y ISSUES & OPTIONS 1 (2003). As Chapter 13 of this volume demonstrates, the devil is in the details. Specifically, the doctrine surrounding the marital deduction in the estate/gift tax profoundly affects the existence (and form) of interspousal transfers. For example, the fact that the Code allows a trust giving

To sum up this section, economics does not offer a persuasive case against some form of tax on gratuitous transfers.

Conclusion

This chapter offers a traditional academic (i.e., detached) perspective on whether wealth transfer taxes are desirable, and, if so, what form one should take. Perhaps unlike most academic pieces, this chapter examines these issues from a multiplicity of norms of interest to the academic community and, in a looser sense, society at large (which the academic community ostensibly aims to understand and improve). A principle characteristic of a norm is its "sharedness" in the relevant community. An appeal to a shared norm has the potential for the persuasion of other members of the community or society. A norm-based approach contrasts with, on the one hand, an approach based on some ultimate value (e.g., that of a particular religion or philosophy, such as libertarianism or welfarism) and, on the other hand, the goals of a particular group. Conflicts among groups are mediated by the legal and political system. Although so-called advocacy pieces on behalf of groups are likely to perform less of a persuasive function relative to other groups (and decision makers), they are well suited to perform the internal function of rallying the troops and the external function of presenting the social "facts" for all to see in a new light.

To summarize this chapter, the primary rationales for a tax on wealth transfers are (1) an ability-to-pay fairness norm for taxes generally (or at least nudging the system as a whole to a closer alignment with an ability-to-pay norm) and (2) as a curb on excessive concentrations of unearned (i.e., gratuitously received) wealth. Both rationales command that the tax on gratuitous transfers be imposed on the transferee, either through an income-inclusion approach or an accessions tax. Both approaches encourage the dispersal of wealth, especially among those who are not well-off on their own. The choice (if any) between the two depends on whether one prioritizes the ability-to-pay fairness norm or the instrumental curb-excessive-inheritances norm. Actually, one could have both: an income-inclusion approach combined with an accessions tax with a very large exemption and high rates.

A transferee-oriented tax would not really conflict with freedom of testation, although the testator would not be able to shift the tax burden among beneficiaries, as can be done under the estate tax. Testators dealing with transferee-oriented tax systems might perhaps be sensitive to the tax situations of beneficiaries and adjust gratuitous transfers accordingly. "Private" redistribution would be encouraged.

Ultimately the notion of a wealth transfer tax collides with social attitudes about inheritance, which is intensely desired by both wealth owners (as a monument to their priorities and accomplishments) and potential legatees (as ripe fruit waiting to be harvested), as evidenced by both the deep political support for high exemption levels and the extremely high threshold for escheat under state intestacy law.[131] Nevertheless, inheritance is an obstacle to achieving a society

---

the surviving spouse only an income interest (as opposed to a fee interest or an income interest coupled with a general power of appointment) to qualify for the marital deduction has resulted in near universal use of this device (i.e., the QTIP trust) by wealthier spouses potentially subject to the estate tax.

131 For an overview of the role of inheritance as an institution in the United States, see Stephen J. McNamee & Robert K. Miller, *Inheritance and Stratification*, *in* INHERITANCE AND WEALTH IN AMERICA, *supra* note 87, at 193–210.

based on equality of opportunity.[132] Just as shifting allegiance from clan or tribe to nationality marks an advance in civilization, so would curbing family dynasties based on inherited wealth.

Curbing family dynasties would not be an attack on families themselves. In the legal sense, a family (as distinguished from a voluntary or even contractual association) entails a "status" relationship that imposes redistributive financial obligations. Interestingly, the strongest of these obligations (i.e., child support) has little relevance to estate planning: although such support is not a gift for gift tax purposes, it is also the case that support does not entail a true wealth transfer, nor does it appear that people incur child support obligations to avoid taxes. In contrast, marital property rights do result in wealth transfers, and any transfer-tax marital deduction or exemption is bound to have a major impact on estate planning. A transfer-tax system that is marriage neutral would not provide any such deduction or exemption, and would need to override community-property law. Since there is no political constituency for marriage neutrality or overriding community-property law, some form of marital tax privilege appears to be inevitable. Accordingly, whether the marital tax privilege distorts behavior by inducing people to marry for tax reasons (or other reasons relating to government or private entitlements) is a nonissue in the political sense. Of course, academics can question the political status quo, but, in the case of marriage, its redistributive aspects would need to be addressed, as would the relevance of tax-subsidized, interspousal redistribution within the top 1 percent of the population. Or, is the real issue the economic power of women (in which case we are back to politics)?

As the next chapter illustrates, the form of the marital tax privilege matters a lot. Doctrinal reform that seems beneficient on its face (both the 1981 changes to the marital deduction and recent enabling of "portability" of a spouse's unused exemption) can have unintended consequences. Or perhaps the consequences are understood only too well by the promoters of these "reforms."

132 *See supra* note 102.

Chapter 13
Portability, Marital Wealth Transfers, and the Taxable Unit

Bridget J. Crawford and Wendy C. Gerzog

Prior to 2011, the most efficient estate tax planning for married couples required a minimal level of asset equalization. In order to take maximum advantage of all existing wealth transfer tax exemptions and credits, each spouse needed to own, in an estate tax sense, enough assets to be able to fully utilize the estate tax credit or applicable exemption. This changed with the enactment of estate tax portability in the Tax Relief, Unemployment Insurance Reauthorization, and Job Creation Act of 2010, which became permanent under the American Taxpayer Relief Act of 2012. "Portability" refers to the ability of a surviving spouse to make full use of his or her predeceased spouse's unused exemption from estate tax. In an era of portability, if the less-wealthy member of a married couple dies first, he or she no longer "wastes" that exemption. It simply "ports"—or carries over—to the survivor.

At first glance, portability appears to implicate theoretical concerns, as it functions as a modern-day coverture that "merges" spouses into one unit. Furthermore, portability discourages some lifetime transfers of property to the less-wealthy spouse, who is more likely to be female. On the other hand, portability simplifies tax planning and benefits both spouses in a marriage. Portability was envisioned as a congressional "kiss" to a loving couple who sees itself as a unit. Yet the tax benefit is available regardless of whether the couple does in fact function as an economic unit, raising tax policy questions about the appropriateness of using the married couple as the primary tax unit. On balance, however, portability is a salutary addition to the law of wealth transfer taxation that minimizes complexity in estate planning and likely reduces the use of certain QTIP trusts, which minimize the autonomy of the surviving spouse, typically the woman, because a QTIP trust allows the marital deduction for one spouse's transfer of the underlying property to a third party and not to the other spouse.

Background to the Estate and Gift Tax Applicable Exemption

Legislative Flux 2001–2012

The period of 2001 through 2012 was one of great legal instability for estate planners and their clients. With the Economic Growth and Tax Relief Reconciliation Act of 2001[1] (EGTRRA) came a series of gradual increases in the estate and gift tax applicable exemption amount from $1 million to $3.5 million over a nine-year period. EGTRRA also lowered tax rates over the same period and provided for a temporary, one-year repeal of the estate tax in 2010. After 2010, pre-EGTRRA law was scheduled to spring back into effect, but ultimately that did not happen. At the end of 2010,

1 Pub. L. No. 107-16, 115 Stat. 38.

Congress enacted the Tax Relief, Unemployment Insurance Reauthorization, and Job Creation Act of 2010 (2010 Act).[2] That law (retroactively) made elective EGTRRA's 2010 one-year repeal of the estate tax, increased the applicable exemption amount to $5 million (indexed for inflation), and further lowered tax rates—to 35 percent—but only through 2012. The 2010 Act also introduced into the wealth transfer tax system the concept of portability—the ability of a surviving spouse to make use of a predeceased spouse's unused exemption amount—which is referred to as the "deceased spouse's unused exemption amount."

All of these changes contained in the 2010 Act had been scheduled to (and did) sunset on January 1, 2013. Just a few days into January 2013, Congress enacted permanent wealth transfer tax legislation with the American Taxpayer Relief Act of 2012 (ATRA).[3] ATRA permanently codified the 2010 Act's applicable exemption of $5 million (indexed for inflation), raised the top wealth transfer tax rate to 40 percent, and made portability a fixed part of estate tax legislation. For the first time since 2001, then, estate planners and their clients now can enjoy a relatively stable legal landscape.

Pre-Portability

To understand the importance of portability and its extraordinary impact on much estate planning for married couples, one must first understand some wealth transfer tax basics and how the estate and gift tax applicable exemption worked prior to the 2010 Act.

Under Code § 2010, each taxpayer has a credit against gift and estate taxes. That credit is equal to the tax liability on a particular dollar amount of cumulative lifetime and death-time transfers, often colloquially called the "applicable exemption amount." From 2003 to 2009, the applicable exemption amount was: $1 million in 2003; $1.5 million in 2004 and 2005; $2 million in 2006, 2007, and 2008; and $3.5 million in 2009. In these years prior to the 2010 Act, in the case of a married couple seeking to minimize wealth transfer taxes on their combined assets, both members of the couple would need to own (in an estate tax sense) assets at least equal to the amount that could pass tax free (i.e., the applicable exemption amount). Otherwise, all or part of the credit would be wasted.

To illustrate, consider a hypothetical married couple, *X* and *Y*. For simplicity purposes, assume that *X* predeceases *Y* at a time when the applicable exemption amount is $5 million and estate tax is imposed at a flat rate of 50 percent.[4] *Y* dies four months later, with no changes to the law. Assume that neither *X* nor *Y* has made any lifetime taxable gifts, the value of assets does not change over time, and no assets are consumed. Estate planners typically encounter several common estate planning mistakes made by a couple such as *X* and *Y*.

First Common Mistake: Leaving All Property Outright to Survivor

To illustrate the first common estate planning mistake, assume that *X* has $5 million in assets in *X*'s own name and *Y* has $10 million in *Y*'s own name. Further assume that the couple has no joint assets. If *X* leaves her $5 million outright to *Y*, the transfer qualifies for the marital deduction, and thus *X* does not use any of her estate tax credit under Code § 2010 in order to achieve an estate tax

2 Pub. L. No. 111-312, 124 Stat. 3296.

3 Pub. L. No. 112-240, 126 Stat. 2313 (2013).

4 Compare these figures to the actual 2014 exemption amount of $5.34 million and a flat estate tax rate of 40 percent.

bill of zero. *X* thus is said in the pre-portability era to "waste" the advantage of her credit because the applicable exemption amount dies with *X* and cannot be used later by *Y*. When *Y* subsequently dies with $10 million in his own name and the $5 million he inherited from *X*, only $5 million of that aggregate $15 million can pass tax free. Instead of *X* passing $5 million tax free and *Y* passing an additional $5 million tax free, the couple shelters only $5 million from estate tax. At the assumed rate of 50 percent, the real tax "cost" of this mistake is $2.5 million.

Second Common Mistake: Not Having Enough Assets in One Spouse's Name

A second common estate planning mistake that a couple like *X* and *Y* might make in a pre-portability era is failing to make maximum use of the wealth transfer tax exemption. Assume that *X* has $1 million in assets in *X*'s own name and *Y* has $10 million in *Y*'s own name, and that the couple has no joint assets. Even if *X* leaves her estate in a nonqualifying form, making it possible for *X* to fully use $1 million of her $5 million exemption, she still "wastes" $4 million of exemption because she did not have enough assets to fully soak up the full $5 million exemption. A more effective tax strategy would be for *Y* to transfer $4 million to *X* during her lifetime. That transfer would qualify for the gift tax marital deduction and thus would not attract any gift tax. Now with $5 million in her name, *X* can fully utilize her $5 million exemption at death by making her own outright, nonspousal transfers. *Y* also can utilize his $5 million exemption at death. Together, the couple passes $10 million tax free to their beneficiaries. The couple has saved an additional $2 million in taxes by *Y*'s transfer of $4 million to *X*.

Third Common Mistake: Jointly Owning All Property

Consider a third common mistake that *X* and *Y* might make in a pre-portability era—owning all assets jointly. Assume, for example, that *X* and *Y* own $10 million in assets as tenants by the entireties. Upon *X*'s death, *Y* automatically becomes the sole, outright owner of the couple's $10 million in assets. This is true regardless of what *X*'s will says, as the jointly owned property passes outside the will. There will be no estate tax due upon the death of *X* because the transfer qualifies for the marital deduction. When *Y* subsequently dies, leaving $10 million to the couple's child, only *Y*'s $5 million exemption is available. Like the couple making the first common mistake, this couple has also "wasted" *X*'s $5 million exemption, at a tax cost of $2.5 million.

Pre-portability, "use it or lose it" was a phrase that aptly applied to the estate tax exemption. In that era, a married couple seeking to minimize the overall wealth transfer tax burden had a financial incentive to "equalize" the spouses' estates, or, at a minimum, to make sure that the less-wealthy spouse had enough assets in her (or his) own name to take maximum advantage of the exemption amount.

Portability

Estate planners will report that, in the pre-portability era, it was not uncommon for married couples to commit one or more of the errors ascribed to hypothetical couple *X* and *Y*: failure to use the exemption that one has, failure to have enough assets in the "poorer" spouse's name to make full use of that exemption, or owning all assets jointly. However, with the enactment of portability in the 2010 Act, later made permanent by ATRA, these potential mistakes were eliminated. Under existing law, it does not matter if the poorer spouse has any (let alone "enough") assets in her (or his) own name. When the first spouse to die simply does not have enough wealth to employ some or all of his or her exemption, the unused portion, called the "deceased spouse's unused exemption" or "DSUE," becomes fully usable by the survivor.

Portability was designed to benefit the typical married couple where one spouse, usually the husband, owns all or a majority of the couple's property during their joint lifetimes but wants to leave all of his property to his wife when he dies. Portability allows *X* and *Y* to be treated taxwise like a couple in a community property state. At the 2008 hearing before the Senate Finance Committee, Shirley L. Kovar, testifying on her own behalf and on behalf of the American College of Trust and Estate Counsel (ACTEC), called portability "the best estate tax planning idea for a surviving spouse since the unlimited marital deduction in 1981."[5] She said that although it is commonly believed that a married couple's estate tax exemption is twice that available to a single individual, that perception is wrong. If all assets are transferred to the surviving spouse, then the couple's combined exemption is only equal to one spouse's exemption because the deceased spouse's exemption is lost. Thus, portability was enacted to help couples in that situation, both to simplify their transactions and to retain each spouse's exemption amounts.

Therefore, those wealthy spouses who write "I love you" wills, wherein the wealthier spouse leaves "too much" under the pre-portability estate tax rules to the poorer spouse, are not disadvantaged taxwise. Likewise, portability allows these couples to avoid complex trusts and couple estate planning. They do not have to create a credit-shelter or bypass trust that limits the surviving spouse's interest in, and control over, property placed in that type of trust.[6] Portability allows the surviving spouse to own the couple's property outright after the first spouse dies. With a credit-shelter or bypass trust, the surviving spouse may be the income beneficiary, but a third party owns the remainder interest after her death. That split inevitably "raises issues of fiduciary duties owed to the remainder beneficiaries by the trustee" even if the trustee is the surviving spouse.[7] Portability obviates the need for any trust for the surviving spouse. This is especially helpful in the case of a married couple that considered assets to be "theirs," even if the assets were formally titled in the wealthier spouse's name. For example, the wealthier spouse might have purchased a car, titled it in his name, and then given it to his wife as a de facto gift but never transferred title to her. The couple might have consistently referred to the car as "her" car, and would have been surprised that, on his death, the car would have been included in his estate because he had forgotten to retitle it in her name. Portability takes the tax sting out of such a scenario.

5 *Outside the Box on Estate Tax Reform: Reviewing Ideas to Simplify Planning: Hearings Before the S. Fin. Comm.*, 110th Cong. 121 (2008) (prepared statement of Shirley L. Kovar, attorney at Branton & Wilson APC, fellow of ACTEC, and chair of ACTEC's Transfer Tax Study Committee). The legislative proposal was unanimously passed by ACTEC's Board of Regents on March 10, 2008.

6 Kovar also pointed out that without the necessity of drafting a credit-shelter or bypass trust, there would be no need for: (1) the complex marital-deduction-formula clause common in those trusts; (2) a separate trust with its own taxpayer identification number and separate income tax return; and (3) a preliminary trust created with its own taxpayer identification number and separate income tax return to hold the assets until after the estate tax return is filed and the credit-shelter or bypass trust is funded. *Id.* at 122.

7 *Id.* at 123.

Estate Tax Portability, Gender, and Structural Inequality

Identifying the Poorer Spouse

In 2010, the average life expectancy at birth for people of all races in the United States was 76.2 years for men and 81 years for women.[8] Among whites, life expectancies were slightly higher than for people of all races.[9] The average white man's life expectancy at birth was 76.5 years; the average white woman had a life expectancy of 81.3 years.[10] For blacks, average life expectancies at birth were 71.8 years for men and 78 years for women.[11] The differing life expectancies for men and women are built into the assumptions that private insurers make. In 2007, for example, the federal government calculated that a 62-year-old woman was 35 percent more likely than her male counterpart to survive to age 85.[12] Insurers price annuities and other mortality-based products accordingly. The federal government, too, gets into the mortality business. There are rules requiring mandatory withdrawals from IRAs and retirement plans, and the calculation of the required amount may depend on a spouse's life expectancy where the spouse is a sole beneficiary and more than 10 years younger than the account owner.[13] The same tables are used to calculate the wealth transfer tax value of retained life estates and remainder interests, except in certain circumstances.[14] Thus, for estate and gift tax purposes, age matters.

Because women tend to live longer than men, gender also matters when it comes to life beyond actuarial tables. Available economic data suggests that women earn less than men,[15] own less than men,[16] and have fewer assets than men at retirement.[17] According to IRS estimates, there are approximately 2,290,000 people in the United States having gross assets of $2 million or more.[18] Of these, 1,320,000 (or 57.6 percent) are male and 970,000 (or 42.4 percent) are female.[19] Of the estimated 470,000 individuals having gross assets of $5 million or more (roughly, the population that would be subject to estate tax for years 2013 and after), 281,000 (or 59.8 percent) are male and 189,000 (or 40.2 percent) are female. Of the estimated 184,000 individuals having gross assets of $10 million or more, 112,000 (or 60.9 percent) are male and 72,000 (or 39.1 percent) are female. Across the entire sample pool, wealthy women were more likely to be widowed than their

---

8 Donna L. Hoyert & Jiaquan Xu, *Deaths: Preliminary Data for 2011*, NAT'L VITAL STAT. REP., Oct. 10, 2012, at 3 tbl.A.

9 *Id.*

10 *Id.*

11 *Id.*

12 Elizabeth Arias, *United States Life Tables, 2007*, NAT'L VITAL STAT. REP., Sept. 28, 2011, at 3.

13 *See Retirement Topics—Required Minimum Distributions (RMDs)*, INTERNAL REVENUE SERV. (Apr. 29, 2014), http://www.irs.gov/Retirement-Plans/Plan-Participant,-Employee/Retirement-Topics---Required-Minimum-Distributions-%28RMDs%29.

14 *See, e.g.*, I.R.S. Pub. No. 1457, Actuarial Valuations: Version 3A (2009). Where Code § 2702 applies, however, retained interests are valued at zero.

15 Neelakantan Yunhee Chang, *Gender Differences in Wealth at Retirement*, 100 AM. ECON. REV. 362 (2010). The older a couple is, the larger the gap there is in earned wealth. *See* Lucie Schmidt & Purvi Sevak, *Gender, Marriage, and Asset Accumulation in the United States*, 12 FEM. ECON. 139, 156 (2006).

16 MARIKO LIN CHANG, SHORTCHANGED: WHY WOMEN HAVE LESS WEALTH AND WHAT CAN BE DONE ABOUT IT 2 (2010) (indicating that women own 36 cents for every dollar of wealth held by men).

17 Chang, *supra* note 15.

18 Brian Raub & Joseph Newcomb, *Personal Wealth, 2007*, STAT. INCOME BULL., Winter 2012, at 169 tbl.1.

19 *Id.* at 171 tbl.2, 173 tbl.3.

male counterparts.[20] Even among wealthy individuals, men have a greater average net worth than women do, although the median net worth was similar across the genders, suggesting the existence of a small number of ultrawealthy men.[21] What the IRS data do not reveal is how many wealthy individuals are married to other wealthy individuals. Whether some of the men subject to the estate tax (roughly those with more than $5 million in gross assets) are also married to women subject to the estate tax is unknown. Absent additional information, then, it appears that the "poorer" spouse is more likely to be the wife.[22] Portability removes any pure tax incentive the wealthier spouse would have had to make equalizing (outright) transfers to the "poorer" spouse. To be sure, though, even in a portability scenario, there will be many wealthy spouses who view their marriage as a partnership, putting all assets into a joint account, or others who choose to make substantial lifetime gifts of property. For these couples, the presence or absence of portability will not impact their sharing behavior.

It is worthwhile to note that portability's "merger" of the two spouses into a single tax unit for purposes of the wealth transfer tax exemption resembles coverture, the common-law doctrine that caused a woman's legal personhood to merge with her husband's upon marriage:

> By marriage, the husband and wife are one person in the law: that is, the very being or legal existence of the woman is suspended during the marriage, or at least incorporated and consolidated into that of the husband; under whose wing, protection, and cover, she performs everything; and is therefore called … a feme-covert.[23]

The legal disabilities of married women were not changed until the nineteenth century with the enactment of married women's property acts, which allowed women to own property in their own names.[24] The effect of portability is to treat the two members of a married couple as "one person" for purposes of wealth transfer taxation. Portability in effect suspends the "tax existence" of the poorer spouse, in the event that the poorer spouse dies first. (If the richer spouse dies first, the exemption will be fully utilized.) In that sense, when the poorer spouse is the first to die, the first decedent's exemption is "incorporated and consolidated" into the survivor. Because the law of estate tax portability—unlike coverture—is gender-neutral on its face, it is not immediately implicated in gender concerns. Coverture works to merge wife into husband, whereas portability merges the (exemption of the) first spouse to die with that of the second. Nevertheless, portability should be understood as part of the U.S. tax system's embrace of the marital unit as the appropriate taxable unit. This makes the United States a relative outlier, as very few other developed countries

---

20 *See id.* at 165 ("Most wealthy individuals of both sexes were married, although a significantly higher proportion of wealthy females were widowed compared to widowed wealthy males.").

21 *Id.*

22 It is not clear how interests in qualified terminable interest property (QTIP) trusts or discretionary trusts figure into the IRS estimates. Estimates appear to be based on data derived from the "complete listing of a decedent's assets and debts" contained in the estate tax return. *Id.* at 156. To the extent that the value of a QTIP trust for the benefit of a surviving spouse needs to be reported on the survivor's estate tax return upon his or her subsequent death, the IRS methodology would appear to capture QTIP trusts. With respect to wholly discretionary interests created by a third party, the results are different. Because the decedent's executor is not required to include the value of the wholly discretionary interest in the trust in the decedent's gross estate, that value will not be included in estimates of the decedent's wealth.

23 1 William Blackstone, Commentaries *430.

24 Richard Chused, *Married Women's Property Law: 1800–1850*, 71 Geo. L.J. 1359, 1425 (1983).

treat married couples as a single taxable unit, even among countries that permit joint returns (i.e., those that calculate tax liability on a per individual basis).[25]

Portability and the QTIP Trust

One way in which portability benefits the "poorer" spouse, typically the wife, is that lifetime qualified terminable interest property (QTIP) trusts will be less common. In the pre-portability context, rich men who did not want to make outright equalizing transfers to their wives instead funded lifetime QTIP trusts. This allowed them to make a transfer that would "count" as the wife's property for estate tax purposes but would give the wife very little economic interest (and likely zero control) over the trust property. QTIP trusts secured the benefit of the wife's exemption in the unlikely event of her earlier death, and the rich husband was also able to ensure that those assets would then pass to persons of his own choosing. Portability eliminates the need for these trusts, which are inherently sexist.[26]

Since its enactment in 1981, the QTIP marital deduction trust has become the most popular form for taking advantage of the marital deduction. The QTIP provisions are an exception to the marital deduction terminable interest rule, which generally requires an outright (or equivalent) transfer to obtain the benefit of the deduction. Unlike the other transfers that qualify for the marital deduction, the QTIP exception allows the wealthy spouse to receive the benefit of a marital deduction without ceding control or ownership of the transferred property to his spouse. The fiction of the QTIP as a marital transfer is thus intrinsically deceptive.

The QTIP provisions allow a gift tax (or estate tax, if the QTIP is created at death by the wealthy spouse) marital deduction for the full value of the underlying property, even though the transferee spouse only receives a qualifying income interest for her life from the trust property. The QTIP provisions require the donor spouse to make a timely election to benefit from the marital deduction; unfortunately, however, QTIP decisions do not require the transferee spouse's participation. In a QTIP trust, the donor, or decedent, spouse alone determines the ultimate beneficiary of the property. Yet, although the recipient spouse will possess only a lifetime income interest in the property, which has a relatively small value, the QTIP provisions provide that for marital deduction purposes the entire QTIP property will be treated as if it has passed to the donee spouse and that no part of such property will be deemed to be owned by the ultimate beneficiaries of the trust selected solely by the donor.

Unlike the paltry interest and power in a QTIP given to the donee spouse, portability may be viewed as bestowing at least some power to the "poorer" donee spouse should she also be the first spouse to die. With portability, the executor of the first spouse to die must make the "portability election," even if the estate of the deceased spouse would otherwise not have to file an estate tax return. While it is unlikely that the financially strapped spouse will actually hire her own attorney, at least in theory she could. She could amend her will and insert a statement that would not automatically allow the "porting" of her exemption. She could alternatively provide that her executor be prohibited from filing an estate tax return for portability purposes unless her estate has a value above a specified threshold. In each instance, it would seem that her executor would be bound to carry out her wishes, even if the executor is the surviving spouse. But query whether

25 *See, e.g.*, Anthony C. Infanti, *Decentralizing Family: An Inclusive Proposal for Individual Tax Filing in the United States*, 2010 Utah L. Rev. 605, 623.

26 *See* Wendy C. Gerzog, *The Marital Deduction QTIP Provisions: Illogical and Degrading to Women*, 5 UCLA Women's L.J. 301 (1995); *see also* Joseph M. Dodge, *A Feminist Perspective on the QTIP Trust and the Unlimited Marital Deduction*, 76 N.C. L. Rev. 1729 (1998).

this would be a mostly symbolic exercise of power—and one with negative tax consequences. Denying a surviving spouse the deceased spouse's unused exemption amount burdens the ultimate beneficiaries of the second spouse to die. To the extent that those beneficiaries are shared, then the first spouse to die has simply created a larger tax bill for her own beneficiaries, too.

In the portability era, wealthy individuals have no wealth transfer tax incentive to make outright transfers or to fund lifetime QTIP trusts for the less-wealthy spouse. Portability also discourages the use of credit-shelter or bypass trusts because no longer will the first spouse to die need to "use or lose" his or her exemption. Previously, a wealthy spouse would have funded a bypass trust with, say, $5 million to make sure to fully utilize the exemption. A typical bypass trust would be structured as a pot trust for the benefit of the surviving spouse and descendants, with the surviving spouse having no mandatory interest of any kind in the trust. To the extent that portability discourages the use of lifetime QTIP trusts and credit-shelter or bypass trusts, then, portability produces welcome results because those strategies inherently limit the interests and powers of the poorer spouse. Increasing women's economic independence during marriage also increases their power, offering some increased insulation from the worst of abuse and dysfunction that can occur in relationships.[27]

A good way to encourage inter vivos transfers to the poorer spouse—who, statistically speaking, is more likely to be female—is to reinstate graduated transfer-tax rates above the threshold for tax-free transfers. After applying our large current exemptions, we now have a flat tax rate. However, if we returned to progressive rates either by lowering the transfer-tax exemptions or by adding progressive tax rates applicable above the current exemption amounts, we would thereby encourage spousal sharing. That is, in order to "run up the lower brackets" of *both* spouses in a world with graduated tax rates, the wealthy spouse would be encouraged to make lifetime transfers to his spouse. That would affect the very wealthy as this benefit would adhere primarily to taxable estates (i.e., those couples whose assets exceeded the couple's combined exemption amounts). This strategy known as "estate equalization" was one of the two main options that used to be urged by practitioners to lower the couples' combined estate taxes.[28] And the steeper the progression, the greater the tax savings when the couple shares their assets during their lifetime. Progressive rates and estate equalization encourage the wealthier spouse to engage in lifetime asset sharing.

Unintentional Benefits of Portability: Help for Some Marginally Rich

The congressional Joint Committee on Taxation in 2008 identified certain unwarranted advantages that portability could also produce.[29] Specifically, a couple with a total amount of assets at the death of the first spouse that is lower than the maximum individual exemption amount might be able to transfer more property free of estate and gift taxes than they could have transferred using pre-portability estate planning techniques, if their assets greatly appreciate between the death of the first spouse and the death of the surviving spouse.[30] For example, assume a married couple owned a total of $3 million in assets at the first spouse's death (all titled in the name of the first spouse). Assume that the first spouse left everything to his surviving spouse, and the exemption amount at that time was $5 million. Further assume that the first spouse's executor elected portability. When the surviving spouse dies, perhaps many years later, her estate would add a total of $5 million of

27 *See* Chang, *supra* note 16, at 8.

28 Dodge, *supra* note 26, at 1737.

29 Staff of J. Comm. on Taxation, Pub. No. JCX-23-08, Taxation of Wealth Transfers Within a Family: A Discussion of Selected Areas for Possible Reform (2008).

30 *Id.* at 10.

unused spousal exemption amount to the surviving spouse's own exemption at the time of her death (as long as the exemption was at least $5 million at that time).[31] This essentially allows them as a couple to have a portable credit for assets not held by either of them at the time of the first spouse's death.

By comparison, absent portability, if the first spouse held all of the assets and those assets were valued at $3 million, that spouse would have made a taxable transfer to third parties (e.g., the couple's children, or to a trust for the benefit of the surviving spouse and the couple's children, which would not qualify for the marital deduction) that would have taken maximum advantage of the couple's then-available $5 million exemption, and that would have been the extent of the couple's available exemption. If the surviving spouse then won the lottery, she would have been limited to her own $5 million exemption. Portability thus raises a fairness question of whether couples should be able to benefit from an apparent "fluke" of good fortune, as two couples with similar assets at the time of the first spouse's death would be taxed differently for no apparent reason other than the "luck" of having died during portability. This result, which appears to be completely unintentional and unwarranted, could be resolved by requiring the couple to hold at least $5 million (or even $10 million) as a couple at the time of the first spouse's death.

Moreover, this serendipitous result also makes us wonder about what constitute "a couple's" assets: do they include assets acquired after one of the spouses becomes a widow or widower? At that time, the surviving spouse is treated as single for most purposes.[32] Does portability extend the marital unit potentially well beyond the end of the marriage? It would appear that is the case.

A Final Word on Portability

Practical Consequences

It has been asserted that portability is most beneficial for those couples with assets greater than one exemption amount but not greater than their two exemptions in total. In other words, the estate plan of a married couple with, say, $7 million of assets is much simpler in the era of portability than it was pre-portability. That couple need not draft wills containing a bypass trust in order to preserve the exemption of the first spouse to die. As long as the first decedent's executor files an estate tax return electing portability, the exemption will be available in the estate of the second spouse to die. The survivor will either consume the assets or die owning less than the couple's combined exemptions, and, in either event, will owe no estate tax. With portability, the administration of the

31 I.R.C. § 2010. The entire amount of the exemption is available to the surviving spouse because the transfer from the first spouse would have been shielded from estate tax by the marital deduction and not the credit against the estate tax. *Id.* § 2056. By contrast, if the first spouse left all of his assets of $3 million to third parties, there would only be an extra $2 million that could be added to his surviving spouse's applicable exemption amount at the time of her death.

32 After one spouse dies, the couple may file a joint income tax return but only for the year of the decedent's death. *Id.* § 6013(a)(2). In the two years following the decedent's death, the surviving spouse may continue to use the tax rates applicable to married couples filing jointly if he or she maintains a household that is the principal place of abode of his or her dependent child (i.e., if the surviving spouse is a "qualifying widow(er)"). *Id.* §§ 1(a), (c); 2(a). Many of the benefits provided to widows or widowers are limited to those with that "qualifying widow(er)" filing status; however, there are some Code provisions that assist surviving spouses regardless of whether or not they have dependent children. *See, e.g., id.* §§ 72(s)(3) (surviving spouse annuity beneficiary), 121 (special rule for sales of principal residence by certain surviving spouses).

first decedent's estate is simple: there are no bypass trusts, just a transfer to the surviving spouse. The surviving spouse has total control over the couple's assets. Portability thus has a significant impact on these couples.

In contrast, for those with greater wealth—couples having assets that exceed the value of their combined exemptions—portability may not change their estate plans. Where each spouse has significant wealth in his or her own name and there are descendants of the marriage, the estate plan likely will include a bypass trust to which the first decedent allocates his or her exemption. The assets in the bypass trust are available to the surviving spouse as one of the trust's discretionary beneficiaries, but in the ordinary course of events, the assets will continue to appreciate free of tax for the benefit of the descendants.[33] The bypass trust "freezes" the transfer-tax value of the assets in the trust, freeing those assets from estate taxation on the appreciation in their value that occurs between the two spouses' deaths. The benefit of "freezing" the asset value in a bypass trust motivates most wealthy couples to obtain traditional estate planning incorporating a bypass trust for the exemption amount and some kind of transfer qualifying for the marital deduction for the amount of assets above the estate tax exemption.

Theoretical Consequences

In a theoretical sense, portability raises questions about the tax system's use of the married couple as the appropriate taxable unit. It is not obvious that the state should be channeling financial benefits into relationships that are presumably sexual.[34] Perhaps the strongest argument for allowing married couples to constitute a taxable unit is the difficulty of tracing assets to a particular spouse because they may commingle their assets without keeping track of deposits and withdrawals.[35] Curiously, though, the married couple is enshrined as the unit regardless of whether, in fact, the spouses do commingle assets. Those who cannot or choose not to marry but who do commingle assets court tax trouble if they do not track deposits and withdrawals. The marriage license exempts married couples from the burden of such record-keeping requirements.

On the one hand, portability allows married couples to achieve what previously required estate planning for them to do (and more). Discussing the advantages of portability, the Joint Committee on Taxation described the difficulties involved not only in engaging a lawyer to create a credit-shelter or bypass trust, but also in the constant retitling of assets to ensure that each spouse has sufficient property to fund that trust fully:

> Even where couples do have such [credit-shelter or bypass] trusts in place, if the first spouse to die does not have sufficient assets titled in his or her own name at the time of death to fund the trust up to the amount of the then-applicable exemption amount, a portion of such spouse's exemption amount may be lost.[36]

On the other hand, portability further entangles marriage, the tax system, and economic benefits.

33 *See Outside the Box on Estate Tax Reform*, *supra* note 5, at 122–23.

34 For a powerful critique of the state's role in policing sex and intimacy, see Laura A. Rosenbury & Jennifer E. Rothman, *Sex in and out of Intimacy*, 59 Emory L.J. 809, 817 (2010) ("states continue to play a role in channeling sex into particular forms of intimacy").

35 *See* Gerzog, *supra* note 26.

36 Staff of J. Comm. on Taxation, *supra* note 29, at 10.

Portability and First Principles

From this consideration of estate tax portability, there emerge two significant underlying tax norms. The first is the importance of identifying the correct taxable unit. Estate tax portability reflects a further reification of the married couple as the taxable unit, although this chapter raises questions about the correctness of that choice. With the *Windsor* decision,[37] the blatant discrimination in the tax laws against same-sex married couples has been eliminated. This is a salutary change to the law. Yet the ongoing reliance on a (presumably) sexual relationship as the correct determinant of the taxable unit deserves further study and scrutiny. Most developed nations have moved toward a single-taxpayer unit for taxation, and it is far from obvious that the married couple is the correct or even best taxable unit.

Like Joseph Dodge in Chapter 12 of this volume, we are concerned about the distortive effects of current wealth transfer tax laws. Portability has minimized the need for lifetime QTIP trusts and bypass trusts for married couples with less wealth than their combined exemptions. But the incentives to use these trusts remain for some taxpayers. In that sense, portability shores up what Dodge calls the redistributive effects of the gift and estate tax system in the form of transfers "from the very wealthy to the moderately wealthy," presumably in the form of fees for estate planning and similar professionals.

The search for a nondistortive system with respect to marital transfers might be enhanced by a shift to an accessions tax or a personal income tax system that treats gratuitous transfers as income combined with a cash-flow consumption tax. Under each system, the receipt by one spouse of outright transfers from the other could be tax free. But of all the systems Dodge mentions, the reformed federal estate and gift tax may be the most practical. The fiction of the decedent's bearing the brunt of the tax—it is obvious that the heirs bear the brunt of any estate tax—is a tolerable one for two reasons. It centralizes the administration and reduces some practical problems when there are many taxpayers. We might do well to consider supplementing the estate tax system with a "realization on death" rule for income tax purposes. The choices need not be either estate tax or income tax; the tax system could accommodate both.

This chapter highlights how estate tax portability likely functions in the lives of married couples who are subject to the estate tax. Admittedly this is a small and financially privileged group. But whether a particular law applies to many or few taxpayers, it is important to investigate the law's likely impact: who benefits and why. To the extent that a law privileges marital relationships over nonmarital relationships, or one member of a married couple over the other, it is worthwhile to expose and interrogate the law's structure and function. Too often, the so-called "detached" or "academic" perspective turns a blind eye to power and privilege. In putting people—mindful of gender, race, sexual orientation or other identities—at the center of the analysis, one can become more attuned to inequalities exacerbated, reified, or perpetuated by the tax law. Nondiscrimination is a norm to which the tax code should aspire.

37 United States v. Windsor, 133 S. Ct. 2675 (2013).

Index

FSC
www.fsc.org
MIX
Papier | Fördert
gute Waldnutzung
FSC® C083411

Kolibri 360 GmbH
Ferdinand-Jühlke-Straße 7
99095 Erfurt, Deutschland
produktsicherheit@kolibri360.de